27.00

D0408797

JERRY HERMAN

ALSO BY STEPHEN CITRON

Play It Again, Sam—By Ear! A Piano Method
The Paderewski Memoirs (editor)
The Inn and Us (with Anne Edwards)
Songwriting: A Complete Guide to the Craft
The Musical from the Inside Out
Noel and Cole: The Sophisticates
The Wordsmiths: Oscar Hammerstein 2nd and Alan Jay Lerner
Sondheim and Lloyd-Webber: The New Musical

782.14092
H551J
C581j

JERRY HERMAN

poet of the showtune

San Diego Christian College
2100 Greenfield Drive
El Cajon, CA 92019

stephen citron

yale university press / new haven and london

Copyright © 2004 by Stephen Citron.

All rights reserved.

This book may not be reproduced, in whole or in part, including illustrations, in any form (beyond that copying permitted by Sections 107 and 108 of the U.S. Copyright Law and except by reviewers for the public press), without written permission from the publishers.

Designed by Mary Valencia

Set in Minion and Franklin Gothic type by The Composing Room of Michigan, Inc.

Printed in the United States of America by Vail-Ballou Press.

Library of Congress Cataloging-in-Publication Data

Citron, Stephen.

   Jerry Herman : poet of the showtune / Stephen Citron.

       p.   cm.

   Includes bibliographical references (p.   ) and index.

   "Songs, shows, music in print, and recordings": p.   .

   ISBN 0-300-10082-5 (cloth : alk. paper)

   1. Herman, Jerry, 1933– .   2. Composers—United States—Biography.   I. Title.

ML410.H5624C58 2004

782.1′4′092—dc22

                                                   2003027632

A catalogue record for this book is available from the British Library.

The paper in this book meets the guidelines for permanence and durability of the Committee on Production Guidelines for Book Longevity of the Council on Library Resources.

10 9 8 7 6 5 4 3 2 1

For Alexander Citron:
my son, my student, my colleague

CONTENTS

ACKNOWLEDGMENTS

In November 1999, when I first began to write this book, I invited Jerry Herman to my apartment in Manhattan for a brunch interview. When he arrived at my door, I could not see the man for the three towering gray baker's boxes he bore. That afternoon I began to understand that Herman's magnanimity with Danish pastry, doughnuts, and muffins was typical of his forthright quality as a man and an artist. I had long acquaintance with the generous output of music and lyrics that has made him a major force in the American musical theater. He is that rare subject, a joy for a biographer, possessed of total recall and never too busy to answer a question. Honest but never hurtful in discussing colleagues, giving but not controlling. For his permission to quote generously from his work, I am deeply indebted; for his magnificent oeuvre, the world is much richer.

Because of his big-heartedness and lack of vitriol (in a profession noted for its acrimony), Herman is much beloved, and fortunate to have many close friends, all of whom lent a hand in getting to the essence of the man as presented in the pages that follow. Chief among them is Sheila Mack, who has been his secretary/cook/major domo, confidante, and friend for most of his life. Sheila, who keeps extensive and immaculate files of Herman's career, was most helpful in digging out facts as well as photos, many of them never before published. For open-ended interviews, her insight, and generosity, a deep bow.

Many thanks also to Herman's agent, Samuel "Biff" Liff of the William Morris Agency, who volunteered opinions, facts, and figures about Herman's career. Thanks also to Jack Hutto, Herman's agent during the *Mame* era and beyond.

Priscilla Morgan was Herman's first agent. It was she who looked after him during the late 1950s and early 1960s. She came back into his artistic life in the 1990s with his television special *Mrs. Santa Claus*. For several in-depth interviews, my deep gratitude.

Edwin H. Morris has been Herman's publisher since the beginning of his career. I am most grateful to Peter Silvestri there, and to his associates

David Bogart and Daniel Sokol, for their help in clearing rights to the many musical and lyrical examples in this book.

Mitchell Douglas is not only an outstanding artist's representative but a close friend, and a knowledgeable theater man. He most generously supplied me with recordings and videotapes of some rare Hermaniana—many of which were out of print. For all this, and more, my deep appreciation.

Thanks to Mary Lynn Potenteau, Nicol Friedland, Ray Fisher, Dan Kalmanson, and Kent Lantass for information on Herman's college days at the University of Miami, and a special tip of the hat to Linda Scott, who sent me photos of the university—then and now. Herman's fraternity brothers Dr. Robert Hutner and Louis Hertz were most helpful, giving me long interviews recalling their college days together. Zeta Beta Tau fraternity brother Burton Litwin sent me a splendid photo, and the executive director of ZBT, Jonathan Yulish, gave me permission to publish it. To both of them, my thanks. And Professors Paul and Margery Nagel, puppeteers in their college days, told me about the shows they did with Jerry at the piano.

Herman's many pre- and postuniversity collaborators were also very helpful in chronicling my subject's output. Alice Borden, who was often called upon to make a demo or perform at an audition, has almost total recall of Herman's life from the early days at Stissing Lake Camp to the present. I thank her for a handful of interviews, both formal and informal. Phyllis Newman gave me much information about the early shows she and Herman put together in Jersey City and New York, while Jim Paul Eilers and Charles Nelson Reilly told me about The Showplace and the first Herman show, *Nightcap*, in Greenwich Village.

Peg Houtchens was the conductor and music director of *Madame Aphrodite*, which, although premiered after *Milk and Honey*, was composed before the Israeli musical. She re-created most of that lost score for me, and we had some splendid discussions about the work. For her informative musicianship, my sincere thanks. I am indebted also to Tad Mosel, who wrote that work's libretto and gave me insight into its creation and performance.

Gerard Oestreicher, the producer of *Milk and Honey*, Herman's first Broadway show, is no longer living, but his widow, Irma, who was deeply involved in the show's creation, helped me understand how the show was put on its feet. Thanks, too, to Robert de Cormier, who did the splendid choral arrangements, and to Madeline Gilford, who cast and supervised the road company. She is a dear, long-standing friend, as well as a fountain of knowledge about the American musical theater. Thanks also to Ronald Holgate, who played the rabbi in this show, and who costarred in *The Grand Tour*. He gave me an extended interview during which we discussed both of these musicals. Speaking of *The Grand Tour,* I should like to thank Florence Lacey, who played Marianne, for her help.

For information on the chapters on *Hello, Dolly!* my thanks go to Carol Channing and to Charles Nelson Reilly, and in the pages discussing *Mame,* first mention must go to Richard Tyler Jordan, whose delightful and informative book, *But Darling, I'm Your Auntie Mame!* was most helpful. Jerome Laurence, who cowrote the libretto for this and *Dear World,* is a dear friend and gets my thanks for his help. Angela Lansbury and Bea Arthur were kind enough to take the time from their very active theatrical careers to answer some of my questions. A deep bow to them. My thanks also to the incomparable Sally Ann Howes, who starred in the recent revival of *Dear World.* Of her performance In the New York City Opera's revival of *A Little Night Music,* Stephen Sondheim said, "She *is* Desirée." I would add that she *is* Aurelia, the not-so-mad Countess of Chaillot. She has definite ideas about that show. I am grateful to her for sharing them with me.

Michael Stewart, librettist for three Herman musicals, is no longer with us, but I am still indebted for his friendship and the splendid musical books he left behind. I want to thank his sister, Francine Pascal, who rewrote his *Mack and Mabel* libretto and who talked to me often about her brother's work and her own involvement in revising that musical. Thanks to Jon Wilner, a longtime Herman champion, who produced *Mack and Mabel* in England and gave me an interesting interview about that show, and to Marcia Selligson, who oversaw the recent Reprise revival in Los Angeles. Don Pippin, a friend of long standing, has conducted most of Jerry Herman's Broadway musicals. Moreover, he understands Herman's music more than anyone. I thank him for an informative interview.

I am indebted to both stars of *La Cage aux Folles,* George Hearn for a telephone interview and Gene Barry for an in-person one. Harvey Fierstein, the show's librettist, and Arthur Laurents, its director, were also very helpful.

Leila Martin, one of the original Jerry's Girls, gave me information about the genesis of the show off Broadway, and Leslie Uggams and Chita Rivera, both longtime friends of Herman, told me much about the Broadway run. I am grateful to all of them.

Long-standing friendships are a part of Herman's life. Some of the elders (now retired to Florida) with whom he is still in frequent touch gave me interviews and answered questionnaires about my subject's youth. They are Lily Sepenuk, Elise Bailyn, and Lil Feinberg. I thank them all. Thanks also to Sylvia Hersher, a theatrical encyclopedia, to Mimi Engel, a musical one, and to Claire Tannenbaum, who was Herman's first musical chum.

Jerry Herman has no blood family living, but one must consider Sheila Mack, Alice Borden, and Jane Dorian his surrogate relatives. The roles the first two play in his life have been mentioned in these acknowledgments, but his goddaughter Jane Dorian, who is as close to him as a daughter might be, has not yet been thanked. She supplied me with plentiful anecdotes as well as many candid photos. For her generosity and total recall, my deep gratitude.

Herman's second love (after music) is interior design. Charles "Chuck" Fultz, Herman's longtime associate, is his right arm in these ventures into the reconstruction of homes. I thank him for candid interviews during which he told me a great deal about my subject.

Dr. Gary Blick is a renowned authority on HIV and AIDS. He took hours away from research and a busy practice to explain this scourge to me, and to report on Herman's condition so that I might discuss its effects on my subject. For this, my sincere thanks.

Michael Kerker is the ASCAP Director of Musical Theater, but beyond his imposing title, he is a knowledgeable theater man. He leads a busy life shuttling between two coasts; still, he is never too busy to dig out a fact or to answer a question. For his help and friendship, a special thank you.

Many others helped me in various ways and I should like to thank them: Dr. Leo Altshul, Jim Amlotte, Billy Barnes, Mark Bramble, David Brown, Sally Carr, Irene Clark, Michael Feinstein, Ian Marshall Fisher, Susan Granger, Sheldon Harnick, the late Al Hirschfeld, Louise Kerz Hirschfeld, Mary Vann Hughes, Evan Hunter, Larry Kramer, Jerome Lawrence, Richard Lawrence, David LeVine, Elizabeth Markowitz, Terry Marler, Dick Moore, Karen Morrow, Robert Osborne, Bernadette Peters, Jane Powell, Douglas Rae, Rex Reed, Robert Shanks, Rose Tobias Shaw, Thomas Z. Shepard, Leonard Soloway, Leonard Stern, Jerry Stiller, Haila Stoddard, Dr. Joseph Sumo, Ion Trewin, Simon Trewin, and Caroline Underwood.

I am beholden to my editors at Yale University Press, and in particular to Harry Haskell, who saw the need for an in-depth biography of one of the American musical theater's most enduring composer-lyricists, to my interim editor, Mary C. Traester, and to Keith Condon, who took over the editorial reins after Mr. Haskell retired and saw the book to completion. Hearty thanks also to Dan Heaton, the manuscript editor, who contributed much more to the pages that follow than manuscript editors generally do. I would also like to thank Brian A. McKay, who is in charge of publicity. A hearty handclasp and thanks too to Tom Wallace, who represents my work in the United States, and to Christopher Sinclair-Stevenson, who looks after my writing abroad.

Photos throughout the book came from several sources. I got much help selecting them and securing reprint permission from Howard Mandebaum at Photofest and Marty Jacobs and Margeurite Lavin at the Museum of the City of New York. The greatest theatrical photographer of our time, Martha Swope, was very helpful and generous, and I cannot overlook Jerry Herman himself, who contributed several pictures from his private collection.

My son, Alexander Citron, himself a fine musician, has always been a sounding board for my writing. In this book he was able to re-create some of Herman's early unpublished songs from tapes, so that words and music could be included. He is also responsible for the many musical examples the book contains. For all of this, my deep appreciation.

Last, and most important, to my wife, Anne Edwards, a sterling biographer and an eagle-eyed editor, my unqualified praise and gratitude. She put aside work on her own book again, and yet again, to read through and edit my chapters, always giving cogent and constructive suggestions. For her devotion to this book, the words "thank you" are hardly adequate, but they will have to suffice. I gave her my enduring love years ago.

S.C.
Beverly Hills, California
March 2004

1

if you believe

In November 1961 *Milk and Honey*, the first musical set in the young state of Israel, opened to splendid reviews. It was Jerry Herman's Broadway debut as a composer-lyricist. Less than two months later, his next musical, *Madame Aphrodite* (written earlier, but its production delayed), had its premiere at the Orpheum Theatre off Broadway. This time the critiques were dreadful, and the eerie musical about a crone who sells fake "beauty cream" hoping to "scar the world" closed after thirteen performances.

Milk and Honey was doing capacity business and would remain firmly ensconced at the Martin Beck Theatre for the next fourteen months. Its acclaim would do much to offset the blow Herman's Greenwich Village fiasco had dealt his ego.

Herman has never lacked optimism, and so by the following spring, with the failure of *Madame Aphrodite* fading in his memory, he looked forward to beginning another show. Small of stature and compact of frame, usually wearing a winning grin beneath his smiling brown eyes, he looked like someone who had just graduated from high school. At thirty-one he was the youngest of the composers then represented on Broadway, which made good copy for the newspapers. Herman reveled in his newfound fame, and neither he nor his publicity agent bothered to correct the error when papers and annals printed his age as twenty-nine.[1]

Although hugely ambitious and protective of his work, Herman remains inordinately shy with strangers. "If I go to a party and somebody comes over and talks to me, I am just fine," he confided to me. "In fact, I usually end up using that person as my security blanket for the whole evening."[2] Because Herman hated meeting new people, the *Milk and Honey* cast, most of whom he had coached in their roles, became his family. The Martin Beck turned into his hangout and Molly Picon's cluttered dressing room his special warming place. Hiring this star of Second Avenue's Yiddish theater for her musical debut uptown on Broadway—the librettist Don Appell's inspiration—had paid off handsomely at the box office. It also had provided Herman, whose own mother had died before he had achieved any major success, with the maternal figure he would always yearn for. Herman has spent the greatest part of his career writing about women: strong, idealized, maternal women like Dolly, Mame, Countess Aurelia in *Dear World,* or even Zaza, the mothering drag queen in *La Cage aux Folles.* Molly Picon was the closest to his actual gregarious, theatrical, singing Jewish mother, Ruth.

Herman was elated and somewhat astonished when May came and *Milk and Honey* was nominated for a Tony Award as Best Musical. It was a foregone conclusion that Frank Loesser's *How to Succeed in Business (Without Really Trying)* would sweep all the awards, but to have his show proposed on the same ballot as Richard Rodgers and Loesser was exhilarating. He felt doubly honored knowing he had been nominated in the Best Composer category as well. Fellow nominees for that award were all experienced hands. Richard Adler had been nominated for the exotic *Kwamina,* Loesser for the superhit *How to Succeed.* Rodgers, the undisputed master of musical theater, having recently lost his partner, lyricist Oscar Hammerstein 2nd, dauntlessly carried on by writing both music and lyrics to *No Strings,* thereby winning the award for best score. (Not until the next year were separate awards given for composer and lyricist.)

Even though *Milk and Honey* won no Tonys, Herman derived intense pleasure in seeing his name gleaming from the Martin Beck's marquee as he made his nightly visits to the theater. So all-consuming was his ambition that Herman could think of almost nothing else but what his next project would be. He scoured *Variety, Billboard,* and the other trade papers and talked to as many Broadway insiders as he could find to learn what musicals were scheduled to be produced that fall or the following spring. He was especially interested in those in their early planning stages, even those still embryonic.

Priscilla Morgan, his agent, had paired Herman with Appell, and the libretttist had introduced him to the producer Gerard Oestreicher, who had gotten *Milk and Honey* to Broadway. But Herman, who had heard that David Merrick was looking for a composer and lyricist to write the score for his musicalization of *The Matchmaker,* did not believe that Morgan had the clout to arrange a meeting for him with one of the most prominent producers on Broadway. Herman was acquainted with Leo Bookman of the powerful William Morris group, and he prevailed on Bookman to make the momentous phone call to David Merrick.[3]

Merrick had been told about Herman's gifts by the librettist Michael Stewart, who had come down to Greenwich Village during the short run of *Madame Aphrodite* and had admired the sensitivity of this unusual score.* Stewart, who had written the first draft of what would eventually become *Hello, Dolly!*, knew that the producer was looking for a composer-lyricist who could capture the Gay Nineties sound in old New York, and who could write hard-hitting showtunes tailored for Ethel Merman, the star he had in mind. He had rejected the slim current crop of those who wrote both music and lyrics as "too angular" and the well-established ones as "too fustian."

Now, urged by Bookman and Stewart, Merrick went to see *Milk and Honey* and had his secretary call Herman the next day to set up an appointment.

"I went up to his office in the Sardi building with great anxiety and terror," Herman said, aware of Merrick's well-known temper. (The producer's sobriquet on Broadway, "the abominable showman" was to come later, when his venom and spite were as renowned as his many successes.) "I was doubly apprehensive when I went into his private lair because I had not gone through my own agent," Herman noted. "The way Merrick presented himself, standing behind a gigantic desk with gargoyles on it, with his black hair combed to one side, terrified me. The walls of the room were felted in blood red and the wall-to-wall carpet was the same vibrant color. The room was quite stunning but very off-putting because it made his jet hair, cut in Hitler fashion, his black moustache, and eyebrows stand out against his pasty skin."[4]

"I went around the corner and saw your show last night," Merrick told Herman rather offhandedly. "I was impressed," he added, "but I don't know if you're *American* enough for this play—a Thornton Wilder piece. Have you ever seen *The Matchmaker*?"

---

* Michael Stewart (1929–1987), born Michael Rubin, was one of the American musical theater's greatest librettists. He learned the craft of comedy as a writer for Woody Allen. In the 1950's he contributed to several *Shoestring Revues*. In 1960 he wrote the book for the smash hit *Bye Bye Birdie*. The next year he had another success with his libretto for *Carnival*. Then *Hello, Dolly!* (1964), *Seesaw* (1973), *I Love My Wife* (1977), *Barnum* (1980), and (with Mark Bramble) *42nd Street* (1980). In addition to *Hello, Dolly!* he collaborated with Herman on *Mack and Mabel* (1974) and *The Grand Tour* (1979).

Herman had to admit that he had not, but Merrick's slur, implying that his music might be too Jewish, got his dander up. "With two parents who were schoolteachers, I consider myself to be the most American person that ever was put on this planet," he retorted. "I don't blame you, Mr. Merrick, after seeing *Milk and Honey,* my Israeli operetta, for thinking I'm a little Jewish kid who can only write this kind of music—but aside from that show all my other work has been as American as apple pie."

"I saw the script on his desk. It had a tattered cover, red—what else? And I made out the title upside down: *Matchmaker Draft #1.* And from somewhere I mustered the courage to say, 'If you would give me that and let me spend a little time with it, I would be very happy to present some of my work to see if you like it.' That was on a Friday morning and I promised to have the script back to him by next Monday afternoon, three days later."

"Keep the script, I have plenty more," Merrick offered, "but I'd be curious to see what you can come up with in that time."

Herman was ecstatic. He hurried home to his apartment in Greenwich Village, eager to begin working on Stewart's libretto. He stopped for weekend provisions at the deli on the corner of his one-room walk-up on East Tenth Street and laid in a stock of Baby Ruths and O Henrys. Herman is a chocoholic who frequently rewards himself after writing a song by devouring several of these, his favorite candy bars.

First, he read the mimeographed script three times. Then he called all his friends to tell them the news and to ask them "not to phone me, because I'm going to work all weekend." Finally, he rang Alice Borden, a young singing actress he had known since her childhood. Alice, a quick study, possesses a lovely voice and had frequently done backers auditions—performances to raise capital—with him. He asked her to come over on Sunday to learn the new songs he was about to write—and to keep Monday free, when they would perform them for Merrick.

Then he sat down at the piano and began to work out the songs. Herman composes his songs at the keyboard by playing and singing them over and over. Once an extended section satisfies him, he makes notes—first of the lyrics, later of the melody—on music paper. Although he has never been trained to make a full piano-vocal score, he can notate a melody, add the chords by name, and put his lyric under the melody line, essentially making what is called a lead sheet.

The first song he wrote for this new project was to become the cornerstone of the first act, "Put on Your Sunday Clothes." "I wrote it word for word the way it is when you hear it in the show," he says. And no wonder it was the first piece he turned to. The stage direction in the script would intrigue any composer. "The Feed store moves, and we arrive at the Yonkers Railroad Station," Stewart writes, "where we find the other passengers dressed in their Sunday best. During the song the train arrives, is finally boarded, and we're off to New York."[5]

This scanty outline encompassing the themes of "Sunday best" and "train" had enough kinetic energy to inspire an opening melodic line that works against an ostinato (a small repeated figure) that suggests a locomotive. Herman kept the chugging first six bars of the song to the single chord of D. Does it sound like it might get boring? Not at all, for his melodic line has tremendous rhythmic energy and ends on a most unexpected note. That very note has an urgency that further propels the music.

This song has been led into by Cornelius, the clerk in the Yonkers feed store who wants to intrigue his assistant, Barnaby, into joining him in playing hooky from their jobs. Cornelius sings the verse broadly:

> Out there, there's a world outside of Yonkers,
> Way out there beyond this hick town, Barnaby,
> There's a slick town, Barnaby . . .

and then, as Barnaby sits mesmerized at his feet, Cornelius captivates him with the chorus:

> Put on your Sunday clothes, there's lots of world out there,
> Get out the brilliantine and dime cigars.
> We're gonna find adventure in the ev'ning air,
> Girls in white in a perfumed night
> Where the lights are bright as the stars.

After an opening in which the rhythm of the locomotive would make rhyme redundant, Herman bombards us with what is almost a quadruple rhyme (*white, night, bright,* and even *lights,* for the *s* is sung as part of the word *are*) in the consequent eight bars. And he carries on this feat throughout a twelve-minute musical scene which becomes the raison d'être for the entire musical. Herman's lyric builds from Cornelius's promise to Barnaby, "and we won't come home until we've kissed a girl," to the conventional plot device of musicals—this time intriguing his bucolic coworker: "and we won't come home until we fall in love." Could any teenager resist such an invitation? Of course Barnaby would be hooked and eager to get into his Sunday clothes and get out of Yonkers.

Next, Herman went back and tackled the very opening of Stewart's script, limning Dolly, making her almost a cartoon character, without turning her into a buffoon. Her song "Call on Dolly" gives us the idea of this enterprising woman's matchmaking ability. It is followed by her boasting "I Put My Hand In," which goes even deeper into her meddling in other people's lives—always for their own good. An excerpt from the lyric will give an idea of this remarkable woman's style.

> And a girl over six-foot-three
> Loves a man who comes up to her ear,
> Surely it's obvious she'll never be seduced
> Till some kind soul condescends to give her beau a little boost!
> So I put my hand in there,
> I put my hand in here.

With the opening, a big brassy number, and the incipient plot out of the way, Herman could concentrate on the gentler aspects of Stewart's script. The next scene takes place in a hat shop in New York and climaxes when Dolly tries to teach these two oafs from the hinterlands to dance. Their partners will be Irene Molloy, the owner of the shop, and her assistant, Minnie Fay. The two couples, immediately attracted to each other, become the romantic focus of the entire musical. "Dancing," a lush waltz in the old-fashioned tradition—but not déjà vu—is a director-choreographer's dream. When staged by Gower Champion, who eventually became one of the driving forces behind *Hello, Dolly!*, the number was beguiling.

The mature Herman admits to a certain elation at having written this number because the subject of dancing has always been painful for him. As a child, small for his age, he didn't always do what other youngsters were doing. When everyone else was playing baseball, he was playing the piano. And when he was a teenager and everyone else was dancing, he was still the one who was playing the piano.[6] Dancing was something he had stayed away from because, as he says, "I never felt comfortable doing something I couldn't do really well. In four years of college I never got out on the dance floor—I was always at the piano—where I felt like somebody.

"Looking at this script, I was charmed by the way Dolly is able to take a clod like Cornelius and turn him into a dancer. That's why I wrote that song, because it's really me wanting to dance and not having the guts to try it."[7]

Adding to his weekend accomplishment, Herman next tackled a solo for Irene Molloy that would precede "Dancing." Modeled after an old English ballad with an Irish lilt, the song tells the audience that Irene is a young widow who still cherishes the memory of her late husband. It opens with the circuitous line, "I still love the love that first I loved when first in love I fell." Although intended as a pastiche, the song's melody has a wistful charm, but its unwieldy lyric dooms it to the reject pile.[8]

Polishing the lyrics and playing these four songs over and over, Herman was working on pure adrenaline. "I was like a crazed person, pacing up and down in the middle of the night, scribbling down lyrics and popping candy into my mouth," he said. Herman was desperate to have this show because of the strong title character Dolly represented, but more so because he adored Ethel Merman, and thought it would be the apogee of any songwriter's career to have the opportunity to write for her.

It was essential that "Sunday Clothes," which was to be sung by Cornelius and Barnaby, be performed with two voices, and the other songs he had written sounded better when sung in harmony. So that Sunday afternoon, when Alice Borden joined him, he taught her the harmony part of all the songs. They worked around the clock, memorizing their parts for presentation to Merrick the following day.

"It was an enormous amount of material to learn," Alice remembered, "and Jerry wanted our performances, without referring to any music, to be perfect." "We were both full of energy," Herman says, recalling that day, "and I wanted this happy, brightly colored, American musical more than anything in the world. We practiced Sunday night until about 2 A.M. and met the next morning at 11:30 in front of Merrick's office on 44th Street."[9]

"God, was I scared!" Alice reported, "when we went up in the little elevator in the Sardi Building and finally into Mr. Merrick's red office. He was so imposing and so frightening. Mike Stewart was there and Neil Hartley, his stage manager, and I don't know who else."

"Jerry said, 'Mr. Merrick, I would like to present you with four songs,' and Mr. Merrick did not look happy because [he thought] nobody could write four decent songs in three days."[10] The impatient producer reluctantly plopped down in his big chair, his gaze challenging. Then Jerry said, "This is my idea for the opening number," and he and Alice performed "Call on Dolly" and "I Put My Hand In." At the end of the sequence Mike Stewart applauded. Merrick mustered a quiet "very good."

"I started tapping out the rhythm of the train on the piano, and Alice and I performed the whole sequence of 'Put On Your Sunday Clothes,' after which everybody applauded," Herman recalls. Alice then sang the old English type ballad to polite applause. (This quasi-Irish song was eventually replaced by the winsome "Ribbons Down My Back.")

Then they did the entire "Dancing" sequence. Incredibly, these numbers have remained in the score essentially as they were performed that morning, and except for "Ribbons Down My Back," "Motherhood March," and "Before the Parade Passes By" they constitute the musical portion of the entire first act of *Hello, Dolly!*

Before Merrick could say "stop," Herman again played the choruses of all four songs. Reprise—a technique he had learned in cabaret, and one that would become a Herman trademark—seemed to tie up the presentation as a kind of minimusical. "They were all speechless," Herman says, "and when I finished, Merrick stood up from behind his big desk and spoke the line that might easily have been written for a Garland-Rooney picture of the 1930s, 'Kid, the show is yours.'"

"Bursting inside, Jerry and I were very cool," Alice recalled, "and remained that way except for the grins on our faces when we got into the elevator. But when we hit 44th Street, we went crazy. It was a sunny afternoon, and I think we danced all the way up Eighth Avenue until Jerry stopped, his eyes filling with tears as he said, 'Oh, if Ruth could see us now.'

"I, too, was affected at the thought that his mother was not there to see his triumph, but I was not about to let any sadness spoil our victory. 'I'm starving,' I said, 'and you promised to buy me a lovely lunch.'"[11]

2

early days

Whenever Jerry Herman's songwriting was accepted enthusiastically, his thoughts harked back to his mother, for it was she who had fostered his music, who had insisted that he study piano, who was never too busy to listen to his early work. Not that his father and the rest of the Hermans were philistines. Quite the contrary, but he had a tendency to think of them as visually rather than aurally gifted.

David Herman, Jerry's grandfather, born in 1880 in Poland near the Russian border in a small town on the outskirts of Minsk, was not unmusical, for he sang in the synagogue choir as a young man. But he was much more attracted to the visual arts. Life was hard for the ghetto residents living in their shtetls, subject to frequent and senseless pogroms. In 1895 young David, manly, stalwart, and ambitious even at fifteen, decided that he could not face a future filled with imminent disaster; he would make his way to England—with hopes of coming to what was then called the *Goldena Medina,* America. David had been apprenticed to a painter and had, in addition to his acceptable ear for music, a true eye for design, especially trompe l'oeil. He could paint a panel on a plaster wall and make it look like textured ash or oak. He could just as easily sketch a tasseled drapery bordering a window that looked so real one was tempted to go up and touch what appeared to be fabric. He was, in short, among the stylistic artisans known as "grain painters" who were much in demand for decorating synagogues and churches in ersatz woods, faux marble, and deceptive draperies.

It was the custom in those early days of the twentieth century for immigrants who had established themselves in the States to billet and feed greenhorns newly arrived from the native village until the newcomers could get jobs and support themselves. Tall, bright, and able to speak Polish, Russian, Hebrew, and—once he had spent some time in the New World—even acceptable English, David was welcomed into the Rosenfeld family in a New York Lower East Side tenement. The blue-eyed teenager got to know the Rosenfelds' middle daughter, Ida, a small dynamo who had come to America some time earlier. Three years older than David, who towered above her, and already somewhat of an entrepreneur, she ran her father's Bowery saloon with an iron fist; she extended no credit to "rummies," and sometimes even threw them out herself. She doted on David, his erudition, artistic talent, and especially his good looks. Wasting no time, they were married three months after their first meeting.

Ida may have been small physically, but she had grandiose ambitions. She was convinced that life would be easier for her and David away from the East Coast, with its crowds and competition. Jews were leaving New York by the score and settling in the open port of Galveston, Texas. Many who had run from the pogroms and reached South America now had easy entrée across the Gulf of Mexico and were streaming into this welcoming harbor. Knowing a burgeoning city would need additional synagogues, Ida envisioned her husband decorating many of them.

But within months, Ida, who was rarely happy with her lot, found the teeming Texas port steamy and insect ridden, with very little work for David. Now, yearning for El Dorado, she soon talked her husband into traveling to Los Angeles. After all, she argued repeatedly, this brand new area, too, would soon need a raft of synagogues and churches, in each of which David could turn base plaster into apparent marble.

So they trekked cross-country from Galveston to Los Angeles, where Ida opened another bar, setting down what looked like permanent roots, and began raising their family. Harry, their firstborn, was born in Los Angeles in 1901.

When Harry was only ten, Ida, who could not have been easy to live with, decided that economics dictated a return to the East Coast. Because the family could not afford to live in New York City, they rented an apartment across the Hudson River in Jersey City. With apartment houses mushrooming in cities across America, and with landlords offering three, sometimes four months' free rent, it was a tempting time for lessees, and Ida—never able to resist a bargain—moved the family frequently. One of her sons remembered coming home from school and finding a note pinned to the apartment door announcing the new address to which he should go for his customary milk and cookies.[1]

As he grew into manhood, Harry became ingratiating and amusing—what his son Jerry was to call "the life of the party, a funny, gregarious man." A daredevil, full of jokes, master of most sports, Harry was that rarity, a Jewish jock. During his college days, he became known for accepting any challenge. He would do headstands and handsprings even before the proverbial hat was dropped. During the winter session, Harry was employed as a gym teacher, but he always looked forward to the summers and jobs as a *tummeler* at Catskill hotels.* It was there, when he was in his mid-twenties, that he met Ruth Sachs, seven years his junior. Ruth was also on the staff of the hotel, as singer, accordionist, pianist, even children's music teacher. She had given a few performances on the local radio in her hometown of Jersey City, and with her multiple talents she was a boon to the owners of the hotel. Attractive, dark-haired, with heavily lidded eyes and a fulsome smile, she looked like a young Barbara Stanwyck.

Ruth, whose interests lay far from the tennis court or golf course, was nevertheless captivated by Harry's dauntless nerve and swarthy look, and the couple fell deeply in love. After the summer, when life returned to normal, they kept up a correspondence. After Ruth got her certificate as an English teacher two years later, they were married, in June 1928.

The young couple moved in with Ruth's parents, hoping eventually to have their own house. Ruth's mother, Pauline, though she had three children of her own—Belle, Manny, and Ruth—doted on Harry, so good-looking, so handy with screw-driver and hammer, and—proud as Pauline was of her hearty Jewish cooking—such a good eater.

In the mid-1920s, with Jersey City showing early signs of urban sprawl, teachers were much in demand. Ruth had a brilliant academic record and enjoyed her teaching job at the local high school, while Harry plodded through the academic year coaching teenagers, playing basketball, and waiting for spring and life outdoors. The first summer after they were married he introduced Ruth to life at Camp Colang in Pennsylvania—she, as music counselor, he as sports director. After the season he shared his dream with her that one day they would own just such a venture. Harry knew that these establishments could be successful only if the owners were gregarious,

---

* Each of these many summer resorts needed a staff of practical jokers. Young wags, generally college students, served as masters of ceremonies and were also expected to manufacture excitement for their guests, creating a tumult (from which the Yiddish word descends). They would act as swimming and tennis instructors by day and dancing partners for the daughters of guests at night.

Jerry Herman's grandmother, "Bubbie" Pauline Sachs. Photograph from Jerry Herman's private collection.

dedicated, and unafraid of hard work. He was certain there was money to be made in such an endeavor, and he sensed that Ruth's personality, her musicality, and especially her maternal nature were right for a summer camp.

The Hermans saved their money and soon were able to move into their own apartment at 413 Central Avenue. Its location, above a mattress store in a teeming commercial area, distressed Ruth, but she reconciled the need for living frugally with her and Harry's hope of being able to buy into a thriving camp.

Throughout the early years of their marriage the couple summered— working as counselors—at many camps in the Northeast. They used their tenure to investigate other camps in the area and learned how to spot the failings of each of these establishments. Either the lake was too muddy, the bunks rundown, the kitchen insect-ridden, or the location too remote for the camp they envisioned. Yet such an enterprise remained their dream— however deferred.

Theirs was a serendipitous lifestyle until Ruth's father, Louis Sachs, suffered a stroke while standing at the top of a staircase and tumbled headlong to his death. It was a tragedy of enormous proportion for Pauline, for, at forty-five, Louis was still a young man. Of course, Pauline (and even Aunt Belle) came to live with Harry and Ruth. At the same time, Ruth found herself pregnant.

Dr. William Jacobson, Pauline's youngest brother, had by this time become a famous gastroenterologist, with offices on East 72nd Street in Manhattan. Uncle Willie took a keen interest in his favorite great-niece and in her pregnancy. When she told Uncle Willie that she was planning to have her baby in a hospital in Jersey City, he insisted that she go instead to Dr. Goldblum, the head of obstetrics at Manhattan's Polyclinic Hospital. Uncle Willie supervised everything, even to selecting Ruth's private room that overlooked Broadway. Looking out of her hospital window, Ruth Herman could not suspect that thirty-five years later there would be a line of customers halfway around the block of the Winter Garden Theatre below, waiting to purchase tickets to *Mame,* her son's hit show.

Gerald Sheldon* Herman was born on 10 July 1931. He was, according to neighbors and friends, a loving, bright child from the beginning. He was central in his parents' thoughts from his earliest days, although they frequently vacationed alone, while Bubbie Pauline took charge of house and child. "I always had my mother, father, and grandmother in the same house. Life was regularly a very warm thing. My grandmother cooked Jewish food, and my mother was a great American cook. "It's a wonder," says Herman, who today maintains the same 136-pound weight of his college days, "I didn't wind up weighing three hundred pounds."

The youngster, who would become a specialist in chronicling the lives of strong women, was surrounded and nurtured by them throughout his growing years. Besides his mother, grandmother, and Aunt Belle, great-grandmother Dora Jacobson came from Brooklyn to visit them every Passover. In her eighties, she was still chipper, and young Jerry loved her and the stories of her arduous life in Russia. This matriarch spoke only Yiddish, and the youth so longed to communicate with her that he learned to speak a kind of pidgin Yiddish—a great asset in Broadway musical theater especially, Herman remembered, "when I was writing *Milk and Honey.*"

Dora had had nine children and somehow scrounged together enough money to send each of them, one after the other, to America to study. The youngest was dear Uncle Willie. Young Jerry relished hearing the story of how all his eight siblings—émigrés themselves, with very little cash to spare—contributed time, money, and lodging so that their youngest brother might go through medical school and internship, and how proud they were to have "a doctor in the family."

Herman remembered that a trip to any of the Jacobsons' was lively, warm, and musical. There was singing, with most of his uncles, aunts, and cousins joining in, at the frequent gatherings of the entire clan. Herman is convinced that his musical acumen is directly descended from this side of his family. The composer, who has collected many awards for interior de-

---

* Herman has always disliked his middle name, and from his earliest memories refused to use it. He spelled his first name Jerry because he thought it less pretentious than the way it was written on his birth certificate. In late September 1961, shortly before the opening of *Milk and Honey,* when his name was to be set in lights on the marquee of the Martin Beck Theatre, he had it changed legally to Jerry Herman.

sign, feels just as strongly that his considerable visual and architectural prowess stems from his paternal genes.

Both Ruth and Harry enjoyed people, and they often entertained their large circle of friends. Herman owes the title and spirit of one rousing song from *Mame* to his mother: once, coming from school and finding masses of hors d'oeuvres in the kitchen, he asked what the occasion was. "It's today," Ruth Herman replied. It was an optimistic response that was to steer his life.

But even when there were just the three of them, the Herman household rang with music from the shows his parents attended. Most evenings they played Rodgers and Hart, Kern, Porter, Gershwin, always the best of theater music. Harry managed an acceptable saxophone, and Ruth was a whiz on the accordion and piano. By the time he was six, Jerry was picking out tunes he had heard his parents playing the night before, and Ruth helped him to master the difficult section of any song. It seemed like fun to the child, but his mother, a born teacher, knew after instructing him for a few weeks that this was an extraordinarily gifted boy. She was torn between giving him proper piano lessons and just sitting by to help when he asked how a tune went. Since her son enjoyed being with his mother at the keyboard, could easily repeat any melody she played, and had an abhorrence of reading music, she opted for the fun of musicmaking and didn't structure his piano-playing hours.

In the summer of 1936 the Hermans drove up to Pine Plains, New York, about three hours north of New York City, and fell in love with Stissing Lake Camp, off New England's scenic Route Seven. The location was easily accessible to parents who wanted to come up for a day, yet remote enough to give campers a true sylvan experience. Stissing Lake was a small mirrored gem that separated the boys' quarters from the girls'. It was here that Jerry would spend every summer from the age of six until he turned twenty-three. Max and Lydia Horowitz, who owned the camp, were in their sixties and eager to retire. They had started the camp and built it into one of the best equipped in the Northeast, with a splendid and devoted staff. They trusted the young couple, promoting them after a season from counselors to head counselors. In 1937 the Hermans, who had saved their money rather than entrusting it to a now-crumbled stock market, were able to invest $2,000 to help the Depression-depleted Horowitzes open for the season. It was a propitious move, for the Hermans' small stake bought a large share of acreage and equipment. The 1930s, disastrous for most summer camps, brought only a small setback for Stissing Lake, which catered to a smart upper-middle-class

The athlete Harry Herman, Jerry's father, at Stissing Lake Camp, where a teenage Herman presented his first shows. Photograph from Jerry Herman's private collection.

Ruth Sachs Herman in gypsy costume for Parents' Day at the camp. Photograph from Jerry Herman's private collection.

camper. Those with "old money," the nouveaux riches, and the alimony heiresses could still afford to send their children away for the summer.

The next year, with the Depression easing and the camp enrollment having risen, Ruth was able to quit teaching and concentrate on her summer role as camp mother. Harry stayed on in the public school system for two more years before leaving to devote himself to running Stissing Lake full-time. The Horowitzes moved to Florida, and Stissing Lake Camp now belonged to Ruth and Harry.

The Hermans took naturally to camp life, for Harry, besides being able to organize sports activities, was a jack of all trades who could fix a toilet, rewire an electric socket, or paint a ceiling in a single afternoon. Jerry remembered him as "on a tractor all day, mowing. And my mother was the social Auntie Mame of the camp. She greeted all the parents on weekends. They were a very good combination.

"Every June, the three of us would go up with a group of workmen to open the camp. The men would put the two rafts out on the water—one for the boys' camp and one for the girls' on the other side of the lake. My mother would go through the cabins, cleaning and polishing everything and stocking the kitchen. My job was changing the light bulbs. I would go around the entire camp with a big basket of bulbs and a ladder. That was our summer vacation, and it started with us getting the place ready for the kids who would be arriving in three weeks. I suppose it was work, but my parents made it fun, wonderful fun."[2]

As the camp prospered, so did the Hermans. Now they could afford their own home, with more rooms than they needed, in a residential section of Jersey City called Greenville. The house had the two assets Ruth had always dreamed of: a large sun porch with a tiled floor, and a backyard. "Since they loved to entertain, my father made an enormous living room by breaking down a nonbearing wall," Herman recalled. "It was big enough to have both an organ and a piano. It soon became the party room for my parents' large circle of friends." But even when the small family was alone, they would invariably go to that room after dinner and play Rodgers and Hart and all the rest of the theater songs.

Across the street in this upper-middle-class neighborhood lived the Perlmans, the only other Jewish family in the area. Naturally Ruth and Rosetta Perlman became friends, and Claire, their daughter, an only child, three years older than Jerry, bonded with him from their first meeting. Even at eight, Claire was passionately maternal. It was she who held five-year-old Jerry's hand and walked him to P.S. 24 on his first day of school.

The children, ardent movie buffs, anticipated Friday nights because they were allowed to go to the local Loew's. Afterward they sat for hours in the corner drugstore over ice cream sodas, rerunning the film they had just seen, acting out their favorite parts. The next day, Jerry would play Claire— by ear—the songs from the movie. They were both, Claire admits, "starstruck. We collected glossy autographed pictures of the movie stars and hung them up on all the walls in my attic, or we wrote stories and plays, put on puppet shows, and played duets."[3]

Jerry had attended several stage musicals with his parents, and he could sit at the piano and play the songs he had heard. Besides his instinctive sense of melody, the boy had a natural affinity for harmony and theatrical flourish. Anyone who heard him, mostly friends of his mother, was astounded at the power and bravura, the sheer energy, coming from such a small-boned child.

His mother had taught him how to play most things in the key of F—her own favorite key for playing by ear. One day she showed him how to move his fingers over one note to the right to create the same sounds a tone higher in G. She explained that if he took out the B flat, which was part of the key of F, and substituted an F sharp, an essential in G, the music that came out was the same, but more suitable for a voice with a higher range. The child understood this rudimentary lesson in music theory and soon was showing off by playing his songs in F and then switching to G for a second chorus. Ruth, realizing his extraordinary talent, decided it was time to give her son proper lessons.[4]

"She hired Ethel Pesin, who taught Claire and most of the kids in the neighborhood," Jerry remembered, "and she came to my home. She said, 'In a few weeks you're going to be able to play this.' Then she sat down and played 'The Happy Farmer,' you know, the Schumann piece. Very simple, with two notes in the left hand. I said, 'Oh, that's very pretty,' and I went over to the piano and played back to her what I had just heard but with much more flourish and more interesting chords. Never heard it before in my life."

The staid music teacher was not impressed with the smart-alecky child, and they got off to a rocky start, but Ruth Herman was persistent enough to pressure Pesin into continuing with formal musical training for her son. Eventually, as Jerry recalled, the music teacher told Mrs. Herman, "'I don't know what to do with him. He's not looking at the notes, and he's playing these things [popular songs] by ear.' She was almost frightened by it. And that was my entire experience with piano lessons."[5]*

"My mother then took me to a wonderful man, the man who wrote the Army Air Corps Song. His name was Professor Crawford and he listened to me and said, 'I have some advice for you Mrs. Herman. Let him alone. Let him develop. Something's happening that's very interesting. He's using odd chords, and if he learns they are not the normal chords to use, he won't use

---

* Ethel Pesin remembers her experience of teaching Herman differently: "Jerry was not very impressed with classical music, but interested in popular songs. I wanted him to start traditionally learning to read music with the Thompson book [a standard, but very boring manual for beginning children]. I worked with him in half-hour segments for a period of about three months. I could never develop an interest in the music I taught him, for he simply refused to practice it." Author telephone interview with Ethel Pesin, 10 September 2000.

them. And I don't want that to happen to him.' He talked her into allowing me to develop on my own, and it was the wisest thing that ever happened because I flowered, not having to sit and work with notes at four o'clock every afternoon after being at school all day."

Like Irving Berlin and Noël Coward, Herman does not read music. "By way of compensation," he told me, "I tried to play with all the flourish of an orchestra." The composer is indeed a superb pianist who instinctively understands orchestral color and can obtain the exact shade he desires from his orchestrator. Ultrasensitive to vocal color and balance, as an accompanist he is without parallel. Alice Borden, for whom he has played since his youth, says: "He sounds like a full orchestra, yet when you're singing softly, he's sensitive enough not to overwhelm you. I think I was really spoiled having him play for me at such a young age. Nobody can live up to that."[6]

Preparing the camp for its opening, having his parents all to himself, and being the center of attention was fun for the child. But once the other children arrived, Jerry was moved out of the lovely guest house he shared with his parents and was treated as a run-of-the-mill camper. Now friction arose between the boy and his father, who forced him into a sports-oriented routine. Their relationship would remain fraught with resentments until Jerry developed a successful career.

"I had an athletic father who wanted his son to be an athlete too," Herman recalled. "What he got was a son who sat at the piano. I hated to be the cause of arguments between my parents, but my mother would always back me up. She would take my side by saying: 'Leave the kid alone. Let him do what's natural for him.' But my father wouldn't listen. He was always trying to get me out on the baseball field, and I would say to him, 'Look, Dad, I don't want to play baseball because I don't know how to do it well. I don't throw a ball well, and I don't catch well, and I feel uncomfortable in front of the other kids. Why can't you just let me do something that I can do?' I was trying to tell him that when I was on the baseball field, I was nobody. But when I played the piano I was somebody. He never understood."

Faced with this constant problem, one day eleven-year-old Jerry announced his "emancipation proclamation. I wanted to go to the camp social hall and play the piano, but my father insisted I had to play in a baseball game," he remembered. "My father dragged me onto the field and put me in left field position. I stood there in this huge open field and when the ball came right to me, I just stood there. The ball landed right at my feet and I just stood there. All the kids were screaming, but I just stood there. I wanted my father to know that I was going to have no part of baseball. I also wanted him to know that he was not going to do this to me ever again."[7]

"Harry never accepted Jerry for who he was, and what he could be," Alice Borden recalled, "whereas Ruth accepted everything about Jerry. But Harry wanted Jerry to become a gym teacher or something like that, and take over the camp."

One can understand the impulse of Harry, born into near poverty, to make the way easier for his only issue. Before he and Ruth bought into the camp, when they just made do on their teachers' salaries, but now the camp suddenly brought them an income that was, according to Herman, "quite extraordinary. They bought a splendid green convertible and took their first trip to Europe. And they did it in style. I guess my father wanted me to have enough money for a comfortable life."[8]

As tense as summers at Stissing Lake were, they nevertheless represented a change from the routine life in Jersey City during Jerry's early years. After a day at grammar school, his only escape from reality was the piano. He would quickly dispose of his homework and rush to the instrument. So alienated was he from his classmates that he did not try to join the school orchestra, instead keeping his piano playing to himself. His inability to read music allowed him to explore his own musicianship from the inside, but it left him out of reach of school music teachers; the musical arrangements the orchestra played were performed from the written score.

At eleven, when Herman began Hebrew School to prepare for his Bar Mitzvah, he had his first encounter with anti-Semitism. Going to cheder meant he would have to leave the shady tree-lined section of Greenville and travel to the seamy part of Jersey City. After some ruffians threw stones at him on his route home one day, he entered the house crying. Ruth and Harry were sympathetic and explained that being Jewish was "special," and that others did not always understand that. The next time Jerry went for his Hebrew lesson and ruffians pelted him with epithets, he simply remembered "being special," held his course, and walked by.

"This was long before I had any idea that I was homosexual," Jerry confided, "but I also must have known there was something a little different about me—that I didn't want to play basketball, that I wanted to come home and sit at the piano. The difference wasn't just that I was younger, shorter, and smaller-boned than my classmates. I was a loner. Oh, yes, I might have felt an attraction for an older classmate, but I couldn't verbalize it or even dare let myself think about it." Herman's sexual feelings were, he

Bar Mitzvah boy, Herman in 1944. Photograph from Jerry Herman's private collection.

said, "typical of many gay youths of the 1940s. Repressed. Rather than think about sex, I filled my life with distractions. If I was not playing the piano, I was making what I would call 'a display.' I would put some Christmas bulbs into a translucent vase and then I would light them up to show my parents. My father would look at me as though I was from another planet, and my mother would say, 'Oh, wasn't that creative?'"

It is curious how writers squirrel nuggets of experience for later use. Regarding his parents' differences of opinion about his Christmas display, one thinks of Zaza's verse in *La Cage Aux Folles,* "I Am What I Am" when he sings:

> I bang my own drum
> Some think it's noise
> I think it's pretty.

In 1946, when *Annie Get Your Gun* opened on Broadway, Jerry's parents took him to see it. He was mesmerized. It was not only the music and lyrics and the romantic story that intoxicated him, but the presence on stage of a larger-than-life female, Ethel Merman. He decided that very night that writing those kind of songs for that kind of woman was what he hoped to do with his life. Irving Berlin was the genius he wanted to emulate. Even to-day, he describes his idol's work with reverence: "So few words, music that goes right to the point, with so few notes. Songs you take home with you. Deep, unpretentious, memorable." For weeks after he saw that show he would go to the piano and play selections from the score. "They Say That Falling in Love Is Wonderful" and "I Got Lost in His Arms" were his fa-vorites. Eventually he was able to master "There's No Business Like Show Business," performing it more fluently than his mother played it from the sheet music.

"I didn't think it was anything terribly special," he says, "because, when you can do something and it's easy and it's fun, you don't realize that you have that special gift. I thought, 'Well this is just something wonderful that I'm able to do, and I'm happy because it gives me a lot of pleasure.' But I didn't realize how unusual it was until many years later."

As he listened to the songs of Berlin and other Broadway composers, and began to play variations on them, Herman began writing his own. He had, and still has, a strong, low tenor voice. Although he has never had voice lessons and doesn't think of himself as a vocalist, he is a splendid interpreter of his own songs. His very first, a ballad he dismisses and was reluctant to show me, was composed when he was about thirteen. Called "It's Not My Fault," all it evinces is that the youngster knew how to handle ABAC (or "showtune") form. In the final analysis "It's Not My Fault" presents a com-poser who is able to write a commercial melody no better or worse than the derivative ballads inserted in Twentieth Century–Fox films featuring Alice Faye or Betty Grable that were fodder for Herman and Claire.*

The next year, at a party at the Jewish Community Center, the teenager was introduced to another Jersey Cityite, Phyllis Newman. Fourteen, she had been in show business since the age of five. Phyllis could sing, dance, and choreograph with great energy and virtuosity. She was, according to Jerry, "not only beautiful, but very talented, and I knew she could put over my songs." Phyllis was looking for a regular accompanist, and Jerry, who could by now play anything by ear, fit the bill. He agreed to accompany her to auditions, and she, in turn, would learn the songs that he was just begin-

---

* Even though his melody uses the cliché-ridden I VI II V sequence, the very opening which leads to a suspended G chord is striking (see example, page 22). Then at (*) Her-man lands on the 9th of the D chord, and at (**) the melody falls on a B making a 13 chord. Certainly none of this sophistication was done consciously, but all of it is indi-vidualistic and quite interesting.

ning to write. It was a symbiotic compact, and in the process they became lifelong friends.

With a young professional on his side, the fourteen-year-old Herman was eager to write a show. *Step Right Up*'s wisp of a plot concerns a boy and girl who meet and fall in love at a carnival. It was written and given a single performance at the Jewish Community Center auditorium in Jersey City. It had only six songs, beginning with "Step Right Up, It's Carnival Time." Only one, "How to Be a Clown," gives Herman any pride today. "The rest," he explains, "are similar to songs I had heard." But this one is steeped in Herman's habitual showbiz greasepaint and has tremendous rhythmic drive. I quote from the beginning and the end:

> Just laugh and laugh until you're sore,
> Then take a breath and laugh some more.

Wear a smile but never a frown,
And that's—How to be a clown . . .

So keep that nose painted red,
And keep that smile from the top of your head
To the tip of your chin, and all the way down
And that's—How to be a clown.

Now that Jerry was a young adult, he could take a more active role at camp, hoping to turn it into a place where music and theater would play an important part. He began looking forward to coming to Stissing Lake each summer, for his creativity was appreciated by the all the campers. He would play the piano in the recreation hall as the kids sang along, which gave him a sense of self-importance. He soon began to write parodies of popular songs to be sung around the campfire, and he sharpened his skills at writing his own songs, mostly revue material which he brought to agents in New York. Phyllis Newman remembered "Jerry with a portable typewriter on his knees pecking out a clean copy for the audition on the bus ride from Jersey City. The songs were good, but we always got rejections. Yet we were persistent."[9]

Things were easier at Stissing Lake, for now there was blanket acceptance. "My father soon realized that I was turning his sports camp into a dramatic camp, and the children would come back until they were sixteen or seventeen to be in my shows."

He graduated from high school the following spring (two years younger than most of his classmates, having skipped two grades), and that summer he talked his father into allowing him to do a major camp show. He chose *Oklahoma!* "I went to the Drama Bookshop for scripts, and to theatrical suppliers for makeup and props." At camp he cut down the script and worked all summer on staging the show as a big event of the season. He used the older campers and some of the waiters for major roles and tried to get as many youngsters into the production as possible. It was a great achievement, so successful that many of the campers wanted to come back the next year to be in another musical.

"I can't stress strongly enough how much I picked up from putting on that show," Herman said. "When you put on something like *Oklahoma!* you learn how a good show is constructed. After *Oklahoma!* I did *Finian's Rainbow,* and the following year, *A Tree Grows in Brooklyn.* And, as I read books about the theater, the shows got more and more lavish. Once I asked my father to buy me a scrim. He said, 'What's a scrim?' I said, just let me pick it out, and you'll see. And I installed theatrical lighting—I mean, I had shows going on there that were as good as the summer stock productions in that area. And I learned from it. . . . I accompanied the shows and tried to make my old camp spinet sound like three pieces. And it was a wonderful way to grow up musically and theatrically."

Alice Borden remembered that she was only ten when Jerry chose her to play the role of Frannie in *A Tree Grows in Brooklyn*. "Being singled out was special—when the older kids in my bunk would go to sleep, I would be allowed to rehearse in the rec hall. It looked huge and the stage looked huge. Jerry actually took a song called 'Don't Be Afraid of Anything,' which is supposed to be sung by the father, and gave it to me. In the last part, when Frannie graduates, I wore a white satin graduation dress that Jerry found in an antique shop in town.

"Jerry did everything. He played the piano, he did the scenery, costumes, and directed the show. He was a one-man operation. We gave two performances in camp, and then on Sunday night invited the townspeople from Pine Plains. I sort of have this picture of Ruth Herman and my mother standing in the back and crying, since both of their children were involved in this beautiful show."

That autumn was an auspicious one for Jerry, who had registered for the Parsons School of Design in New York. His mother, however, was still trying to get him to take his original compositions more seriously, especially some of the clever, revue-type songs he had written. In January 1949, after Herman had completed a semester at Parsons, Ruth arranged, through a friend of a friend, an interview with Frank Loesser. Jerry was reluctant to go but finally asked Phyllis Newman to sing the songs from *Step Right Up* (plus some new ones) for the renowned Broadway composer-lyricist.

Loesser approached the neophyte in an atypical manner. Like Jerry, he was a talented artist, addicted to cartoons. He took out a big pad and some colored drawing pencils, and proceeded to sketch a freight train, making all the cars different colors. "A song is like a freight train," Loesser said. "It has to have a locomotive or hook—and the whole body of the song has to follow that. They all have to go where the locomotive is going. And then comes the most important thing, the red caboose that ends the song with a twist, a little surprise."

After discussing each of the teenager's songs, Loesser leaned back and asked, "What are you doing at a school of design? Why aren't you writing music? It's a tough field, but I think you can make it. There is genuine talent here."

Herman was euphoric. He never forgot the lesson of that afternoon. Many of his lyrics get their sense of locomotion from the title and proceed with a sense of inevitability that inhabits them from beginning to end. The essence of an off-kilter love song like "I Won't Send Roses," the ungallant soul, is stated at the outset. It serves as the song's engine that drives the work to its conclusion: "And roses suit you so." In this and other songs, Herman, when he begins, is always aware of the caboose that Loesser talked about. It follows in due course, never trivializing the work with the punchline of a cabaret song, the surprise ending that cloys on repeated hearings. A good example of Loesser's lesson is Herman's "Let's Not Waste a Moment" from *Milk and Honey*, whose title is clearly the locomotive. It ends

> When you face a short forever, there's no right or wrong,
> I can only face forever if you come along.
> I can only find my way
> If you're there to lead me on,
> So let's not waste a moment,
> Oh, look, another moment's gone!

When Jerry reported Loesser's encouragement, Ruth was ecstatic. "Why not try songwriting for a couple of years?" she asked. "You'll always have your room in this house, and I will slip you couple of bucks whenever you need it." His father still wanted him to come in with him on the children's camp. But when Jerry got up the courage to ask for help in something *he* wanted to do—to pay his tuition at a university that taught theater arts, rather than what his father had chosen—Harry Herman realized his dream was different from his son's and agreed to undertake the cost of his schooling.

Finishing out that school year at Parsons gave Herman a chance to dig deeply into his songwriting skills while looking for a college that was known for its theater department. He also sought a school that was far enough away from home that he could break the parental tie.

Poring over the catalogues of most liberal arts universities in the South or West, he settled on the University of Miami, which had an avant-garde theater department for its time. His decision to enroll there became his passport to emotional freedom and musical success.

3

college and beyond

Even though its marquee made it look deceptively like a nightclub from the outside, in 1949, when Jerry Herman matriculated there, the University of Miami in Coral Gables had a serious curriculum. The school put its ten thousand students through a rigorous schedule of classes in all forms of theater arts leading to a bachelor of arts degree.

"It had a progressive drama department that made you *do* theater instead of just talking about it," Herman says. "You didn't just sit in the classroom or work only in your own field. You also learned how to act, direct and design a show."[1]

Students also built scenery, designed costumes, made props, and were taught how to light a show. The composer remembered thinking how unnecessary were his lessons on the different kinds of lighting effects available through the use of gels. But years later, when sitting next to Tharon Musser, one of Broadway's finest lighting designers, who was working out the lights for Angela Lansbury's climactic solo of "If He Walked into My Life" in *Mame,* the knowledge he had acquired in those classes saved the day.

"Tharon was having a hard time getting the exact feel of autumn in Connecticut into the scene," he remembered, "and I asked her to try something warm like an amber gel. She looked at me with the strangest expression on her face. I could actually see her thinking 'now the songwriter thinks he's the lighting expert.' But she picked up her microphone and told the technician to 'try an amber gel on Miss Lansbury.' Then she added a gobo [a revolving gel with cut-outs that throws patterns of light on the stage], which made the backdrop look like swirling leaves, and the scene was absolutely gorgeous."[2]

At Miami, Herman turned into quite a different person from the shy, retiring boy who had daydreamed after school while playing the piano in his mother's parlor. From almost the first day, when he was walking by the lake after classes, he was drawn to Carol Isaacson. Isaacson later described Jerry as "the skinniest person you ever saw," adding, "but I was skinny too." She walked on by that afternoon. But that night, at a campus get-together for new arrivals, she found him again. She stayed next to him at the piano all evening while he played and she sang. They bonded that night, and Herman felt that now he had a real friend. Throughout their college days and beyond, their careers and lives were intertwined. They laughed uproariously at the same jokes and made wonderful music together—later, she even appeared in some of his shows. And when he wrote a new song, she would be the first to hear it. Their relationship, always platonic, was nonetheless intense. When she married, her husband, Bob Dorian, became Jerry's pal. Their children, Jane and David, were to become his godchildren, and Jane's daughter, Sarah, his great-goddaughter. Herman's close relationship to Carol was the key to his sense of fulfillment during his early months at college.[3]

Now he joined the school's dramatic society and also began writing articles for the university paper. The nineteen-year-old soon pledged to Zeta Beta Tau, familiarly known as "the Zebes," an upper-class Jewish fraternity whose members saw the advantage of recruiting this piano-playing expert. The university did not have individual fraternity houses, but Jerry moved from the regular dorm into the fraternity dorm. Some seventy members of ZBT shared suites in this section of the dorm, some with two bedrooms and others with three. Jerry's had two, and he shared his room with Martin Stone. Dick Edwards and Louis Hertz occupied the other bedroom. The suite's living room boasted a piano, lent by one of the roommates, and this site soon became one of the most popular on campus. Herman was adept at all the pop songs of the day, as well as Broadway showtunes and college songs, and, wanting desperately to do a social about-face and be accepted, he was eager to share his talents.

He began performing at parties and dances. "Playing for dances was something that I could do very well," Herman said recently, "and I found people who appreciated my talent, and later, my creativity." Two of those people were Paul and Margery Nagel, a young married couple, juniors when Herman was a freshman. The Nagels were fascinated with puppets. They had studied the art under the renowned Sue Hastings, who had retired to Coral Gables and taught puppetry in the university's drama department. As part of their course the Nagels gave shows in elementary schools in the area.

Paul wrote the scripts, Margery made the puppets, and the couple operated them together. "Jerry provided all the music," Margery remembered, "on whatever passed for a piano in each school, making up slightly different accompaniments each time, like the old-time pianists did for silent movies."[4]

Carol was Jerry's pal, but all his fraternity brothers had girlfriends, and finding one was easy for this campus dynamo. Early in his stay at Miami he got to know Sally Singer—pretty, petite, sophisticated, and knowledgeable about theater. She came from New Rochelle, and her father was the head of the elegant fur salon at Bergdorf-Goodman, New York's most chic department store. The Singers, on Sally's instigation, often attended the theater, and were especially fond of musicals. Sally was a "belter," with a strong chest voice, and she handled the comic role of Meg Brockie to fine account in the university's production of *Brigadoon*. "She was," according to Herman, "red-headed and adorable; full of spunk—the perfect companion for me." Sally was very supportive of Jerry's songwriting and admired his creativity. Fifty years after his college days, he still occasionally dips into a tattered copy of *Walker's*, the only rhyming dictionary he owns—a gift from Sally.[5]

Women were not allowed into the dorms, but, by their sophomore year, when Jerry and Sally were "going steady," Herman and Louis Hertz found a way to get into bed with their girls. They rented a pair of rooms at the affordable Prince Michael Hotel, an establishment near the campus that was not too fussy about IDs. There Jerry, Sally, Hertz, and his girlfriend enjoyed what Hertz called "a glorious weekend of heavy fucking."[6]

The Phi Sigma Sigma Honorary Society sponsored a yearly event called Potpourri, a musical competition for fraternities and sororities. A typical performance was little more than a skit or two with music. "My fraternity brothers, knowing of my creative aspirations, put me in charge of Potpourri," Herman recalled, "and my first show in 1951 was about a college on Saturn whose chorus line all wore antennae." The skit featured the song "The New U of M in the Sky," with lines like "And after classes when our work is done,/ To get a tan we rocket to the sun." If the material was jejune, it was performed with serious professionalism. Herman rehearsed his fraternity brothers diligently, just as he had done the campers at Stissing Lake; he also supervised the painting of the minimal scenery, directed, and accompanied. The Zebes easily walked off with the trophy.

The victory was cathartic for Herman: "I seemed suddenly well-liked, and it didn't hurt that my campus mates would go around singing my songs long after the contest was over. I had learned how to use my talent not just to write songs but to make a place for myself. For the first time in my life, I felt that I really belonged."[7]

The next year he got more ambitious and put on a show called *In the Red,* which had *kazatskas* and other Russian dances mixed with anti-Soviet jibes and barbs. Now Herman had a more elaborate set, and one of his fraternity brothers, Wally Levine, a music major, wrote out his score and orchestrated it for the semblance of a pit band. Again, Jerry created the script and the music, supervised painting the scenery, and even conducted from the piano. *In the Red* was much more mature in subject matter and style than its predecessor. And again, ZBT trounced the other Potpourri entrants.

This seemingly unquenchable talent and ambition led to another show in Herman's junior year, *An Apple for Venus,* which Herman calls "my first real musical." It was the Box Theatre's experimental musical, and it won him the drama department's annual award. Written before John Latouche and Jerome Moross's *The Golden Apple* (which reached Broadway in March 1954, the year Herman graduated from Miami), *An Apple for Venus* shares with that well-respected Broadway musical an antique setting. "My show had some cute songs, but was a fledgling work," Herman says.

By 1953 the Potpourri committee met with Herman and told him that the annual competition would have to be suspended because there simply weren't enough entrants. Few dared to compete with the Zebes.

"Why don't we write a revue in which everyone can take part?" Jerry suggested to the committee. "Let anyone audition, and let it be our varsity show." They agreed heartily; Potpourri was retired and replaced with a more inclusive and mature title: Sketchbook. Yet although the songs and sketches in this musical revue were open to the entire senior class, that edition was almost wholly a Herman creation.

Herman had grandiose ideas for the first Sketchbook, which was scheduled for two performances in March 1953. It had a cast of ninety-six on stage and needed twenty-two students backstage, all combining their talents for this topical revue. More locals and parents of the performers wanted to attend than the Ring Theatre on campus could accommodate, so the huge Dade County Auditorium was booked.* Sketchbook had nineteen

---

* In 1974 the university built a splendid new theater, one that can be adapted to open, thrust, or proscenium stage. To honor its most famous alumnus they called it the Jerry Herman Ring Theatre.

original songs, all written by Herman, and all in the tradition of college entertainment. "The Gal with the Bumpiest Profile," "Ode to Chlorophyll," and "Viva la Revival" poked irreverent fun at breast endowment, latest scientific news, and the current Broadway season.

Herman treated performers and crew in a most professional way. Intense daily rehearsals began six weeks before the performances in a rented facility near the campus paid for by the fraternities and sororities. Because students needed to keep up with their academic training, all rehearsals were scheduled after class hours and in the evenings. But Herman was a demanding taskmaster, expecting faithful attendance, promptness, and, above all, complete memorization of lines by the second rehearsal. Cast and crew practiced scenes and songs, went through numerous costume fittings, and posed several times for publicity photos.

On the two big nights, the orchestra and cast, who had been solidly rehearsed, went through their paces with professional aplomb before sold-out houses. Sketchbook's material may have been somewhat naive, but it was performed with such theatrical polish that it became one of the highlights of Miami's academic year. Still called Sketchbook, the University of Miami's annual revue is a tradition that flourishes today. Largely because of that show, Herman, a junior, was listed in *Who's Who in American Colleges*.

In his senior year, Herman's abiding interest in writing and directing a more sophisticated musical revue, similar to those he had seen in Greenwich Village, transformed Sketchbook. Twenty-two new songs and skits were presented under the title of *I Feel Wonderful*. With song titles like "I Fell in Love with the Blues," "Share and Share Alike," and "Don't Go to the Movies," this was certainly a less campus-oriented show. With an eye to transferring his revue eventually to Manhattan, he inserted a hilarious skit called "Theater on a Stool." The number mocked the revues at New York's posh Upstairs at the Downstairs, which always included a few singers sitting on stools and acting oh-so-blasé.

By graduation time, Herman had collected many other awards besides his listing in the collegiate *Who's Who*. In 1954 he was elected to Iron Arrow, the university's leading honorary society, and to Omicron Delta Kappa, a national honor society. In recognition of his contribution to theatrical life at the university he won the coveted Snarks Playwriting Award. That year the campus yearbook, the *Ibis*, was dedicated to him, as somebody who had made a mark.

Herman calls that time "nourishing," for he was never to lose the friendships, male and female, made in his years at college. Paramount among his college friends were Carol Dorian, who appeared in most of the college musicals, and of course Sally Singer, to whom he had become engaged. But although Herman has said that Sally "was madly in love with me, and we were sleeping together," intending to marry upon graduation, he was not sure of his own feelings for her.

"Back during my sophomore year some part of me knew there was something wrong," Herman said, "but I wasn't sure what it was. I was a little naive, but my awakening happened during an expressionist play by Gerhart Hauptman called *The Ascension of Hanele,* in which I played a beggar boy. A very handsome young man named Hal Vaughn had the lead. He's deceased, but I don't think he would have minded my relating the story.

"He was very, very friendly to me during the rehearsal period. Once the show opened I would stand in the wings and wait for my entrance with Hal. We were alone on stage left surrounded by heavy black drapes. One night, without any warning he leaned over and kissed me. It was the most amazing awakening, like something out of a novel, because I knew in that second—it was longer than a second—that I liked it. And that kiss told me two things: that something was missing with Sally, and that I was not some kind of freak. I understood at once that there were others like me in the drama department.

"I probably had looked at some guys, but never dared do anything about it. Now it turned me on. And that was the beginning for me. I went on stage that night in an absolute stupor. I didn't know what I was saying. And after the show Hal asked me if I would go out and have a cup of coffee with him. I don't drink coffee, but I said I would be delighted to. And later he took me back to his place, and that was my first real experience with a man. It was under the best circumstances because he knew he was dealing with a novice. He was very gentle and easy with me. He didn't try and push me in any direction that I didn't want to go, and he made it very lovely. And I saw him many times. He was charming, a very bright man. And we kept in touch even after graduation.

"I knew now I had to say farewell to Sally. But I was really frightened of telling her the truth. So I told Sally that I was about to embark on a very difficult journey of trying to become a songwriter for Broadway, and I knew that I would have great difficulty in supporting my own self, and I certainly couldn't support a wife. I said, 'You just have to let me find my way and we'll see what happens.' And I ended my relationship with Sally on that note. It was the wisest thing I ever did because, had I married her, I would have been in a situation that would have been wrong for me, and I would have ruined her life and mine. This way I was free to go on and live the life I've lived, which has been exciting and very fulfilling. I have enjoyed being gay. I have enjoyed it so tremendously. I have the same group of friends that I have had for years. I've had a few major romances, and since Sally, I have never lied about my proclivities."[8]

His junior and senior years at the university, once he had broken his engagement to Sally, became a time of liberation for Jerry Herman. With friends both gay and straight, he was much applauded for his creative work.

On Herman's twenty-third birthday, he was back at Stissing Lake, putting on shows and writing parodies to well-known songs. But with the approach of autumn back in Jersey City, this fledgling holder of a bachelor's degree in theater didn't know where to turn.

Eventually, his mind was made up for him. Although World War II had long since ended, Herman was drafted to serve in the army. Aberdeen Proving Ground in Maryland was a distressing experience for both the soldier and the army.

"I became a liability. The army was not in need of soldiers, certainly not one who was sick all the time. I was not eating properly and lost twenty-five pounds. When my parents came to visit me after I had gotten one of my bronchial attacks and was in the infirmary (my weakness healthwise has always been in my chest), they saw a skeleton who weighed about 100 pounds. My father was so upset with what was happening to me that he told me, 'I'm going to get you out of here.' He had no influence, but he didn't have to do much but wait until I was called into the colonel's office. I thought I was going to be chastised for not being a good soldier, but this gruff voiced man said, 'Sit down, son,'—he called me 'son.' And then he said very gently, 'I don't want you to be disappointed, but not everybody's cut out to be a soldier.' Then he added, 'We're going to send you home so they can fatten you up.'"

What impressed Herman most about that experience was the about-face of his father, who had told his son when he was drafted, "This will be a good experience for you." At the time, Herman had resented his father's insensitivity, his refusal to recognize that his son was not army material. Now, at least, he realized his father cared about him. It was the beginning of a growing relationship that the mature Herman was to cherish. Eventually, the antagonism that had existed between them simply melted away.

Grandma Pauline and Ruth lost no time restoring his trim frame to its pre-GI state. With his health regenerated, his old ambition returned. The "gee-whiz" kid, completely imbued with the Garland-Rooney mystique, decided to put on his own show. Remembering the success of *Step Right Up,* written for the YMHA and starring Phyllis Newman, he enlisted her again, promising this time to "bring it to New York."

His burgeoning trust in Harry Herman after his army experience led Jerry to involve his father in producing the show, and Harry in turn cajoled the parents of campers and local businessmen he knew into investing in his son's revue. With the songs culled from Jerry's varsity show at the University of Miami, only the title, *I Feel Wonderful,* was new.

I Feel Wonderful opened at the Theatre de Lys (now the Lucille Lortel) on Christopher Street in Greenwich Village on 8 October 1954 and closed on 28 November after forty-nine performances. It was not a rousing success. Brooks Atkinson, critic for the *New York Times,* while taking the composer's youth into account, wrote that "most of Mr. Herman's music and lyrics are imitations of work by mature craftsmen." Atkinson went on to note that "although his numbers are long on style, they are short on content."[9] But second-stringer William Hawkins of the *New York World-Telegram* wrote that he had "spent a thoroughly agreeable evening" and predicted that "twenty-two-year-old Herman [he was actually twenty-three] will be heard from in the future."[10]

Hawkins's review was enough to attract an agent, someone who would become an important part of the young songwriter's life. Priscilla Morgan, tall, rail-slim, and the epitome of worldliness, remembered: "I was separating from my husband and I moved to a lovely garden apartment. I then had my own agency and I represented many authors for television and theater.

"I had an affair with the painter René Boucher, who was very close to de Kooning, et cetera—very glamorous. We were spending the weekend in my apartment, and one Sunday—in the autumn of 1954—Don Appell called me and said, 'There's a very talented young guy down at the Theatre de Lys with a new musical. Just your kind of smart material. The show is called *I Feel Wonderful.*' I was very nervous because René was so very knowledgeable, and I thought he's not going to like this showbiz. When we came in there were only about five people. It was so incredible. First of all he had produced it, he cast it, he wrote everything, all the lyrics all the music, all the sketches. And he played the piano in the pit. I couldn't believe what I was listening to. We put back our heads and roared. I laughed so hard I thought I was going to be sick. Those were the days when we wore long gloves, and I took one off, put out my hand, and said, 'I'm Priscilla Morgan, and I'm an agent, and you are so talented, I would like to represent you.'"[11]

Morgan knew that "other agents were going to go after him," so she put

Bob Miller and Phyllis Newman in twenty-three-year-old Herman's first off-Broadway show, *I Feel Wonderful*. Photofest, Inc.

the pressure on him to sign with her. "I entertained him [actually, *he* entertained] at parties in my spectacular garden apartment replete with sculptures by Isamu Noguchi." The young musician, still living at home in Jersey City, was duly taken with Priscilla and her urbanity.

Herman now had an agent who believed in his work, one who could introduce him to New York café society to help his career take off, and who could find him jobs writing special material. But it was not to be a time of unmitigated joy. Jerry's beloved mother had gone to a local dentist for a routine tooth extraction. "The wound didn't heal, and the dentist sent her to a specialist, who did a biopsy and found it was cancer," Herman recalled mistily. "If it had happened today they would have cured that in three months with radiation, but it was before all that was available. It spread like wildfire and it went into her head, her brain, and she died a few months later. She was forty-four years old, a beautiful, vital woman. My father was as devastated as I was, for he truly loved my mother."

Ruth Pearlman, a close friend, recalled taking Ruth to New York Hospital for chemotherapy. "Members of her large circle of friends formed teams: one would drive and park, the other would escort Ruth. Each one thought of this activity not as a duty, or a favor, or a mitzvah, but rather as an honor, a distinction—so much was Ruth loved, revered, and respected. She was the president of the Jersey City Hadassah. At the time, I remember people said anybody could be president, but there was only one Ruth Herman, who played the piano and accompanied rank amateurs, shifted to any key, wrote lyrics in English and Yiddish satirizing anything. I knew her more as a friend and a hostess who laughed and told jokes. She wasn't laughing when Jerry's show opened at the Theatre de Lys, but she was terribly proud. I can picture her with her swollen jaw, sitting on the aisle in the second row. And I remember the day before Ruth died. The bed was in that vast living room, and I was at her bedside when Jerry came in from school. And she asked, being barely understandable because of the condition of her mouth, 'Did you take your vitamins?' Is that a memory? My best friend was dying and her only concern was for her son."[12]

Trying to express the tailspin his mother's death plunged him into that December, and aware of the depth of his own emotion, Herman said recently: "I know it sounds like a cliché, a gay boy who loves his mother, but my loving relationship with my mother played a huge part in my life. She was the first, and maybe the most important, of the influences that shaped me." Ruth Herman's death in December 1954 was a blow from which Jerry Herman never recovered.

For close to a year he sat listlessly around the house. "I went into serious grieving," Herman admitted. "I stopped doing everything, wrote no new songs, didn't even feel like playing the piano. My father and my grandmother were afraid I was never going to come back to myself."

Eventually, when he decided to try to get a job playing cocktail piano in

New York, his father gave him enough money to put down a month's rent for a small third-floor walk-up apartment on East Tenth Street in the Village. Jerry took his mother's piano and the bed from his room in Jersey City and some other furnishings. His father built closets and put up necessary fixtures. Father and son bonded closer.

Aunt Belle, Ruth's younger sister, who upon her sister's death had taken Jerry's grandmother to live with her in New Jersey, visited frequently. She became, if not a surrogate mother, "that special warm and loving person I could always talk to and share things with."

A year later Harry Herman asked his son whether he had any objection to his father's dating a distant cousin who like himself was "widowed and lonesome." Jerry thought it was very dear of him to ask, and he encouraged him to see the woman, because he felt his father was a lost man without his mother. "He depended on a woman, so when he and Edna were wed, it was a very good second marriage."

Jerry Herman's first jobs in New York were at ordinary cocktail lounges, so many that he does not even remember their names. But eventually he landed at the chic supper club RSVP. He was only the intermission pianist, playing soft music-for-talking-over after the headliner left the stage. The star who made the room her own was the doyen chanteuse Mabel Mercer.

"Mabel Mercer never possessed a great voice," Herman was to say, "but watching her night after night was an extraordinarily valuable course in song interpretation. She acted those wonderful ballads she sang with a fierce passion and intelligence that forced you to listen to every word. Because she was such a great actress, she became the definitive delineator of the *meaning* of the song."[13]

Students of singing, Frank Sinatra included, often came to hear her and emulated Mabel Mercer's sense of phrasing. As a lyricist, Herman, too, was fascinated with Mercer. She had such exquisite taste and chose only the best and most sensitive musical theater repertoire. Her songs invariably were a marvelous wedding of words and music, and Mercer, because her voice quality was secondary—some said nonexistent—compelled the listener to attend to the way the words sat on the music.

When Mercer finished, Herman would take over. "I got this job through an elderly gentleman who booked me because he liked my style and my looks. He told me to play floridly and to look romantic to create a mood. So I played, Gershwin, Rodgers, and Berlin mostly, quietly, but trying to encompass the whole keyboard with lots of arpeggios. I knew most of the songs by ear and could generally fill customers' requests. I was paid $90 a week, and to me that was a fortune. The only thing about the job I didn't like was the hours, because I like my mornings for songwriting, and since I'd sometimes not leave the club until three A.M., I'd have to sleep through the mornings."

As he grew more assured at his job, Herman began accompanying some of the customers, frequently celebrities, often tipsy, who came to hear Mabel Mercer. They soon found out about his compositional gifts and asked him to write special material for them. He wrote "My Type Is Coming Back" for Tallulah Bankhead ("Fads that have gone away/Find that they're on their way back . . . /We've been thru Gina, Lena, Donna, Lana,/Those who won't and those who wanna") and one called "Washington Square" for Ray Bolger. Hermione Gingold soon heard about him and asked him to write a song to open her act. It was full of allusions to different kinds of gold, like old gold, rolled gold, white gold, and fool's gold. In performing it with her elegant lisp, she flashed the audience a mischievous smile, eliciting a titter when she announced the punchline: "But the best gold is Gingold!"

Some pianists, like Cy Walter at the Byline Room or Barbara Carroll at the Carlyle, become permanent fixtures of the nightclub scene. They develop a following and stay for years, entertaining the same clientele. Jerry Herman had too much ambition, perhaps too many bridges uncrossed, to remain more than a year as a background mood pianist. He soon began looking for work in cabarets where he could move to center stage and perhaps have some of his original songs performed. A year later he lit on The Showplace in Greenwich Village, which was run by an irrepressible actor-model, Jim Paul Eilers.

Eilers, young, attractive, and canny, a native of Indianapolis, had poured his savings from posing with cigarettes, hats, and shaving cream into a town house on West 4th Street in the Village. Wanting to open a cabaret, what he needed now was a liquor license. He applied and had one transferred from a defunct Mafia-run bar called Le Chantilly, where a murder had been committed. This valuable license became his passport to success. Since Eilers had a liquor license and no police record, he was permitted to convert his house into a duplex cabaret. Later he bought the building, living on the top floor in the apartment that had once been the hideaway of New York's playboy mayor, Jimmy Walker.

The Showplace itself operated on the two lower floors. The lounge on the street floor was a mecca for budding talent. For the price of a drink, a neophyte singer could take a turn at an open mike backed by a pianist who could transpose any song to accommodate the singer's range. Upstairs was a seventy-five-seat theater with an eight-by-ten-foot stage, perfect for the intimate revues that were all the rage in the fifties. The Showplace was Greenwich Village's answer to Julius Monk's flourishing stainless steel and black vinyl midtown cabaret, Upstairs at the Downstairs. When Jerry Herman came in to audition (an audition he passed easily), he sang a funny song called "Skip the Opening Number," a satire on the mindless curtain raisers in which girls come out and kick. Then he plunged into an irresistible greasepaint towel number called "Two a Day." Its melody, an easy soft shoe, does not need to be quoted here, but in its nicely rhymed lyric which is all of one piece, all the lines head (or in Frank Loesser's metaphor, locomote) toward the finale:

> I was born to play the two a day:
> The hoke, the corn, the empty matinee.
> And so, I know that vaud'ville's just asleep,
> And so I gotta keep on dancin' till I rake it up, and dig it up,
>   and wake it up.
> I get no thrill from this atomic age,
> My home is still upon the Palace stage.
> Where life's a song, as long as I can say
> "I belong to the wonderful world of the two a day!"

To cap off his audition, Herman then plunged into the can't-fail rouser that was his signature song at the time, "Showtune in 2/4."*

Eilers listened attentively and was impressed enough to hire Herman on the spot. But, desperately in need of a pianist for the downstairs room, he said, "I'll do your show, but it has to follow the revues I have lined up."

According to Eilers, Herman was the best pianist he ever had in the lounge, far better than the future actor Warren Beatty, who had preceded him. He was also deeply attracted to the young man's compact frame, good looks, and patient manner accompanying even the worst amateurs who came to sing along, or worse, solo.[14] But Herman saw only the brighter side of his job. "Working at the Showplace Lounge," he recalled, "was like going

---

* "Showtune in 2/4" is typical of the deceptively simple melody at which Herman excelled. The rising intensity of each phrase—especially at the end of the seventh bar—where the melody is a B flat against the B natural of the chord, creates a kind of Herman signature. The dissonance is not forced because the melody rises from A to B flat to B and finally lands on a C. Herman originated those wide skips to dissonant landings, a technique later borrowed by Cy Coleman and John Kander.

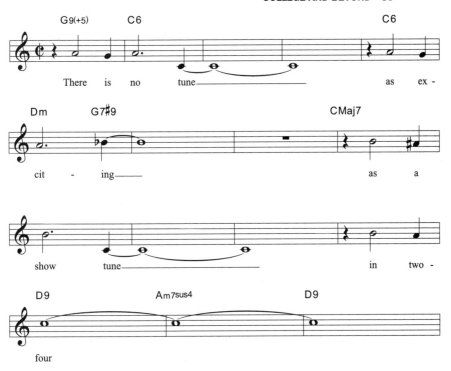

to a party every night. People came in and I played for them. I became an expert at accompanying."[15]

In 1957, when Herman had been working the lounge for more than a year and the upstairs show was Rick Besoyan's popular *In Your Hat*, Besoyan and Eilers decided to expand one of its most successful sketches to a full evening-length show. They called it *Little Mary Sunshine* and transferred it to a proscenium theater, where it ran for almost eight years.

"Boy, you better get that material you've been talking about ready," Eilers remembered telling Herman before the transfer, "because once *In Your Hat* moves, I'm going to need a show." Herman dawdled, rewriting his material to make it more timely. Eilers, in a bind, marked time by opening a dull show called *Two by Four*.

Herman's new show, *Nightcap*, was built on the theme of life in New York. Lasting about an hour, it was intended as an after-theater diversion. As was his custom by now, Herman wrote the sketches, cast, directed, supervised the scenery (created by Hal Jacobs) and the costumes (by Nilo), conducted, and played the piano. He even designed and created the advertising sandwich signs to lure customers from the sidewalk into the theater. In keeping with his shoestring budget, he made a colorful set out of ribbons and balloons artfully lit. For movement and dance, the only element in which he was inexpert, he called on his friend Phyllis Newman. *Nightcap,* which opened on 18 May 1958, received a splendid review from *New York Post* critic Richard Watts, who said, "It's worth a trip down to the Village to hear this wonderful new material."[16] The show chalked up a most respectable two-year run.

Watts's rave was enough to bring the uptown crowd down to The Showplace to see what all the furor was about. In his memoir Jerry tells a story about trying to shoo away the people he thought were waiting to get into the restaurant next door. He was angry with them for blocking the show's advertising billboards he had designed. Actually, they were lining up to buy tickets to *Nightcap.*[17]

"There was never a slow night," Eilers remembered. "If it looked like there were only a few reservations, Jerry's father and stepmother called parents of their campers and told them to hurry over to The Showplace." Eilers marketed the show cleverly. Since customers hesitate to enter a cabaret unless it is somewhat crowded, he had life-size cardboard silhouettes made to give the appearance to passersby that there were people at each table. These cut-outs folded down when the tables were occupied. "From the doorway," Eilers remembered, "it always looked like the place was jammed. Then I got a mannequin, dressed her up, and put her out on the street in front of the place. Some kids stole her, and, offering a tremendous reward, I got the papers to write about it."

Charles Nelson Reilly, who was entrusted with the show's comic material, remembered his first meeting with Herman: "Phyllis Newman and I had the same voice teacher—I was trying to be an opera singer—and she told me about the show. So I went down to Jerry's one-room apartment— the size of a pool table. There was no dining table, but a board attached to the wall which could serve as a table or could fold down. It had a stick to hold it up. When I went to audition, his grandmother's fine china, service for eight, was on it. I was so nervous that I accidentally kicked the stick, and the whole table fell and all the dishes were completely destroyed. He didn't get upset. I thought, 'What does someone in such a small room need with service for eight?' So I sang, 'There But for You Go I' from *Brigadoon,* and I said to Jerry, 'I can't have anyone look at me when I sing, so I'll sing to the wall. And I sang with this phoney opera baritone. And he told me, months later, that he laughed so hard he wet himself. I thought I was going to be the next Robert Merrill. So he says right away, you're in the show. And at the rehearsal I find out that I'm not the leading baritone—that I am the comedian.

"We played Wednesday through Sunday, with two performances per day over the weekend. Dom de Louise was The Showplace bartender, but on the nights we didn't play he would do his magic act, with Ruth Buzzi as Shakuntala, his assistant.

"Wash-and-wear shirts had just come in, and you could buy French cuffs with one layer of cloth, not like today's fancy cuffs which are folded over. Jerry would play the piano often so violently that his cufflinks fell out. I was in charge of putting in the cufflinks on opening night—and it was also my job to hunt for them after every show."

Reilly, who was given all the comic material, remembered his duet with Jane Romano about the recent grim plays that were standard Broadway fare that year. The song, called "Jolly Theatrical Season," seemed a bit dated after the play *The Visit* closed. "And I said we have to update it, and just to show you how brilliant Jerry was, he came back with '*Sweet Bird of Youth* is a comic sensation/Of dope, hysterectomy, rape, and castration.'

"There was an off-Broadway rule. We scheduled a Sunday matinee at 3 o'clock, but we canceled the performance if we had less than seven people. I would peek through the curtain and announce, 'There's only three. Now there's five, and its almost curtain time. Shit! Five people just came in.' But most Sundays we didn't get to seven, so we would walk a half-block to a restaurant called Portofino, which had a young pretty waitress named Elaine Kauffman, who eventually owned Elaine's, Manhattan's premiere showbiz-celebrity restaurant. She spoiled us and gave us two drinks for the price of one. And we would order the cheapest thing on the menu—spaghetti. On most Sundays Bill Cosby would come in. And we'd say, 'My God, there's Woody Allen, and then Dick Cavett. They didn't get seven either.'"[18]

Herman had a knack for picking talent, and he knew the kind of "show-voices" he needed in addition to Reilly to put over his songs. He chose Kenneth Nelson, a brilliant song-and-dance juvenile, as the romantic lead and Jane Romano and Fia Karen, both belters.*

---

* Charles Nelson Reilly went on to have a splendid career, notably creating the role of the wicket company's nepotic nephew in *How to Succeed* (for which he won the Tony Award as Best Supporting Actor in a Musical), and later as Cornelius Hackl in *Hello, Dolly!* Kenneth Nelson starred in *The Fantasticks* and *Seventeen;* Jane Romano went into the Fay Bainter play *A Swim in the Sea.*

The show was packed with trenchant material and seems to have had very little dross. "Confession to a Park Avenue Mother," which was written for Reilly, is a teenage snob's admission to his mater, who set foot on the West Side only when she sailed for Europe, that he had fallen in love with a girl who lived on the wrong side of Fifth Avenue. His nervousness, transmitted to the trembling teacup he held, made the song hilarious.

> If the stork in this tragic case
> Had just dropped her on Sutton Place,
> For in every other way she's made to order
> But cruel fate had her conceived across the border.

"Nice Running Into You" and "Your Good Morning" were the kind of whimsical songs that Herman would later develop into high art. The former concerns a girl singing to her imaginary ex. With lines like "The years must *go* well/You look *so* well," it reached for, and almost arrived at, the moving kind of torch that Herman ballads would eventually attain. The latter was a jaunty, wholesome duet for a boy and girl who pass each other, say good morning, and begin a relationship.

Nightcap also sported some raunchy spoofs like "Naughty Forty-Second Street" and "The Producer Didn't Hire Me," quite appropriate to what uptowners thought should be heard in a soi-disant den of iniquity like The Showplace.

Early Herman melodies first introduced in *Nightcap,* often only partially completed, would be rewritten and reappear, sometimes decades later, in their definitive form. "I Wish I Could Say" became *Dear World*'s "I've Never Said I Love You," and the opening phrases of "Showtune in Two-Four," one of the first tunes Jerry played for Eilers, ended up in *Mame* as part of "It's Today." "It's Gotta Be a Dream," with its lyric transformed to "Love Is Only Love," was beautifully sung by Barbra Streisand in the film version of *Hello, Dolly!*

Business stayed brisk throughout the run. When the original cast moved on to other venues, Rita Gardner, Estelle Parsons, and Bobo Lewis stepped in as replacements. Finally Jerry even replaced himself. It was time to move on.

"I knew other agents were going to go after him," Priscilla Morgan recalled, "so I was as supportive as I could be for his career to move ahead. Jerry was ambitious, he wanted to do a Broadway musical like crazy. But I couldn't make it happen; I was so afraid I was going to lose him because I wasn't able to get him to Broadway where he wanted to go. So I said, 'Just do another revue. Or add some new material to this one. You have a wonderful showplace for your talent.' And I went practically every night. [The theater critic] Otis Gurnsey used to come down, and 'Yip' Harburg, the lyricist of *Finian's Rainbow,* frequently dropped in to hear what new material Jerry had added. Meantime I was trying to get Jerry together with [the television producer] Fred Coe to commission him to do something. At my frequent parties I'd get Jerry to play all his music. Then Frank Loesser heard about him and told me he wanted to sign him to his own music publishing company. But I wasn't about to let that happen."

One night Herman's friend the producer Larry Kasha dropped in to see *Nightcap* and aired his views that "with a couple of changes and some more material it could get out of the nightclub and play in an off-Broadway theater." Kasha said he wanted to "enlarge it" and set up a handsome-looking production. Herman augmented the score with even more topical numbers, while Kasha retained the same cast, only substituting for Jane Romano the comic Dody Goodman, a zany comedienne who appeared frequently as a guest on Jack Paar's *Late Show.* What to call it? Herman, always in love with panoply and processions, found the apt word: *Parade.*

Gary Smith, now a successful TV producer, at that time was an avant-garde designer. He created an all-white set, contrasting the backdrop with magically colorful costumes. "After my ribbon-and-balloon shoestring set, this was real scenery," Herman recalls.

Herman, not yet thirty, had written all the sketches, *and* the music and lyrics of the songs, half a dozen of which are still valid today: no mean achievement. But the young composer's bubble burst after opening night, 20 January 1960, when the critic from the *New York Times* came down to the Village and wrote a scathing review, calling *Parade* "sophomoric."

Still, producer Kasha so believed in the material that he invited Larry Kapp of Kapp Records to come down to the Players' Theatre on Macdougal Street to listen to the revue. Herman was ecstatic when Kapp said he'd like to make a recording of the show and asked Herman to design the album cover. Herman produced a poster of a pack of balloons with one that had gotten away from the multihued pack, floating free in air.

Listening to the recording, one notices at once Herman's poetic penchant for word identity and alliteration in lines like "touch me, and nothing can touch me at all" from "Your Hand in Mine" and "a piece of the past for your mantelpiece" from "The Antique Man." (This is in contrast to early Stephen Sondheim, who avoided alliteration and has observed that his counterpoint book called the device "the refuge of the destitute."[19] Young

Dody Goodman, *Parade*'s zany clown, in her Valentine sketch. Photofest, Inc.

Sondheim preferred the trick of confusion between words with the same sound, such as *know* and *no*.[20])

Later Herman became more subtle with language, but what these songs lack in craft is made up for in élan. *Parade* included some now-dated songs that at the time were considered smart, Manhattan-type material—most of

Richard Tone, who introduced "The Two-a-Day," Herman's first showtune, the hit of *Parade*. Photofest, Inc.

which was happily omitted from the recording. A song entreating the city fathers not to tear down the Village landmark, "The House of Detention," is rather amusing, but others are adolescent: spoofs about how Hollywood actresses find their names, Maria Callas in showbiz, and TV commercials. Perhaps the most philosophical song of this early period is "The Antique Man," whose title character invites the audience into his shop with

Come in, look around, would you care to browse?
You say it's a relic you seek
To give you a glimpse of another time,
A priceless, authentic antique,

and then goes on to list his wares as Davy Crockett hats, mah-jong sets, ration books or Hula-Hoops, items from the recent past. The song ends with an appropriate message:

You see that the past is but yesterday,
Last year is last month, is last week.
So wake up and live each today today,
For today is tomorrow's antique.

Toward the end of the revue there is the obligatory tear-stained ballad, called "Another Candle on the Cake," whose title tells it all. It elicits some sympathy for an aging ingenue, and the recording and show end with what would become a Herman trademark, a reprise of most of the revue's twelve songs.

The show limped along through ninety-five performances, a fairly respectable run for a fledgling composer. But in spite of the *Times* pan, *Parade* was Herman's steppingstone to Broadway.

4

milk and honey

Although several claim credit for the inspiration and genesis of Herman's big hit of 1961, *Milk and Honey,* the subject of Israel—its birth, its economic woes, its struggle to green the desert, its efforts to exist with hostile neighbors—was simply in the air. This was not the usual stuff of musical comedy, but since Hammerstein had shown that subjects like miscegenation, murder, and a bombing raid during World War II made for exciting musical theater in *Show Boat, Carousel,* and *South Pacific,* why would a musical about the Jewish state's birthing struggles be taboo?

With *Parade* running, albeit to half-empty houses, Herman had a showcase for his work, but his ambition to write a show for Broadway had not abated. He kept pestering Priscilla Morgan to put him together with someone who could turn out a proper libretto. Almost as a last resort, she thought of Don Appell, a former writer for Sid Caesar in the Borscht Belt.

A dozen years older than Herman, Appell was not well known to the public, having written only a few TV plays and one unsuccessful Broadway show, *Lullaby.* But Morgan believed he was capable of writing in almost any style and personable enough for her to sell him with ease.

Trying to hide his homosexuality, Appell always introduced his Mexican lover as his son. Priscilla, however, knew him well enough to see through the deception, and sensing that Don and Jerry might share their gay sensibilities, their Jewishness, and their ambitious natures, she invited Appell to a performance of *Parade.*

"I got so worried that Jerry was going to give up writing because he wanted to get a musical on Broadway that I put them together," she recalled. At that time I had fallen in love with Isamu Noguchi, and I said to Jerry and

Don, 'Why don't you do a musical about a couple who have a hard time coming together?' Isamu was doing a most unusual garden in Israel, and so I said, 'You might think about Israel.'"[1]

While conceding that "Priscilla brought us together thinking we might collaborate," Herman remembered the origin of *Milk and Honey* quite differently. "The whole project started in an Italian restaurant. We threw around some terrible ideas until, all of a sudden, Don said, 'What about a musical set in Israel?' We all knew he was right. *Exodus* had been a big thing, and the hora dancing scene had been the most entertaining part of *Fiorello!* Since my mother had taught Hebrew music at the local YMHA, and I had absorbed much of what she taught, I saw it as an opportunity to write an exciting Israeli score."[2]

Still another version is offered by the widow of *Milk and Honey*'s producer, Gerard Oestreicher, who had invested heavily in the Broadway production of Appell's *Lullaby* in 1954. "In 1959," Irma Oestreicher said, "Don called Gerry raving about this revue, *Parade,* and the talented fellow who had written it. So we went down to the Village to see it. And it truly had some funny and some sad songs. Then we came up and talked to Jerry—who looked like a kid at the time. Don was there and he told my Gerry they had an idea about an Israeli musical. My husband was excited and became almost immediately involved."[3]

Since the incipient musical, first called *Shalom,* had nothing more than a location and the hazy concept that it should be a love story, Priscilla felt her two clients needed to take a trip to Israel to scout for ideas. "Don talked to Oestreicher and he put up half the 'seed' money, and after I talked to Bob Sauer at BMI, we got the other half. And then we sent the two of them to Israel to absorb local color and work out ideas."

"The Israeli government people were so thrilled that we weren't going to write a play about Israel-embattled-with-gun-in-hand," Herman remembered, "but rather one that might encourage tourism, that they rolled out the red carpet and had a black limousine at our hotel every morning." Oestreicher had gotten El Al airlines to invest some money in the musical and had cleverly scheduled their trip to coordinate with Israel's thirteenth Independence Day.

Herman and Appell observed life in Jerusalem, Tel Aviv, and Haifa, but were more impressed by the kibbutzim, the thriving farms and desert settlements. They admired Israel's success in taking a barren part of the world and turning it green. But it wasn't until they took off in a car on their own, and saw people living in fear of being shelled in the middle of the night, that the danger and heroism in this new locality began to thrill them. They wanted to show some of that, and in addition were determined to add a naysayer to their plot, so that the musical, albeit optimistic, would not be a simpering valentine.

Appell was impressed by the number of couples living together, even bringing up children, without benefit of marriage. The new state was a study in contrasts. Many Israelis were deeply religious, respectful of ritual and tradition, while others were freethinkers, atheists, or communists. Appell wanted to depict all these persuasions in the musical's libretto. Having had to camouflage his sexuality all his life, Appell admired the Israeli people's freedom from restraint enough to make it the raison d'être of his musical.

Even before they left the United States, the collaborators decided that a platoon of Jewish widows traveling through the new land would make an amusing subplot, and early on Don had suggested Molly Picon, the reigning star of the Yiddish theater, as one of the widows who finds a mate while on the tour. For his main story he chose the bittersweet romance of two Americans, the young widow of a symphony conductor, Ruth Stein (the name was an homage to Herman's late mother), and a retired builder, Phil Arkin, whose marriage has been a failure. They fall in love and defy convention at first, but in the end they seek a way to be conventional. The tempestuous story of Phil's daughter, married to a Sabra, or native Israeli, is woven into the musical and provides the youth and verve necessary to contrast with the middle-aged widows and the two slightly younger protagonists.

Milk and Honey's score is rich in Middle Eastern themes. A large portion of the production numbers, much of its dance music, and several songs begin in minor keys. But because we are in a Broadway theater and not a synagogue, they soon modulate to the traditional major.

Opening on a street in Jerusalem, the score introduces Ruth to Phil in a clever way—a canon or round.* A disgruntled shepherd sings in Hebrew when his sheep are barred from going up a main thoroughfare. Ruth wants to know what he is saying, and Phil, who has been watching the scene and

---

* It is uncanny how Herman, with no training in counterpoint, theory, or advanced music composition, could come up with a score containing such variety and sophistication. It is true that he had help from Genevieve Pitot, who arranged the sometimes frenetic ballet and dance music, Robert de Cormier, who did the exquisite choral arrangements, and the orchestrations by the redoubtable Hershey Kay. But all of these were supervised by Herman, who may not have known how to get it, but knew exactly what sound he was looking for in every instance, and persisted until his collaborators gave it to him.

Robert Weede translates shepherd Johnny Borden's song for Mimi Benzell in *Milk and Honey*'s opening scene. Herman's first Broadway show was a hit that ran 543 performances. Museum of the City of New York.

has been instantly attracted to Ruth, steps up to translate—two measures later.

This gives Phil the chance to introduce himself to the audience, to tell us that he is a retired builder, and to sing perhaps the show's best-known song, "Shalom." Because the word means both "hello" and "good-bye" Herman has written the happiest minor-key waltz in all of musical theater. But it has a deceptive ending. On the words

> And even when you say goodbye,
> If your voice has "I don't want to go" in it,
> Say good-bye with a little "hello" in it,
> And say good-bye with Shalom,

Herman slows the tempo and switches his melody into a major key (a technique he may have learned from Tchaikovsky), creating an eye-misting emotional tug—the first of many in this score.

By the next scene we have met the subplot widows and have singled out the star, Clara Weiss—to be played by Molly Picon—as well as Barbara, Phil's daughter. Ruth has toured the area with Phil and Barbara and has seen some of the countryside. We learn that Phil has lied to Ruth, telling her that he is unmarried when in fact his wife, living in Paris, has no intention of divorcing him. Then, since she is aware of the mutual attraction between her father and Ruth, Barbara invites Ruth to stay at her house in the Moshav, a cooperative farm.

On the farm, Phil, hoping to protect his daughter, tries to talk Barbara and David, her Sabra husband, into going back to Baltimore with him. He offers his son-in-law a job in his construction business and points out that life in Israel is—and will always be—difficult and threatening. But the native-born Israeli vows his devotion to his country and is joined in its praise by his neighbors in the rousing "Milk and Honey." The lone dissenter is the cynical Adi, who claims he would be better off in the city, and he makes his views known in a counterpoint to David's positiveness.*

---

* Adi's comments are the token naysaying that Appell and Herman had promised their consciences. Herman owned that "the show came out a valentine, but I was proud of Adi's comments, that gray shadow that made it truthful."

DAVID	ADI
This is the land of milk and honey,	The honey's kind of bitter
This is the land of sun and song.	And the milk's a little sour.
This is a world of good and plenty	Did you know that pebble was
Humble and proud, and	The state's official flower?
Young and strong.	What about the tensions,
This is the place where	Political dissensions?
The hopes of the homeless and	And no one ever mentions
The dreams of the lost combine.	That the scenery is barren
This is the land that heaven blessed, and	And torrid, and arid, and horrid.
This lovely land is mine!	How about the border when the Syrians attack?
This lovely land is mine!	How about the Arab with the rifle in your back?
	How about the water? What there is of it is brine,
	But this lovely land is mine!

David and the chorus are not to be dissuaded and end the song optimistically, including a large dose of Israeli chauvinism:

> What if the earth is dry and barren,
> What if the morning sun is mean to us,
> For this is a state of mind we live in—
> We want it green and so it's green to us.
> For when you have wonderful plans for tomorrow,
> Somehow even today looks fine.
> So what if it's rock and dust and sand,
> This lovely land is mine!

As Ruth's two-week tour is nearing its end, Phil asks her to stay on, even offering to build a house for them to share. He sings "There's No Reason in the World," the score's most operatic moment, a song of sixty-four bars, double-the-usual-length, which begins tentatively. Once the title is announced, the melody begins creeping up by half-tones, as though Phil is unsure what Ruth's answer will be. Eventually, when he reaches the release, somewhat startling in its wide skips and appoggiaturas, his passion spills over into an intense proposal for Ruth to stay with him. The song ends as Phil sings

For there are wis - er men and young - er men. I
There may be wis - er men and young - er men and

woud - n't blame you if you walked a - way. But I feel
men with more im - por - tant things to say. But there's no

wis - er now and young - er now and
kind - er man or warm - er man, he

so, with all my heart I ask you "stay."
touch - es me and rea - son runs a - way.

For I feel suddenly alive,
Aware that I've been touched by something warm and new.
I think you ought to know
If I never let you go,
That I'd have every reason in the world—
You!

This aria (and Ruth's reprise in act two), which employs a range of al-most two octaves, demonstrates why *Milk and Honey*'s lead roles needed voices of operatic caliber.

Now it is time for comic relief, and by coincidence the widow ladies just happen to be visiting the Moshav. When they see these virile young farmers, each fantasizes about her hopes of finding a suitable husband. Their far-fetched daydreams are shattered when the men tell them that they are mar-ried, but Clara, still optimistic, sings "Chin Up, Ladies (Somewhere over the Rainbow There's a Man)."

Phil tells Ruth that he has bought property for the home he had talked

Molly Picon, as Clara Weiss, is lifted aloft by two of the stalwart sabras on the kibbutz her character is visiting. Museum of the City of New York.

about, and she sings her approval. She recounts how being in love and in this new environment has energized her and made her slough off the past:

> But that was yesterday, that was yesterday,
> But my equilibrium returned
> And there's not a chance of a backward glance
> Over all the bridges that I've burned.

Barbara is shocked at her father's deceit and urges him to tell Ruth about his marriage. He does so reluctantly with an ardent plea, "Let's Not Waste a Moment," another intense song, replete with Herman's most cogent advice on mature love. This time it is a duet that could be the theme song of every middle-aged member of the audience—urging that they avail themselves of every minute. "When you face a short forever, there's no right or wrong," Phil sings, adding, "I can only face forever if you come along."

Attending a wedding ceremony for three couples—marriages in

Moshav must be performed in groups, for the rabbis are busy—Ruth and Phil, influenced by the romance around them, express their deep love for each other and, heedless of the consequences, go off together as the act ends.

If the end of the act leaves some doubt about Phil and Ruth's sexual activity during the intermission, the opening of act two is reminiscent of the Cheshire-cat grin on Scarlett O'Hara's face the morning after Rhett has carried her up the stairs. Phil's song "Like a Young Man" clearly tells how energized his relationship, presumably carnal, with Ruth has made him. Phil cultivates an optimistic chimera until Barbara tells him that Ruth, realizing the consequences of living with a married man, has lost her courage and has run off to Tel Aviv. Phil hurries to find her and bring her back. David, sensing that Barbara is unhappy on the farm, sings one of the show's most poignant ballads, declaring that his love for his wife means more to him than his love of country.

The quasi-Hasidic minor key melody has a liturgical ring which makes it sound like a Hebrew incantation. The tessitura is purposely high, cantorial, extracting full meaning from the words

> I will follow you.
> I am ready to
> Go wherever you happen to lead me
> Just in case you might happen to need me,
> All that you'll have to do
> Is turn around
> For I'll be following you.

Phil finds Clara at a café in Tel Aviv, but she refuses to tell him where Ruth is, saying, "when she wants to find you, she will." Then Clara and an older gentleman, Sol Horowitz, discover that they are mutually attracted, and Clara sings her show-stopper, a joyous tango called "Hymn to Hymie," a comic precursor to the pivotal number in *Hello, Dolly!* in which Dolly asks her late husband for the right to cast off her mourning and enter an amorous relationship:

> How can you expect a woman to exist
> When there's just one lonely lambchop on her shopping list? . . .
> I'm not a horse, I'm not a pony so my problem is acute
> I am too old for Hialeah and too young to shoot . . .
> Because I'm half a family, half a team
> But still I haven't grown too old to dream.

I know that once you've met him, you'd like this fellow Sol
And so I'm asking for the last time, Hymie?
[cups her ear to his answer]
Yes?!!! You're a doll!

Now, in soliloquy, Ruth tells Clara about her life with her late conductor husband:*

I was married to a man who needed me
To cater to his every whim.
To organize his life he needed me
And so I needed him.
I loved the little things I did for him,
His breakfast and his cup of tea.
He needed all those things I did for him,
But never really me.

She ends the scene with a reprise of "There's No Reason in the World (To Feel the Way I Do)." Suddenly the word *reason* takes on the meaning of *sanity,* and the wisdom sprinkled through Herman's poetry emerges, coupled with the sensuality of the song. One also feels Phil's and Ruth's overpowering mutual magnetism as an overwhelming love affair, the kind that will be absent from *Dolly, Mame,* and Herman's later shows; the kind that will not reappear in his work until *La Cage aux Folles.* For true to her heart, Ruth comes back to Phil. Her reason? She does not explain, but changes the subject with a kind of female logic in song:

If it's your home, it's my home
My world is where you are, wherever we two are.
Don't ask me to leave you, for this is the answer I'll give,
If you're here then I'm here, I'm with you as long as I live.
It's as simple as that.
Just as simple as that.

Appell's libretto has the courage to sidestep operetta's formulaic happy ending, for now it is Phil who has his doubts. With deep respect and the knowledge that Ruth is the kind of woman who needs marriage, he realizes that he must tell her to leave. It almost breaks his heart.

At the Lydda Airport outside of Tel Aviv, the touring widows are prepar-

---

* Ruth's soliloquy, added in Boston, was in place of a long scene in which she goes to ask the advice of a rabbi.

ing to board the aircraft. Ruth and Phil have their final moments together, after which he promises to fly to Paris and plead with his wife for a divorce. Ruth does not believe he will succeed until he sings a reprise of one of the show's big ballads "Let's Not Waste a Moment" with more intense lyrics:

> There's a short forever
> That begins tonight
> And a long tomorrow
> Till the time is right
> But you'll hear the doorbell ring
> And you'll look and there I'll be,
> You see, a short forever with you
> Is long enough for me.

Ruth boards the plane hoping that somehow Phil will succeed, and she will then be able to come back to him. The widows enplane after her, and, as the curtain falls, they and the ground crew join in a reprise of "Shalom."

With the book and score completed and director Albert Marre hired, casting could begin.* There was never any doubt about who would portray Clara. Molly Picon had appeared successfully on Broadway opposite Sir Cedric Hardwicke in *A Majority of One,* but only Second Avenue had seen her at her best, in musical roles.

Risë Stevens was the front-runner for the key role of Ruth, but her contralto range did not have enough brilliance for the score. Next came Patricia Morison, but she lacked the ethnic quality for the role.† At last Mimi Benzell, the Metropolitan Opera coloratura, who was Jewish, was given the role. Herman felt that Benzell resembled his mother, who was the prototype for the role. Robert Weede, star of the Metropolitan opera, famous for his Rigoletto as well as Tony in Frank Loesser's *The Most Happy Fella,* eagerly accepted the part of Phil, and no one else was auditioned. Perhaps the most surprising of the principals was Tommy Rall, formerly a soloist with the Ballet Theatre but better remembered for his dancing role in *Seven Brides for Seven Brothers.* Rall is also a singer of uncommon operatic quality. He

---

* Albert Marre (1925–) was the artistic director of the New York City Center and has directed many shows on Broadway, among them *Kismet, The Chalk Garden, A Cry for Us All, Saint Joan, Time Remembered,* and the long-running *Man of La Mancha.*

† Morison performed the role to critical enthusiasm with the St. Louis Municipal Opera Company in 1964.

took on the key role of David and brought down the house at every performance with his rendition of "I Will Follow You." (Shortly after the opening
his name was elevated to costardom, along with those of Weede, Picon, and
Benzell.)

Besides assembling an all-star cast, producer Oestreicher lavished great
care on the project by hiring top behind-the-scenes professionals, such as
Howard Bay to create the glorious sets and Miles White to do tasteful costumes. The ballets were the work of Donald Saddler, who created a full scenario for each ballet.* Herman found his producer "a tough guy, but not really knowledgeable in music theater, and [I] was grateful that he listened to
me about the score, for by this time, I knew who were the outstanding professionals in the field."

Oestreicher wanted a concert pianist he knew, a man Herman describes
as "a sort of Liberace," to do the orchestrations, but he bowed to Jerry's request for someone who was more professional. "I needed a classically ori-
ented orchestrator to make my score sound like I wanted, and so I talked
him into hiring Hershey Kay.† I was very shy, but somehow I found I could
exert enough strength to protect my work."

The all-important choral arrangements were done by Robert De
Cormier, who handled the operatic writing with professional aplomb. The
composer, who had never written for a full chorus, says, "He retained my
harmony and gave the songs added power with his exquisite part writing."

Herman reveled in the theatricality of the process. He and Alice Borden
performed the show for prospective investors in the Oestreichers' sumptuous living room in the Carlton House. After several backers auditions, by
July the Martin Beck Theatre had been reserved, and the show, budgeted at
$400,000—a pittance today, but a lavish allotment then—was set to go into
rehearsal. Molly Picon and her husband were on tour with *A Majority of
One,* and Herman flew down to Miami to present her with "Hymn to
Hymie" which he had just written for her.

Picon remembered: "After we finished the tour we went into rehearsal
in earnest—from eleven to seven, and we had lots of work to do just with

* Donald Saddler (1919–) began his career as a member of American Ballet Theatre.
He has won Tonys for his choreography of *Wonderful Town* and *No, No, Nanette* and
received Tony nominations for his work on *On Your Toes* and *Much Ado About Nothing.*
† Hershey Kay (1919–1981), composer, arranger for ballet, and, beginning in 1944,
one of the most sought out orchestrators of Broadway musicals. Some of his successes
in this field were *Peter Pan, The Golden Apple, Candide, Juno, Once Upon a Mattress,
110 in the Shade, Coco, A Chorus Line, On the Twentieth Century, Evita,* and *Barnum.*

the machinery. One of our props was a genuine tractor. We also had to work around bales of hay, plows, and real live animals. In one scene, Phil had to milk a goat. That meant getting one star goat, fully equipped with milk, plus one goat understudy—who also had to be bulging at the teat."[4] Oestreicher spared no expense, paying $750 a week for the animals. Picon and the rest of the cast considered that a small fortune for perhaps two minutes of stage business and one laugh.

The show opened inauspiciously at New Haven's Shubert Theatre on 8 September 1961. "It was a wonderful experience to work with people like De Cormier and Saddler," Herman said. "And the rehearsals, hearing sounds coming from the stage and orchestra that I had only heard in my head, were a revelation. I clung to Mimi Benzell a great deal because she had the look and the charm of the mother I had just lost. And oddly enough, Mimi died of cancer not too long after the show. Weede was a joy, so reliable. He treated me as if I were Richard Rodgers and wanted to be sure that he was singing everything the way I wanted it. I was treated with such respect by all these people even though I was a novice, just thirty. I owe a great deal to them because I was a beginner and they made me feel like a pro."

After two weeks in New Haven it was clear that the show was badly in need of cutting. That was reserved for the next stop, Boston. The early scripts made Ruth, who vacillates morally, even more erratic by having her go to a rabbi to ask God's forgiveness. Trying to lighten the show and build up Picon's role, director Marre removed the synagogue scene. According to Molly, with it went "the temple set where they had introduced a dancing rabbi. 'Out! Out!' shouted director Marre, and along with the rabbi went a hundred thousand dollars' worth of scenery."[5] But the show was now short enough to fit into the commercially feasible two-and-a-half-hour Broadway time slot.

Ron Holgate, who was hired to understudy Tommy Rall and given the rather extensive role of the rabbi, felt his scene was the only one the Boston critics cited as "ringing true." In the wake of the praise, he said, "I thought, 'They're going to build up my part.' But when I came in the next day they said, 'We're playing the scene with Mimi and Molly alone.' Now I only had the small role of the policeman in the first act, so I left the show after three months."[6]

Cutting that long dramatic scene also meant deleting Mimi Benzell's big act two soliloquy to God, "Give Me a Word." By the time Herman saw the number on stage, he sensed that it was too serious even for an operetta, but he was "still a little shaky when it was cut from the show and—I had to find a way to tell Mimi." He kept some of the recitative to flesh out Ruth's character and substituted a reprise of the quasi-operatic chorus of "There's No Reason in the World," its lyric altered and the melody arranged in a higher key, to show off her voice. This became one of the major emotional moments of the show.

Herman, who is frequently criticized for overuse of reprise, appreciates its power. In this he holds a contrasting opinion to that of Stephen Sondheim, who feels that by the time the audience comes to the reprise, the show has moved along so far that the song is no longer applicable.[7] Here we can see one of the essential differences between these two masters of musical theater. Herman wants the audience to take the songs home with them; Sondheim wants them to take home the meaning of the play. "Reprise is so successful," Herman contends, "because it teaches the audience the song by letting them hear it again. Very few people know its value or how to use it artfully. By changing a word here and there to switch the meaning, one can broaden the concept. To me reprise is the glue that holds the whole score together."*

As the out-of-town performances progressed, Molly Picon became more cantankerous and critical of the other performers. She found Weede technically flawless but lacking warmth. Although he had had a big success with *Most Happy Fella,* she said, "He was uncomfortable on the musical stage and it showed." Picon admitted that she, too, was struggling with her big number, "Hymn to Hymie," and hadn't gotten it down yet. She felt the song needed something flip, especially when Clara cries "Look Hymie, I'm young!" Finally she negotiated with Jerry to work her trademark somersault into the number.[8]

It was Herman's first experience "on the road," and he relished almost everything—the cutting, the adding, even the "cold-tea-hotel-room-song" that had to be written overnight. Since "Hymn to Hymie" does not come until late in the second act, Molly Picon needed another big number in the first. The marching song, "Chin Up, Ladies (Somewhere Over the Rainbow There's a Man)," is the least effective number in the show, but Picon, with her ineffable style, was able to sell it to her audience. Besides, as Luther Hen-

* Herman often uses reprise to move the plot along. Sometimes, as in *Mame's* act two opening, he will take a previously stated melody and outfit it with appropriate words to indicate the passage of time. Elsewhere, a song introduced earlier can become the climax of the act, as when *La Cage's* "We Are What We Are" is transmogrified into "I Am What I Am." At the ending of most of his shows, however, Herman simply lets the audience wallow in the by-then-familiar tunes as a parting gift.

derson, one of Broadway's great orchestrators, maintained after listening to the score, "With an opening like 'Shalom,' the almost frenetic 'Independence Day Hora,' followed by the rousing 'Milk and Honey,' by the time they came to Molly's number, the show had the audience in its pocket."[9]

Preparing for the opening in New York, the cast was in peak form, except for Robert Weede, who had developed a case of laryngitis a week earlier. It looked as if the opening would have to be postponed, but on that very afternoon, October 10, 1961, his malady miraculously disappeared and he was in fine voice.

In every way, except for the absence of his mother, it was a perfect opening night for Herman. His grandmother, his Aunt Belle, his father, and his father's new second wife were all there. "The audience laughed and cried and clapped their hands in rhythm with the songs," he remembered. "And when the curtain came down, we all ran backstage for a small party in Mimi Benzell's dressing room."

Ron Holgate described the official opening-night festivities as "incredible. Oestreicher rented New York's finest restaurant, the Four Seasons, and had an open bar and a line for food that went right through the kitchen, with all the chefs waiting there to serve you. The whole restaurant became our party." It was a wonderful place to wait for the reviews, which were on the streets by 2 A.M.

First out was the *New York Times*, whose headline, "All 'Milk and Honey' at the Martin Beck," read aloud by Oestreicher, elicited cheers. Howard Taubman, the critic, continued by lauding the musical's "heartwarming integrity [which] shines through . . . an endearing asset in any theater work, it is remarkable in a musical." The *Journal-American*, though it could muster only "workable" when describing Appell's libretto, called the show "sumptuous, melodic and rousing, with haunting ballads." Walter Kerr, writing in the *Herald-Tribune*, also appreciated Herman's score but was dismissive of the libretto, saying, "It seems to have been written by that stiff and self-conscious fellow who composes travel books." The *Mirror* noted the show had "some of the best dancing you're likely to see this season." On the whole the critical fraternity found the songs, settings, costumes, and movement exemplary, but cared less for the direction or the book. All the cast received kudos, with critics typically singling out Tommy Rall as being "outstanding" and Molly Picon as "a bundle of energy."[10]

Oestreicher was so elated that he rushed over and embraced Jerry warmly, exclaiming, "We're a hit!" After another gala party, this time in the producer's hotel suite, Herman went back alone to his third-floor walk-up.

In his memoir he remembered: "It was the middle of the night. Everyone else in the show had gone home to their families and loved ones. I was all by myself. I had nobody to talk to. I didn't even have a pet. But I remember standing there and thinking: *'You have a hit show on Broadway!'* It was absolutely the most extraordinary feeling in the world."[11]

Milk and Honey was a surefire hit. The box office was $16,000 the day after it opened, topping even *My Fair Lady.* By its thirty-fifth week it was still earning $50,000 weekly.

But Molly Picon had been offered $40,000 plus expenses per week to appear as Frank Sinatra's mother in the movie version of Neil Simon's play *Come Blow Your Horn.* Since filming would take a maximum of ten weeks, and because her six-month contract to play the show had run out, she was free to accept the offer and planned to leave at once for Hollywood.

Because Robert Weede, Tommy Rall, and even Molly (when she finished the movie) would be going on the road, the New York production had to be recast. Madeline Gilford, who was given the job of signing new cast members, chose as Molly's replacement her understudy, Dianne Goldberg, an excellent but unknown actress. But with Molly gone from the New York roster, the receipts suddenly plummeted. The well-known Hermione Gingold was quickly hired to fill in. The few critics who wrote about Gingold as Clara noted her comic timing but deplored her clodlike dancing. The role needed a pixie and had gotten a leviathan instead. By its forty-third week the show was on half-price tickets and losing momentum fast. It was not helped when Mimi Benzell, who was not well, bowed out.

Herman was in for more discouraging news when a songwriter in the Midwest filed a lawsuit against the composer and the producer, claiming that his song "Shalom" had been sent to NBC and that Herman and Oestreicher had stolen the idea. The two men had to fly to Detroit to defend the suit and prove that there was no similarity between the songs. The case was quickly thrown out of court when the judge realized that there are hundreds of songs built on the idea of "Shalom"; in any case, the law states clearly that one cannot copyright a title. It was an annoyance that Herman and Oestreicher didn't need when the troubled Broadway company required their attention.

Gingold tried valiantly to keep up the excitement in the musical, but ticket sales were so spotty that the show almost closed. When Picon returned eight weeks later, business picked up, but then Molly suffered an appendicitis attack and remained hospitalized for two weeks. By the time she

When Molly Picon took a leave of absence to make a movie, Hermione
Gingold, right, took over the starring role. Here she clowns backstage to
Tommy Rall, Mimi Benzell, and Robert Weede. Museum of the City of New
York.

was well enough to reappear (mildly piqued because doctors forbade her
doing her stock-in-trade somersault), the wind was out of the sails of *Milk
and Honey*.

The show finally closed in January 1963 after playing 541 performances. One would think that with such a long run *Milk and Honey* would
have turned a large profit, but due to the huge cast, high salaries for the
principals, and half-empty houses during Picon's absences, the show never
regained its initial popularity and paid back only 90 percent of its cost. It
was the first show in Broadway history to have run that long without turning a profit. Herman feels that "Picon's leaving throttled the show. It took a
year off the life of the musical."[12]

In 1994 Richard Sabellico addressed the problems of the libretto when
he directed a revival of the musical for the American Jewish Theatre in New
York. The production starred Ronald Holgate (the original rabbi, whose

role had been deleted) as Phil, Chevi Colton in the Molly Picon role, Katy Silverstone as Barbara, and Jeanne Lehman as Ruth.

Because the theater was so small, Sabellico eliminated the dancing and used a three-piece orchestra with no amplification. It made for an intimate, almost chamberlike performance. In an attempt to show the ethnic conflict and antagonism, he changed the shepherd in the opening scene from a young Israeli to an Arab. In many spots he lowered keys, and he lightened the dialogue to update the story.

"Freed of its visual distraction," wrote the *New Yorker*, "the story rests on the merits of its music. Herman's patented tunefulness, which, in later incarnations, tended to cloy and curdle, is, in this instance, refreshing. Sabellico plays down the overexuberance that pops up naturally in Herman's score."

But *Milk and Honey* is pure operetta, and its exuberance is a large part of its charm. If the 1961 critics dismissed the book, it was because its outdated heroine vacillates, choosing not to live in an unmarried state with a man she loves. But those were the conventions in force at the time. Appell's libretto is an honest picture of the era and particularly of first-generation Jewish-American women in the late fifties. What makes the musical unsuitable for revival in a major Broadway house—which its sumptuous score demands—is the cartoonish, demeaning, and dated treatment of the widows. They set off on a tour, ostensibly to imbibe culture, but in reality they are only out to trap men. Particularly distasteful are all the ethnic jokes, out of fashion long before the nineties.

Still, the score, despite its lack of humor, is complex and opulent, different from anything Herman would write in the future. It truly reflects a youthful composer willing to take chances with counterpoint, harmony, and form. Ardent and effervescent at times, sensitive and romantic at others, it is never sentimental. In his *American Musical Theatre* the respected music critic Gerald Bordman writes that "although Herman was destined to have even greater success, none of his future scores was as melodically inventive or memorable."[13]

Herman's next show, *Madame Aphrodite*, with a libretto by the Pulitzer Prize–winning Tad Mosel, had its first night only six weeks after *Milk and Honey* debuted, although its writing was begun years before.* *Aphrodite*'s genesis was in an unproduced twenty-five-minute radio script. "I expanded

---

* Mosel's play *All the Way Home* won the Pulitzer for Drama in 1961.

that to an hour show that was televised in the mid 1950s," Mosel remembered. Herman, then fresh out of college, had seen the show and found it charming, but was sure that music would improve it. He never forgot the play and began thinking of songs for it, working them out on "spec."

He asked Priscilla Morgan, whom he knew was also Mosel's agent, for an introduction to the playwright in an attempt to sell Mosel on the idea of setting the story to music. After a conference they both agreed that *Madame Aphrodite*'s fantasy could be transformed into a musical. Herman wrote eight songs, and Mosel expanded the plot to accommodate the music.

Morgan interested Howard Barker, Cynthia Baer, and Robert Chambers, the producers who had had such success with *Little Mary Sunshine*, in presenting it; they planned to open at the Orpheum Theatre in Greenwich Village in February, months before *Milk and Honey* debuted. But, as is often the case off and off off Broadway, the necessary $25,000—then an enormous sum—could not be raised.

The story has aspects of the fable of *The Enchanted Cottage* as filtered through the *Twilight Zone*. It opens with the introduction of Barney, a sincere, but naive boxer, who is too gentle to hurt his opponents, being hired by Madame Aphrodite. She is a blowzy old woman who spouts malapropisms while boiling up a concoction she calls her Magical Skin Creme. It is made of "candle wax, lard, and a touch of lavender oil," and she sells it to unsuspecting ladies in neighborhood saloons. Ugly herself, the bitter fraud hopes her "beauty treatment" will deface her clients by giving them skin ailments.

Barney peddles the cream from door to door in the belief that it is as good as advertised. He sells a jar to Rosemary, a plain young woman who has fallen for the good-looking boxer's spiel. After two applications her faith in the cream's supposed beautifying properties raises her self-confidence. She suddenly feels beautiful enough to enter the local "Miss Euclid Avenue Beauty Contest." (The song "Beautiful," which Barney sings at this point has an exquisite musical motif that will be fully developed in "And I Was Beautiful" in Herman's 1969 musical *Dear World*.)

Rosemary's pep talks, in turn, fill Barney with enough assurance and zip for him to talk all the women in the nearby housing project into buying Madame's cream. When he sells it all and comes to Madame for fresh supplies, he catches her at her iron cauldron whipping up a new batch, and he realizes the concoction's ingredients are not beauty enhancing. He is doubly conscience-stricken because he has fallen in love with Rosemary and fears he may have ruined the looks of Rosemary and the women in the housing project. But after rushing to her, he finds her as beautiful as ever—and tells

He thinks I'm love - ly. He thinks I'm love - ly, and he's
warm and won - der - ful and wise.

her so. When he leaves, she sings the musical's best song, "The Girls Who Sit and Wait," one of Herman's most mature lyrics, coupled with what might be called "musical onomatopoeia." (In bars three and four, the "waiting and waiting," when the tune seems to be marking time, creates a kind of slow-motion delay.)

> The girls who sit and wait and wait and dream away the day
> Will never know the moment till the moment slips away.
> And then, when time has passed them by
> They look around and wonder why.
> So I'll go out and find my love and tell my love that he
> Was only made to share his love and spend his life with me.
> And time will never pass me by
> For in his arms I'll know that I
> Was not too slow; not too late.
> "Come follow me,"
> I'll call to all the girls who sit and wait.

Now Barney decides he must turn Madame in—only to discover that she has been paying off the police all along. So it is he they arrest and put in jail as the act ends.

The second act begins after Barney's brief time in jail. He has changed his outlook on life and has decided to go back to boxing. The outlook is favorable for Rosemary too, for she seems to be leading in the beauty contest. Even Madame is doing well, for the housing project's women are calling for more of the beauty cream, and when Rosemary offers to endorse it, Madame dreams of becoming rich.

A few days later, when Barney has won his boxing match and presents

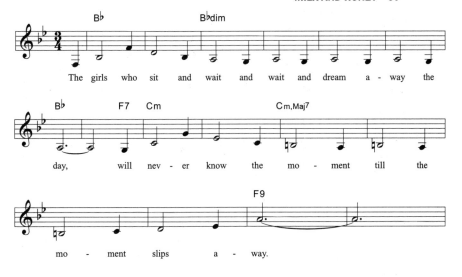

The girls who sit and wait and wait and dream a - way the day, will nev - er know the mo - ment till the mo - ment slips a - way.

Rosemary with his winnings, he tells her that she was beautiful all along and that the cream has no effect on anyone. Rosemary now sings the ballad that found most approval with the critics, "Only, Only Love." The song's lyric sums up the meaning of the whole musical, but the melodic line seems to hover, masquerading as an art song, around a tiresome minor theme.

> There once was a girl with the magic
> To grow as lovely as lovely can be,
> But that perfect smile was, all the while was only, only me.
> She thought she had some special power
> That made her dreams and her fortunes come true,
> But that something strong was, all along was, only, only you.
>
> She wished and she found herself climbing
> To heights she'd never been capable of,
> But that thrilling climb was, all the time was, only, only love.
> Not magic, not power, not fortunes, not wishes,
> But only, only love.

After this happy denouement, Barney tells the old curmudgeon that she need not be ashamed of her cream, that it contains nothing truly harmful. She explains to the others (and the audience) why she created this phony beautifier. She says that as a child she was always taunted for being fat and ugly, and so she stole $5 to send away for a beauty product which turned out to be nothing but a chin strap, a piece of gauze, and a rubber band. But the aunt who raised her forced her to wear the contraption to school for a full month. Ridiculed by her classmates, she only wanted to make the rest of the world as unattractive as she could. Now, close to tears, showing emotion for the first time in the musical, she opens a jar of cream and dabs some on her face while the background chorus sings

> The firefly believes and becomes a star.
> You can become anything,
> Anything your heart believes you are.

As the curtain falls there is a hint that Madame may be effecting a transformation in and on herself, but it comes too late for the audience to care much. This ho-hum attitude toward the story was echoed by the majority of the critics, although Herman's score received enthusiastic thumbs up. Frances Herridge, writing in the *New York Post,* found the "songs the best part of the show," calling them "melodic and skillfully inventive." John McClain of the *Journal-American* concurred, terming the score "the one flicker of light in the evening." Whitney Bolton of the *Morning Telegraph* called "Only, Only Love" a fine song and said that "And a Drop of Lavender Oil" had a "fine sardonic air about it." The normally dismissive Thomas Dash wrote in *Women's Wear Daily* that "Herman has composed a number of sprightly and tuneful songs which lend verve to the proceedings." He singled out several others that he felt would "enliven even a good Broadway musical" but complained that "most of the songs seem smothered in the whirligig of the non-musical libretto."

Mosel came in for a terrible drubbing from all the critics; the story was called "silly and saccharine" at best and "pretentious, dismal, and humorless" by the majority.* Consequently, there was no line around the block as was the case for *Milk and Honey,* and *Madame Aphrodite,* which opened at the Orpheum Theatre on 29 December 1961, closed after thirteen performances.

---

* Some of the sugariness of the musical was occasioned by having an off-stage chorus, used as an adjunct, sing the thoughts of characters. Herman wanted to tinker with the usual form of musicals in general. Off Broadway seemed a likely place to experiment. But the venture was not wasted on the sophisticated critic for the *New Yorker,* who wrote, "At the opening of the second act an offstage chorus, which accompanied the action all the way through, sang an overture, reprising some of the songs of the first act and hinting at songs to come that was absolutely wonderful."

In a conversation a few years ago, Mosel took all the blame for the musical's demise. "My script should have been more fanciful," he admitted, "and less protracted. It started as a short play, but as the work grew longer it became more and more attenuated. What it mostly lacked was lightness. I wanted to pull out halfway in the rehearsal period and kept making changes, but these things are like a juggernaut, impossible to stop.

"Jerry had not yet written *Milk and Honey* and was only in his midtwenties, and when we began working on *Aphrodite*, I don't think he had had anything produced but his college work, not even *Parade*. But he had all the talent in the world and wrote a fantastic score. Not being that well known, we had to wait until *Milk and Honey* came out and I had a hit with *All the Way Home*. Then it was a shoo-in for us to get a production of our earlier work."[14]

Herman is remarkably taciturn on this musical, but he admits that *Madame Aphrodite* is "a strange piece. Tad is a wonderful writer," he adds, "but he had never written the book of a musical. We had producers who had done *Little Mary Sunshine*, and they just took over. They hired a director [Howard Turoff] who didn't know what he was doing; they hired a set designer [David Ballou] who was wrong for it. It wasn't even well cast. Nancy Andrews was a vaudevillian, and Madame is written as a strong person. She should have been played by an older Meryl Streep. The reason I don't talk much about it was that it wasn't a good show and it was heartbreaking after the success of *Milk and Honey*."

One of the reasons Herman was so devastated by the failure of *Madame Aphrodite* was the lack of support and compassion he received from his father—on whom he had come to rely after the death of his mother.

"My father was angry with me. Although he hadn't invested in the show, he felt I should have known better. I told him he should have been sympathetic, but he still was angry. 'You can't expect everything I do to be nominated for a Tony,' I said.'It's not going to happen.'

"Actually, Aphrodite was a very brave thing for me to do. It was a dark piece, something more suited to early Sondheim than it was to me. I did some interesting things in it, but the book and direction didn't work. I was very thrilled that a writer of the stature of Tad Mosel would work with an untried composer like me, but it wasn't Tad's or my fault; it was just the wrong element coming together."

When asked whether *Madame Aphrodite* might be rewritten and revived, Herman shrugs and says, "When you've created a show like *Mame*, where every line of dialogue, every costume, every orchestration, and every song is right, why would you want to go back to a work that you think is so flawed?"

Herman's disdain for what he considers less than his finest work was to be evidenced in his next project. *Hello, Dolly!* would become Herman's greatest success, and, until surpassed by *Fiddler on the Roof,* the longest-running show of the decade. But it is not Herman's best musical; not even his most critically applauded one, and certainly not his personal favorite work. And record-breaker that it would become, its creation remains to this day Herman's continuing nightmare.

5

a damned exasperating woman

Jerry Herman could hardly contain his joyous excitement the first time he left producer David Merrick's scarlet domain. But six months later, after Herman presented the almost complete score to Merrick, he left the office crestfallen.

"Mike Stewart was there, too," Herman recalled, "and after I played the last few numbers and Mr. Merrick had approved of the whole score, he said he was going to call Ethel Merman and ask her when she wanted to come to hear the songs. My heart was in my mouth as he dialed the number. After all, I had written every note of Dolly's part with her voice in mind. I even worked several of the numbers so they led up to her 'money note'—the great C natural she holds in 'I Got Rhythm,' where she goes '*aaaaaaah*'—and you can hear her voice as far away as Podunk."*

Merrick was on the phone for an inordinately long time, smiling jovially as he exchanged pleasantries with "the queen of Broadway," and Herman remembered how the producer's face dropped and gloom enveloped the room as he and Mike heard Merrick repeat several times, "Are you sure, Ethel? Are you absolutely sure?"

When he finally cradled the receiver, his face ashen, he stated flatly. "She says she doesn't want to hear it because she might be intrigued by the material and she's made a momentous decision. She doesn't want to spend any more of her life in a dressing room. When everybody's going out and having fun or sitting down to a lovely dinner, she says she's putting on her makeup,

---

* Merman's voice had dropped considerably in the years since 1930's "I Got Rhythm." When she eventually did play *Hello, Dolly!* in 1970, keys had to be set for her range, which then topped out on B or, more often, B flat.

or out there singing her lungs out. She's done it for so many years. She's had enough."[1]

Herman's letdown was monumental, yet, since the show's groundwork had been securely laid with Mike Stewart's impeccable script and Gower Champion had been contracted to direct, he knew the project would go forward—with or without Merman.* Still a theatrical neophyte and ever optimistic, Herman salved his disappointment by speculating that Merman's mind might yet be changed.

Merrick, however, was fuming. He was not accustomed to being said no to—even by a superstar like Ethel Merman—and he did not take rejection with equanimity. His temper tantrums were notorious on Broadway. Many talented designers, choreographers, composers, and lyricists had been the brunt of Merrick's anger—some had even been reduced to tears as he pulled them inches from his blazing black eyes and hissed, "You're ruining my show."

Born David Margulois on 27 November 1911 in St. Louis, he had studied law, but after attaining his degree, he found himself happier spending his days in theaters rather than courtrooms. Possessed of an intense manner and panache, the calculating young man had courted and married a wealthy local socialite who was also interested in theater. When her mother died and left his wife a small fortune, the couple moved to New York. In 1940, almost immediately after his marriage, he changed his name to Merrick, announcing half-jokingly that if things didn't work out on Broadway he could always escape creditors by moving back to St. Louis under the name of Margulois.

He apprenticed in the office of Herman Shumlin, a well-known producer—having bought his way in by investing $5,000 of his wife's money in the Shumlin production of James Thurber's *The Male Animal*. The play's success turned the $5,000 into $20,000—deposited in his own, not his wife's, private bank account.

His first production, *Bright Boy*, cosponsored by Arthur Beckhard, opened in 1944 and ran only sixteen performances. Its final scene featured a long anti-Fascist diatribe that critics found almost laughable in its naïveté. The reaction taught Merrick that "message plays" were anathema at the box office, and so he set his vision on escape and comedy. He did not produce a

---

* In the fall of 1962 Harold Prince directed a revival of *The Matchmaker* for the Phoenix Repertory Theatre. It was so successful that Merrick offered him the direction of *Dolly: A Damned Exasperating Woman*. Prince turned it down, saying he "did not care for the score, particularly the song 'Hello, Dolly!'"

solo effort until six years later, when he found *Clutterbuck,* a genial English comedy. It received tepid reviews, but its run of 218 performances was a personal triumph, a lesson in how publicity and advertising can turn a turkey into a mild hit.[2]

Using sexual innuendoes and doggerel verses of his own composition, Merrick placed intriguing ads in the *New York Times* and managed to interest the public in this frothy play about the British on a cruise in the Caribbean. Throughout his life he cared more for publicity, fame, and theatrical notoriety than he did for theatrical values.

Merrick's first real success as a creative producer occurred five years later when he secured the stage rights to *Fanny,* Marcel Pagnol's lusty film trilogy set in Marseilles. He thought he could interest Rodgers and Hammerstein in writing the soaring score needed for this romantic story—*Fanny* is in love with Marius, who is in love with the sea—but they refused to touch the project.[3] At last, he enlisted Ezio Pinza and Walter Slezak, and the two stars, with an assist from Harold Rome's atmospheric score coupled with Merrick's uncanny sense of publicity, were able to propel *Fanny* into a two-year run.

The show that established Merrick as a producer of classy material was an English production of an American play—a revival of a flop play that Herman Shumlin had produced during the 1938–1939 season, Thornton Wilder's *The Merchant of Yonkers.*

Wilder had adapted *Merchant* from a little-known play, *Einen Jux es Sich Machen* (1842) by the nineteenth-century Viennese comic writer and performer Johan Nestroy, who had himself adapted it from an 1835 English comedy, John Oxenford's *A Day Well Spent.*

The adaptation transposed the farcical events of a single day in Vienna to the hinterlands of New York of the 1890s. Wilder made a most significant change by adding a scheming aggressive woman, Dolly Gallagher Levi, the role written for the diminutive American star Ruth Gordon.[4]

Shumlin's 1938 production was directed by Max Reinhardt, a distinguished refugee from Hitler's Germany who spoke little English. His heavy-handed manner and Teutonic bossiness bristled Ruth Gordon, and she withdrew from the cast. The role went instead to Jane Cowl, a serious actress unskilled in frothy comedy. Undermined by Cowl's forthright performance and Reinhardt's *mittle europishe* direction, the play opened in 1938 and closed after thirty-nine performances.

Fourteen years later Tyrone Guthrie, who had directed Gordon in London, was looking for another project for her and decided on *The Merchant of Yonkers.* He scheduled it for the Edinburgh Festival, of which he was the artistic director, and arranged for the British run to be produced by Hugh "Binkie" Beaumont. He asked Wilder to do a modest rewrite which would build up the part of the leading lady, a master of all trades, and thereby take the emphasis away from the merchant. Retitled *The Matchmaker,* it was an instant success in Scotland and later in London. A prescient Kenneth Tynan, England's most perceptive critic, found in it "the impact of a musical comedy from which the music has been discarded as superfluous."[5]

During the 1955 London run Merrick came abroad to scout new productions, and, properly entranced, went back to Gordon's dressing room after the show. The personable young producer said he would like to coproduce the play with the Theatre Guild and bring her and *The Matchmaker* to New York. Gordon insisted that it must be done with the entire British cast. "If you change one thing, it affects the whole balance of the production."

Brooks Atkinson came over to critique the show for the *New York Times* and wrote a rave about the ensemble performances.[6] That settled it. Merrick decided to hire Americans only as understudies and in minor parts and somehow was able to talk American Equity into allowing an unprecedented number of British actors to appear in the New York production of this very American play. The raves he received for this production increased his reputation as a producer of quality theater.

Opening on December 5, 1955, *The Matchmaker* had a glorious two-year run, with David Merrick's name blazing on the marquee atop the Royale Theatre eclipsing those of Ruth Gordon and Thornton Wilder below.* The St. Louis dynamo had indeed joined the pantheon of Broadway producers.

Shortly after the play closed, the farce was made into a charming movie starring Shirley Booth, Shirley MacLaine, and Anthony Perkins. The film, released in 1958, only added to Merrick's luster, for during *The Matchmaker*'s run on Broadway, he had moved fast. Four productions *(Look Back in Anger, Romanoff and Juliet, Jamaica,* and *The Entertainer)* in the 1957–1958 season; six *(The World of Susie Wong, Epitaph for George Dillon, Maria Golovin, La Plume de Ma Tante, Destry Rides Again,* and, with Leland Hay-

---

* Although he wrote only three major full-length plays and half a dozen one-acters, Thornton Wilder (1897–1975) is considered one of America's greatest playwrights. In 1938 he was awarded the Pulitzer Prize for his examination of small-town life, *Our Town,* which is one of the world's most read and most produced plays. Wilder won the Pulitzer Prize again in 1942 for his daring, nonnaturalistic allegory of the human race, *The Skin of Our Teeth.*

ward, *Gypsy*) in 1958–1959. Although he had his share of flops, in succeeding seasons Merrick produced some of Broadway's finest plays and musicals, among them *Take Me Along, A Taste of Honey, Becket, Do Re Mi, Carnival, Subways Are for Sleeping, Stop the World—I Want to Get Off,* and *Oliver.* These led up to his busiest season, 1963–1964, when Merrick opened a record eight productions (*The Rehearsal, Luther, 110 in the Shade, The Resistible Rise of Arturo Ui, One Flew over the Cuckoo's Nest, The Milk Train Doesn't Stop Here Any More, Foxy,* and what would become his biggest hit— until *42nd Street—Hello, Dolly!*).

Merrick's immediate need was to cast the role of Dolly with a star performer of the caliber of Ethel Merman. Gower Champion first suggested Nanette Fabray, the snub-nosed ingenue who had starred in musicals from *Let's Face It* to *High Button Shoes* and *Love Life,* and was now achieving more renown on the Sid Caesar television show. Fabray's audition revealed a talented singer and performer, but one who lacked the strength and charisma of a Merman. Carol Channing who, in a way, Champion had actually discovered, was their next choice. Although the director acknowledged that Channing might be difficult to work with, he knew she was capable of giving a splendid performance.

Born in 1921 in Seattle, the daughter of a prominent newspaper editor who was active in Christian Science, Channing had attended Bennington College in Vermont, majoring in theater. Five feet nine inches tall, when the standard ingenue of the time was at least six inches shorter, Channing made it hard to find a leading man to play opposite her. Her voice, which could change abruptly from a girlish squeak to a baritone growl, got her a role off Broadway in Marc Blitzstein's 1941 musical *No for an Answer.* When it closed after a brief run, she retreated to the West Coast to be with her family. Luckily, Marge Champion was auditioning singers there for husband Gower's first theatrical assignment, the revue *Lend an Ear.* She recommended Channing, who scored in this revue as Pearl White, as an opera prima donna, and, especially, as "The Gladiola Girl," a spoof of twenties musicals. From *Lend an Ear* Channing catapulted into the lead role of Lorelei Lee in the musical version of Anita Loos's broad satire *Gentlemen Prefer Blondes.* Loos herself selected Channing as the flapper who insists that "Diamonds Are a Girl's Best Friend," a role that brought her the stardom that was never to desert her. In 1955 *The Vamp,* an opulent musical about the silent movie era, followed, and although Channing was trapped in a charmless extravaganza that ran only a few months, her unique interpretation of the lead role added to her personal cachet. Then in 1961 she starred in another revue, *Show Girl,* a sort of retrospective of *Lend an Ear,* always portraying irrepressible flappers—which seemed, by now, to be her stock in trade.

During the summer of 1963, the summer when Merman declined what would become *Hello, Dolly!,* Channing was appearing in the Theatre Guild's production of Shaw's *The Millionairess.* Champion suggested that he, Merrick, Stewart, and Herman go and see whether she would be right for their new musical.

"I went with very little enthusiasm," Herman recalled, "because when you write a score for Merman, you don't expect anyone else to hold a candle to her. But I had no choice. We all wanted to see what she sounded like and how she moved on stage, and I must say that by the end of the first act I understood what Gower was getting at. I knew she couldn't sing half the songs I had written, but it didn't bother me because she had a distinctive comedic presence. I also knew it would be a very different show from the one I started out writing. Frankly, it turned out to be a more distinctive show than it would have been with Merman. When I saw what Carol could do, I sensed it would be a very funny show, more of a cartoon—which was very healthy for the book. After the performance we went back and I met Carol, who was just adorable, and it was love at first sight between us."

A few days later at Herman's apartment on Tenth Street they met again, and Herman told her "that I had a bunch of very rangy songs that I might have to alter for her. But before she sang a note, she apologized to me, saying, 'I hope this won't upset you, Mr. Herman, because a composer usually hears his songs sung in a certain way, but, you know, I sing lower than most of the men in your show.'"

Herman laughed, but after they had tried the first song, "I realized she wasn't kidding.* Then I think I told her that I had one song that I would just have to eliminate, and she said, 'Would you do that for me?' And I said, 'I have only one goal and that is to make you comfortable, because if you're comfortable, I'm going to look good.'

"I had learned from Molly Picon and a few others to be flexible in my writing. In *Milk and Honey* there were a couple of very high notes for Mimi Benzell that I brought down an octave lower because she was past the point

---

* Along with the prompt book for *Hello, Dolly!,* Tams-Witmark publishes Dolly's songs in the keys Channing uses on the cast recording. They are usually four or five full tones below the keys in the piano/vocal score—that is, the keys originally written for Merman.

in her opera career where she could hit them without straining. I made Mimi sound good, and so when I said the same thing to Carol, it established a warmth between us that I know she appreciated."

Over the next few days Herman and Channing worked well together as he tailored the almost completed score to her personality and vocal range. He even cut "World Take Me Back," a moving song, but one that he terms "very, very Merman."* While teaching Carol the music, he recorded the changes he made to suit her voice permanently into the score.

With a strong seal of approval from Herman, Channing was invited to David Merrick's office, ostensibly to sign contracts. But before getting down to business Merrick bluntly told her his reservations about her mannerisms: "I don't want that silly grin with all those teeth that go back to your ears," he said. Channing ignored the slur, for she was passionate for a role that she knew well from having studied *The Matchmaker*. She told Merrick of her admiration for Wilder's revision of *The Merchant of Yonkers*, saying that "in Dolly he had poured his intense belief to affirm life."

As she saw it, Dolly Gallagher was an Irish woman born on Second Avenue who fell in love with Ephraim Levi. Her years as Mrs. Levi "turned her into a Hadassah lady, and she turned into Ephraim when he died." She planned to base the slight accent she would give the role on the rhythms of turn-of-the-century New York Irish modified by the Jewishness of Levi.[7]

Merrick agreed with that interpretation and hired her. Then he told her about the other principals he was signing, at the instigation of Champion. David Burns, who had won Tonys for his performances of Senex in *A Funny Thing Happened on the Way to the Forum* and the Mayor in *Music Man*, made an irascible Horace Vandergelder, Yonkers's half-millionaire. The role does not demand a lot of singing, but it needs an actor with expert comic timing. Herman found Burns "grumpy and endearing at the same time," adding, "I've seen a lot of Vandergelders, but Davey Burns could growl and make you love him because he was harmless—like a little pet tiger."

After Burns, most at ease in cameo roles, first read for Vandergelder, he complained that this costarring role was "too long." He asked his friend Jack Gilford to help him find a way to refuse the role without offending the all-powerful David Merrick.

"Ask for more money," Gilford advised. And they gave it to him. "Ask for star billing," was Gilford's next suggestion. And they gave it to him. "A big

---

* The song was reinstated in 1970, when Merman, the last of the major Dollys, took over the role.

song at the end of the first act" was Burns's major complaint. "Ask for a piece of the record; they'll never agree to that," Gilford assured him. But they did, and a reluctant Burns accepted the part, which he played happily for two years.[8]

Charles Nelson Reilly, who had worked with Herman in *Nightcap* and *Parade,* did an about-face and brought sensitivity to the key role of Cornelius Hackl, making him much more than an excited country bumpkin on the town for a day. Completing the quartet of principals was Eileen Brennan, fresh from garnering awards for her performance as *Little Mary Sunshine.* Brennan had shown dramatic acting ability in the role of Annie Sullivan in the touring company of *The Miracle Worker,* and her sensitivity and comedic talents would be put to good use in the ingenue role of Irene Molloy.

By September 1963, with the casting of even the minor parts out of the way, the company began an intense rehearsal period in New York, readying the musical for previews in what was then a frequently chosen tryout city, Detroit. Champion's directorial style allowed his actors much leeway, but as a total professional, he was aware that in essence, with this show his career was in jeopardy. He had won a Tony for *Lend an Ear* back in 1948 but afterward had become mired in a number of forgettable Broadway shows. *Bye Bye Birdie* in 1960 catapulted him into the top echelon of Broadway choreographer-directors. Fiercely competitive, he felt that since he had lost out on the Tony for his recent work on *Carnival,* he must regain his preeminence as a director of musicals and was determined that the new Dolly show would be hugely stylized and contain as much dancing as he could put into two and a half hours. At the outset of his career, when he had formed a dance team with Marge, Gower, being of short stature, could not do conventional lifts. Instead he devised routines that included comedy and self-satiric numbers. By now he was a master of that technique, and since his leading lady Channing was a strong comedienne and singer, but no more than an adequate dancer, he knew that satire, cartoon, and mayhem must be the backbone of this production, with the major part of the dancing falling to the ensemble.

Working with David Merrick would not be easy, for Champion was well known as a director who kept polishing a show until he got it right, no matter how much it cost the producer. When Champion tinkered with *Carnival,* which had received excellent reviews in Philadelphia, Merrick was enraged. He backed Champion up against the wall of the theater, lifted the

Gower Champion, who directed two of Herman's shows: *Hello, Dolly!,* which was a super hit, and *Mack and Mabel,* Herman's favorite of all his oeuvre, which was a near failure. Museum of the City of New York.

shorter man off the ground so that their eyes met, and screamed at him to restore the show to exactly the condition it had been in Washington.

Why did Champion continue to work with such a despot? Because he knew that Merrick sincerely loved things theatrical, was not cheap, and would give him the production he wanted. Even more, Merrick loved hits and Gower Champion wanted a string of them after his name. He reveled in the thought that in spite of his physical size he had risen through the ranks from a lowly hoofer to a director whose name would be written in the annals of showbiz history. But now he needed more than a Tony nomination, more than a mild hit like *Carnival.* He needed a smash.

Dolly: A Damned Exasperating Woman, as the show was called when it opened in Detroit, is a true farce, and Champion, like any good director, wanted to let the audience know it at the outset. Jerry Herman remembered how Champion communicated to the viewers "that it was okay to laugh and have fun at the show.

"Mike and I were having a hamburger somewhere near the rehearsal studio when Gower hit us with his idea. 'I'm thinking of opening the show by having a horse pull Dolly's carriage on stage,' he said. 'Only I want it to be a goofy-looking horse with two showgirls hidden inside.'"

Herman and Stewart thought this was a stroke of genius: after seeing that funny horse with long seductive painted eyelashes, an audience would accept any zany business. "Once Gower got his horse," Herman added, "he was free to direct the whole show in wild, poster colors—bright, happy, unsubtle—which had been his idea all along."

To help create a seamless continuity, Champion arranged for a ramp to be constructed around the orchestra pit. It recalled the old fashioned runways popular in the Gay Nineties that led from the stage into the first few rows of the theater. The ramp created intimacy by bringing the characters within arm's reach of the audience. It also created a diversion, for it allowed the viewers to concentrate on the activity in front of the proscenium while scenery was flown or dropped in behind.

The musical, whose first scene is a street in New York, opens without an overture.* An omnibus pulled by the flamboyant horses Champion envisioned bears an ensemble of Yonkers ladies singing Dolly's credentials as a matchmaker (Call on Dolly/She's the one the spinsters recommend . . .).

---

* An overture was added later, but it was not planned as part of the original New York production.

When Dolly, who has been riding on the back of this horsecar, descends and walks the ramp, she interrupts the number and tells the audience about herself, establishing a device (extracted from Thornton Wilder's play), that will be continued throughout the evening and be consistent with most of the leading characters—soliloquy. We empathize with our heroine from the start, especially since she has told us—with no sense of self-pity—of the hardscrabble life she had led since the death of her beloved husband, Ephraim.

Noël Coward said you can make the public accept any theatrical convention if you introduce it at the beginning of your play. So as each of these characters speaks half to himself or herself and half to the audience, we believe their sentimental soliloquies—a respite from the farce going on around them.

After the chorus completes "Call on Dolly," we are introduced to Ambrose Kemper, a young painter, in love with Ermengarde, the niece of Horace Vandergelder. When Kemper questions Dolly's occupation, she simply says, "Some people paint, some sew . . . I meddle."

Now she gets to sing her first solo, a chance to tell us of her qualifications as a meddler and a matchmaker, "I Put My Hand In," in itself a tour de force of witty rhyming:

> My aplomb at cosmetic art.
> Turned a frump to a trump lady fair,
> She had a countenance a little bit like Scrooge
> But oh, today you would swear the Lord himself applied the rouge.
> I put my hand in here,
> I put my hand in there . . .

In her ensuing soliloquy she does not dwell on the penny-pinching side of her life as a widow but turns serious when she confesses movingly that she has resolved to marry Vandergelder herself, as soon as she gets a sign of approval from her late husband.

Champion brings the sentiment to a close seamlessly by having a band move on, sending the horsecar on its excursion to Yonkers, while an oleo behind changes the scene to Horace Vandergelder's feed store, where we will meet the irascible curmudgeon. Through his soliloquy we learn of his intention to march in the 14th Street parade on his way to court Irene Molloy, a young widow to whom he has been introduced by Dolly. Crafty as she is, Dolly realizes that this time his intentions are serious. She tries to discredit his choice of Molloy by intriguing him, improvising a fiction, an heiress with a name she dreams up: Ernestina Money. As the tightwad bites on her

Dolly (Carol Channing) makes her entrance on a cart driven by John Anderson and pulled by Jan LaPrade and Bonnie Mathias, director Gower Champion's "goofy horse." Photofest, Inc.

bait of Miss Money, Dolly, sure that she will ensnare him in the end, confides to her late husband that she plans to have the bedroom in Horace's house done over in blue.

Vandergelder now expresses his philosophy in a typical "list" song, "It Takes a Woman," replete with alternating images of delicacy and earthiness:

> It takes a woman all powdered and pink
> To joyously clean out the drain in the sink,
> And it takes an angel with long golden lashes
> And soft Dresden fingers for dumping the ashes. . . .
> The frail young maiden who's constantly there
> For washing and blueing and shoeing the mare,
> And it takes a female for setting the table,
> And weaning the Guernsey and cleaning the stable. . . .
> And in the winter she'll shovel the ice,

And lovingly set out the traps for the mice.
She's a joy and treasure, for practic'lly speaking,
To whom can you turn when the plumbing is leaking?

Vandergelder's song is frequently interrupted by comments from his chief clerk, Cornelius Hackl, and his juvenile assistant, Barnaby Tucker, and even—always consistent with Champion's fantastically unrealistic direction—the appearance of "an instant glee club" (which comes and goes at the director's will).

Carrying a box of chocolates and eager for his rendezvous with the young Irish beauty, Irene Molloy, Vandergelder departs for New York, where he has arranged to meet Dolly at Molloy's hat shop. The clerks decide that they too want to have an adventure, to see some of the glittering big city only a short train ride away. They explode some tomato cans in the basement of the store purposely to create a pungent odor, dress in their Sunday clothes, shutter the store, and are off on a spree of their own.

As the scene shifts to New York City and the exterior of Mrs. Molloy's Hat Shop, we are privy to her assistant Minnie Fay's own soliloquy, with comments on everything from modish headwear to the current state of marriage. Later, when Mrs. Molloy appears to unlock the shop, we learn of her dissatisfaction with her life as a milliner, which explains why she is willing to marry a much older Vandergelder—and, although she is about to settle for security, we sense that Irene is a modern woman with a healthy thirst for adventure and love.

Using a line Stewart had cribbed from Wilder, indicating that the mode in headgear that year of 1890 was no longer cherries and feathers, but "ribbons down the back." Herman creates one of his finest ballads. The phrases of the gentle song begin in minor keys but end up neatly in majors. This ruminative melody was originally intended for the score of *Milk and Honey* but was not appropriate to any of the major characters. It fits perfectly into the voice and character of Molloy.

In the release, where the tune is solidly in a bright major key, the sensitivity of the lyric combines perfectly with the rustling melodic activity.

And so I'll try to make it easier to find me in the stillness of July,
Because a breeze might stir a rainbow up behind me
That might happen to catch the gentleman's eye.

After the fluttering, almost windswept, music on "rainbow up behind me" the song returns to its opulent main theme as Irene lets us know that she is not ready to settle down with a cold-hearted Horace Vandergelder.

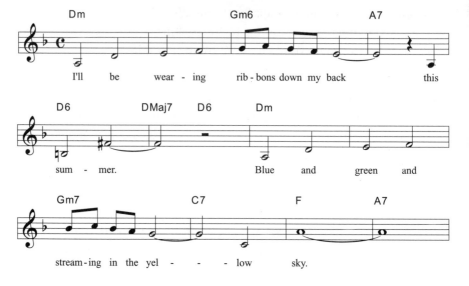

I'll be wear - ing rib - bons down my back this sum - mer. Blue and green and stream - ing in the yel - - - low sky.

She wants a different kind of man, one who will smile and take her by the hand, making her recall in a momentary recollection of her first husband, "how lovely love can be." She concludes the song, singing almost to herself:

> And so I will proudly wear
> Ribbons down my back,
> Shining in my hair,
> That he might notice me.*

Dolly arrives late for her meeting with Vandergelder. The clerks, Cornelius and Barnaby, having stumbled onto the street of the hat store (where would musical farce be without a healthy dose of coincidence?), see their boss coming and take refuge in the shop. They pretend to be wealthy roués interested in the then shocking act of purchasing women's hats. When Vandergelder enters the store, the clerks hide, one diving under a table, the other into a large armoire, but Vandergelder, sensing a masculine presence in the shop, wants to search the room.†

When the pair are finally discovered, Vandergelder leaves in a huff—off

---

* Herman opts to end this melody on the fifth of the major key rather than the expected tonic. It reinforces the feeling of incompleteness, leaving an open door into Irene's love life.

† The "Motherhood March," which occurs at this point, was not added until previews.

to the parade and his next conquest, Ernestina Money. Irene is upset that the appearance of these two young men has spoiled her relationship with Horace and orders them out of the shop, but Dolly flimflams her into having dinner with the pair. As a suitable restaurant she suggests the Harmonia Gardens, where there is dancing. Cornelius says that would be impossible because "I have absolutely no sense of rhythm." Dolly counters, "Absolutely no sense of rhythm is one of the primary requirements of learning dancing by the Gallagher-Levi Method." And so we are led neatly into one of the show's most infectious and charming sections, "Dancing."

It is always amusing to see a clod slip and fall but eventually end up an adequate dancer, and Gower Champion knew the empathy these oafs would create as they learned to waltz, all the while forming a tentative romantic attachment with Irene and Minnie. The song fits easily into Stewart's dialogue, spoken mostly in rhythm as the quintet—Dolly, the clerks, and the two women—warm to each other.

One gets an idea in this deceptively simple waltz of Jerry Herman's ability to hone sharp, original-sounding melodies out of harmonic clichés. Although his chord sequences have been used by hundreds of composers in thousands of songs, Herman's particular choice of 6ths, 9ths, 11ths, and 13ths for his melody notes creates harmonic freshness as the tunes rub against the traditional harmony. Herman also creates tension by giving us an unexpected modulation (not unlike Richard Rodgers's swirling waltzes) in the second half of "Dancing's" release.

With "Dancing" the high spot of this section of the musical, and Dolly acting as the force to bring these two young couples together, the play now has its subplot well in hand. The practically penniless clerks, committed to taking these two ladies to New York's most expensive restaurant, bring enough excitement to propel their story into the second act. To keep the suspense going we have the unknown quantity of Ernestina Money, the unresolved love affair of niece Ermengarde and her painter swain, and, of course, the match between Dolly and Horace. Champion brought act one to a close with a song during which Vandergelder talks about the beauty of thrift, recounting his rise to riches while he is holding a charity auction. According to Herman, "Gower staged the sale with items passing from person to person, anything from feather boas to grandfather clocks—all of which turned the stage into a riot of color."

At the time, Herman thought it was the most exciting production number he had ever seen, but it was not until the company got to previews in Detroit that, in Herman's view, "the audience told us that they missed their

Dolly—they had fallen in love with the character played by Carol Channing and wanted to know what she was thinking, not what Horace's past had been." Unfortunately, one of Herman's most humorous songs, a veritable cartoon, "Penny in My Pocket," had to be cut:

> I put a penny in my pocket and in a little time
> That penny in my pocket had grown into a dime.

And in a little longer, a quarter jingled out,
I put that quarter in the teapot and I waited till my teapot had
     a dollar in its spout.
I put the dollar in my mattress and had some pleasant dreams,
Till suddenly my mattress was bursting at the seams.
And that's how I acquired the wealth I now possess.
That little penny is the secret, yes, that penny is the secret of
     my success.

Then Vandergelder gives us more details about his life, but always with
the sense of caricature:

I had a penny in my pocket and not another sou,
And with my only shirt-tail I shined a rich man's shoe.
He threw me down a nickel, admiring my skill.
I gave the nickel to the blind man and the blind man left me all
     his meager savings in his will.

I bought myself a wagon and started hauling ice,
I cut the ice to ice cubes and got a higher price.
I crushed the ice to ices for still a higher fee,
A rich tycoon said "Very enterprising in your organizing, son,
     you must come work for me."

En route to work next morning, I helped a lady cross.
The lady was (you guessed it) the mother of the boss.
The boss said, "You're promoted, I need you by my side,"
And then I met the boss's daughter, and I wed the boss's
     daughter, and quite suddenly she died.

I bought myself an acre, a silo, and a steed.
All Yonkers started buying my grain, and hay, and feed.
And now I've half a million, but proudly I confess
That in my pocket is that penny, it's that shiny little penny,
     that's the secret of my success.

Keeping the excitement of the auction in abeyance for a few minutes,
we get a soliloquy from Dolly, impatiently awaiting a sign from Ephraim,
but the pensive mood is soon dispersed as we are plunged into the thrill of
the upcoming 14th Street Parade which concludes the act.*

* Dolly's concluding number, "Before the Parade Passes By," replacing "Penny in My
Pocket," was not written until the show was in Detroit.

Act two, whose centerpiece will be one of Broadway's most famous songs, "Hello, Dolly," opens as Cornelius and Barnaby are still trying to convince Irene and Minnie that the rich and truly elegant do not take hansom cabs, nor do they take the streetcar—they walk. So the quartet head on foot to the Harmonia Gardens while the oleo spins behind them. The song, "Elegance," that accompanies this trek, was not written until the show was in previews.

When the four arrive and the setting changes to the plush interior of this restaurant in Battery Park, we are treated to the show's best dancing sequence. In anticipation of Dolly's long-awaited return to her favorite restaurant, the maître d'hôtel, Rudolph, is putting his waiters and busboys through the sort of drill that only a top-notch choreographer could devise. They come and go in hysterical groups with breathtaking near-collisions. Two, bearing food en brochette flambée, engage in a duel; others supply percussion by clapping silver salvers together. Large trays are employed as shields and mountainous stacks of dishes are passed between them without the loss of a single plate. This meticulously designed mayhem, repeatedly interrupted for plot development, is called "The Waiters' Gallop," and along with the Keystone Kops ballet in *High Button Shoes* and *Oklahoma!*'s "Dream Ballet," reaches the pinnacle of the Broadway musical's choreographic art.

The boys (even though Cornelius is in his early thirties, he still acts like a boy), soon throw all caution to the wind and order a private dining room, curtained, on the opposite side of the stage from the one where Ernestina, Vandergelder, and, later, Dolly will be dining. The farce grows more zany as we switch from one curtained room to the other, always interrupted by the waiters' shenanigans. Vandergelder loses his purse, and of course Barnaby finds it, and he and Cornelius order lavishly as the excitement builds.

Helped by the somewhat frenetic Offenbachian music, this frolic is punctuated by the gentler strains of "Dancing," but the gallop theme, which seems to fit the 1890s Harmonia Gardens to a tee, finally wins out. Now Rudolph blows his whistle to inform the waiters of Dolly's arrival.

And there she is at last, immaculately coiffed, standing spotlit at the top of the carpeted stairs in a blood-red glittering gown.* The moment always elicits prolonged applause as she descends and begins to sing slowly, "Hello, Harry, well, Hello, Louie,/It's so nice to be back home where I belong."

---

* Michael Stewart and Freddie Wittop, the costume designer, chose the color to represent the return of life and blood to the heroine's existence. They were more than dismayed when Barbra Streisand, filming the musical, insisted on a gold sequined gown for her costume.

Herman amplified the meaning of this song, which has become one of the most popular theater anthems of the century: "I wanted the musicalization of her return to the human race to be as touching as possible. It had to make me feel that I was writing something important, not just a dizzy comedy, so I opened it by using the names of people I loved, Harry, my father and Manny, my uncle. When I played it for Mike Stewart, he said, 'This is going to make such a wonderful statement.' He didn't recognize—nor did I— that this was going to be a popular song; I was just musicalizing Thornton Wilder's and Mike's scene."

The song itself is almost too well known to demand quotation. Its melody, easily remembered, is not particularly adventurous, but it does fit into the style of the Harmonia Gardens and the musical. The lyric, with phrases like "lookin' swell," "goin' strong," and especially "golly, gee, fellas" is highly anachronistic, smacking more of the flapper twenties than the show's Gay Nineties.

Even though "Hello, Dolly!" is not the high point of the show for me, one cannot deny its place in the hierarchy of musical theater. As Martin Gottfried maintains, "It teaches a lesson that should never be forgotten. This is the lesson of directness. Such a song sounds corny to many a musical theater sophisticate, but no song that comes out and wows an audience is corny. Such directness is the essence of showmanship, and without showmanship, there is no musical theater."[9]

The song builds the scene dramatically, as all the waiters and diners join in. For Herman, it is not the song but Dolly's return to life that thrills him. "What I wanted to capture," he admits, "was the moment when this lady, who has locked herself away from life, finally gets the guts to put on her old finery and walk down that staircase to face the world again."

As we return to the plot, and it now becomes time to pay the bill, Horace discovers that his wallet is missing and becomes embroiled in a general melee, and the principals, staff, and several customers are arrested.

The scene changes to a courtroom, and Dolly—handing the judge a card that reads "Counselor at Law"—pleads the innocence of all her clients except Vandergelder. Cornelius comes forward with an impassioned speech about love and adventure, saying that had he stayed in Yonkers he would have "missed that important, minute, no, moment when one knows his life is forever changed." The song, "It Only Takes a Moment (To Be Loved a Whole Life Long)," is top-notch Herman, for the composer sets his title to follow natural speech patterns. But then almost immediately, on the words "for your eyes to meet—and then," he climbs a scale which ends on a note

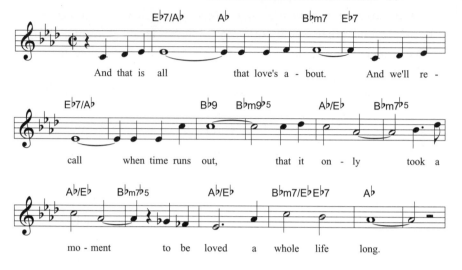

out of the key. It is as unexpected and beautiful as the moment one falls in love. As romantic and original as this chorus is, my favorite is the coda in which Cornelius is joined by Irene.

By the end of the song the judge is in tears and dismisses all the defendants except Vandergelder, whose interest Dolly piques when she sings her goodbye song, "So Long, Dearie":

> For I can hear the choo-choo callin' me on
> To a fancy new address . . .
> I'm gonna learn to dance and drink and smoke a cigarette
> I'm goin' as far away from Yonkers as a girl can get.

By this time, although he struggles and flips like a hooked flounder, Horace—and the audience—realize that Dolly will be his mate, when he echoes her lines said in the scene before: "You go your way, and I'll go mine," pointing twice in the same direction.

From the courtroom, the scene changes to the feed store back in Yonkers. Cornelius and Barnaby come in for their back pay, adding that they intend to open a competitive emporium across the street in real estate that Dolly has rented them. Ermengarde and Ambrose are to be married, and the niece, too, asks for the dowry her mother had entrusted to Vandergelder. Horace fumes, then goes reluctantly upstairs to get everybody's cash from his safe, as the talk downstairs turns to the responsibility of having wealth. Dolly observes that her late husband used to say, "Money is not worth a thing unless it's spread around, encouraging young things to grow." And then, assured that Vandergelder will marry her, she repeats for the last time her request for permission from her late husband. That sign looks like it is forthcoming when Horace instructs the paperhanger he has hired to use blue paper in the front bedroom. Now, shrewd business woman that she is, Dolly persuades Horace to avoid competition by taking Cornelius in as partner and promoting Barnaby to chief clerk.

To tie the plot up, Stewart has Horace echo Dolly's quote of Ephraim's words about money, this time comparing it to manure—worthless unless spread around. Dolly heaves a sigh, saying, "Thank you, Ephraim," and we are into the finale—reprises of "Hello, Dolly," "Dancing," "It Only Takes a Moment," and "Put on Your Sunday Clothes."

David Merrick had a great many other shows in progress and was unable to attend rehearsals of this musical, but he promised to "catch up with it" when it opened for previews in Detroit. And so, with a month of previews scheduled, *Dolly: A Damned Exasperating Woman* headed out of town for its break-in period.

It was to be the worst theatrical experience of Jerry Herman's life.

6

hello, dolly!

David Merrick arrived in Detroit in the autumn of 1963 after the dispirited opening—and abrupt closing after seven performances—of his Broadway production of *The Resistible Rise of Arturo Ui*. He was generally hypercritical of his shows out of town, but this year with *The Rehearsal, Luther,* and *Arturo Ui,* each a *succès d'estime* but failing at the box office, he was more testy than usual.

The audience at the first preview of *Dolly: A Damned Exasperating Woman* was not enthusiastic, and after Merrick read the local reviews, one of which was headlined "GOODBYE, DOLLY," Merrick began to scream at Herman, Stewart, and especially Freddie Wittop, the costume designer.

"The next day we had a full cast rehearsal with Merrick in attendance," Herman recalled, "and at the end of it I found Freddie sitting in the back of the theater with his head down in his arms. We all had heard Merrick yell 'I'm ashamed of these costumes!' at him.

"I thought they were very joyous and beautiful. So I came to him after Merrick had stormed out of the theater, and said, 'Freddie, when we began the "Put on Your Sunday Clothes" number, there was no singing, no dialogue, hardly any orchestra, just a vamp, and a parade of your glorious costumes—and you heard that rousing applause. Who do you think the cheering was for?'"[1]

"Mike Stewart was able to stand up to Merrick." Herman remembered, "Once we were in an elevator and he said something slurring to Mike, the two of them trading insults so loudly and getting so red that I thought a fight was going to break out. But Mike never backed down. Gower had a different technique. He would either leave town or go to the movies." Some of

"I'm ashamed of these songs!" producer David Merrick, known on Broadway as "The Abominable Showman," shouted at Herman during the creation of *Hello, Dolly!* After the hit show opened, he apologized. Photofest, Inc.

Stewart's defiant manner communicated itself to Herman, who recalled how the producer flayed him in practically the same words he had used with Wittop: "I am ashamed of these songs."

"But, David," Herman summoned the courage to answer, "these are the same songs you begged Ethel Merman to come and hear. The same songs you've praised me for and that you've been touting all over. I just don't understand."

Still, Merrick never would back down. "The songs are just not working," he fulminated.

Champion, too, although he was usually more diplomatic than Merrick, felt the show was "only three-quarters there" and needed repair, especially at the end of the first act and the beginning of the second. "He would sometimes demand new lyrics overnight, in front of the whole company, instead of coming to me privately," Herman recalls. He had a manner that Herman term "like a sergeant."

At one point Merrick became "maniacal," threatening to close the show in Detroit, but Champion called his bluff. When he bragged that he and the cast would buy the producer out, Merrick retreated.[2]

Now, with his back to the wall, not knowing who was his ally, Merrick phoned Bob Merrill, who had written the score of *Carnival.** After a blow-up with Merrick, the composer had sworn that he would never work with the producer again. Now Merrick offered to give him a full 1 percent of the show if he would come to Detroit to fix this score, and perhaps even offer a few suggestions for the book.[†] Knowing what a liar Merrick was, Merrill wiggled out with the excuse that he was busy writing the lyrics for *Funny Girl.* Then Merrick pulled his trump card, saying, "Both Jerry and Gower need you and want you to come."[3]

With an urgent plea he believed came from both Herman, whose score he had heard and admired, and Champion, a director he considered a close friend, Merrill could only acquiesce. Of course, the 1 percent of the show that Merrick had offered him also carried influence.

When Herman saw Merrill in the lobby of the Detroit Park Sheraton Hotel, he turned ashen. Merrill knew at once that Merrick had lied. Later, in Merrick's office, Herman stood his ground; he was deeply humiliated by

---

* Bob Merrill (1920–1998) started his career by writing pop tunes in Hollywood. After the successes of "If I Knew You Were Comin' I'd've Baked a Cake," and "How Much Is That Doggie in the Window?" he began writing for Broadway. His most important works were the music and lyrics for *New Girl in Town* (1957), *Take Me Along* (1959), *Carnival* (1961), *Funny Girl* (1964, lyrics only), *Breakfast at Tiffany's* (1966), *Henry, Sweet Henry* (1967), and *Sugar* (1972, lyrics only).

[†] The customary composer's royalty for writing a complete score is 1½–2 percent. This is calculated on the gross box office receipts, and with a hit show it can add up considerably. What Merrick was offering Merrill was a disproportionate share for simply "doctoring" the show.

Merrick's suggestion he collaborate "for the good of the show," saying, "I didn't sign to do this show with anyone else."

"Take it or leave it." Merrick spat. "Ultimatum."

Merrick's calling in Merrill to rewrite Herman's work has spawned a smear campaign—promulgated by at least two books devoted to the musical—that should be set to rest.*

"The truth is," Herman maintains, "Bob Merrill did not want to interfere with my work. He started off by saying, 'I really don't like being in this position because I love the stuff you've done. If you believe we need a song to open the second act, we'll just write one together. I have an idea, and I'm going to give you a little bit of it, and if you like it, you write the rest of it.' And he wrote, 'Hey, New York, it's really us/Barnaby and Cornelius.' (He stretched it out to Cor-nee-lee-us [instead of Cor-*neel*-yus]. Then he wrote, 'All the guests of Mr. Hackl are/Feelin' great and look spectacalar.' I would never write that. I would never syllablize a name to get a rhyme, or twist a word ['Hackl are' and 'spectacalar'] to make it fit, especially since Cornelius doesn't talk that way in any other part of the musical. My rhymes have to be perfect, and my people always sing in the language that fits their character. It's a small point, but important to me.) Bob gave me the first eight bars of 'Elegance' and those opening lines. Then he left me to write the rest of the song." One of Herman's favorite original couplets is

> All who are well bred agree
> Minnie Fay has pedigree

and his special favorite is

> Exercise your wildest whims tonight
> We are out with Diamond Jims tonight

which he calls "so Jerry Herman that anybody in his right mind would know I wrote it. And I enjoyed writing it—in fact for the movie I wrote a third chorus that is not in the show. I think of 'Elegance' as a fifty-fifty job even though I get no ASCAP royalties for the song. David Merrick insisted on giving my royalties to Merrill, now the Merrill estate."†

---

* Stephen Suskin's *Show Tunes* attributes the authorship of the music, and coauthorship of the lyric of "Elegance," to Merrill (p. 325). It attributes "Motherhood March" to Merrill and Herman. Ethan Mordden, in *Open a New Window*, mistakenly states, "Bob Merrill wrote two *Dolly!* numbers, 'Elegance' and 'Motherhood'" (p. 144).

† Giving away someone's royalties is not unique in the annals of songwriting. Accord-

"Elegance," may be the kind of number needed for the opening of the second act, but it is among the weakest moments in the show. Its sentiments and language are hardly likely to be initiated by these two bumpkins from Yonkers, and the concept is a pale tracing of "He Had Refinement" from *A Tree Grows in Brooklyn,* written more than a decade before, coupled with a crib from an even earlier song, a Cole Porter comic number, "It Ain't Etiquette" from *Du Barry Was a Lady* (1939). Musically, with its ricky-tick syncopations in the verse section, "Elegance" smacks more of 1920 than the rest of the score, and although the quasi-refrain is catchy, its approach without a pitch or harmonic change is simply boring.

During the time Merrill was in Detroit, Champion decided to amplify the hat shop scene in the first act to strengthen the female characters' resolve and patriotism at the same time that he augmented the suspense in the clerks' hiding in the armoire and under the table. The added number was the "The Motherhood March," another Merrill-Herman collaboration.

When Vandergelder asks Dolly, Minnie, and Irene to stand pat while he searches out the men, they revolt, and ask him to produce a search warrant. Again we have a cartoon, a pastiche with a lyric mostly by Merrill:

> I stand for Motherhood, America, and a hot lunch for orphans.
> Take off your hat, sir, Betsy Ross's flag is passing.
> Do you see him on the hill at Gettysburg,
> 'Neath that great triumphal arch?
> If you see him as he's tramping through the grapes of wrath,
> Stand up and march, march, march!

This unnecessary song (for the men are found out shortly afterward) is practically "through-composed"—its melodic themes are not repeated. That technique leaves the listener with only a strong martial rhythm and clear-cut harmony to cling to—certainly not a Herman-type melody. Herman says that he and Merrill worked on "Motherhood March" together. "The lyric, which has only the most rudimentary rhyme, was mostly Bob Merrill's idea; what I wrote completely was the counterpoint: Remember the Alamo. I regret that I've one life to give for my country, etc." The num-

---

ing to Michael Kerker, director of ASCAP's Musical Theatre Department, "In exchange for singing a composer's songs, well-known recording artists frequently cut themselves in on the work. Alimony recipients too, sometimes have copyrights and payments of exes assigned to them" (author telephone interview with Michael Kerker, 11 September 2002).

ber is so patched together and so patently different from the rest of the score one wonders why Merrill, Champion, Stewart, or even Merrick didn't cut it.*

But Champion, who had commissioned the number, had to save face, and Herman was constantly in fear that Merrick was going to replace him, even though he, like the rest of the creative team, had a standard Equity contract and, according to union rules, couldn't be fired.

A dispassionate look at *Hello, Dolly!* reveals that these stylistic inconsistencies weaken the entire musical and that these two songs are the dullest spots in a score that is otherwise hit tune after hit tune. But Herman was insecure, young, and malleable enough to be cowed by Merrick's interference. The composer is the first to admit that such a situation could not happen to him today.

By the time Merrill left Detroit, it was clear to Champion that the only major problem left to solve was the unsatisfactory ending of the first act— too many of the audience were not interested in learning how the auction turned out, and "Penny in My Pocket," while amusing, was not stirring enough to make the audience return to their seats after taking a breather. Clearly, they missed Dolly, who did not reappear until the middle of act two. Davey Burns was delighted to have his big number eliminated, since he had always felt his part was too arduous and "far too long."[4]

Because Stewart's libretto had included the line about Vandergelder marching in the 14th Street parade, Champion suggested that the replace-

---

* As musical supervisor of the cinema version of *Hello, Dolly!*, Herman went on record as saying that he "hate[d] the 'Motherhood March'" and insisted the number not be included in the film.

ment song take that as its cue. Stewart rewrote the essential lines that close the act and told Herman, "We need a song about a parade passing by." Before allowing Herman a crack at the concept, the director and Merrick, still concerned about Herman's ability to deliver a hit song, called in composer Charles Strouse and lyricist Lee Adams, the team with whom Champion and Stewart had worked so smoothly on *Bye Bye Birdie*.* It was another humiliation for Herman.

Overnight they came up with a song Herman never heard. Herman recalled, "They played it for Champion, who listened to their song and dismissed them. He said to me, 'It's up to you, kid, because I don't like what they did and I sent them home.'"

"I remember it was late evening when I went to the piano in my room at the Park Sheraton Hotel. I gritted my teeth and repeated to myself, 'Nobody's going to write this moment in *my* show.' I was planning to write a song for Dolly, about her joining the parade because Mike and I had had long meetings about using the movement of a parade passing by as a metaphor for her joining the parade of life. I heard the opening notes in my head as a kind of fanfare. After all, my first show was called *Parade,* and I loved the theatricality of that image.† The concept for the song had been in my head for weeks, and I called it, 'When the Parade Passes By.' I wrote the song in about forty-five minutes, but I played it over and over, quietly because by that time it was the middle of the night. Finally I got the chorus and all the lyrics clearly in my head, and I imagined how it would sound in Carol's voice.

"When I could bear it no longer, I called her, and speaking very quietly I told her I had finished the song. She came down to my room at once in the hotel's white terrycloth bathrobe, and I played and sang it for her. I could see the tears welling up in her eyes as I got towards the end, which is quite exhil-

---

* Charles Strouse (1928–) wrote the music and Lee Adams (1924–) the lyrics for several hit shows: *Bye Bye Birdie* (1960), *All American* (1962), *Golden Boy* (1954), *It's a Bird . . . It's a Plane . . . It's Superman* (1966), and *Applause* (1970). *Annie* (1977), Strouse's biggest hit, one of Broadway's blockbuster musicals of the seventies, had lyrics by Martin Charnin.

† Parades seem to have been on other musical minds in addition to Herman's that season. The Merrill-Styne *Funny Girl* score featured "Don't Rain on My Parade," and Sondheim's musical *Anyone Can Whistle* included "There's a Parade in Town." Sondheim's ends with a lame punchline about the singer missing the parade while getting dressed for it. The Styne-Merrill effort is exciting but totally self-involved, while Herman's song, with its carpe diem theme, is truly inspiring.

arating. Then I played it again, this time in her key, and she began singing softly what she remembered, but almost unable to control herself with the excitement of the moment—gradually growing—as we repeated it, she sang louder. Twice more through and she had memorized it. By then—I guess it was about four in the morning—she said, 'Let's wake Gower up.' And so we called his room. He soon joined us—also in his terry bathrobe. And then I played and sang it for Gower, and he jumped up on the sofa in my little room and said, 'That's it! That's exactly what I want!' By this time he was yelling. 'I don't care if I wake up the whole hotel,' and I played it again and he started running around the room throwing out ideas about how he was going to stage it. Finally he shouted, 'I'M GOING TO GET NEW SETS AND NEW COSTUMES!' It was like something out of an MGM musical, and we put that song into the show in five days, literally. We had Freddy Wittop design new costumes, and until they were all finished some of the cast even played in leotards."

Herman maintains that instead of digging into his own pocket Merrick "gave away 50 percent of my royalty on this number to the other team for their time and trouble, journeying to Detroit."

Since then, two respected theater historians delving into ASCAP files have been misled by the 50 percent royalty arrangements paid to others for "Before the Parade Passes By," attributing the composition of this song to Adams and Strouse.*

This misattribution for one of his finest songs—not the fact that half of the income due him goes to others—has so frustrated Herman that he asked Charles Strouse for a letter certifying Herman's authorship. Perhaps its inclusion in this book will set to rest the misapprehensions about an exceptional Herman song.

"Before the Parade Passes By" is masterful and doubly moving as the metaphor for the entire show, coming as it does after Dolly's speech bemoaning the lack of color in her life since the death of her beloved husband. Her extremely moving soliloquy (written by Wilder and adapted by Stewart) mentions a faded oak leaf that had fallen out of her bible. She had

---

* Mordden again mistakenly writes, "Charles Strouse and Lee Adams wrote 'Before the Parade Passes By,' which Herman reworked" (*Open a New Window*, p. 144n). Suskin writes, "Strouse and Adams came up with a big number to end the first act, 'Before the Parade Passes By.' This version was not used though; instead, Herman wrote his own song with the same title. ASCAP, which licenses songs by their members, lists 'Before the Parade Passes By' as by Adams, Herman, and Strouse" (*Show Tunes*, p. 326).

220 CENTRAL PARK SOUTH, NYC 10019

To whom it may Concern

Jerry Herman wrote the music & lyric for "Before The Parade Passes By"

Charles Strouse

Letter from Charles Strouse certifying Herman's authorship of "Before the Parade Passes By."

placed the once vibrant leaf there when Ephraim asked her to marry him. "I suddenly realized that I was like that oak leaf," she continues. "For years I had not shed one tear nor had I been filled with the wonderful hope that something or other would turn out well. And so I've decided to rejoin the human race, and Ephraim . . . I want *you* to give me away."
And then she begins very slowly,

Before the parade passes by,
I'm gonna get in step while there's still time left.

The song breaks off to go into dialogue, with the others encouraging Dolly to come join the parade, but she continues, singing two choruses with mounting intensity:

Before the parade passes by,
I'm gonna go and taste Saturday's high life.
Before the parade passes by,
I'm gonna get some life back into my life.
I'm ready to move out in front,
I've had enough of just passing by life,
With the rest of them, with the best of them,
I can hold my head up high!
For I've got a goal again, I've got a drive again,
I'm gonna feel my heart coming alive again,
Before the parade passes by!

As the act ends, Dolly reprises her resolute song at the top of her lungs:

I'm gonna raise the roof,
I'm gonna carry on.
Gimme an old trombone,
Gimme an old baton,
Before the parade passes by!

The melodic theme of the song, which attacks a tonic triad and ends on the most active note of the scale (the leading tone), is like a clarion call. This, coupled with the rhythmic verve of the idea, an upbeat leading to a triplet which finally brings us to a strong downbeat (♪ ♪♪♪|♩), makes for an extremely rousing motif. Lyrically, too, the song is a study in positiveness: the first three repeated phrases all ending with *life* ("high life," "my life," and "by life"). The melody soon shortens itself into punchy phrases, maintaining a high tessitura as Dolly continues to sing about facing the competition of living. We know from this song that this woman is now prepared to bring about any lifestyle she chooses. Herman says it is Dolly's song about second chances. It is more than that, for it is a reaffirmation of the continuum of life, and as such is the most important message of the play—and certainly the most moving.*

---

* Herman wrote an appropriate quatrain for Chita Rivera to sing in *Jerry's Girls*. The verse reads: Before the parade passes by/I've got to get in step while there's still time left./ Before the parade passes by/Before it all moves on and only I'm left." An alternate line is apt for Rivera in her middle years: "While I have one more 'I'm still in my prime' left."

Victory over this situation, coupled with having written a rousing hit song, wrought its adjustments. Champion's attitude changed; he began to ask Herman's advice about the last-minute tuning that was now necessary for the production's journey toward Broadway. Even more important was David Merrick's stand.

Herman credits Champion as the catalyst for that change. "Gower was so impressed with the song that he never went back to sleep after he left my room," he remembered. "He insisted that Merrick go right up and listen to the new song, and told him—yes, didn't ask him, just told him—that the song and new sets and costumes were going into the show whether he liked it or not!

"Merrick came in, listened, approved, and for the first time patted me on the back and started treating me like his own protégé. I had written 'So Long, Dearie' overnight and now this song overnight and somehow that professionalism under fire gained his respect. If David admired anything, he admired theatrical craft."

It was also in Detroit that the title of the show changed from *Dolly*, with a subtitle, *A Damned Exasperating Woman*, to *Hello, Dolly!* because of the release of Louis Armstrong's recording.* Herman remembered that "someone from my music publishing company in New York got on a plane and showed up at my hotel room in Detroit clutching a 45 RPM record. I had no equipment for playing recordings in my room so I took him to the Fisher Theatre, where the company was rehearsing, and waited until Gower called a break. Then we let all the company hear it. The melody I had written was sort of swaying; I had based my recollection of the Gay Nineties on Alice Faye as Lillian Russell in an old black-and-white movie. It was a sweet, old-fashioned, long-white-gloves kind of tune.

"But, without changing a single note or rhythm, Louis Armstrong had made it New Orleans Dixieland. He had taken the parochialism out of the number and substituted a universality. Everyone in the room could tell that this record had 'hit' written over it. The music publisher was the first to speak after Armstrong's growl faded away. 'There's the title of your show,' he announced. 'This record's going to sell a million copies.'"

He underestimated it by far. Two years after the show opened, according to *Variety*, "Hello, Dolly!" had sold half a million sheet copies and Armstrong's recording had sold three million records. The record has gone plat-

---

* Herman had actually written a tongue-twisting song around the subtitle called "You're a Damn Exasperating Woman."

inum many times over, and there have been more than 350 recordings of the song in twenty-two languages. ASCAP lists it in the top ten of its top one hundred most successful songs of all time.

With its new numbers in place and the last Detroit audiences according the show a totally different reception from those who saw its early performances, a rechristened *Hello, Dolly!* moved on to a two-week preview engagement in Washington before Broadway. The show was "frozen" from its final Detroit performances; Champion would allow no further changes so that it would continue to play smoothly and professionally.

The Washington opening was glorious. The show was stopped several times, notably after "Before the Parade Passes By," "The Waiters' Gallop," and especially "Hello, Dolly!," when the audience did everything but tear up the seats.

Washington proclaimed the musical a genuine hit, giving the cast prolonged ovations nightly. By the time the show was ready to open in New York, the word of mouth, along with local critical hosannas, had created a healthy advance that seemed to promise a long run for *Dolly*. Jerry Herman was elated, but he still worried that Broadway critics might not accept the stylization and the mayhem that Detroit and Washington audiences now found so exciting.

After only two preview performances (for lighting and sound adjustments), *Hello, Dolly!* opened at the St. James Theatre in New York on 16 January 1964. Herman was ecstatic, with his father, grandmother, and Aunt Belle in the audience. He invited many of his mother's friends, and maybe that was a mistake, for they pointed up the absence of the one he missed most.

Herman remembered, "After the laughing, swaying, clapping, I was whisked out of the theater to the festive opening-night party David Merrick had arranged at Delmonico's," a venue mentioned in the lyric for "Put On Your Sunday Clothes." "The party was glittering and every few minutes Gower came over and said, 'We'll know soon,' and then, around midnight, David got up on the small stage and read the *Herald-Tribune* revue, which was the first to come in."

Walter Kerr raved about everything in the show, especially the dancing, the direction, and the star, saying, "Composer Jerry Herman has torn up a hurdy-gurdy and scattered its tinkling waltzes and mellow quartets and tipsy polkas all over Union Square. The musical numbers are solid gold brass."[5] Howard Taubman in the *New York Times* at first praised "a musical shot through with enchantment." Then, writing more cautiously, he found fault with Stewart's book and Champion's taste. It was a grudgingly mixed review.[6]

Stewart's book also was criticized by Richard Watts Jr. in the *New York Post:* "The story . . . interrupted the songs and dances instead of giving them entertaining support."[7] But Watts, like all the others, was enchanted by the score. Most of the critics raved about Carol Channing, Champion's direction, and the joyousness of the music and lyrics.

In all the jubilation of probably the single most exciting night of his life, Herman remembers Mike Stewart "running across the room to me yelling 'Jerry! Jerry! Jerry, *we're rich!*' That was when the enormity of it all really hit me. *Hello, Dolly!* was not just a hit like *Milk and Honey* had been. It was a huge, once-in-a-lifetime hit, and I knew that at that moment my life had changed forever."[8]

What does one do when his life has changed forever? For Herman, who appreciates being well dressed, it meant, first, buying a few suits at Paul Stewart, the chic Madison Avenue clothier, and then negotiating the purchase of a house. He wanted to move from his small apartment at 6 West 10th Street to a proper house, and for some time had had his eye on Edward Albee's town house at 50 West 10th. The two-story town house with basement had been converted from a firehouse into living quarters by the actor Maurice Evans, then redone with heavy, dark woods by the playwright Albee, who was moving to Montauk, on Long Island. The white brick edifice had handsome wooden doors, wide enough for the engines that used to pass through them. Herman's first move was to set them off with lanterns. He reveled in the fact that the weekly royalties on *Hello, Dolly!* brought in enough for him to indulge his passion for decorating, a passion he had since those days at the Parsons School of Design. He worked for three solid months to eradicate the dark somberness that Albee found congenial, and to transform his new quarters into a sunny, entertaining party place.

Meanwhile, *Dolly* made the cover of *Life* and most other magazines. Louis Armstrong's recording of the title song was ubiquitous. Sammy Davis's "It Only Takes a Moment" and other songs from the show monopolized the airwaves, and articles about Channing, Herman, Champion, and Merrick filled the media. It seemed like *Dolly* had delivered the whole country out of the doldrums into which it had plunged after the assassination of President Kennedy months before.

Then in the spring came the theater awards. *Hello, Dolly!* won an unprecedented ten Tonys, a record that stood until 2001, when Mel Brooks's

The Producers won twelve.* *Hello, Dolly!* also won the Drama Desk Award and the Outer Critics Circle award for Best Musical. Herman was proudest when the score won a Grammy.

Everyone wanted to see this show. With a seating capacity of only 1,600 at the St. James Theatre, tickets were sold out months in advance, and scalpers cashed in. The original cast recording soon went to number one, and Armstrong's single of "Hello, Dolly!" toppled the Beatles' "I Want to Hold Your Hand," which had been leading the charts for sixteen weeks. For the non–theater goer, that was the ultimate accolade.

Jerry Herman was suddenly Broadway's hottest composer, and soon shows that were having difficulty sought his advice. *Ben Franklin in Paris*, a musical starring Robert Preston, was in trouble on the road, and the composer Mark Sandrich asked Herman to write a ballad prior to the opening in the autumn of 1964. "I hated the whole idea because of what I had just been through," Herman remembered, "but since this request for a ballad came directly from the composer, I went to see the musical.[†] There was an Oliver Smith set with a gorgeous multicolored air balloon with wires that went down to a basket where the couple stood. It moved against the background, and when I saw it, I said to myself, 'Boy, is this a setting for a romantic ballad?'" Anonymously, Herman contributed a Cole Porterish song, "Too Charming," and the lovely "To Be Alone with You," of which one critic remarked, "If the rest of the score were of this quality the show might stand some chance."[‡9]

It has been mentioned before, but perhaps the reader needs reminding

---

* *Hello, Dolly!* took awards in the following categories: Best Actress in a Musical (Carol Channing), Best Book of a Musical (Michael Stewart), Best Director of a Musical (Gower Champion), Best Producer of a Musical (David Merrick), Best Score (Jerry Herman), Best Conductor and Best Musical Director (Shepard Coleman), Best Costume Design (Freddy Wittop), Best Choreography (Gower Champion), and Best Musical. Actually, by today's judging standards, under which separate awards are given to music and to lyrics, Jerry Herman would have won two awards and *Hello, Dolly!* would have won eleven.

† The experience was also serendipitous because working on the score put Herman in contact with conductor Don Pippin, with whom he found he saw "eye to eye on orchestration." Herman asked Pippin to conduct his next musical, and Pippin answered with a resounding "Yes!" Herman has never since done a musical without Pippin at the orchestra's helm.

‡ Uncredited to Herman during the run of the show, these songs are now listed with Herman's works in the ASCAP file.

Robert Preston and Ulla Salert go off in a balloon in the Sandrich-Michaels *Ben Franklin in Paris,* a show for which Herman interpolated the ballad "To Be Alone with You." Photofest, Inc.

that Herman's melodic gift depends not on complex chord relationships, as is usually the case with Sondheim or even late Arlen, but rather on taking a harmonic cliché and infusing it with life and color. In this ardent melody each of Herman's phrases centers around a restless 9th: G against an F chord (see * in the example) in his first phrase; A against a G minor 7th (see **) in the second; and reaching into the stratospheric, a high D against a C minor 7 with flatted 5th (see ***) for the section's climax.

Herman might have lived very happily in this euphoric state of hit-show composer and musical-doctor had not his lawyer called some months into the *Dolly* run with the news that Mack David (brother of Hal David, lyricist for Burt Bacharach) felt that the first two phrases of "Hello, Dolly!" used the same notes as his 1948 country hit "Sunflower."* David's attorney claimed that Herman had heard his client's song and unconsciously re-tained the notes in his brain. After all the debilitating (and now seemingly

---

* The first ten notes and the rhythms of both songs are identical. "Sunflower" had sold, according to *Variety*, a respectable 300,000 copies of sheet music and a million copies of its recording.

unnecessary) collaborations forced on him by Merrick's lack of belief in his innate creativity, this slap at his honesty and artistic integrity plunged him into despair. "I would not steal two notes from my own mother," he told his friends laughingly, but the accusation stung enough to elicit his righteous anger when he had to give a deposition to Mack David's lawyer.

"I was seventeen years old when Mr. David's song came out, and not at all interested in what we then called 'country and western,'" Herman said in his deposition, "so there was no chance I would ever have heard that song. Besides, the only notes that stay in my brain," he said acidly, "are from songs that I love and admire." He went on, describing how easily melodies came to him and that he had no need to borrow anyone else's:

"When a melody comes to me, I don't usually write it out or put it on tape. I just live with it for a while, playing with it in my head. If it doesn't stay with me, I toss it out. I must have lost a hundred melodies in my time, but they don't matter to me. I care only about the ones that stay with me and work their way into my heart. When a melody grabs me that way, I may take the time to tape it or write it out. Sometimes I don't even bother because, if it's a melody that I really care about, I will play it from time to time and retain it through the years."[10]

Even today, the subject of this long-ago accusation angers Jerry Herman, who told me, "Don't you think, if I were aware of his song, I could have inverted two notes to make mine different? It would have been the easiest thing in the world."

When the news of the suit was published in the trade papers, Herman's friends, knowing he was a font of melody with no need to plagiarize, were supportive. Even other songwriters called to sympathize. Richard Rodgers, hoping to denigrate Mack Davis's song, went on record in the papers saying, "The difference between me and Jerry Herman is I steal from the best." Jule Styne, one of Herman's idols, telephoned to say, "Kid, you're not a full-fledged composer until you've gone through this kind of baptism by fire." Then he went on to point out that "Oh, You Beautiful Doll," starts note for note like "I'm Just Breezing Along with the Breeze," and that the Gershwins and Irving Berlin had been accused of the same embezzlement. Styne ended his call by listing several cases in which he had been accused of pilfering from other composers. Then he said he hoped "the whole thing will be settled in a week and you'll be able to get back to work."[11]

That was the way it should have worked out; it should all have blown over, but at the time David Merrick was in serious negotiations with Twentieth Century–Fox over the screen rights to *Hello, Dolly!* Herman was suddenly deluged by calls from Merrick and his other collaborators saying that Fox could not offer them contracts on the film version "while there is a legal cloud over the property."

Gower Champion was the first to phone. "Jerry," he said, "my heart is broken for you. This must be more painful than all you went through in Detroit, but we've all worked very hard, and you've got to see that this is our big chance to make some real money." Then Michael Stewart called saying essentially the same thing, adding, "This is our *only* chance. Styles change so fast in Hollywood. One day musicals are in, next day they are out. If we don't make this movie deal now, we may never get another chance."

"I want to resolve this more than anybody," Herman answered him, "but if I settle out of court I can't fight these charges of plagiarism." Yet at last, after much reflection, fearing that he was depriving his collaborators and his producer of their chance at a piece of the $8 million that was offered to film *Hello, Dolly!,* he gave in.

The case was settled out of court for $200,000, paid completely out of Herman's pocket. Not a fortune today, but a very considerable sum in 1964. When asked why Stewart and Champion, who had as much to gain as Herman by the movie sale going forward, didn't chip in, at first the composer took all the blame.

"It was my song, and my suit," he explained.

"Did you resent their not coming forth with an offer to split the cost of the bogus suit?" I asked.

"Yes, in my heart of hearts I did. But I understood them," came the gentle rebuke.

Once this lawsuit was out of the way *Hello, Dolly!* and the title song resumed their places as accomplishments Herman could revel in, and he visited with the cast almost nightly. His one slight worry was how long Carol Channing, with whom he had become extremely close, and who had an eighteen-month contract, would stay with the show. When she left to take another company on tour throughout the United States, who could possibly take her place in New York?

David Merrick was the first producer to believe that with a star of the first magnitude he could inveigle audiences, even those who had already seen the show, to come back and buy tickets again. With that in mind he started negotiations with Ginger Rogers in May 1965, and in June the stage and screen star finally accepted his offer for a one-year contract with a six-month renewal clause. Not one to throw money around, he had her come to New York ten days before she was to open, insisting that she rehearse with

In August 1965, before Channing left town to head the touring company, she visited Ginger Rogers in her dressing room to welcome her into the company. Rogers starred in the role on Broadway for two years. Photofest, Inc.

the company one scene at a time, never giving her a full run-through, which would have meant canceling a scheduled performance.

Because of this, Rogers was extremely tense on her opening night, 9 August 1965. The evening veered near disaster when Merrick, again trying to economize, persuaded one of the dancers to fit Rogers's wig. Ginger flew into a tizzy when, minutes before she was to go on stage, she tried on the custom-made wig she was to wear throughout the performance. "It looked like I had a red floor-mop on my head," Rogers seethed. "It wasn't till I threatened not to go on that a professional hairdresser was rushed to my dressing room. She found that the wig had been put on my head backwards. After she straightened it and combed it, everything was fine."[12]

Things may have been fine for Rogers that night, but not only did she not play out the year of her contract, she rarely sold out the theater, and she missed a lot of performances. Merrick devised a foolproof way of keeping the audience in the dark as to whether they would be seeing their star. He had the conductor give the downbeat for the overture at the precise moment an announcement was made that "tonight the role of Mrs. Levi will be played by Bibi Osterwald, Rogers's understudy. The ticket window would be slammed shut at the same time.*[13]

Champion restaged the show to emphasize Rogers's dancing. In her prime she was known to toot her own horn with the line, "I did everything Fred Astaire did, and I did it backwards and in high heels!" By this time she was far beyond her prime, but though her steps were rudimentary, to many in the audience she was the epitome of the Hollywood glamour, a star who had delighted them in so many movie musicals. She needed only to break into a simple time-step with two chorus boys supporting her to have the theater erupt in spontaneous applause.

Herman got along very well with Rogers, and with all the Dollys except Martha Raye, who took over the role from Rogers on 16 February 1966. "Even though I sent her flowers and telegrams, she simply never forgave me for not coming to see her performance. I was in the hospital with severe hepatitis for months during her run," Herman recalled, "and I told her about it, but she never believed me."[14]

Herman's childhood idol, Betty Grable, was the next to take over this

---

* This was before Equity ruled that cast substitutions had to be posted in the lobby and that the full name of the character (for example, Dolly Levi, not simply Mrs. Levi) be announced from the stage. The box office also had to remain open to allow time for any audience member to receive a refund.

plum of a role. She had starred in a touring company before coming to play it in New York throughout the summer of 1967. Each of the stars who took over the title role underlined another aspect of Dolly; Grable brought a vulnerability to the role that most of the others lacked. Audiences went wild when, during the dance sequences, she flashed those million-dollar legs.

On her days off Grable would often come to Herman's house on Fire Island. In his memoir he wrote lovingly of her: "It was such a thrill for this little Jewish boy from Jersey City, because when I was seven or eight years old, I was in love with Betty Grable. She was the musical comedy star of all those Coney Island and Wabash Avenue movies my mother used to let me go to on Saturday afternoons. I would send away to the movie studios for autographed photographs, and I used to send her fan letters. And here was Betty Grable herself, standing in my kitchen in a *schmatta,* doing the dishes and lounging around my pool with her hair dripping wet."[15]

As business began falling off, Merrick came up with an even more astonishing idea. He organized an all-black company of *Hello, Dolly!,* with Pearl Bailey as the star and Cab Callaway as Vandergelder, to tour, play Washington, and eventually open in New York. With racial tension rife throughout the cities of the United States, a company starring a black Irish-Jewish busybody was not the sort of thing the civil rights movement was encouraging, even though it provided jobs for dozens of black performers.

Bailey herself was not too eager to go back on stage, preferring the more lucrative venue of nightclubs, but Merrick offered her a handsome contract and convinced her that when the show previewed in the nation's capitol she would be performing in a theater where formerly she would only have been allowed to sit in the balcony. As Dolly, she made the role her own, adding her customary ad libs and curtain-call chitchat.

When this energetic company opened to splendid critical reviews in November 1967, Merrick thought that this new shot in the arm could keep *Dolly* running forever. In the driver's seat because his contract specified that the film could not be released until the show had closed on Broadway, he perversely told the moguls at Twentieth Century–Fox that he would try to have *Hello, Dolly!* break the record for longest run by a musical.

Nevertheless, on 13 February 1968, under the direction of Gene Kelly, a much-too-young-for-the-role Barbra Streisand began filming the musical. It was only her second film, directly following *Funny Girl.* The producer, Ernest Lehman, who had worked for three years to make the screenplay believable, had his hands full managing Streisand's well-known tempera-

In 1968 Merrick revived interest in *Hello, Dolly!* by mounting an all-black production starring Pearl Bailey. Here she spouts to Cab Calloway the famous "You go your way and I'll go mine" line, pointing twice in the same direction. Photofest, Inc.

ment, especially when she tried to transform the character so that the total spotlight would be directed to herself.*

Early in the filming she realized she was not old enough to play the widow as she was portrayed by Channing on stage, and she asked to be replaced. Lehman mollified her by telling her that Kelly would work it all out. Yet this major flaw in casting could not be remedied, and caused friction between her and her director.

Then, realizing that three stars had already recorded the score—Carol Channing, Pearl Bailey, and Mary Martin (who headed the London com-

---

* Lehman had written the screenplays to three of Hollywood's highest-grossing musicals: *The Sound of Music, The King and I,* and *West Side Story.*

The show-stopping "Waiters' Gallop," one of the highlights of *Hello, Dolly*'s second act. Here the waiters are caught in midair. This number showed Gower Champion's choreographic genius. Photofest, Inc.

pany)—and that whoever played Irene Molloy had two of the show's best ballads, while Dolly had only three solos, Streisand asked Herman to write additional songs for her approval: a fast one to open the movie and a ballad.[16]

"Just Leave Everything to Me," a replacement for Dolly's first number, "I Put My Hand In," seems to fit the movie version better, as it has a far more contemporary feel. Its basic motif, a three-note idea with accents falling on different parts of the bar, was perfect for Streisand, whose voice and diction in rapid tempo are exemplary. The lyrics are truly funny; I quote from my favorite, the last verse, ever appropriate to the 1890's:

> If you want your children coddled, corsets boned or furs remodeled,
> Or some nice fresh fricassee,
> If you want your bustle shifted, wedding planned or bosom lifted,
> I'll discretely use my own discretion,
> Just leave everything to me.

The same number as choreographed by Gene Kelly for the film, far more grandiose but much less exciting. Photofest, Inc.

The other new song, "Love Is Only Love" had been written for *Mame* but had been dropped in Philadelphia because that show was overlong. It is an exquisite ballad, planned for Angela Lansbury, but one that seems more suitable for Streisand's voice. Lehman was furious that the song was a retread, in violation of Jerry Herman's contract, but Streisand okayed it. She appreciated the aptness of the melody and the freshness of the concept and lyrics.

> Don't look for shooting stars,
> For love is only love.
> You touch and still you touch the ground.
> Don't listen for those bells,
> For love is only love.
> And if it's love you've found,
> Your heart won't hear a sound.
> And when you hold his hand, you only hold his hand.

The violins are all a bluff.
But if you're really wise, the silence of his eyes will tell you
Love is only love,
And it's wonderful enough.

The inclusion of "Love Is Only Love" may have given the film a healthy up-to-dateness, but it did nothing to smooth the course of shooting this $25 million musical. Streisand had her differences with almost everyone in the key Harmonia Gardens scene. A cause célèbre was the design and color of the gown. She rejected a beautiful scarlet one that Irene Sharaff had designed and whose blood-red color the producer and playwright felt was psychologically essential to Dolly's return to living. In the press Streisand reasoned that Carol Channing's Dolly had worn a similar one and had been photographed again and again in it. The star refused to leave her dressing room until promised that a new design in gold would be forthcoming. At last Sharaff presented her with a richly beaded topaz dress that pleased her.[17]

Star and costar Walter Matthau did not hit it off from the start. Matthau is quoted in Anne Edwards's biography *Streisand* as having said he found it "painful to adjust to her personality, particularly as she made no attempt to adjust to mine." Gene Kelly felt the same way, especially as he expected a certain respect for his position and his long experience in films.

But at last the film was completed and in the can waiting for the Broadway production to close. It had cost $25 million and was largely responsible for the huge downward spiral Fox was now facing. Again Merrick threatened the motion picture backers with an indefinite extension of the Broadway run. "After Pearl Bailey," he promised, "it'll be Liberace coming down the staircase in that red dress."*

Not quite Liberace, but the zany Phyllis Diller took over the role for a few months beginning in December 1969. Herman was afraid she would do the part crazily, injecting the script with some of the raunchy humor she was famous for in her nightclub act. But she played the role simply and honestly, no gimmicks, completely professionally.

---

* The film version of *Hello, Dolly!* was released in 1969 after Fox paid David Merrick nearly $2 million to eliminate the release clause in his contract with them. It did not do well at the box office or with the critics, possibly because cinema is such a realistic medium, anathema to cartoon or pastiche. Fantasies are the essence of theater, especially musicals.

Always a step ahead of the game, David Merrick invited Ethel Merman to see Phyllis Diller in the show, with the understanding that she would have the opportunity to take over the role. He did not mention Herman's disappointment that she had snubbed the role written purposely for her, nor that, contrary to what she had told Merrick then, she had already returned to the stage in a revival and tour of *Annie Get Your Gun*. He intrigued her by saying that hers would be the final word on Dolly. Nobody could fill her shoes, and nobody would succeed her in the role. She said she heard that Herman had written a couple of songs that Channing "couldn't handle, and if you will let him put them back, I'd be interested."

After seeing the show, before signing Merrick's three-month contract, she said, "I wanna hear the songs"—the two that Channing "couldn't handle." The next thing Herman knew, Merman, whom the composer had never met, was on his doorstep.

"Always my idol, the queen of showbusiness, I couldn't believe she was there, tall and intimidating," he remembered, "and she came wearing a simple black crepe dress. Even her jewelry was intimidating. She wore a huge pin that was like a sunburst of diamonds and rubies."

After he played and sang the songs, written for her seven years ago, she said, with typical Mermanesque dispatch, "I can handle 'em." Both songs are appropriate to the older woman that the show was designed to star, but the plaintive "Love, Look in My Window," is a wistful gem, a request from any lonely person to be visited by that emotion. The personification of love as an old friend one might invite to tea adds to the song's sensitivity and uniqueness, not unlike "Good Morning, Heartache," a lament popularized by Billie Holiday. Herman knows how to make Dolly's plea more effective by using minor chords, flatted ninths, and sequences to hit us in our emotional centers.

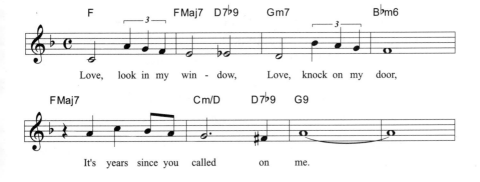

Love, look in my window, Love, knock on my door,
It's years since you called on me.
How I would love hearing your laughter once more,
So, if you should ever be—in the neighborhood
Let's talk about old times, Love, pull up a chair,
How I miss your friendly smile.
Love, look in my window, Love, knock on my door,
Oh, Love, come in and stay a while.

Since it was decided to end act one with "Before the Parade Passes By," the other Merman song, "World, Take Me Back," whose theme is obvious from its title, seems redundant. The two songs say almost the same thing. But Merman wanted to sing it, and although her addition of these two songs added ten minutes to the running time of *Hello, Dolly!,* she invariably brought the house down and tripled the audience's enjoyment with this one. Imagine the following resolute final lines in Merman's clarion voice:

My step has a spring and a drive,
I'm suddenly young and alive
You wonderful world take me back again!

On her opening night, 26 March 1970, Herman hurried backstage as the curtain fell to congratulate Merman on her splendid delivery of these two numbers. Herman reports that the star "was flattered by my approval. 'I told you I could handle 'em, didn't I?' was all she would say."

With Ethel Merman extending her three-month option to nine months, *Hello, Dolly!* finally shuttered at the St. James on 27 December 1970. With 2,844 performances in almost seven years, it outran *My Fair Lady,* its nearest competitor, by more than a hundred showings.* The last years of its record-breaking run were partly due to David Merrick's marketing know-how, especially his combative nature, which allowed him to dictate to the Fox movie people just when he was ready for them to release the film. But the end of the Broadway run was certainly not the end of *Hello, Dolly!* Carol Channing, having finished her stint on Broadway, crisscrossed the United States in the role she had made famous, and she starred in several revivals over the next twenty-six years.

Mary Martin, who also had toured with the show throughout the United States, brought a different, perhaps more vulnerable quality to the

---

* This long-run record was broken several months later by *Fiddler on the Roof,* which closed with 3,242 performances.

Ethel Merman, the last Dolly, on stage in the part originally written for her. Here she is with the waiters on the walkway surrounding the orchestra pit. Photofest, Inc.

role, starring in the London performances, Japan, and even Vietnam. (Martin was eventually replaced in London by Dora Bryan.) The show was a huge hit in Austria, Germany, Poland, and Australia. There was even a company touring Russia, for which, according to Herman, "nobody got any royalties. My collaborators said, 'This is terrible,' but I said, 'We don't need the money from Russia, I consider it a great compliment that they wanted our show.'"

Besides all the New York Dollys, the indestructible title role has been played on tour by Eve Arden, Dorothy Lamour, and even the female impersonator Danny La Rue.

In 1989 Herman supervised a production that originated at the Houston Grand Opera. It starred Carol Channing, with Florence Lacy as Irene Molloy. The composer recalled that he tried to retain all the excitement and brilliance of staging "that Gower [who had died in 1980] put into the original. One thing I wanted to change was the orchestration of 'Ribbons Down

Gene Kelly teaches Walter Matthau how to dance for the film. Photofest, Inc.

My Back,' which I hated. I thought it was vapid and empty and had no romance, and so I got that great orchestrator Phil Lang to do it my way, and it became so beautiful and moving." This production, which eventually went on to New York, was Herman's first foray into directing. He refused to take the credit for this role but says, "Getting the production the way I always wanted it was reward enough."[18]

Carol Channing was still portraying Dolly on Broadway and on tour in

1996 when she was in her late seventies. In its long history *Hello, Dolly!* has to be considered not only one of Broadway's greatest successes but also one of the most successful touring box-office attractions in the history of the American musical.

Today, while *Hello, Dolly!* awaits its next major revival, the musical has become a staple of high school and college productions for many reasons. It employs a very large cast, and its big design is pastiche or cartoon, which works very well with less-experienced singing actors. Cornelius, Barnaby, Minnie, Ermengarde, Ambrose, and even Irene Molloy are juveniles—easily impersonated by other juveniles.

Yet although *Hello, Dolly!* holds the record for the longest run in Herman's oeuvre, the tall shadow that David Merrick cast on the show during its pre-Broadway ordeal, the disputed origins of several of the songs, and the false accusation of plagiarism always prevented Herman from fully reveling in its great success. By the time *Dolly* closed on Broadway, Herman had written two more musicals: *Mame,* perhaps his most outstanding score, and *Dear World,* a very sensitive fantasy with much-applauded music and lyrics that has developed a considerable cult following. But neither of these, or even his later success with *La Cage aux Folles,* struck the chord of recognition that makes one's name a household word like *Hello, Dolly!*

7

mame

When Patrick Dennis, né Edward Everett Tanner III, wrote *Auntie Mame: An Irreverent Escapade,* he had no idea that this character would take her place in the forefront of theatrical heroines, much less become a generic household word for a sophisticated relative in charge of a youth. The author's choice of the name Mame Dennis for his heroine was purposeful. Tanner was looking for a name that would suggest "mamma" in a super-cosmopolitan way; to balance the Christian name he had settled on he chose Dennis from the Manhattan telephone directory because of its elegant ring. He liked it so well (and hated his own ostentatious name so violently) that he legally adopted it and used it as his pen name throughout his prodigious career. The change made Tanner the fictional nephew of the character he created.[1]

The book, his third novel and the first under his new nom de plume, was not an easy sell. He made his way through the alphabet of publishers, being rejected by nineteen of them before he reached the Vs and acceptance by Vanguard Press. The frothy fiction became immediately popular and quickly rose to bestsellerdom, remaining on the list for more than two years.

But even before the book's rapid ascent, the producers Robert Fryer and Lawrence ("Jimmy") Carr sensed, when they read its middling review in the *New York Times* in January 1955, the theatricality inherent in the zany title character. They immediately optioned the novel for the stage. Fryer and Carr had Shirley Booth, who had starred in their production of *The Desk Set,* in mind to portray the aunt who takes charge of a young boy's life and inculcates him in her own bohemian lifestyle. As they looked more deeply into the character of the chic and eccentric Auntie Mame, they felt the madcap, sometimes biting role called instead for Rosalind Russell's cool and frequently acid wit.

At forty-three and a bit over the hill by Hollywood standards, Russell had seen her popularity rejuvenated by raves in the Bernstein–Comden and Green *Wonderful Town,* produced under Fryer's aegis. After the musical closed and Russell returned to the West Coast, Fryer and Carr had kept in close touch. As soon as the contracts were signed and the property of *Auntie Mame* was truly theirs, Fryer offered her the role.

Russell hedged, at first insisting that the play be set in the 1930s, although the drama of Mame's losses in the 1929 stock market crash is a turning point to the story. She claimed that the flapper dresses and toques did not flatter her. Then she demanded that the director Morton Da Costa, who had pulled together another fragmented book, *No Time for Sergeants,* be engaged. Fryer and Carr acquiesced to all her demands and brought in the respected playwright Sumner Locke Elliot, who eventually presented them with a script that set the action a decade ahead and built on the actress's strong points. The dreary thirties and wartime forties were not a time for madcap comedy, and, it being obvious that Elliot's scenario was out of kilter with the basic story, his script was rejected. After months of delay, Patrick Dennis decided to adapt his own book. He turned in a rambling, discursive play which ran to several hundred pages and, after joking, "That's the first act," even he admitted defeat.[2]

By this time, almost a year after publication of the book, Russell still hadn't signed, and it was rumored around Broadway that the episodic novel of *Auntie Mame* defied dramatization. In order to retain their star, Fryer and Carr had to align themselves reluctantly with Russell's husband, Frederick Brisson—a crusty producer who drove such hard bargains that he was known to theater people as "The Lizard of Roz." Now, at last, Russell signed, and the project became active again.

Except that they had no play.

In their frantic search for a writer to dramatize the book, the producers received turndowns from Irwin Shaw, Moss Hart, Noël Coward, and Truman Capote. Finally Jerome Lawrence and Robert E. Lee, whose *Inherit the Wind* was then playing to standing-room-only audiences, came forward and asked for an opportunity to dramatize the novel, which they found "hilarious."[3]

Carr, Fryer, and Brisson agreed, and again the project went ahead, this time with amazing speed. Under Morton Da Costa's direction, Lawrence and Lee's play was completed in a few months. *Auntie Mame,* which opened successfully on Broadway on 31 October 1956, ran almost two years, with Russell playing the title role for fifteen months. The highest praise for the play came from Patrick Dennis himself, who wrote that "Lawrence and Lee have caught—far better than I—the moments of heartbreak that are also in *Auntie Mame,* and placed them on stage so deftly that between the guffaws and sniffles, snickers and snorts, there are audible sobs and visible tears at each and every performance."[4]

Of course, such kudos made all involved immediately think of musicalizing the play—but not yet. *Auntie Mame* had more mileage in it before it would be transformed by Jerry Herman into *Mame.*

When Rosalind Russell, who owned 15 percent of the production, had had enough of Broadway, she returned to Hollywood to oversee this hit play's transformation into a hit movie, asking the producers and writers to close the New York production. Russell was annoyed when instead they hired the film star Greer Garson to play the role for several months. Garson was followed by Sylvia Sydney, who brought a tearfulness, and, later, Beatrice Lillie, who injected her own zaniness into the part. Meanwhile, Constance Bennett and Eve Arden toured with the play.

Lawrence and Lee would have been the natural choice to adapt this playscript for the screen. But Russell's pique at their collaboration in the producers' refusal to close the play influenced Warner Brothers to refuse them the opportunity to write the film scenario. The studio chose Betty Comden and Adolph Green, who had successfully adapted *Wonderful Town* for Russell, to do what little conversion was needed. They stuck close to the Lawrence and Lee script, adding a scene or two when the heroine, broke after the crash, has to get a job, and such amusing bits as Mame refurnishing her Beekman Place town house with futuristic furniture.* This was all to the good, for the public adored the Mame it knew, and the picture, which opened at the end of 1958, was a great hit with critics and public alike—the highest-grossing film of the year.

Of course, the musical, at first entitled *My Best Girl,* was next.

It was obvious to the producers that Russell would be ideal if she would agree to re-create her role. Although her voice was a low baritone, she was

---

* The most amusing new scene was one in which Mame is employed as a saleswoman for the then popular pressure cookers, and the pot she is demonstrating predictably explodes, shooting brisket, vegetables, and gravy all over the set and the customers. Unfortunately, the scene was left on the cutting room floor.

eminently musical and had had great success singing in *Wonderful Town*. Fryer and Carr traveled to Connecticut, where Russell was staying, to recruit her. She not only turned them down with an acerbic "I don't like to eat last week's stew" but actually tried to stop the musical from going forward, saying that she and Patrick Dennis had a much more lucrative offer in mind—a television series of *Auntie Mame*. Undeterred, since they owned the dramatic rights, the producers persisted.

By this time Mame had become a beloved character, a camp heroine like none other, dear to everyone whose childhood had been influenced by a favorite aunt. She was especially important to the gay community as the chic maternal figure with whom many homosexual men could identify. Capable of bitchiness but never a bitch, with plenty of money, taste, beauty, and a forgiving nature, Mame *is* the person many long to be. Throughout the play there is no father figure to insist Patrick come outdoors for a game of baseball, no other sibling to divert his mother figure's attention. Best of all, although she is *My Best Girl*, she presents no sexual threat—in fact, Mame would be happy if Patrick never leaves her.

When Russell said no, the producers were faced with the search for another musical superstar. Ethel Merman, who had declined Jerry Herman's *Hello, Dolly!*, was in temporary retirement, and Gwen Verdon was scheduled to appear in *Sweet Charity*. The inevitable choice now was Mary Martin.

The word *inevitable* is not chosen lightly. Martin was a beloved musical superstar, perhaps the only one who could singlehandedly keep a show running. Now forty-two, six years after she was hardly believable as the young postulate in *The Sound of Music*, she could no longer play ingenue roles and was the right age to interpret Dennis's bohemian Auntie. She had a very close relationship with Josh Logan and had influenced the producers to engage him to write and direct the musical. Why was Logan, a mercurial talent who was notorious for changing his mind and wiping out stage directions he had sworn by the day before, elected? Again, the producers, hoping to curry favor with Martin, passed over Lawrence and Lee, opting for Logan, who had turned *South Pacific* into a Mary Martin spectacular.

Lawrence and Lee, whose contract for the original playscript at least specified that they had the right to oversee the musicalization of the show, swallowed the likelihood that Logan—notorious for changing authors' lines—would rewrite their play. Hoping to exert their influence in the choice of composer-lyricist, they called the composer of *Hello, Dolly!*, whom they had never met in person, and invited him to lunch at Sardi's. No sooner had they exchanged pleasantries and sat at the table than they made their offer. Herman, usually a quiet man, let out a memorable yell—the kind that would be long remembered at this frequently volatile theatrical meeting place. It was just the kind of project he had been waiting for.[5]

Lawrence and Lee's splendid choice of Jerry Herman was not as altruistic as it sounds, for a musical of *Auntie Mame* without Russell would have had a hard time raising the considerable monies that the scheduled lavish production would be costing. With a score by the composer of Broadway's reigning hit, capitalization for *My Best Girl* became easy.

Herman wrote several songs, and the script, including Logan's changes, was sent to Martin.* She approved of the songs but did not sign—pending the final score. Herman went ahead and composed the rest of the music—again, as he had done for Merman with *Hello, Dolly!*, with his star's voice, this time Martin's, in mind. Logan had assured Herman and the producers that he could deliver the star, and he was so sure Mary Martin would be their Mame that scripts were actually printed with her name on the cover.[6]

At that time Martin and her husband Richard Halliday were living at their ranch in Brazil, where they raised bananas, avocados, mangos, and pineapples. Herman remembered that he and Fryer "flew to Rio de Janeiro and took a plane to a small city. From there, we boarded a Jeep that took us through rough and frightening jungle to visit her hacienda and to play the score for her." She said she would accept the role gladly, but she still balked at signing the contract, first complaining that she was not particularly excited by the songs and later saying that she did not want to play a part so identified with Rosalind Russell. Herman feels, "It was the same as with Merman. She simply did not want to go back on stage."

Now, with the Winter Garden Theatre already engaged, the search for a Mame became desperate. Eve Arden, Patrice Munsel, Bette Davis, Katharine Hepburn, Greer Garson, Lauren Bacall, Susan Hayward, Arlene Francis, Tammy Grimes, Constance Bennett, Ann Southern, Doris Day, Ginger Rogers, Olivia de Haviland, Lucille Ball, Irene Dunne, Beatrice Lillie, Julie Harris, Margaret Leighton, Elaine Stritch, Lena Horne, Jane Morgan, Geraldine Page, Dinah Shore, Maggie Smith, Georgia Brown, Kitty Carlisle,

---

* Logan changed Beauregard Burnside, Mame's great love, into Lord Bolingbroke Burnside, making her, on his demise, the Duchess of Burnside, doyen of the horsey set. He also had Patrick's father drop dead of a heart attack on stage early in the musical, but worst of all, he insisted on the exorbitantly costly and totally unnecessary casting of three Gooches.

Nanette Fabray, Gisele MacKensie, Simone Signoret, Dolores Gray, Janet Gaynor, Phyllis Diller, Lisa Kirk, Barbara Cook, Kaye Ballard, and Judy Garland were all mentioned as possible Mames. Many of them were invited to audition, but none seemed an exact fit for the role.

When Angela Lansbury, whose only prior Broadway singing role had been the Mayoress in the short-lived Sondheim-Laurents musical *Anyone Can Whistle* of 1964, heard of Mary Martin's withdrawal from the *Mame* sweepstakes, she approached her old friend Jerry Lawrence, whose house was near hers in Malibu, and arranged for an audition. She even offered to pay her own fare to New York. Her agent arranged for her to be heard at the Lunt-Fontanne Theatre.

The auditorium was dark when Fryer, Carr, Herman, Logan, and assorted gofers arrived. One of the assistants had forgotten to turn on the lights, and in accordance with the strict union codes of Broadway, no one in the party had the temerity to touch the lighting panel. The stage was lit with a single arc light, so someone opened the street doors to let in a little daylight.

Lansbury groped her way to the stage and began to sing, but had not gotten very far when she heard Logan's booming voice shouting, "It's too dark up there." One of the assistants drew the arc light closer to her. She managed somehow to finish her song and was asked to read lines from the play. Again the darkness was a distraction, and Logan suggested she tape the script to the spotlight. At last, the group marched up on stage, closing in on her, as Lansbury put it later, "in all those raincoats and dark glasses."[7]

After the audition, speaking for the group, Carr thanked her and said they were undecided. Then he promised she would hear from him, although he added that "her singing was not as strong as we want." But Jerry Herman preferred Lansbury, who was his vision of Mame, over all the other applicants, even though she had not been at her best.

Shortly after Lansbury's audition, the fortunes of *My Best Girl* turned around. The reports from Boston, where *Hot September*, a musical based on William Inge's *Picnic* directed by Logan, were dire, and his direction was said to be one of the problems. Carr and Fryer flew there to see whether Logan was really the right choice to direct their musical. When their worst fears were confirmed, they spoke with Oona White, their choreographer, about getting a new director. "You know I love Josh," White was forced to admit, "but I'm not thrilled about working with him." When Carr asked whether she had any other ideas for a director, she said she had just finished doing *Half a Sixpence* with Gene Saks, whom she described as level-headed and smart. At the time Saks was also in Boston, directing *Generation,* starring Henry Fonda, so the producers went over and talked with him. After watching a rehearsal, they told him they liked what they saw of his work and offered him the job.

"*Auntie Mame?*" he asked. "Hasn't that already been done as a musical?"

When Carr assured Saks that indeed it had not, and showed him the new script, he agreed to consider the job. At their first meeting in the producers' office, Saks handed them Logan's revised scenario and asked, "Why do we need this ridiculous thing?" Tossing that script on the coffee table, he picked up Lawrence and Lee's original play, *Auntie Mame,* and said, "why can't we stick to this one?"

Eventually the director erased all the brittleness Logan had injected into the character (although Logan came in for a 1.5 percent royalty of the show's gross), and it was left to Herman's songs, most of them joyous, but several trenchant or moving, to carry the musical forward.

Herman, still feeling Lansbury was the best choice for the title character, suggested that she come east and audition again, this time for the new director. He suggested that she arrive a day early because he wanted to show her the two songs he felt would clinch her audition. He was well aware that Larry Carr, "a charming man, but very opinionated, thought that Lansbury was the type that could [only] play someone's mother." He remembered telling Carr that "Angela can be beautiful—and she *can* dance."

"The bell rang in my apartment on Ninth Street, and this stunning woman was standing there," Herman remembered. "We had an absolutely delightful lunch at Longchamps on Fifth Avenue, and I remember that at the end of lunch I turned to her and did something so terrible, so wrong. I said, 'You have to have this part. You're going to think I'm bananas, but my instincts are so strong that you will be absolutely smashing.'

"I said, 'If you walked out and sang my two best songs, they'd absolutely fall out of their seats,' and she said, 'Let's do it! I won't even hold a paper, I'll learn the words.' Well, the next day the stage manager announced, 'Miss Angela Lansbury,' and she walked out on stage and tossed her mink coat on the chair. I had gone down the back stairs on the pretense that I was going to the men's room, and I came up through the orchestra pit, played the introduction to "It's Today," which she sang with great elan. Not as well as she eventually would, but better than any auditioner has a right to expect. Then she blew them away with 'If He Walked into My Life.'"

Actually, the producers were not "blown away." They were impressed with Lansbury's theatricality but still felt that she lacked the star drawing power of a Merman or a Martin. They were not sure about her dancing abilities and felt she was a bit overweight to be the acerbic comedienne who might replace Rosalind Russell. They dismissed her with a "we'll call you" and threw the final decision into Gene Saks's lap.

Saks agonized over the decision. He discussed it with his wife, Bea Arthur, who was then playing Yenta in *Fiddler on the Roof* on Broadway. For a little while Saks even considered the possibility that Bea would play Mame, for she had many of the baritone qualities of Rosalind Russell. She certainly could be hilarious with double takes, and to top it all, she could be very moving. But upon reflection, in a feat of brilliant casting, Saks wisely chose her to play Vera.*

Saks was still not sure of the actress for his leading role and called Lansbury for yet another audition, her third. Gritting her teeth, she came over to the theater, sang the songs, and read lines again for him. To Jerry Herman, she looked exasperated, but when he caught her eye, he begged her to have a little more patience. She left the theater quietly but inwardly seething.

The next morning she called Carr and reminded him about how long this had been going on. "I am going back to California," she said firmly, "unless you tell me—I mean—let's face it . . ." She paused, trying to retain her composure, "I mean—I have *prostrated* myself. I must know before I leave New York. I'm not coming back again!"[8]

A half-hour later Saks called Carr and told him that unless they wanted to re-create the brittleness and pastiche comedy which he felt was in the Russell interpretation, and which he felt his wife could handle beautifully, they had better go with Lansbury.[9]

Carr went over to Lansbury's hotel, up to her room, and told her, "We are offering you Mame." After twenty-three years as a professional actress, having performed secondary roles in thirty-six movies, twenty-six television plays, and one earlier singing part on Broadway, Angela Lansbury would at last be starring in a multimillion-dollar Broadway musical built around her. It would catapult her to the superstardom she had heretofore only dreamed about.

To prepare herself for the role she went on a diet, took singing lessons, and attended dance classes until the six-week rehearsal period for the show

---

* Stinging and acid as she can be, Arthur joked on her own television spectacular, "They wanted to call the musical *Vera*, but Jerry Herman couldn't think up anything to rhyme with Vera." Then after the laugh died down, she quipped, "Stephen Sondheim could have."

began. And then, almost before anyone knew it, they were in previews in Philadelphia.

After the rousing overture, *Mame* begins with the "terrifying lights of the city: a huge, gartered showgirl's leg kicking, a bubbling champagne glass, and a flashing red neon arrow." Ten-year-old Patrick and his terrified nanny Agnes Gooch are on their way to Three Beekman Place.* We hear the roar of traffic in the background as Patrick rereads the letter, giving the audience the information that his father has died and he is to be reared by his only living relative, his Aunt Mame. Frightened to be responsible for the child in what she perceives as a wicked city, hoping for salvation by a wrinkled spinster in an antimacassared parlor, Agnes sings

> St. Bridget deliver us to Beekman Place
> Away from the wicked and depraved.
> A gray head is peeping through the curtain lace
> Calling "Come ye inside where you'll be saved."
> She's baked him a cherry pie and glazed a ham,
> Her dear arms reach out for his embrace.
> So if you have pity on this poor lost lamb, God love you,
> Dear St. Bridget deliver us to Bee-e-e-e-e-e-eek-man Place.

Patrick joins her in a reprise of the second half of this entreaty, which wanders in and out of unexpected minor chords that give it a liturgical feeling. Herman ends this litany with a lovely melismatic line.

Now, as the pair enter an elegant vestibule, Ito, Mame's Japanese butler, tells them, "You wait here. Madam having affair." The music soon turns syncopated as we are plunged into the second scene, in Mame's sumptuous and

---

* Norah Muldoon is the nanny in the play *Auntie Mame*. The character of Agnes Gooch does not appear until act two, when she comes in as Mame's stenographer. Combining them in the musical was an economic as well as an artistic inspiration.

somewhat eclectic living room. A spot hits the top of the freestanding stair-case, and we discover Mame, in midparty, a bugle at her lips as she sounds the opening phrase of his old signature song, "Showtune in 2/4," now called "It's Today."

Light the candles,*
Get the ice out,
Roll the rug up,
It's today.
Though it may not be anyone's birthday
And though it's far from the first of the year.
I know that this very minute has history in it:
We're here!

If the main theme of the melody of "It's Today" came from Herman's teenage years, the lyric sprouted from wellsprings even farther back. The composer explains the song's genesis:

"I had already worked out a rough structure with my collaborators, so I knew there was going to be a song at the beginning of the show that was to take place at a big party. Well, I hate writing party songs. What can you say about a party? 'Have a good time, everybody?' Boring! It is also the hardest kind of song for me to write because I get my musical ideas from character, not from situation. Ask me to write a song about a garden and I really won't know what to do, but ask me to write a song about a woman whose life is wrapped up in her garden because her lover has left, and I know exactly how to do it."

Besides crediting the title of this song to his party-at the-drop-of-a-hat mother, Herman even used his mother's line—"Parties can happen whenever you feel the urge, even on a weekday"—to introduce Vera Charles, America's most revered pseudo-British actress; in *Mame*, she is a superannuated stalwart of musicals, and a confirmed lush. She sings:

Life can also be lived on a weekday,
So don't depend on a holiday date.
If you need New Year's to bubble

* The original opening offering was "Pass the peanuts," far too plebeian for one of Mame's soirées. Other tidbits rejected from this menu were "deviled lobster, pickled herring, have a radish." The original second chorus had an interesting, time-setting quatrain: "And it isn't the Fourth of October/When Calvin Coolidge and Grace took the vow/But it's a time, I might mention, deserving attention/It's now!"

Young Patrick Dennis (Frankie Michaels) greets his Auntie Mame (Angela Lansbury) in her boudoir after a late-night party. Photofest, Inc.

Then order a double
And wait.

Patrick and Gooch make their entrance as the party guests are dispersing. Gooch is horrified, but Patrick is mesmerized. Now we get our first glimpse of Mame's sensitivity when she slows the tempo and draws Patrick to her.

Someone gave me a wonderful present,
Something I needed—and yet never knew,
So start the whistling and clapping
'Cause under the wrapping
Was you.

During ensuing scenes Mame inculcates Patrick into her bohemian way of life and the two get on famously. But Mame's authority over the boy is shared with the Knickerbocker Bank's Willard Babcock, a stuffed shirt. Babcock points out that the will of Mame's late brother specifies that Patrick is to have a conservative education. But Mame has other ideas about his schooling, and after mollifying Babcock and getting him to leave, she sings the boy one of Herman's jauntiest melodies, "Open a New Window." The situation reminds one of Cornelius's inveiglement of Barnaby, intriguing him to come and taste life in *Hello, Dolly!*'s "Put on Your Sunday Clothes." But where Cornelius's exhortation is static, Mame's counsel is all-encompassing. Opening all possible new windows for Patrick, she takes him to an art class that includes a naked model, then to a modern dance group. They ride to a four-alarm blaze in the fire engine, and then visit a speakeasy which is raided shortly after they arrive. At last they are arrested, and in the paddy wagon they hug, apparently overjoyed at these life-enriching experiences.

> Open a new window, open a new door,
> Travel a new highway that's never been tried before,
> Before you find you're a dull fellow punching the same clock,
> Walking the same tightrope as everyone on the block.
> The fellow you ought to be is three-dimensional,
> Soaking up life down to your toes.
> Whenever they say you're slightly unconventional
> Just put your thumb up to your nose,
> And show 'em how to dance to a new rhythm, whistle a new song,
> Toast with a new vintage—the fizz doesn't fizz too long.
> There's only one way to make the bubbles stay:
> Simply, travel a new highway, dance to a new rhythm,
> Open a new window every day.

The dance arranger, Roger Adams, did a splendid adaptation of this catchy, scalelike melody in 6/8 time. Throughout the ensuing production number the music becomes more animated by segueing to constantly rising keys. This, coupled with Don Pippin's four-part choral harmony involving the whole cast, made for a most difficult musical number—requiring extra rehearsal time. But once perfected, the number was thrilling and invariably brought the house down.

Babcock, Mame's nemesis, believes only in "opening traditional windows" and is furious when he discovers that Patrick is happily enrolled in a progressive school called The Laboratory of Life, where nude students and teachers are playing a game called "fish families." He throws a coat over the naked boy and drags him home, tells Mame that he has enrolled her nephew in his own alma mater, St. Boniface in Massachusetts, and orders her to have

Auntie Mame (Lansbury) takes Patrick (Michaels) to a speakeasy, where she teaches him to dance the tango. Photofest, Inc.

Patrick ready to leave the following day. Going off in a huff, he vows that he will "turn this kid into a decent, God-fearing Christian if I have to break every bone in his body!"

Mame is disconsolate upon losing Patrick, and doubly depressed when Vera comes in with the news that the stock market has crashed and she is broke. Vera offers a solution, a bit part in her new operetta about a lady as-

The "Man in the Moon" number in *Mame.* Bea Arthur is the lady astronomer, center with the conical hat. Lansbury's squirming on the moon-seat will momentarily cause a catastrophic collapse of the scenery. Museum of the City of New York.

tronomer. In the finale, Mame is supposed to be the "Moon Lady," riding the rising crescent. Vera illustrates as the scene changes and she sings her big solo before the moonrise. Its chorus begins:

The man in the moon is a lady,
A lady in lipstick and curls.

The number does not quite come off, perhaps because it is too camp, or maybe because it's simply a one-joke song whose punchline is given away at the start of the chorus. It was, however, amusingly mounted on a luminous blue stage with truly hilarious mayhem that ensues when Mame misses her cue, finally takes her moon seat, and is so terrified as it quickly jerks her up high that she causes the scenery to collapse. Vera orders the stagehands to ring down the curtain on this disaster. During curtain calls, Mame's jewelry becomes enmeshed in Vera's dress, thereby ruining the star's bows.

As a tearful Mame, chewed out and fired by her best friend, sits alone on the darkened New Haven stage, Patrick, who has hitchhiked from school with Ito, finds her. "Nobody liked the stinky old show till you came in," he says. When Mame calls herself a failure, he counters, "No you're not. Not to me. Not ever." Then he sings "My Best Girl," the first song Herman wrote for the show. This is a moving ballad in 3/4 with one of Herman's very best and most adventurous melodies. It has great harmonic and melodic freshness.* The lyric is artless and pure, and the song's placement in the musical is masterful. It makes us care about Patrick, whose character in the second act will not be as exemplary as it is now. His bonding with Mame cannot but bring a tear to even the most jaundiced eye.

The next scene moves to a fancy salon *pour messieurs,* where Mame has been hired as a manicurist. Her first customer is Beauregard Jackson Pickett Burnside, a wealthy and most attractive plantation owner. As she files his nails down to the quick and massacres his cuticle, she falls in love with him,

---

* The old cliche—I, VI, II, V, known as the "Heart and Soul" vamp—has been transformed into I, III, II, V for the A section, and is almost unrecognizable. Additionally, the B section (using the same harmonic design) plunges us gracefully into and out of a fresh key, a third higher. Meanwhile, the frequent use of the flattened fifth, almost sounding incorrect (see the fourth bar) and cleverly placed so that it falls on the word "wrong" gives the melody great originality as well as tremendous pathos.

and Beau, with true southern gallantry, does no more than wince. Mame so mangles his hands that she is fired. But losing jobs is nothing new to her. As she arrives at the Beekman Place apartment, now denuded of its artworks and most of its furniture, she finds Patrick home on a mid-December holiday weekend. Overjoyed but broke, she begins to weep and stops herself. "Hell," she says, "we don't have any Kleenex."

Always able to best any situation, she declares, "We need a little Christmas!" and brings out small gifts she had bought for everyone three jobs ago, "before I was tempted to spend it on something foolish—like food." Agnes and Ito present her with a spindleful of paid bills as their present and Patrick gives her a rhinestone bracelet which he got at a pawnshop in exchange for his bugle.

The moment is lovely and warm, and the song, slightly reminiscent of *Dolly*'s "It Takes a Woman," is just right. Amid the plethora of Christmas songs this one is good enough to have taken its place as a standard and comes around every year. It serves double duty by fitting admirably into the show and being eminently extractable.

> Haul out the holly, put up the tree before my spirit falls again.
> Fill up the stocking,
> We may be rushing things but, deck the halls again—now.
> For we need a little Christmas,
> Right this very minute,
> Candles in the window,
> Carols at the spinet.

When it came to the staging, Oona White's original dance steps made a semi–production number of this simple homespun frolic, until Lansbury, saying that the number should be about "a family that hasn't two cents to rub together," persuaded her to simplify the choreography and go for charm.* Ito and Gooch bring out last year's Christmas decorations, and Mame becomes a living garlanded Christmas tree.

The small household becomes more and more joyous until the doorbell

---

* For all his musicals since *Hello, Dolly!* it is Herman who suggests and shows his orchestrator just which scenes should be underscored—that is, have music under dialogue. In staging scenes, Herman suggests just which theme should be used to point up the emotion of the moment. Phil Lang's tender orchestration of "We Need a Little Christmas," in very slow tempo, adds immeasurably to this scene. Likewise, the "Time Heals Everything" theme played by a solo clarinet at the end of *Mack and Mabel,* and the "He Needs Me" toward the end of *Mrs. Santa Claus,* were all Herman suggestions.

rings, Beau enters, apologizing for having been the cause of Mame's dismissal from the manicure parlor, and insists they all join him for dinner. With a reprise of the song—now called "We've *Got* a Little Christmas"—the scene ends as we prepare for act one's big finale.

Beau wants to marry Mame but first must introduce her to his large southern family at their plantation and get—especially from his grossly obese mother—their approval. Uninvited, but trying to protect her interest, Sally Cato, engaged to Beau since grammar school, comes over to meet the Yankee belle. She maneuvers Mame, who has never ridden, into declaring herself a horsewoman and organizes a hunt for the next morning. Hoping to wiggle out of the ordeal, Mame says she only rides sidesaddle, but Sally Cato comes up with one and reports the news to Beau. "Sidesaddle!" he exclaims, "Too dangerous." But then he reconsiders and says, "Anything Mame says she can do, she can do."

The lights are lowered and raised as a grumpy rooster crows, heralding dawn, and the hunt begins. As with most sporting events, the stage is no match here for the cinema. It relies on reportage, which is never as thrilling as being there. This racing scene might have been stylized, as was *My Fair Lady's* Ascot Racetrack section, which accented British sangfroid. But instead, the excitement of the hunt here is developed by the orchestra at a gallop, and an almost operatic combination of voices. Herman, wishing to create what he calls "contrapuntal pandemonium," worked with his tape recorder and three others, borrowed from friends. He sang one part while he played another, gradually adding more parts to achieve the four-part counterpoint that gives the scene its horserace excitement.

The number is a true tour de force: Patrick shouts, "Fall off," while one of Beau's relatives exclaims,

> Look at her go
> Look at her fly
> Out of the woods
> Into the sky
> Look how she's bobbin' her head, flappin' her feet
> She must be glued to the seat.

Meanwhile, the chorus discourages Mame, and the other relatives stand amazed as she passes the huntmaster, the hounds, and eventually, the fox. At the conclusion of the number, confessing only to Patrick that her riding clothes got entangled on the saddle horn, Mame returns victorious with the live animal. Even Mother Burnside is forced to admire this daring feat.

The banjos start plunking and a proud Beau proposes marriage, saying, "You've done more for the South than anyone since Robert E. Lee." And we come to the title song, a worthy sequel, far superior musically and lyrically to "Hello, Dolly!"

You coax the blues right out 'a the horn, Mame,
You charm the husk right off 'a the corn, Mame,
You've got the banjos strummin' and plunkin' out a tune to beat
    the band.
The whole plantation's hummin' since you brought Dixie back
    to Dixieland.
You make the cotton easy to pick, Mame,
You give my old mint julep a kick, Mame,
Who ever thought a Yankee would put our little Dixie belles to shame?
You've made us feel alive again, you've given us the drive again
To make the South revive again, Mame.*

As the rehearsal pianist Dorothea Freitag kept repeating the song to teach it to the cast, conductor Don Pippin, who attended most rehearsals, became vaguely dissatisfied with its musical ending. After all, this number had to climax the act with a paean to Mame's greatness. So he composed five repeated "Mames" built on intensifying chords (A, F7, D, E47, and A), an almost Hollywoodesque ending of which Herman heartily approved.[†] But choreographer White was not impressed with that extension. "The cast is kneeling around Mame at the end of the number. They can't just stay there like statues," she complained. "What am I to do with all those goddam 'Mames'?" she queried.

Pippin's and Herman's hearts dropped with the thought of losing this glorious finale ultimo until Bea Arthur, who happened to be nearby, piped up, "Why not let them kneel in little groups until the last repeat when they all will be kneeling?" Thus the staging of this number illustrates the collaborative nature of creating a musical.

---

* The patter Herman created for the third chorus is too good not to be quoted. It makes a stunning rhythmic counterpoint against the basic melody: Well, shut my mouth and freeze my face/You've brought some elegance to the place/There's sowbelly, hominy, catfish and tripe/Mame./Well, shut my mouth and damn my eyes/ You've made the price of tobacco rise/The old watermelon is suddenly ripe/Mame./ And down on the levee a beautiful bevy of crinolined ladies has flocked/The way that they're squealin' they give me the feelin' the Robert E. Lee must have docked.

[†] See *suspension* in the Glossary.

Angela Lansbury also volunteered her own ideas about the staging when she insisted that she wanted to have her back to the audience while the number is sung. This being the only production number in which the leading lady *doesn't* sing was bizarre enough for director Saks. But not only did he permit it, he welcomed the bit when he saw how Lansbury performed it.

Jane Connell, who played Gooch, observed from the middle of the ensemble, "You could see from the way she moved her back that the audience was getting the whole impact of the number." Chorus members who were facing Lansbury reported that she stayed in character, overwhelmed that these southern aristocrats were kowtowing to her with such intensity that each cast member was personally energized—which enriched their own performances. Whatever magic Lansbury exerted, this number always elicited an ovation. It drowned out the final short scene in which a forlorn Patrick is comforted by his aunt as she leaves the stage with one arm around him and the other around her future mate, Beauregard Jackson Pickett Burnside.

Act one of *Mame* is about Mame. Act two is about Patrick.

It begins with his typing letters—to the tune of "Mame"—as the couple honeymoon. When Patrick grows older and is replaced by a teenager, we get subtle hints of the snobbery that is becoming part of his character at this restricted school. Rooming with Junior Babcock, son of his repressive trustee, he sings:

> My glands are in a hurry,
> My voice has sort of taken on a roar.
> The girls I date, don't worry,
> Are socially decidedly top drawer.

Patrick's letter writing is interrupted when Mr. Babcock enters bearing bad news. Uncle Beau has met with a fatal accident, but Auntie Mame has escaped injury, and is hurrying home. In fact she is on the phone to tell Patrick about it. Patrick says he already knows and comforts her by singing a reprise of "My Best Girl," now with final lines that are doubly appropriate and moving:

> And if someday when everything turns out wrong
> You're through with the human race
> Come running to me,
> For you'll always be
> My best girl.

Back in the Beekman Place apartment Vera and friend, publisher Lindsay Woolsey, prepare to organize a new life for the wealthy widow. As a sort of occupational therapy, Lindsay has made arrangements for her to write her memoirs, which he will publish. He has even sent Agnes to study Speed-o so that she can stay nearby and take down all of Mame's bons mots in shorthand. Patrick, too, is here to welcome her, but when the men leave, Mame and Vera get tipsy, have a heart-to-heart, and sing the show's funniest number: "Bosom Buddies," perhaps the best forked-tongue song that's ever been written for a musical.

> BOTH   We'll always be bosom buddies,
> Friends, sisters, and pals.
> We'll always be bosom buddies,
> If life should reject you, there's me to protect you.
> VERA   If I say that your tongue is vicious
> MAME   If I call you uncouth,
> BOTH   It's simply that, who else but a bosom buddy
> Will sit down and tell you the truth?

With rhyming zingers like "You should try to keep your hair natural like mine," from Mame and ripostes like "If I kept my hair natural like yours, I'd be bald," it is a no-holds-barred sparring match. But suddenly they become aware of Agnes, who has been listening to all this in amazement. In their semi-inebriated state they decide to make her over. Vera removes Gooch's glasses, and when she howls, "I can't see anything out of my right eye," Vera commands her, "Look out of your left one!" Mame intrigues her to spread her wings and "Live! Live!"—to go out into the world, with her by now oft-quoted line, "Life is a banquet and most sons-of-bitches are starving to death." Then the duo dress this plain, short creature in a sexy red dress and spike heels. A made-over Agnes joins Mame and Vera in a reprise of "Bosom Buddies."

Six months later, Lindsay has dropped over to see how his author is progressing and inquires about Agnes's whereabouts. Mame says she hasn't seen her since she sent her steno out into the world to "Live!" Now Patrick drops by to tell Mame that he has a girl. "Not just a girl, but *the* girl. He plans to bring her over in just a little while to introduce her to Mame, but at that moment Agnes returns in the full bloom of imminent motherhood. When Mame says that Gooch will stay with them until the baby comes, and even after, Patrick thinks better of introducing his girl, Gloria Upson, to his aunt. We get the impression that Gloria might be shocked by Mame's condoning unwed motherhood. Agnes explains how she got into her family way in an endearing ballad. (The music here, while deceptively simple, is really quite catchy; the release takes a fresh tack by moving the key up a third and then down a half-step before returning artfully to the original key):

> With my wings resolutely spread, Mrs. Burnside,
> And my old inhibitions shed, Mrs. Burnside
> I did each little thing you said, Mrs. Burnside,
> I lived! I lived! I lived!
> I altered the drape of the drop of my bodice,
> And softened the shape of my brow,
> I followed directions, and made some connections,
> But what do I do now?
> Who'd think this Miss Prim would have opened a window,
> As far as her whim would allow?
> And who would suppose it was so hard to close it,
> Oh, what do I do now?

Mame is invited to Montebank, Connecticut, to visit the Upsons at their home, insipidly called Upson Downs, for a party in their palatial barn. She is served a daiquiri made with strained honey, which she dispenses into a potted palm, and she nearly gags on an hors d'oeuvre of tuna, clam juice, and peanut butter—this she slips into Patrick's pocket. But she really fumes inside at the Upson's unsolicited bigotry. It is Gloria's twentieth birthday, and at her first introduction to Patrick's aunt, we sense the deb's shallowness and her prejudices in her remark "Everybody at the party is absolutely top-hole."

But Mame holds her tongue, not wanting to upset Patrick's newfound happiness, and lets off her steam, when the elders leave the barn, in dancing with Junior Babcock and the rest of the teenagers. Herman has said that this scene was included not only to give Mame a lighthearted moment before the emotional "eleven o'clock number" but also to show Mame's rapport with the younger generation—and theirs with her. As they dance the Lindy, they find her simpatico and modern. The song is "That's How Young I Feel," a forties-style swing number, not Herman's forte, but one that efficiently serves its purpose.

When the adults return, Claude Upson shocks Mame by spilling the beans about Gloria and Patrick's forthcoming marriage. He also tells her that he has arranged for her to share the cost of a wedding gift for the young couple: the vacant lot next door. This, he assures her, will set the youngsters up in real estate while at the same time keeping Montebank safe from riffraff. Mame takes Patrick aside, and after he puts his hand in his pocket and pulls out the gooey hors d'oeuvre she had deposited there, he inquires, "What the hell is this?" Mame replies, "This is what you're stuck with—for the rest of your life." He is incensed, saying he wants to protect Gloria "from the crazy bunch of screws and nuts . . ." "Like me?" Mame interjects.

But rather than answer his aunt's question as to whether he wants to spend the rest of his life among "the other Babbitts in this ethnically restricted little dandelion patch," Patrick walks out.

Mame is left alone wondering how the obnoxious young man she has just told off could have sprung from the little boy who was so principled and endearing. She sings "If He Walked into My Life," arguably Herman's most intense ballad, and certainly one of the greatest theatrical moments of its decade. The number is pivotal to the sensitivity that exudes from this character: it does much to erase any vestige of the brittleness left over from the Russell portrayal. With the protagonist's self-doubt about her fitness to raise a child, this number solidifies the transformation of the play *Auntie Mame* into the musical *Mame*.

With double-length A sections, as well as a verse, the song weighs in at seventy-two intense and slowly moving bars, and, unlike any other song in Herman's oeuvre, it is sung through only once.* The verse sets the tone— and here Herman's lyric walks the tightrope of extractability, the quality that means a song will fit the musical and be capable of having a life outside the show, for its words could apply to love maternal, gay, or straight.

> Where's that boy with the bugle?
> My little love who was always my big romance? . . .

Moving as the lyric is, we must realize that a song is only as good as its music, and the melodic motif of "If He Walked into My Life" is a masterstroke. Transposed to the mellow key of D flat, eminently suitable to Lansbury's voice, this totally original phrase (built mostly of lower and upper appoggiaturas) sticks in our heads the first time we hear it, along with the words "Did he need a stronger hand?" when it comes to rest on a D flat sixth chord (see * in example, page 144). But when the motif is repeated, this time with the lyric "Did he need a lighter touch?" the composer ends the phrase on an F minor suspension that resolves into a B flat seventh (see **).

Stephen Sondheim has called melody "the heart of a song," but adds

---

* For those who need to know such things, the song breaks down as follows: verse (ten bars), A1 (sixteen bars), A2 (sixteen bars), bridge (eight bars), A3 (sixteen bars), coda (six bars).

that "harmony is its soul," and certainly it is this unexpected emotional harmonic underpinning in dark colors, as well as the suspended melodic note, that elicits our soul's deep emotional response here. One does not have to be musically trained to sense the phrase blossoming through its harmony the second time we hear it. It is emotional magic.

As she digs deeper into her psyche, the questions (and later, the musical phrases) become shorter, tumbling on top of each other, as Mame doubts the efficacy of the bohemian lifestyle to which she has exposed Patrick:

> Were his days a little dull?
> Were his nights a little wild?
> Did I overstate my plan? Did I stress the man
> And forget the child? . . .

And still later, assured she has irreparably broken off the relationship, she sings,

> Should I blame the times I pampered him or blame the times
>   I bossed him?
> What a shame I never really found the boy before I lost him. . . .

The only way to resolve the emotional tension into which this song has plunged us is to black out the scene, allowing us to applaud and then to wipe our eyes before the show can continue. That leads us to the next scene, in which Mame has resolved to patch things up with Patrick and invites the Upsons to dinner. To help her through this ordeal she has asked her decorator assistant, young, pretty Pegeen Ryan, to stay late and help. She has invited Vera, Babcock, and Lindsay, as well as some of her famous bohemian friends. Patrick comes early because he is worried that his future in-laws will not understand Gooch's presence, but Mame assures him that she has been instructed to stay in her room. When he helps Pegeen with the last-minute decorations, they renew old acquaintance, recalling their days at the same avant-garde school. Laughingly recalling that, as naked children, they had played "fish families," he realizes that he is mightily attracted to her.

At last the Upsons arrive with Babcock. Vera enters shortly afterward and mistakes Pegeen for Patrick's fiancée. When Patrick corrects her, she carefully looks over both young women; after a memorable thirty-second stage pause that only Bea Arthur could get away with, she comments acidly, "Pity." If Mame was out of place at the Upsons', they are glaring misfits here on Beekman Place. When Mrs. Upson asks what the delicious hors d'oeuvres are, Mame reprises "It's Today" with the following lyric:

Pickled python, peppered sheep spleen,
Have some owl's eggs,
It's today,
I said "Ito, do something exotic,
Just try a bit harder to please,"
And he's been extra ambitious,
Try these—they're delicious,
They're bees!

The shock of what they have just eaten is nothing compared to the bombshell of seeing Mame's strange cronies and a tent-sized unmarried Gooch. But these visual jolts are quickly dwarfed by the moment when Mame announces that she has just purchased the vacant lot in Mountebank, next to the Upsons'. She stuns the Upsons with the news that she plans to erect there the Beauregard Burnside Memorial Home for Single Mothers. After Gloria and her parents leave abruptly, Mame has her final showdown with Babcock, who yells that her "idiotic nincompoopery has ruined everything [he] wanted for Patrick."

"All you want to do is to slam windows in his life," she fumes, "Well, I won't let you do that to my little one." Turning toward Patrick, she admits, "No, he's not little anymore. And he's not mine. But he's not yours either, Mr. Babcock. And I doubt if he'll let you marry him off to a headful of hair with the I.Q. of a dead flashlight battery!"

Patrick takes all this in thoughtfully, realizing that Mame has just rescued him from a life of bigotry and conformity, and thanks her in a reprise of "My Best Girl."

The last short scene moves us forward to 1946. Patrick and Pegeen, now married, have come to say goodbye to Mame before she leaves on yet another world tour. Their little boy, Peter, has spent a glorious afternoon with his great-auntie Mame, and his parents have come by to collect him. Mame has given Peter a turban and taught him a Hindi phrase. She has also invited the boy to join her on the Indian leg of the journey, and he begs to be allowed to go. His parents decline until the boy says, "The trouble with you two is you don't live, live!" And before Pegeen can clamp her hand over his mouth he insists, "Life is a banquet, and most sons-of-bitches are starving to death!" Pegeen and Patrick look at each other, are forced to grin and give in. "But only," Pegeen cautions, "if he is back for the start of the school term, by Labor Day."

Mame assents, and before the curtain falls, the spotlight picks out great-aunt and nephew having dismissed Peter's parents. Mame is opening new windows for Peter, teaching him how to salaam, while involving him in preparations for their trip.

"Labor Day," she muses as they climb the stairs, "That's sometime in November, isn't it?"

8

mame—and its movie

By the time of its opening in Philadelphia, 27 March 1966, *Mame* was in excellent shape. So good, in fact, that during its previews, Jerry Herman remembered sitting in a movie theater with Angela Lansbury on one side and Bea Arthur on the other. "I suddenly thought of my tribulations with *Hello, Dolly!* in Detroit," he recalled, "and whispered to Angela and Bea: 'You know, we're supposed to be going through on-the-road hell. If anybody saw us now, they wouldn't believe it.'"[1]

But although the first-night audience roared its approval and Herman, an incurable optimist, felt hardly anything more needed to be done before its Broadway debut, the show was far too long, dragged near the ending of act two, and badly needed tightening: at least two songs and much of the dialogue needed trimming. But most of all, the star needed to inhabit the role, as she clearly did not.

Saks had given Lansbury notes about owning the part. "Technically," he had told her, "everything you're doing is great, but you've got to take the stage. You don't yet own it." Lansbury in turn was grateful for the assessment, for she considered her director's advice about her assertiveness essential to her performance. "From that moment on," she felt, "I could make the role my own. That was the beginning for me as a Broadway star." But she was not yet there.

Throughout the Philadelphia performances Saks felt that "Angela was suffering from a real lack of confidence." As a result, Bea Arthur, playing a supporting role, was dominating the show. Saks wondered whether Lansbury could muster the flamboyance needed for this role—and even whether a character actress, which Lansbury had been all her life, could, in middle-age, become a true star, one who eclipses all others.

But he knew *Mame* had the potential to become a giant hit, and, to effect the changes he wanted, he adopted a systematic plan. First, he talked to the composer and librettists, assuring them all that he knew how sensitive what they had written was, and promised them that he didn't intend to chop it up. "We need about twenty minutes of judicious cuts," he explained, "that will not harm the fabric of the piece, and we're going to make those one- or two-minute cuts with each performance."

When he asked for suggestions, Herman spoke up. "We could cut 'Camouflage' and pick up three minutes right there," he offered. This is a very funny scene and song in Mame's bedroom, written for her and Vera to precede the moment when Babcock first comes to order Patrick's strictly conventional schooling. The situation is suspenseful as the duet talks about using makeup and a costume to make Mame into a grandma of whom the trustee would approve. The quasi-minor song, with a sort of silent movie vamp, is definitely Vera's and seems out of style in this show. Cutting this song meant losing some of the suspense of the moment, with Babcock waiting down below to snatch Patrick away, but that loss was outweighed by restoring the balance of songs in Mame's favor. Besides, "Camouflage" was topped by the "Bosom Buddies" duet in act two, which is far funnier.*

Next came "Sterling Silver Boy," sung by Babcock to Patrick. That was an easy cut, for the song created an empathy for Babcock that the playwrights had not intended.

It was harder for Herman to delete "Love Is Only Love," the tender song in which Mame, having given her heart to Beau, explains falling in love to a preteen Patrick. Composers and singers dearly love their ballads and are reluctant to part with them. Choreographers and directors call them "stage waits" and have a hard time finding movement for the actor during their performances. At the time it was decided to cut this one, Herman wrote, "It is a lovely song, and nobody did it better than Angela. Those emotionally rich moments are her specialty, for she can really act. And yet, I remember the first performance after the song was cut.† We went straight from 'We

---

* In 1999, when Columbia–Broadway Masterworks released a new digitally mastered recording of *Mame,* Thomas Shepard, the record's producer, asked Jerry Herman whether he had any audition tapes. Herman found a splendid one he had made with Alice Borden, which included "St. Bridget," "It's Today," "Open a New Window," "Mame," and an acted-out version of "Camouflage."

† "Love Is Only Love" was not lost. It was used in the film version of *Hello, Dolly!,* sung beautifully by Barbra Streisand.

Need a Little Christmas' to the hunt scene, which climaxes in 'Mame' and ends the act. I was surprised how it speeded the show along and amazed that nobody missed the slow number. Without that scene, the act roared along to its conclusion like a steam engine."[2]

The first act finale, "Mame," literally stopped the show on opening night. Oona White, the choreographer, remembers going backstage after the song to find tears running down Lansbury's face. The response had been so great that the star, with her back to the audience, could actually feel their love coming across the footlights to her, and was overcome with happiness.

Part of their applause was due to the audience's familiarity with the title song, for by this time Bobby Darin's recording of "Mame" was high on the charts, and the song had been featured on the popular Ed Sullivan Show. Recordings by Louis Armstrong, Al Hirt, and Pearl Bailey were getting a lot of airplay. Eydie Gormé had recorded "If He Walked into My Life" on her album *Don't Go to Strangers,* which came out in April 1966, before the show got to Broadway. Once the show opened, Herman had another record at the top of the charts. He was amazed that Gormé's rendition, "without changing a note or a word of the lyric," had the power to transform this soliloquy of maternal doubt into a threnody of loss of lover. The public, hearing it as a torch song, bought thousands of copies. The album quickly went gold, and the single won a Grammy Award. A moving moment in a show was changed to a standard—and a standard it has remained.

After three weeks in Philadelphia the show was much tighter when it went on to its last preview city, Boston. Director, author, and composer were still tinkering with the songs, orchestrations, and performances, snipping a word or two of the dialogue or a musical segue, careful not to disturb the flow. Lansbury and White were working on the big second-act dance number, in which Angela jitterbugs with the kids. The number never did take wing, but Lansbury inhabited it, adding kilowatts of energy, and turned it into a personal tour de force which stopped the show.

Most of the Boston critiques were favorable, like that of the *Boston Globe*'s Kevin Kelly, who simply pronounced it "the best musical of the season." The lone dissenter was the doyen critic, Elliot Norton, who wrote that "Miss Lansbury can't sing, but then neither can anybody else in *Mame.* But she gets through most of the songs," he added, "without ruining the melodies." The public paid little heed to Norton, and throughout the Boston engagement there were long lines in front of the Shubert Theatre.

By opening night, 24 May, the company had coalesced and the show was playing as smoothly as it ever would. But Lansbury, still very nervous, fearful that she might not be able to go on, had her husband, Peter Shaw, invite Gene Saks to their apartment for a talk. Saks told her how proud the whole company was of her—and would be—no matter what happened on stage that evening. That seemed to convince her of her superb talent, and a determined Lansbury went to the theater.

The Winter Garden, taking up most of the block between 51st and 52nd Streets on Broadway, is the only legitimate theater except for the Palace directly on "The Great White Way." On this night its marquee was covered with the striking yellow poster logo by Berta of a flapper in an elegant gown and white fur wrap. That this willowy John Held–esque creature was holding a bugle was an interest-piquing inconsistency that affirmed that the show inside was a "class act." The smartly dressed crowds who streamed into the newly refurbished theater to see *Mame* had chosen their evening's entertainment over *Fiddler on the Roof, On a Clear Day You Can See Forever, Skyscraper, Man of La Mancha, Sweet Charity, Superman,* and even Herman's still-resounding hit *Hello, Dolly!*

After Don Pippin led the rousing overture (interrupted several times by applause as the songs were recognized), the theater hushed during the brief opening scene, waiting for the entrance of Lansbury. She soon appeared in gold pailletted pajamas, blowing the trumpet. And when she announced, "All my dearest friends are here—even the ones I haven't met yet," and slid down the glittering banister into her living room, it was as though she was hosting a gigantic party that welcomed everyone on both sides of the footlights. And the audience roared its approval.

By the end of the evening, when she took her final bows in a long white coat wrapped in white fox, there was no doubt that here was the new toast of Broadway. In those days standing ovations were rare, but that night the Winter Garden audience rose to its feet, as one person, to welcome Lansbury into the ranks of the great divas of musical theater: Ethel Merman, Mary Martin, and Gwen Verdon.

After the performance, as she strode into the art deco fantasy that is the Rainbow Room on Jerry Herman's arm for the gala opening-night party, the applause broke out again. Now in the midst of champagne and cheers, there was nothing but to wait for the reviews to come out.

Walter Kerr in the *New York Herald Tribune,* the first paper read, raved about the settings, the pacing, Bea Arthur, and Frankie Michaels, who played young Patrick. He found Lansbury less than a "powerhouse personality," describing her quality as that of "the fastest girl in high school who also turned out to be nice." But he dismissed Herman's score as "standard music that sounds like all other music," softening the blow a bit by adding, "It's not pretentious, and who among the youngsters is doing better?"[3]

Herman fared better in the *New York Times*, where Stanley Kauffman wrote, "Jerry Herman's score has music that is strongly rhythmic and sufficiently tuneful, and lyrics that are generally deft."[4]

Richard Watts Jr., writing in the *New York Post*, observed that "the score is pleasantly tuneful and several of the songs are going to be heard frequently for a long time to come." Like several other critics he complained that the song "Mame" sounded too much like "Hello, Dolly!"[5] (The only similarity I find is that they are both title songs. "Dolly" purposely resembles an old German beer song, while "Mame" is a definite cakewalk.) Herman never let any of these negative comments dispirit him. He held a strong belief in his score and the show's chance of great success.

Even though the reviews were not uniformly sterling, producers Fryer, Carr, and Sylvia and Joseph Harris also sensed that they had a hit. They indulged in the old show-biz cliché: "Nobody liked it but the public." Word of mouth had been excellent, and the show had a healthy advance sale of more than a million dollars. This kind of box office insurance was garnered only by Rodgers and Hammerstein shows.

Mame was produced for $500,000, a heavy outlay for musicals of that time, but it paid back its entire investment in twenty-four weeks. Lansbury's contract for the first year called for her to receive the then-modest star salary of $1,500 per week, but unbidden, she was given a raise to $1,750 after a few weeks. Still, despite the show's long run of more than 1,500 performances, it was not a great moneymaker. The large cast and orchestra represented a sizable expense, and the percentage payoffs to all who had been part of the original creation of *Auntie Mame* were a further drag on profitability. Patrick Dennis, who had written the book, Josh Logan, its original director, and Warner Brothers, producers of the nonmusical movie starring Rosalind Russell, all shared in the receipts. The high costs of maintaining such an elegant show ate up most of what was left of the profit.

The associate producer John Bowab explained: "It wasn't like doing *Fiddler on the Roof,* where, if a costume got a rip in it, you just sewed it back up. The *Mame* production had twenty-six costume changes for Lansbury alone and several for Bea Arthur. The producers had to hire two women who did nothing but sew sequins back onto their dresses."

On 31 May 1966, one week after *Mame's* official opening, the American Theatre Wing announced its nominations for its annual Tonys. Three excellent musicals, *Mame, Man of La Mancha,* and *Sweet Charity,* and one flop,

Robert E. Lee, left, and Jerome Lawrence, right, *Mame*'s librettists, along with Jerry Herman and Angela Lansbury, celebrate the show's rousing success at Sardi's. Photofest, Inc.

Skyscraper, were nominated as Best Musical. The word on the street was that *Mame* would win. Herman was devastated when *La Mancha* took home most of the awards, including Best Score.

It was an unusual ceremony for the Tonys. Because of the recent death of Helen Mencken, president of the American Theatre Wing, the nominees were not voted on by the total membership; ballots were given to the members of the first- and second-night press lists and to the governing boards of Actors Equity, the Dramatists Guild, and the Society of Stage Directors and Choreographers. It was no surprise that this elite group of theater professionals would ignore a traditional musical like *Mame* and choose instead the more intellectual *Man of La Mancha,* whose book simultaneously told the tragicomic story of Don Quixote and narrated the life of his creator Cervantes. Most theater pundits feel that had the entire membership had a chance to see all the nominees and vote, *Mame* would have won Best Musical.*

Angela Lansbury and Bea Arthur, as expected, garnered Tonys for Actress in a Musical and Supporting Actress in a Musical, while little Frankie Michaels, who played young Patrick, won Supporting Actor in a Musical.

It was a stunning victory for Lansbury. After three nominations (and no wins) for the Academy Award, she had taken home the coveted Tony. As Rex Reed reported: "Angela Lansbury is a happy caterpillar, turning—after years of being nose-thumbed in Hollywood in endless roles as baggy-faced frumps—into a gilt-edged butterfly." She would never play a supporting role again.

Lansbury took seriously the trust her producers had placed in her and continued to give deep, driving performances in this demanding role. With only one vacation, two weeks in August 1967, she played the role for two years. Her understudy, Celeste Holm, who also headed the national tour, garnered excellent notices as well. Dan Sullivan, writing in the *New York Times,* said, "Miss Holm makes an aunt that every little boy would love to have."[6]

When it was announced that Lansbury would be leaving, Judy Garland, who was then forty-seven, visited Angela backstage and told her how desperately she wanted the role. Herman, Lawrence, and Lee, and even the associate producer John Bowab, all felt she would have made a splendid Mame. But they were also aware that she was battling failing health and was

---

* Perhaps the unenthusiastic and very recent New York critiques influenced the voting. In contrast, when *Mame* was revived in 1983, all the reviewers welcomed Herman's score as a revered classic.

drug dependent, which posed serious problems. Jerry Herman insisted that she have a chance to try out. He worked with her on the score and in October 1967 played her audition.

"It was beyond comprehension," Bowab remembered, "what she did with the score. When she sang 'If He Walked into My Life,' 'My Best Beau,' and 'It's Today,' it was simply devastating. She must have had the pitch pipes out all night, because there wasn't a crack in her voice except when she wanted it to crack."

But despite that exceptional audition, despite Garland's pleading for the role, the producers Fryer, Carr, and the Harrises knew that Judy—who would be dead in two years—could never sustain the rigors of an eight-performance-a-week schedule that a musical demands.

"To have seen even one performance of *Mame* with Garland would have been worth all the risks," Herman stated at the time. But as he reconsidered, he added, "I realize it was my heart speaking. The producers did the correct thing—they were protecting their show—*my* show." He felt he owed Garland a tremendous debt and recently told me that she "inspired me in ways nobody knows. I heard her singing 'It's Today,' when I was writing it. She has had a deep effect on my life and my work since I keep her voice unconsciously in my brain, and her sound often will influence my choice of a word or a note."[7]

When the producers decided that Garland was too much of a risk, many others auditioned. The top contenders were Jane Wyman, who had a name in the movies, and Shirl Conway, who had starred in the musical *Plain and Fancy*. But neither had enough pizzazz. At last the role went to Janis Paige, who had starred in several Broadway hits, including *The Pajama Game* and *Here's Love*. Of her performance Clive Barnes wrote, "She looks glowingly well, sings, dances, and acts with a sweet enthusiasm. . . . She's less of a character but perhaps more of a performer [than previous Mames]." She played the role for a year before singer Jane Morgan took over "in her good natured show-biz style," according to Barnes.[8]

At last, after a four-year run it looked as if the show would close when John Bowab, who had directed Ann Miller in Zev Buffman's production of *Mame* at the Royal Poinciana Playhouse in Florida, suggested bringing Miller, who had not done a film in fifteen years, to New York.

Bowab called Jerry Herman, who flew down to Florida and caught Miller's performance, which he thought was excellent. Since the show was on the verge of closing on Broadway, he figured they had little to lose in offering to bring in Miller.

Because it was Miller's specialty, Oona White added a quite incongruous tap section to the barn dance scene. "She was sensational," Bowab re-calls, "amazingly fluent in the singing and garnering as good notices as Lansbury." Critics and public were amazed at her sterling performance and energy. Staunch trouper that she was, she kept the show running for almost a year until she caught pneumonia and had to be hospitalized. The Broad-way production closed on 3 January 1970. It had played 1,508 perfor-mances. The show would probably have played as long as *Hello, Dolly!* if it had had a David Merrick at its helm, or if Lansbury had returned to her original role on Broadway. The public simply did not accept other Mames as eagerly as they had flocked to see other interpretations of Dolly. For most audiences Mame *was* Angela, and although others assumed the role, none had the style, warmth, and elegance with which Lansbury lit up the stage.

Seventeen years later, after she had collected three more Tonys (for *Dear World, Gypsy,* and *Sweeney Todd*), Angela Lansbury, now a much beloved musical theater icon, returned to Broadway in a cut-down revival, what one critic called "a low budget touring version" of *Mame.* It was booked into the mammoth Gershwin Theatre (né Uris). This time the critics pulled out all the stops for the star, finding her "at the peak of her form," but criticized al-most everything else about the production—except the score.

Frank Rich, the critic for the *New York Times* whose reviews were noto-rious for lauding new and adventurous musicals, especially those of Stephen Sondheim, found that "the sentimental romance never gets going this time." He attributed it to "insipid" performances by actors playing the young and mature Patrick and the actress (Anne Francine) interpreting Vera.[9] Roshi Handwerger, who assumed the role of young Patrick, came in for more drubbing when Douglas Watt of the *Daily News* found him "one of the more objectionable stage children within recent memory."[10] The other critics soon jumped on the negative bandwagon and this production—which had played to packed houses during the tour—gave only forty-one performances in New York.

Most critiques welcomed the score back as an old friend, but Rich's neg-ative opinion of the Jerry-Herman-musical-for-entertainment-rather-than-cogitation was to generate a feud that would climax at the next year's Tony Awards.* Undermining the value of glamour and diversion, Rich wrote that "the glow of that escapist world can still be found in *Mame,* even if now, more than ever, we're aware that it's provided by artificial light."

---

* The Tony for the Best Musical of the 1983–1984 season was won by Jerry Herman's *La Cage aux Folles* over Stephen Sondheim's *Sunday in the Park with George.*

The "bow dress," specially designed by costumer Robert MacIntosh only to be worn for the curtain calls in *Mame*. Here it is worn by Ann Miller, the last Broadway Mame. Photofest, Inc.

Rich's sour note aside, many critics had found a new and deep appreciation for the score. *Women's Wear Daily*'s Howard Kissel, whose view of the critic's duty to tout the avant-garde was typical of other aisle sitters, put it most succinctly:

"At this point I must make an apology for the many unkind things I have said about Herman's work over the years. At one time I was under the illusion the musical was a thriving art form. Under this misapprehension it seemed my duty to praise the daring and scorn the conventional. It is of course unfair to expect any artist to nourish one's misguided illusions and now that I harbor none, I can acknowledge that I was unduly harsh on Herman. His music and lyrics, as the revival of *Mame* at the Gershwin demonstrate, are winning and zestful. They have polish and craftsmanship—increasingly rare commodities"[11]

The movie was another thing altogether.

In 1970, when filming *Mame* first was discussed, Jerome Lawrence came up with what he considered to be a perfect movie cast. "Of course Angela will do *her* role," he said, "and Bette Davis wants to play Vera—and we will have Carol Burnett for Gooch." No doubt that would have been an ideal trio. But just as Barbra Streisand, at twenty-six far too young for the role, was cast as Dolly, Hollywood saw nothing wrong in starring Lucille Ball, sixty-two, as Mame. It was not Ball's age that signaled this would be a monumental mistake (although years of sunbaking and heavy makeup had wrought such havoc with her skin that to hide her wrinkles she had to be photographed in soft focus—as Frank Rich quipped, "so gauzy that you think you're in a hospital"). It was not even her inability—crucial in a musical—to dance or to sing above a whisper. She simply lacked the joie de vivre, the elegance, the maternal and romantic warmth essential to make the character believable.

The picture's failure is not completely Ball's fault. By 1974, when *Mame* was released, the movie musical genre was dead. *My Fair Lady, The Sound of Music, Mary Poppins, Oliver!,* and *West Side Story* were practically the only successful musicals since the mid-1950s. They were exceptions to the principle that the movie musical format doesn't work any more. After that *Dr. Doolittle, Star!, Darling Lili,* and *Paint Your Wagon* all were box-office and critical duds.

When Warner purchased the rights to *Mame* for the staggering sum of $3 million (second only to *My Fair Lady,* which brought more than $5 million), it determined that only a superstar—like Streisand—would be able to carry the picture. Such a superstar was Lucy, and it was anticipated that her television audience of fifty million viewers would desert their Barca-loungers and run to their local cinema to see their beloved Lucy on the big screen. Ball's 1968 film *Yours, Mine, and Ours,* only a few years earlier, had earned a hefty $20 million and bolstered the studio's confidence in her continuing ability to carry a movie. But in that film she had the much loved Henry Fonda as a costar.

All the Broadway theater pundits scratched their heads when the trade papers announced Ball's casting. They were—and still are—unable to fathom the Hollywood mentality that a Tony is worthless as compared to being a true "Movie Star."*

Robert Fryer, who was producing the movie, said that "at the time Ball was an internationally syndicated television star, which meant that abroad, at least, Warner would get their money back." But Lansbury's loyal fans felt that this casting was a desecration of a great performance, and that Ball absconded with the role that rightly should have been Angela's. Even Patrick Dennis, *Auntie Mame*'s creator, said, "Miss Ball is a good comedienne, but a little too common for the role."[12]

The film was scheduled to begin shooting in 1972, with George Cukor directing, but around that time Ball had a skiing accident in Aspen and broke her right leg in several places. The recuperative period was many months, and by that time Cukor was on another picture. Gene Saks, who had directed the Broadway production, was chosen instead.

When Lucille Ball's leg healed enough for her to walk with only a slight limp, the rehearsals began. Oona White insisted that Ball throw away her crutches and gave her exercises to strengthen her leg. Eventually she designed the choreography to disguise the star's infirmity—but often it appears she is being held up by the chorus boys.

Ball tried to run the show from the beginning. She complained about Bea Arthur's clear nail polish and the lack of care given the props (which she felt she was paying for). Madeline Kahn was hired to play Gooch, but on the first day of rehearsal Ball demanded she "use her trick voice."

"I'll come to the vocal register that suits the role as I get into it." Kahn replied.

"Might as well use it from the beginning," Ball insisted.

Kahn left the room angrily, and her part was given to Jane Connell, who

---

* It has been rumored that Ball, in the hopes of reviving her flagging television career, invested $5 million in the film on the condition that she be cast in the lead.

was as brilliant here as she was on stage. The word on the set, however, was that Kahn was far too pretty to be photographed in this picture alongside Ball.

Robert Preston, the original *Music Man* and star of *I Do, I Do,* was cast as Beauregard. Ball claimed that he was too short and suggested Rory Calhoun or George Montgomery for the part. When the studio rebuffed her choices, the insensitive star bought the dapper Preston a pair of shoes with built-in lifts. Preston was furious and told Ball he would "wear his own elk-skin shoes on the set."[13]

Paul Zindel, who had won the Pulitzer Prize for his script *The Effect of Gamma Rays on Man-in-the-Moon Marigolds* but who had never written a musical, adapted the scenario, which stayed very close to the Lawrence and Lee libretto. With few exceptions—namely, the hunt scene and the "Open a New Window" sequence, which cried to be "opened up" to cinema—almost every scene is inferior to the theater version.

Only marginally better is the moment when a self-centered Vera leads Babcock directly to "The School of Life," while Mame tries desperately to head them off, for that scene provides some motivation for a contrite Vera to offer the now penniless Mame a small part in her new show.

Preston's performance (and Zindel's script) fleshes Beauregard out as a human being. But even the meeting between Mame (as a Macy's saleswoman) and Beauregard fails to ignite sparks between the two. The best Ball can muster is to make cow eyes at her swain. Perhaps the most amusing scene is when Mame, fired from Macy's, blithely skates out of the store. It is Ball, the master clown.

When Mame and Beau are on their extended honeymoon, Beau has a lovely romantic song newly supplied by Herman:

Loving you is snow, and jasmine, and the noise of New Year's Eve,
Loving you is now, and yesterday; is real, and make believe.
Loving you is Rome, and New Orleans, and gazing at the lazy
    summer skies,
Fireworks reflecting in your eyes,
Foolish and improbable and wise.

The song, set visually in different parts of the world as the couple tour incessantly and dance tentatively, fills in the years during which Patrick is growing up. (Several critics of the movie found Mame heartless and accused her of having abandoned Patrick during puberty only to return to control his personality development after Beau's death.)

Although Ball may be faulted for much of the film's failure, one has to admit that what was most lacking in this and so many filmed versions of stage musicals was a fresh point of view. One thinks immediately of the stage and cinema versions of *Cabaret*. Each was true to its genre; each reconceived the material for its medium. Perhaps this was impossible with a prosaic director like Gene Saks, who, understandably, tried to re-create his own successful stage version. Certainly a take-charge director like Bob Fosse or Hal Prince might have brought some freshness to the film. Saks was simply unable to stand up to a tornado like Lucille Ball, who was intent on keeping the musical as it had looked on Broadway.

The film had been scheduled for release at Christmas 1973 in order to contend for that year's Academy Awards the following spring. When the producers viewed the rough cut, they knew it stood no chance, and they planned a blitz advertising campaign and a release date for Easter 1974.

Nothing could help. All the reviewers condemned the picture, citing its misdirection, improper lighting, ugly costumes, and weak dialogue. But they saved their most venomous vitriol for Lucille Ball. Frank Rich in the *New York Times* found her "too thick in the waist, too stringy in the legs, too basso in the voice, and too creaky in the joints."[14] As for her singing, the *New Yorker* impaled her by noting that her sound "is somewhere between a bark and a croak."[15]

"There she stands," wrote the critic for *Newsweek*, "her aging face practically a blur in the protective gauze of the softer than soft focus . . . looking alternately like any one of the seven deadly sins."[16] The other reviews were equally devastating, and although the picture did respectable business during its first weeks in New York, once the word got around that it was a real "bomb," its box-office receipts dried up.

But *Mame* is foolproof, and one can only agree with Richard Tyler Jordan, who observes in his fine book, *But Darling, I'm Your Auntie Mame!*, "If the property hadn't been so indestructible Lucille Ball might have ruined *Mame* forever."[17] The musical has never spent much time away from the theater. It is constantly revived by college and high school acting troupes. In 1996, after her great success in *Murder, She Wrote* and before she began Herman's Christmas TV show, *Mrs. Santa Claus*, there was talk of Lansbury bringing the show back to Broadway.

Shortly after that, when those plans were scrapped, Barbra Streisand picked up the option to play Patrick's bohemian aunt in a television spectacular. At the time the book's author, Patrick Dennis, said, "She will play it—but not well." Fortunately, that did not come about, for Streisand, surely

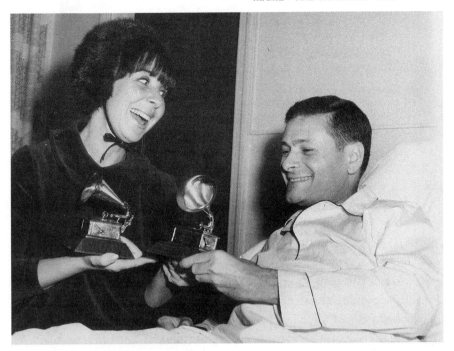

Herman, in the hospital recovering from hepatitis, gets a visit from Edyie Gormé who brought him his Grammy, won for the original cast recording of *Mame*. She also holds her Grammy, won for her recording of "If He Walked into My Life." Photofest, Inc.

one of our greatest pop divas, would be as miscast as Mame as she had been as Dolly. When she dropped out of the running, Cher came into it, and as of this writing she is tentatively slated to star in a television version.

Although it is not his absolute favorite among the eight scores he has written for Broadway, Jerry Herman counts *Mame* near the top of his oeuvre. In my opinion it is one of the finest musicals of the sixties, a golden decade that included *Bye Bye Birdie, A Funny Thing Happened on the Way to the Forum, Camelot, How to Succeed in Business Without Really Trying, She Loves Me, Funny Girl, Fiddler on the Roof, Cabaret, Sweet Charity, Hair,* and *Promises, Promises.* The decade was Herman's heyday, just as the seventies were to be Stephen Sondheim's. In 1961 Herman had had his first hit with *Milk and Honey.* Then through most of the decade he had two shows, *Hello, Dolly!* and *Mame,* playing to packed houses.

Only Rodgers and Hammerstein could rival that record.

9

dear world

With *Mame* comfortably ensconced on Broadway, 1966 was a triumphant time for Herman. He had no reason to doubt his capacity to write hits. After all, he had penned three in a row—two of which would be playing for the next five years. Honors were pouring in from all sides, and offers to collaborate on new projects piled up on his desk. Even today he dubs that time his "golden afterglow of *Mame*."[1] Still, the artist in him, the one who had tackled *Madame Aphrodite*, kept nudging him try to create a work that might be more daring than an adaptation of a popular novel like *Auntie Mame*, or an old-fashioned farce like *The Matchmaker*.

That winter, with the royalties teeming in from *Dolly* and *Mame*, and still no concrete idea of what his next show would be, he decided to take a holiday:

> Sheila Mack and I had gone down to the Virgin Islands to celebrate *Mame*'s success. We were supposed to be on vacation relaxing, but Sheila said, "I have a friend who owns a restaurant down here. We have got to visit him." I said to myself, "Oh, my God, I'll be bored to death." So I asked Sheila, "Do I really have to go with you?" Sheila said, "Oh please! I haven't seen this man in years and I'll be much more comfortable with you." So I said I'd go, but I wasn't happy.
>
> I remember climbing an endless flight of stairs to the restaurant. And there at the top of the stairs was the absolutely gorgeous, suntanned man with dark hair and the most amazing blue eyes. I said, "Oh, my God! *That's* your friend?" Sheila didn't get it. We barely sat down before she started making excuses so we could leave. She thought I was

bored, so she said, "Well, George, it was great seeing you, but Jerry and I have plans . . ."

"No, we don't" I said. "We have all the time in the world, George. What are you doing this afternoon?"

Well, it turned out that we had a three-year relationship. It was a little difficult to maintain, because I live in New York and he lives in St. Thomas. But the airport scenes were very exciting. That was my first serious relationship and it was lovely.[2]

It was on this vacation that Herman decided on his next musical, an adaptation of Jean Giraudoux's *The Madwoman of Chaillot (La Folle de Chaillot)*. He had played the role of the mute when he was a student at the University of Miami, and, as he puts it, had "fallen in love with the play."

From his college days Herman had always felt that this play, a parable, was lyrical, and had hoped that one day he would be able to musicalize it. He was also determined that this work be as far away from the candy-striped colors of *Dolly* or the ultrachic art deco contrasts of *Mame* as possible. This play's heroine lives in a sewer, and her superannuated cronies inhabit the Paris flea market. But like most artists who think they are mining a new lode, Herman invariably reinforced themes stated in his previous works and was drawn to the same title character. The Countess Aurelia is an amalgam of his two earlier heroines. No matter that her clothes are bizarre and her appearance grotesque, she is a doer, like Dolly, and a sophisticated, take-charge person who wants to bring good to the world like Mame.

To understand the play's bizarre title, one must first define the word *folle*, which, in French, leans more toward eccentricity than insanity. The playwright wrote his pithy social commentary when he was living in Switzerland during the early 1940s after the German occupation of Paris. At that time altruistic motives were mistrusted, considered aberrant or *folle*. The playwright himself is a paradox of evil and good, having been given a post by the Vichy government, and rumored, at his death in 1944, to have been poisoned by the Germans because he was, according to Professor John Reilly, "engaged in accumulating documentation on the crimes committed by the Nazis in Paris."[3]

Although Giraudoux's "bad men" are motivated by greed, they are not much more than thinly disguised Nazis in their insouciant annihilation of others. Villainy runs rampant through this play, although its satire is so broad that it softens the fearsomeness of the evildoers. Actually, their plotting is a sham, a cartoon. And because the play is often a preachy comic strip, it is not nearly as frightening as the more realistic anti-Semitism of *Mame*'s Upsons.

Giraudoux believed strongly in his parable and was optimistic that the Allies would eventually win the war. He so trusted the world to "pay attention" to his words that as soon as he had completed the first draft, he phoned the famed French actor Louis Jouvet, then hiding out in Rio de Janeiro, to tell him that the play would be ready for production when Paris was liberated. Presented shortly after the liberation, in August 1944, *La Folle de Chaillot* was a great success in France and was quickly translated by Maurice Valency into English. The whimsical, indomitable title character, on stage almost throughout the evening, was an actress's dream, and the role won a Best Actress Tony for Martita Hunt, who played the Countess during the 1948–1949 Broadway season.

Still, the play is peculiarly French, and the intellectuality and long-windedness of this morality tale did not go down well with Broadway audiences, allowing it only a limited run. After that, the script lay fallow until 1967, when it was selected for filming by producer Ely Landau as a vehicle for Katharine Hepburn featuring Charles Boyer, Edith Evans, and Danny Kaye. Landau decided that the story should be contemporized and had his screenplay written to play out in the sixties. At the time Hepburn found that "updating *The Madwoman of Chaillot* gave it more relevance. The world has gone cuckoo. We're still dominated by greed, and that's what Giraudoux was talking about. *The Madwoman* represents the possibilities of man, she represents hope."[4]

Yet, according to *A Remarkable Woman,* Anne Edwards's biography of Hepburn, the final film failed either to make this point or to be arresting on its own terms. Contemporizing the story bound it to the earth when it should have taken off in enchanted, whimsical fantasy. Although it was well produced, this film failed to capture the charm of the play, and quickly vanished.

The success of Herman's two long-running shows gave him enormous confidence, and in the spring of 1968, for the first time in his Broadway career, he initiated a project. He went to the producer Alexander Cohen, who had used some Herman parodies when he produced his Tony Award shows. Cohen had a reputation for presenting quality, intelligent shows, and Herman intended this to be a chamber musical, itself a kind of art form.

Cohen (and coproducer Hildy Parks) accepted the challenge eagerly, and, armed with a sympathetic producer, Herman went next to playwrights Lawrence and Lee, with whom he had worked so smoothly on *Mame.* They, too, knew and admired the play, and signed on.

"From those first meetings," Herman remembered, "we knew that we did not have the potential for a huge commercial piece. But we all felt the same way; that a career in the theater should not merely go from commercial success to commercial success. There are times when you should just do something you love and believe in. And so we set out to write a musical that would please us."[5]

Herman had pictured "a little group of musicians on stage, playing a concertina, a flute, and maybe a fiddle." That plus a few more musicians in the pit was what he envisioned for his chamber musical. He did not want a full-sized orchestra, an ensemble, or flashy dance numbers. "What I was interested in," he added, "was an intriguing look for the production, and the strange, haunting sound of a Parisian street band."

Since *The Madwoman* depends on a strong protagonist, he immediately visualized Angela Lansbury as the Countess Aurelia. (In truth, the role is much closer to the musical in which Lansbury made her singing debut, *Anyone Can Whistle,* than it is to *Mame,* for this mad noblewoman represents sanity in an insane society.)

Lansbury, who was piqued because she felt that the director, Gene Saks, had not stood up strongly enough on her behalf during casting of the movie version of *Mame,* refused the role. But when Saks bowed out because of other commitments, and Lucia Victor—who, as Gower Champion's assistant, had staged the all-black *Hello, Dolly!* with Pearl Bailey—was hired as director, Lansbury signed on.

Trouble started almost from the first rehearsal, for Lansbury, who by this time was a genuine 24-carat star, was not satisfied with the $1,750 weekly salary she had received for *Mame.* Now she demanded and got $5,000 per week and a percentage of the gross. According to the critic Martin Gottfried, she demanded and was paid the first ten weeks' salary in advance.[6] Producer Cohen, feeling that he needed a bigger venue in order to recoup his star's hefty salary, reserved the Mark Hellenger, where *My Fair Lady* had held forth for six years.

Having one of Broadway's largest theaters meant that the intimate chamber opera Herman had envisioned and the delicate orchestrations Philp Lang had so beautifully written would have to be enlarged. Of necessity, a chorus would be added, and, to balance all this, the principals and orchestra would have to be heavily miked.*

* Back in 1965, Harold Prince felt that Cohen, an extravagant producer who reveled in big productions, had ruined the intimacy of *Baker Street,* which Prince directed, by

Two weeks into rehearsal it became obvious to the librettists and the composer that Lucia Victor did not have the stamina or know-how to direct this snowballing production. Peter Glenville, the British director who had done such a splendid job with *Separate Tables, Becket,* and *Take Me Along,* was brought in. Glenville's direction, "which pulled the show in a cerebral and emotional direction," according to Herman, "was the right one. But he had come in only for a short time as a personal favor to Angela, and had to leave to fulfill other commitments."[7]

Before the show began previewing in New York, Joe Layton, who was basically a choreographer, was hired to direct this nondancing show. Layton was much showier than his predecessors, and according to Herman, "What he brought to our show was more entertainment value, which is not what it needed."

Opening night in Boston was a disaster. According to Lansbury, who dissolved in tears after the curtain came down, audiences were furious and practically booed, expecting another *Mame*. "For me to come out looking like a crone was too much. I wasn't afraid of looking like that in the first place, but I was convinced that I had to modify my look to bleed some of myself into this character." First to go was the huge crooked nose, then the wild wigs and the darkened eyes.

Composer Herman and librettists Lawrence and Lee spent the five weeks that the show played in Boston in frantic rewriting. Even Lansbury offered ideas for improvement and is reported to have insisted on assorted behind-the-scenes changes, much to the chagrin of her fellow cast members. By this time, the script was vastly different from what the playwrights had started with. Whenever a work is consciously designed as "art," there is a danger that its creators will stumble into pretension. The librettists were now frantically rewriting, inserting preachy scenes rather than opting for their traditional simple emotional style.

Cohen insisted that Herman write a title song, one the producer hoped might have the same commercial appeal as "Hello, Dolly!" or "Mame." Herman was dead set against it but eventually capitulated. The result was third-rate Herman, with lines that some have compared to a Hallmark get-well card:

---

booking it into the 1,800-seat Broadway Theatre. "We're defeated," Prince said, when, because of the size of the theater, he had to make such adjustments as a larger chorus and more elaborate sets (Ilson, *Harold Prince,* p. 111).

Please take your medicine, dear world,
Please keep your pressure down, dear world.
Promise to thrive on each word your doctor speaks,
He'll bring the roses back to your cheeks.

"It never worked even for me," Herman explains. "I had envisioned it sung by a young boy, maybe six years old, and having an ingenuous quality. I thought a kid telling the world to "take your medicine" would be charming—but when it was staged by adults it was blown out of all proportion."

But the reader should not assume that the bulk of the score of this musical is dismissible. *Dear World* is simply uneven. It has some of Herman's finest songs with some of his most poetic lyrics, and because of that the weak ones show their flaws more blatantly. Perhaps the creators should have returned to the original conception during the show's unprecedented fifty-nine New York previews, but with a mammoth cast, orchestra, and theater engaged, turning back—so often the hindsight that everyone has after a flop closes—was impossible. The best that could be hoped for was to build on Herman's former successes, and to this end, even a glamorous photo of Lansbury as *Mame* was used in the show's early publicity. The power of Lansbury's new superstardom was reflected at the box office, creating a hefty advance.

The following narrative represents the show as it was originally conceived. This is the musical as created by Lawrence and Lee, and not the very different, much weaker, version that eventually premiered on 6 February 1969.

The musical opens at the Café Francis in the Chaillot section of Paris. It is late morning and the sky, typically Parisian, is threatening. The scene serves to introduce the denizens of the café. Nina, the waitress and ingenue, is the only one given a proper name; the others are Doorman, Waiter, Busboy, Juggler, Deaf-mute, Policeman, and so on.

Enter the Countess Aurelia, venerable but ageless, whose mission in life is to feed the stray cats of Paris with table scraps, chicken bones, and gizzards that Nina generally puts aside for her. Her costume and parasol tell us more than words could about the long-ago world she lives in. Aurelia is in perpetual search for a lost nine-foot feather boa given to her by an admirer.

Business looks bad for the café as storm clouds threaten. But when Aurelia predicts fine weather to come, and the sky almost instantly clears, the

Angela Lansbury as the Countess Aurelia, the Madwoman of Chaillot, in Herman's 1969 musical *Dear World*. Photofest, Inc.

euphoric waiter offers her a drink. "A fine year," she proclaims, as she sips champagne. "Better than next," and she is off into her song. "Through the Bottom of the Glass," a hymn to illusion:

> What a fascinating view through the bottom of the glass.
> A December afternoon looks particularly well
> When you watch it drift along through some sunny muscatel.
> It's the middle of July through the bottom of the glass. . . .
> But in the brazen blazing of the sun
> You feel the pressure and the tension and the hurt.
> In the brazen blazing of the sun
> You see the gossip and the hunger and the dirt.
> But there's majesty and truth in a tall aperitif,
> When a crisis in the world rips my countrymen in half.
> Through the bubbles in champagne they invariably laugh.
> So I simply let life pass
> Though the rose of the rosé
> Through the amber of the rum

Through an endless pousse-café
Through the bottom of the glass.

The lyric is a giant step into the art song for Herman, an indication of his (and the Countess's) poetic capabilities. The lush language, the alliteration, all indicate the poetry to come, and through Aurelia's murky vision we glimpse her message—the dissatisfaction with mundane reality.

Unfortunately, the song was cut, according to Herman, "because it was basically static. We had gone beyond the chamber piece I had originally envisioned. A woman sitting with a brandy snifter in these huge Oliver Smith sets could not be staged interestingly."* An ensemble number that had originally been planned to open act two, "The Spring of Next Year," was put in its place.

Before long we are introduced to the villains of the piece. First, the Prospector, who asks for a glass of water, an unheard of request in France, sips it, and announces that "it has a formidable taste." The waiter rushes to get him another glass, but he waves him away, announcing, "It's delicious."

In the next scene, we meet the President, to whom the Prospector rushes to announce that the Café Francis is built over a lake of oil—he can taste it in the water. Then we meet Julian, who will be our hero. He has had some legal troubles, has been bailed out by the President, and is now in his thrall, in no position to refuse the dirty job of destroying the café so that the President's cartel can get at the oil. As Julian rushes off to plant a time bomb to explode at noon, the Lawyer is called; he, the Prospector, and the President indulge in a gluttonous trio called "Just a Little Bit More":

Taking francs from the rich has a certain allure,
But it's even more fun when you're screwing the poor.
(Just a little bit more)
For each man has a natural desire
To find a plot of earth that he can acquire.
And so to rest my bones the day I retire
I would simply adore

* For the Goodspeed Opera House production in 2000, Aurelia's opening number became "A Sensible Woman," written and discarded when *Dear World* was in Boston. It would illustrate, according to Herman, "her backwards philosophy which shows her form of madness as a kind of reverse intelligence. Her opening lines are 'A sensible woman will walk through the sewers to keep her hat out of the rain/A sensible woman grows spirited flowers by watering them with champagne.'"

Just an acre of ground,
One respectable piece,
Just a little back yard,
Argentina or Greece!

At the café, as the clock bongs twelve times—suspensefully—and
nothing happens, a Policeman runs on. Julian has thrown himself into the
Seine after the bomb he lacked the heart to plant, and the Policeman has
saved him, knocking him out to keep both of them from being dragged under. When Julian opens his eyes and glances up at Nina, he thinks he is in
heaven. The Countess, standing nearby, recognizes love at first sight. To
dissuade the young man—in the untenable position of being in service to
the President—from trying again to take his life, she sings "Tomorrow
Morning," our first real Herman song in this show—a catchy tune which,
with its opening up a triad with a pop on the major 7th, seems genuinely
Gallic.

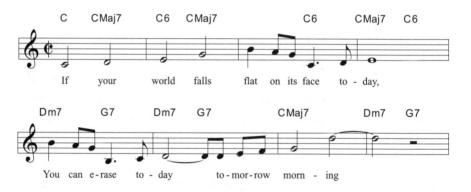

Perhaps the most interesting aspect of this jaunty melody is its spoken
interlude, with music under, taken directly from Giraudoux. In it Aurelia
recalls the lovely thrill of receiving a letter in the mail that you had sent
yourself yesterday, then washing "your face in rose water, and powdering
it—not with this awful rice powder they sell nowadays, which does nothing
for the skin, but with a cake of pure white starch—and you put on your
rings, your brooches, bracelets, earrings and pearls—in short, when you're
ready to receive your morning coffee—and have a good look at yourself—
not in the glass, naturally—it lies—but in the side of the brass gong that

once belonged to the immortal Sarah. . . . Then, you're ready for tomorrow morning."

The President and the Prospector return, hoping to find the café destroyed. They are disappointed to find Julian, who has informed everyone that his bosses want to get their hands on the oil that lies under the café. Julian declares that he wants no further involvement with these men, the Countess protects him, and as the Policeman runs the two baddies offstage, the President threatens to destroy Aurelia as well as the café.

When they leave, the denizens of the café try to convince the Countess of the evil and greed in modern-day Paris, but she covers her ears and sings one of Herman's most intense songs, one he calls "fierce, but beautiful," "I Don't Want to Know." The music, reminiscent of street dances on Bastille Day, is typically Parisian (as distinguished from the Côte d'Azur sound Herman was to achieve in *La Cage aux Folles*). It could be part of the repertoire of the great French song interpreters like Edith Piaf or Jacques Brel. Produced with lighting that went from delicate Parisian blue to blazing red, the melody, built around the major 7th and 6th of the scale, is fierce and impassioned. The A2 section (beginning at * in the example on page 172), an inevitable sequence of the A1, intensifies the ardor, for it is written in a key that is a full tone higher. And then we come to a remarkable release during which Herman manages to modulate back to the key he started out in without losing any of the song's intensity. Now Herman can build up to a final climax which brings the house down at every performance. From its fervor, one would assume that this song would have a tremendous range, but an examination of the score shows that Herman used the economical vocal distance of a 10th to good effect. The tessitura, however, punching out the brutal top notes, makes the song sound high.

> Let me hide every truth from my eyes with the back of my hand,
> Let me live in a world full of lies with my head in the sand.
> For my mem'ries all are exciting.

Aurelia still does not know how to react to the President's drastic threat and decides to enlist the help of her cronies, Constance, the Madwoman of the Flea Market, and Gabrielle, the Madwoman of Montmartre. As she sweeps out on Julian's arm, she leaves Nina alone on stage, and in a feat of dramaturgical ineptitude, with almost no preparation or reason, the waitress sings the musical's only love song to no one. It is, to be sure, quite a

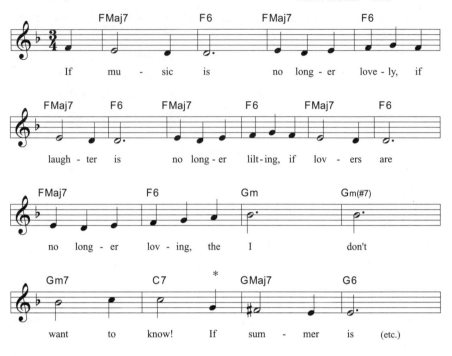

FMaj7   F6   FMaj7   F6

If mu - sic is   no long - er love - ly, if

FMaj7 F6   FMaj7   F6   FMaj7   F6

laugh - ter is   no long - er lilt- ing, if lov - ers are

FMaj7   F6   Gm   Gm(#7)

no long - er lov - ing, the   I   don't

Gm7   C7   *   GMaj7   G6

want   to   know! If sum - mer is (etc.)

charming song, with a fresh lyrical ending, a splendid caboose of the sort that Frank Loesser had talked about years before to the neophyte composer:*

> We'll turn and we'll look,
> We'll nod and we'll know,
> We'll stare and we'll smile
> And then, and then,
> I'll gratefully say "I love you,"
> And when I say, "I love you,"
> He'll know I've never loved before,
> He'll know I'll never love again!

* Herman rarely employs the evaded ending, which can often cheapen a song, but this one, which occurs between the penultimate and ultimate lines, fits the song perfectly. It is beautifully handled here, and fits perfectly with both music and lyric.

In the next scene, at the Flea Market, we meet the other two eccentric and amusing Madwomen.* Constance (Carmen Matthews on Broadway) has no conception of time and is deaf except on Wednesdays. Gabrielle (Jane Connell, who had done such a brilliant job in *Mame* as Gooch) habitually brings along her imaginary dog and wears the long blond curls of the woman she has not been for half a century. As they indulge in petty arguing, Aurelia reminds them that it is time to settle the fate of the world, and to do that she decides to invoke the Sewerman, a kind of all-knowing, all-seeing guru, as close as we get in this musical to a costar. (On Broadway he was played by Milo O'Shea.)

The Sewerman sings a charming habanera, first about the elegant garbage of the past:

Pâté de foie gras, Thursday's gardenias, ribbon and orange rinds.
A volume of Chaucer bound in Morocco, lilies and coffee grinds.
The pit of a peach, the stem of a cherry floating in pink champagne,
There was a time when garbage was a pleasure,
When you found the sound of good and plenty gurgling in your drain.

Then he draws a contrast with today's throw-aways:

Spastic contortions spatter the dance-floor, with flailing arms and legs.
Plastic for breakfast, tin-foil for dinner, pass me the powdered eggs.
Capsules and needles stunning the senses, splitting the mind in two.
Bring back the time when garbage was a pleasure,
When insanity was limited to just a chosen few.

The song with its stylization is better than the dialogue that leads into it, but it is not the tour de force necessary at that moment. As a "social statement" it eventually becomes tiresome, even though it was directed as an insane phantasmagoria, climaxing in a mad bolero. The number reminds one of Samuel Goldwyn's remark: "If you want to send a message, call Western Union."

We are not through with messages, for the Sewerman points out that most of the evil in the world comes from these greedy pimps. The Countess, who recoils in terror at this threat to her world of yesterday, decides to fight these monsters. When Constance says "there are so few of us and so many of

---

* In Giraudoux there are three: Madwomen of Passy, St. Sulpice, and La Concorde, created on the New York stage by Estelle Winwood, Nydia Westman, and Doris Rich, respectively. Great actresses all.

Milo O'Shea as the Sewerman who sings "Garbage," a song in praise of yesterday, to Lansbury. Photofest, Inc.

them," the Countess retorts with "there is no number larger than one," introducing a stirring march:

> One person can beat a drum
> And make enough noise for ten.
> One person can blow a horn
> And that little boom, and that little blare
> Can make a thousand others care.

The song is similar, if superior, to the first-act ending of Andrew Lloyd-Webber and Tim Rice's *Evita*, years down the road. Perhaps what makes it even more stirring is its interlude, which grows in intensity and volume:

> There may be a legion of them
> And only a parcel of us,
> And how can a poor little band fight a mighty regime?
> There may be an army of them

And only a handful of us
But it isn't the size of the fist,
It's the size of the dream.

This leads to a repeat of the "One Person" refrain sung by the entire ensemble, and as the act ends with this big production number, all Paris seems to join in.

Act two begins as the President sings a whimsical waltz in which he tries to intrigue his cronies with a vision of their Paris of the future. The tartness of the music as it climbs the scale, juxtaposed with the propaganda of the lyric, gives the number an élan that the play has been lacking:

There will be a sweet taste in the air,
From industrial waste in the air,
And your eyelids will smart from the sting of the smog
In the spring of next year.

The scene now shifts to the Countess's apartment, where she summons the Sewerman again. She asks him how he keeps order in the sewer, and he tells her he disposes of what he considers garbage. When she asks him to reveal "the secret of the moving stone." He feels the masonry for a brick, finds it, and dislodges it, whereupon a huge section of the wall pivots to reveal stairs into a gaping hole that emits a sickly greenish light. Asked where the stairs go, he replies ominously, "they just go down." The Sewerman touches another stone, closing the passageway, and departs.

Now we are ready for the maddest tea party since the one Lewis Carroll included in *Alice in Wonderland*. On the pretense that Aurelia needs the mature wisdom of the other two madwomen to set up a trial for the miscreants of the world, we get a series of songs, views of life, marriage, possessions, and philosophy that have very little to do with the plot—but serve as surcease from the perpetual agitprop of the story.

First, Aurelia asks Constance, whose late husband was a lawyer, about trying and convicting these dastardly men. Constance rants on about the lecherous seducers she has known, recalling, in a song called "Memory," all their erotic titillations and ending with a punch line, "but I remember absolutely nothing about my husband."

The Countess and Gabrielle now sing a lopsided waltz called "Pearls," whose philosophy about the porous border between fantasy and reality is taken directly from Giraudoux:

Surely you must know when you wear pearls
That little by little the pearls become real.
And isn't it the same with memories?

Gabrielle carries on with the tea party's most amusing section, a hymn to her imaginary dog, Dickie, who her companions say barks too much. The song ends with its own surprise: "The fact is, my dears, that I didn't even bring him today!"

Constance strongly objects to the presence of an imaginary dog and, hoping to answer the Countess's question as to how to get rid of these men who want to rule the world, says she will rush home and consult her "voices."

Chatter, chatter, chatter, there are voices in my closet
Saying, "wear the fuscia gloves and purple veil."
And voices in my piano singing up and down the oriental scale.

Aurelia goes off on her own existential tangent when she proclaims that "everything that was, is. There are other minds here."

Moliere and Keats are enraged and engaged in a row,
Listen to the lovely language.
Every lesson Voltaire ever taught, and every thought that Buddha
   ever thought,
Is right here in this air,
In this house, in this room,
With us now!

Each of these eccentrics repeats her philosophy, creating three-part counterpoint. The melodies are distinct, but only the "Dickie" theme, which is a real melody rather than a contrapuntal exercise, sticks in the memory.

The tea party is interrupted by an excited Nina and Julian, who burst in with the news that these bad men have enlarged their plans. Now they want to blow up the world. After observing that the act "can only be done once," the Countess coolly insists we must "bait a hook, as for fish," and asks Julian to lend her his watch. She scrapes the radium numbers off the dial, puts them in a bottle with some water, and tells Julian to deliver it to the President as soon as night falls. Then, as all depart except Julian, we embark on the tenderest scene in the musical.

Aurelia, who, throughout the play has confused Julian with her imaginary lover, Albert Bertaut, dozes, and as she does, the walls fall away and we are in the park at Colombes.* Concertina music is heard in the background, and then, in perhaps Herman's most heartbreakingly exquisite song, "And I Was Beautiful," we are privy to the memories inside Aurelia's mind. I quote the entire lyric, but for the true emotional experience this song can create, one must hear the sumptuous way the syllables lie on the music when it is sung.

> He stood and looked at me
> And I was beautiful,
> For it was beautiful how he believed in me.
> His love was strong enough
> To make me anything,
> So I was everything he wanted me to be.
> But then he walked away,
> And took my smile with him,
> And now the years blur by,
> But every now and then,
> I stop and think of him,
> And how he looked at me,
> And all at once
> I'm beautiful again.
> For a moment—I'm beautiful again.

This song, about the transforming power of love, gives us an opportunity to analyze the essence of Herman's great gift: the ability to let a lyric phrase climax in a moving thought while it is matched to ideal melodic notes. Cleverly using an ABAC form, Herman begins with a memorable low scalelike phrase, each succeeding repetition of which ends a tone higher. It is almost as if Aurelia believes that this love affair will end happily. She is ecstatic recalling the beauty she sees reflected in her lover's eyes as the melody rises up to the word *anything,* and even more joyous when she announces (on an intense D9 chord) that she was "everything he wanted me to be." But then, plunging down an octave and a half, she recounts the tragedy of her lover's departure with the stunning poetics of how "he walked away,/and took my smile with him" in the second A section. Yet the Countess does not dwell on the betrayal but lets us know that "as the years blur by," when she

---

* In Giraudoux the lover is called Adolphe, and he is very real, having left Aurelia for another woman.

recalls their first meeting, the decades turn to dust, and she is once again that beautiful young girl in the park at Colombes.

As she ends her song and drifts off to sleep, Julian covers her with the nine-foot boa, which he has found. He picks up the bottle, which now glows in the dark, and takes his bicycle across the stage as the set behind him changes to a slice of Chaillot. When he presents the liquid to the President, he and the Prospector believe it to be radioactive.* "Better than oil!" they exclaim, and run off to find the source of this miracle.

We are left with Julian and Nina on stage, and they begin the title song, "Dear World." The others soon join them. Now the bad men come on stage with the glowing bottle. They hurry back to the Countess's flat, and as she presses the sesame brick, the green glow comes on as the door to the basement opens. "Where did this water come from?" The President demands. "I can't imagine," Aurelia hedges, "unless . . ." With her pregnant pause they all troop down. She presses the other brick, and, as the trap door closes, the green light is extinguished.

The show should be over, but the subplot threads have not yet been tied: Nina and Julian are still in limbo. With very little dramatic lead-in, the Countess sings another of Herman's finest songs, "Kiss Her Now," an urgent exhortation whose lyric is self-explanatory. (The memorable minor key melodic emotionality of the opening lines comes from the B in the melody rubbing intensely against a persistent A minor chord.)

> Before you half remember what her smile was like,
> Before you half recall the day you found her
> Kiss her now, while she's young,
> Kiss her now, while she's yours
> Kiss her now, while she needs your arms around her.

Perhaps the Countess's and the authors' carpe diem would be better understood if the song had been placed after "And I Was Beautiful," urging Julian not to let Nina slip away as Aurelia slipped from Albert Bertaut's grasp. But after this number, the sky becomes blue and all Paris seems to smile. As in all previous Herman musicals, we are treated to (or subjected to, depending on your point of view) reprises of most of the lively and optimistic songs.

---

* In the light of the 11 September 2001 bombing of the World Trade Center, the atomic bomb implications of the radium or plutonium in Julian's watch only go to show how prescient Lawrence and Lee's original script was.

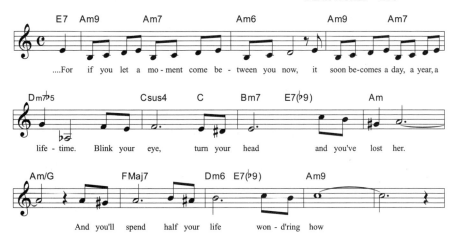

It should be mentioned again that the preceding *Dear World* plot summary is based on the original libretto of Lawrence and Lee. It was seen only for the first weeks of previews in Boston before the wholesale tinkering began. By the time of the New York opening the most stunning bit of change from Giraudoux—the substitution of radioactivity as bait for the villains instead of a pool of oil—had disappeared, "Dear World" and "One Person" had been juxtaposed, and most of the poetry of the libretto had been excised. Before its official first night, Lansbury had been transformed from an eighty-year-old crone to an eccentric but beautiful woman with mascara-rimmed eyes, and the show had been shortened to less than two hours. Even so, the interminable talkiness of the libretto still made it feel far too long.

Herman took most of the blame for *Dear World*'s failure. "Other people may have been technically responsible for choosing the wrong theater," he was to say, "and the wrong style, and for allowing the show to get too big and clumsy, but those mistakes were my fault, too. I could have said: 'Hey, wait a minute everybody! This is not what I set out to do. Let's go back and find that original, wonderful idea we lost.'"

Samuel "Biff" Liff, Herman's agent since the days of *Hello, Dolly!*, gives us some insight into how those original ideas get subverted. "It is because of Herman's positive attitude. He'll say, 'Oh, yes, that will work fine,' and people suddenly think they have the right to do anything, or he'll say, 'Yes, that's a very good idea,' and instead of asking him, 'Do you want me to move ahead with this?' they go ahead on their own. And then they say, 'You said it was OK.' He has a great deal of difficulty going back, once he's given his approval to something.[8]

Dear World opened on 6 February 1969 to blistering reviews. Most critics mentioned the fifty-nine previews, during which the show only got more diffuse; many seemed to be personally offended by the producer's bilking the public by selling tickets to a very troubled show. Clive Barnes in the *New York Times,* after raving about Lansbury's performance, wrote of the show, "The only time it gets off the ground is when it gracefully flounced up airborne by a delicate kick from the adorable Miss Lansbury, who not only can make magic out of nothing, but has to."[9] All the critics came down hard on the book and especially on Herman's score. *Time* magazine incomprehensibly called the songs "a total zero."[10] Walter Kerr found Lansbury's show-stopping number "I Don't Want to Know" banal. He called its melody "a playground-in-the-park Parisian jingle, a pastiche of all those before-Piaf frosty morning tunes that seem to have been born on carousels" with a "hard hitting lyric."[11] And Martin Gottfried, noting that the plot line had been cut to ribbons, found "the story impossible to follow."[12]

With such dreadful notices it is a wonder that producer Cohen did not end the run at once, but stubborn as he was, Cohen refused to close *Dear World* unless the weekly box-office gross dipped below $51,000.* The show, heavily advertised, did rather good business—taking in $74,000 in its first week. But after a few weeks, when even Lansbury's fans seemed to stay away, and the few customers who did come to the show spread bad word of mouth, *Dear World* closed—having given 132 performances.

Herman's reaction was to take a few steps backward into his reclusive past. "I just didn't want to go out, and for a while I went no further than the Mark Hellenger Theatre to watch a performance," he was to say. "Except for the cast, I didn't want to face anybody. I felt I had failed myself and let everybody down."

But although dead, *Dear World* refused to lie down and lives on even now. Because of its splendid score the recording made by Columbia and conducted by Donald Pippin continued to sell to a considerable cult audience for years after the show closed. In the mid-1990s producer Thomas Shepard at Sony remastered and released the recording in "high definition sound," and it is still a favorite of musical theater buffs.

Frequent revivals that attempt to recapture the chamber intimacy of

---

* The Mark Hellenger (now leased as a church) then had a potential weekly gross of $104,000.

the original idea have found an enthusiastic audience, always for the songs, if not for the confused and preachy book. An important revival—supposedly a rethinking, but still one saddled with endless chatter—was staged in November 2000 at the Norma Terris Theatre in Connecticut under the aegis of the Goodspeed Opera Company and starring a glowing Sally Ann Howes as Aurelia. The revival coincided with a staging of *Mack and Mabel* as part of the Los Angeles Reprise Series, and Herman shuttled cross-country to supervise both productions.

"I feel *Dear World* still works," Howes said recently, "but this production didn't come anywhere near it. The problem is that it takes very serious subjects—capitalism, ecology, terrorism—and treats them philosophically. But this production was too gay. The people who are the objects of our scorn were no threat, they were flouncing around. And for this production itself, we cut the song 'One Person' because the director said we had too few people, too few good guys, to sing it properly, so we ended act one with 'Dear World.' When Jerry came back and saw that, he was furious, but it was too late to change it. That left us with nothing to end act two but a reprise of 'A Sensible Woman.'

"We had talk-back afterward with the audience, and they felt—young and old—that they wanted the love story of the young couple to have more prominence and to be concluded. They also agreed with Jerry that the song 'Dear World' should be cut."[13]

Howes and the majority of critics now believe that *Dear World*'s score is of such high quality that with a rewritten libretto it could be turned into a successful musical. The show does not lack for performances by little-theater groups, and it was enthusiastically received in a major revival starring Maureen McGovern in August 2002 at the Sundance Festival in Utah.

Herman, like Sondheim with his critically roasted *Merrily We Roll Along,* or Lloyd-Webber after the unenthusiastic reception of *By Jeeves,* is determined to assist in changing the musical's libretto so that this score, so dear to his heart, can be viable. He plans to eliminate the title song and call the show *Tomorrow Morning*—already an improvement. Certainly this show has more than its share of thrilling musical numbers to make the composer's hope more than a dream. A score that includes "Tomorrow Morning," "I Don't Want to Know," "I've Never Said I Love You," "One Person," and especially "And I Was Beautiful" and "Kiss Her Now" adds up to top-notch Herman.

After the composer noted his disappointment with the critical drubbing and curtailed run of *Dear World,* he said, "I was terribly spoiled; I thought you just wrote a musical and it ran for seven years." But by mid-1969 he had set a new record. It was the first time in recent memory that an American composer-lyricist had three shows running simultaneously on Broadway. Yes, his songs, especially "Hello, Dolly!" "Mame," and "If He Walked into My Life," were on everybody's lips, and his shows had been the most successful ones of the 1960s.

That made it so much harder to face the decade of disillusion that lay ahead.

10

mack and mabel

In the spring of 1969, with *Dear World* still playing (though to half-empty houses) and Angela Lansbury lionized by the trade papers for her Tony Award–winning performance, Jerry Herman's critique-trampled spirits gradually began to rise.* During the few months of *Dear World*'s Broadway engagement Herman ritualized his evenings. He would usually arrive at the Hellinger at about 8:30 to revel in Angela's first-act emotion-packed "I Don't Want to Know" (which the composer feels won her the Tony), then scoot over to the Winter Garden by 9:15 for *Mame*'s rousing act-one-closing title song. Most evenings he would spend the intermissions gossiping in the dressing rooms before strolling down Broadway to 44th Street in time to see the second-act "Hello, Dolly!" number stop that show. And then, after the curtains came down, he would go out for a late-night snack with one or the other of his leading ladies.

Evenings that included three standing ovations and suppers with stars cheered him; so did mornings when the mail brought ASCAP earnings checks and hefty royalty payments from three separate producers. Gradually, he returned to his usual ebullient self. He was also involved in an affair with Joe Masiell, the handsome singing actor who had starred in the revue *Jacques Brel Is Alive and Well (And Living in Paris)* and now had a small role in *Dear World*. Herman admitted that having an emotional relationship with someone in one of his shows was not a good idea, because he "didn't want the other kids to think I was giving somebody preferential treatment.

* Lansbury won the Tony for Best Performance by an Actress in a Musical, but *Dear World* was not even nominated as Best Musical. The award was won by *1776*, with the other nominees being *Hair, Zorba,* and *Promises, Promises.*

But we met, we liked each other, and the emotion won out. So, for a year or so, I had a very fulfilling experience."[1]

Early in 1972 Herman was approached by an old friend, the playwright Leonard Spigelgass. Spigelgass's successful comedy *A Majority of One* had starred Herman's original passport to glory, Molly Picon. He had an idea for a musical set in the early days of the movies and outlined to Herman the stormy romance between Mack Sennett and his personal superstar, Mabel Normand.

Herman is a movie buff but knew very little about the origins of movie-making. But now, intrigued by a musical based on the lives of real people, he began to do thorough research about both Sennett and Normand. Mack Sennett, he found, had made a significant contribution to silent films in the United States, with the frenetic slapstick comedies he introduced. He was one of the industry's first producers, a versatile entrepreneur who recognized and encouraged talent and who created a systematic approach to production that yielded a large quantity of films.

He was born Michael Sinnott to a poor family in Danville, Quebec, in 1880. In his youth he worked as a laborer, although he had ambitions to become a singer. He soon left home for New York City, where he got his first show business job in burlesque, and later he worked as a Broadway chorus boy. In 1908 he was hired by the American Mutoscope and Biograph Company headed by D. W. Griffith as an actor, and eventually he became a scriptwriter. By 1910 Griffith had promoted him to director, and it was on the set of one of his earliest movies that he met and was smitten with Mabel Normand. Mabel, a five-foot beauty with luxurious chestnut hair and expressive dark brown eyes, was born on Staten Island in 1892 (although she always insisted she was born three years later, and her tombstone birth date is engraved as 1895). As a teenager she had posed for such famous illustrators as James Montgomery Flagg and Charles Dana Gibson before becoming an actress at Biograph Pictures. Her modeling experience had taught her to quickly assume a pose that would impart the various feelings her directors sought. Griffith, who had directed her in a bit part, realized that she was not just an actress and a gifted comedienne but an incipient stuntwoman, a fearless high-diver as well. Since he himself was "above" comedy, Griffith assigned Normand to his assistant, Mack Sennett, who directed her first comedy, *The Driving Girl*. Mabel was a sensation and Sennett recognized her popular appeal. So when he left Biograph in 1911 to open his own studios on the West Coast, he had the good sense to take Mabel with him.

Because of Sennett's superb sense of comic timing—illustrated in hilarious chase scenes—Keystone, his company, quickly became the leader in the production of slapstick comedy. His films, often including rude visual humor, made audiences roar. He understood that a snowball knocking off a man's hat is not funny unless it is an opera hat, and that a pie in the face of a shopgirl may elicit a laugh, but the gag is truly hilarious when the victim is a duchess. With his keen eye for talent he hired Roscoe "Fatty" Arbuckle, Edgar Kennedy, Slim Summerville, Chester Conklin, and Ben Turpin, and he was the first to encourage his talented company of comedians to improvise. As his studio prospered, other directors were brought in. But it was Sennett's vision that created the Bathing Beauties, the Kid Komedies (the early precursor of Our Gang), and the memorable Keystone Kops.

In 1913 he discovered Charlie Chaplin and starred him in a series of one-reelers, but two years later, when very short films were no longer popular, his company was forced to become part of the Triangle Film Company headed by Griffith and Thomas Ince. Here Sennett's films became more commercial.

When Triangle folded in 1917, the irrepressible Sennett formed Mack Sennett Comedies, which cranked out longer films that frequently starred Mabel Normand, usually as an innocent maiden in danger. But by this time Normand had begun drinking and causing embarrassing public scenes. She entered a dissolute, drug-filled affair with the director William Desmond Taylor, and after he was murdered, the public conception of her lasciviousness was so strong that her career was ruined.* Normand left the screen in the early 1920s and went on to marry cowboy-actor Lew Cody. She had seven quiet years until she died of tuberculosis in 1930 at the age of thirty-seven. By contrast, Sennett lived a long life, but by 1923, with his best films behind him, he had ceased to work independently. He cranked out films until he retired in 1935 at the age of fifty-five, wrote his autobiography and lived until 1969, dying at the age of eighty-nine.

Those were the bare facts of the lives upon which Herman and Spigelgass would be basing their libretto. The work had hardly begun when

---

* Taylor, one of Hollywood's "artiest" early movie directors, was murdered in 1922. The crime was never solved, although suspicion pointed in several directions. Most suspect were anonymous drug dealers who supplied the victim. The tabloids pointed to Mary Miles Minter, who had replaced Mabel Normand in Taylor's affections, and to Mabel herself. Normand, who had been the last to see him, had broken a date with him and walked out of his house a few minutes before the murder. Like Fatty Arbuckle, a huge star before he contributed to the death of a starlet during one of his coke-filled parties, Mabel's career never recovered from the scandal.

Spiegelgass mentioned a biography of Edward G. Robinson he was working on. He wanted desperately to go ahead and finish it, so he begged to be let off the project and suggested Herman find another librettist. According to Herman, Spiegelgass asked only for "a little piece of the total work," a small percentage of the gross, and billing as "from an idea by."

There was no question about who would write the script. At that time Herman's librettist of choice was Michael Stewart, his "brother," because they had worked so well together on *Hello, Dolly!* He called Stewart at once and said, "I have found our new musical, Mike. You're the perfect writer for it." According to Herman, all he did was describe the idea, and Stewart said, "I love it! Let's meet on Monday and get to work." And so in early 1973 the pair plunged into their first libretto based on real characters, their odyssey of the early movies.[2]

Stewart adapted the Sennett-Normand story freely. While sticking to the broad outline of the pair's history, Stewart and Herman conceived Mack as an "introspective kind of guy, rough and abrasive on the outside, who was obsessive about his moviemaking." He truly loved Mabel but was too inhibited to come out and tell her so, even though he wanted her to know it. She, too, was insecure and needed to know he cared for her and thought of her more than simply as a shadow on the screen who was his comedy star. In a way Mack's tongue-tiedness builds to an epic kind of tragedy—a woman who needs to hear "I love you," and a man whose machismo won't let him say it.

Mack and Mabel begins in 1938. We see a bankrupt Mack Sennett, drunk and indignant, coming onto his studio soundstage the night before it is repossessed. He rails about how little "those modern sonsofbitches with a Victrola back of the screen know about making movies." Under his diatribe we hear a pastiche of the old tintypes that leads to his opening song, "Movies Were Movies," a minor-key vamp, tiptoeing down the scale. And as we are led into the song, the soundstage brightens and comes alive with actors, grips, and extras. We are back making movies in 1910.

The song, with its staccato line, is so reminiscent of the early silents that one can almost see Pearl White and Charlie Chaplin in the music. This driving, urgent credo is also a hymn to the early flickers and makes us come to understand Mack's personal respect for the art. Not since *Milk and Honey*'s "Shalom" had Herman written so apt an opening number:

> Movies were movies when you paid a dime to escape.
> Cheering the hero and hissing the man in the cape.

Romance and action and thrills,
Pardner there's gold in them hills,
Movies were movies when during the titles you'd know
You'd get a happy ending.
Dozens of blundering cops in a thundering chase,
Getting a bang out of lemon meringue in the face.
Bandits attacking a train,
One little tramp with a cane—
Movies were movies were *movies* when I ran the show!

With the lights up we are in Mack's first studio in Brooklyn, and Lottie, his leading actress—a former hoofer—is portraying an innocent with a baby. She stands before an old washtub as Mack yells instructions to the mustached villain like "either she coughs up the money, or you put the baby through the wringer!" Mabel, who is delivering lunch from a nearby deli, stumbles into the scene. She demands her fifteen cents for Lottie's sand-wich, and tripping over props causes hilarious mayhem, during which Mack keeps the cameras rolling, accidentally filming Mabel's first picture. He offers her a job, which she refuses at first. But the next morning, when she sees herself glamorously blown up on the screen, she is entranced with her own charisma and changes her mind.

"Look What Happened to Mabel" is a book song, a genre inserted to move the story along, but one whose melody is not generally "take-home-able." Yet this one, because of its catchy syncopated melody, suggests the early ragtime era so completely that it feels like it could have come from that time. Its lyric, however, beyond the first section, is repetitious and unimag-inative. Although the words lack humor it is a singing actress's dream that creates great empathy for the waif.

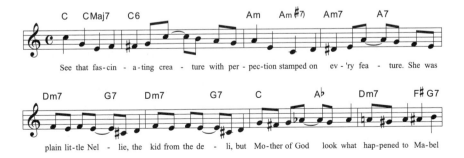

The next song, a production number for the entire company, although quite different in mood, expresses the same feeling of wonderment at the stroke of luck that has befallen the Keystone group. The actors, Mack, Mabel, and Lottie, are joined by producers Kleinman and Fox, who offer to set them up making pictures in Hollywood. As they rejoice at leaving Brooklyn, they sing "Big Time," an even more highly syncopated number than "Look What Happened to Mabel," but much more driving. The number, Herman feels, explains the passion that impelled this little group to move to California.

> This time it's the big time,
> In a short time we can be
> The cherry on the top of the sundae,
> The shiny star on top of the tree.
> So you'd better grab it with your both hands
> When that great moment arrives
> Cause this time it's the big time,
> It's the big time of our lives.

On the train headed for the West Coast, Mabel seduces Mack, first with her poetry and charm, and then with some veal and peppers she has prepared on a cooker in her compartment. After the meal, when he enthuses not about the dinner but about his work, she asks, "Does everything have to do with making movies?" He lets down his guard, but soon he warns her that she must understand his "rules."

The song is "I Won't Send Roses," one of Herman's most moving ballads, a negative, bearish love song, poured into a typical ABAC pattern. The ardent music in the closing C section—at the top of his vocal range—belies Sennett's flinty words. At last, he spills out his feelings in the final line.* Herman creates shattering emotional effects by using simple appoggiaturas (see * in the example, page 189) and suspensions (see **).

---

* In his memoir, Herman acknowledged the difficulty he had—once he had written the opening—of getting beyond the motif of this song: "I must have played the opening of that tune for weeks. . . . But that was all I had—the beginning, I didn't have my middle, and I didn't have my caboose. . . . But I knew what I wanted Mack to say, which is basically 'Stay away, kid,' So I jumped to the last line. Suddenly this same gruff voice comes out and says, 'I won't send roses—and roses suit you so.' That line was so perfect, I lost my mind. . . . I think it says more about those two people than anything in the show" (Herman, *Showtune*, p. 188).

I won't send roses or hold the door,
I won't remember which dress you wore.
My heart is too much in control,
The lack of romance in my soul
Will turn you gray, kid,
So stay away, kid.
Forget my shoulder when you're in need.
Forgetting birthdays—is guaranteed.
And should I love you, you would be the last to know.
I won't send roses,
And roses suit you so.

Between the first and second choruses, preparatory to their first sexual awakening to each other, Mabel insists that they have a token private wedding rite, because, as she says, "When two people get married even for a single night, they need a ring." Mack obligingly puts the napkin ring (stolen from the Union Pacific Railroad) on her finger, then he continues even more intensely, still dwelling on his own character flaws:

My pace is frantic, my temper's cross.
With words romantic I'm at a loss.
I'd be the first one to agree that I'm preoccupied with me.
And it's inbred, kid,
So keep your head, kid.
In me you'll find things like guts and nerve,
But not the kind things that you deserve.
And so while there's a fighting chance, just turn and go.
I won't send roses,
And roses suit you so.

They have reached California, and, as Mack leaves Mabel preparing to debark, she sings her own song of capitulation to this irascible movie workaholic. It ends resignedly, for Mabel now knows the depth of her love for Mack:

And though I know I may be left
Out on a limb
So who needs roses
That didn't come from him?*

In Hollywood, Kleinman and Fox try to talk Mack into making the epics that are all the rage in 1911, but Mack knows where his talent lies and senses his limitations. He sings his doctrine, the jocular "I Wanna Make the World Laugh":

Some have a leaning for dark hidden meaning,
But I wanna make the world laugh.
Let other directors film tragic romance
But I like the hero with ants in his pants.

After a year of producing successful comedies, Sennett's writer, Frank, who secretly loves Mabel, pens a script for her that requires real acting acumen. Mabel protests, "Mack will never let me do it. Besides, it's a feature film and I only do two-reelers." Frank says, "That stultifying despot doesn't respect your integrity as an artist."

Mabel is intrigued by Frank's words, and while Mack directs the ensuing soup-spilling scene, she refuses to move on the counts he has assigned

---

* One should observe Herman's subtle craftsmanship that ends each chorus. Besides the ultimate rhymes of *know* and *so* in Mack's lyric, the penultimate *u*-sound rhyme in Mack's *suit* and *you* is beautifully balanced by the *o* in Mabel's *come* and *from*.

her. "It offends my integrity as an artist," she declares. When he fumes and screams, "One, you turn, two, you reach for the bowl, three, you spill," she grabs a nearby custard pie, throws it at him, and says, "How's that for four?" She has spawned a pie-throwing melée, and soon the whole troupe is covered with custard and meringue. A contrite Mabel apologizes for losing her temper, but Mack is delighted with this new comedy technique she has invented.

In the next scene at the Hollywood Hotel, Mabel meets the director William Desmond Taylor, who is powerfully attracted to her. When Mack calls him a phony, she replies, "It was nice being talked to for a change instead of being bellowed at." When Sennett bellows that shooting will start at the beach in ten minutes, "with you or without you," she walks out. One gets an idea of the intensity of her fury in her exit song, "Wherever He Ain't," a minor-key presto, from the opening lines of its chorus:

> I gotta give my life some sparkle and fizz,
> And think a thought that isn't wrapped up in his.
> The place that I consider paradise is
> Wherever he ain't! Wherever he ain't!

Despite Mabel's departure, Mack almost immediately continues filming, inventing his Sennett Bathing Beauties. He sings another syncopated melody, but this one, replete with little eclectic phrases, seems to indicate that Sennett is groping for new ideas and new people in his life. "Hundreds of Girls" gives the show a much-needed production number before the ending of act one. As the semidressed girls come on one by one, Mack sings:

> I'll make a star and a half out of that one,
> The one with the dimples, the redhead, the fat one.
> How 'bout the one on the blanket, the one playing ball?
> Let's take 'em both—Ah, to hell with it.
> Let's take em all!
> What gives a man ginger and snap?
> Goin' through life with his little ol' lap
> Full of hundreds and hundreds of girls!

The song, which contains one of my favorite rhymes—"Till every fella from Duluth to Atlanta sees/All of his fantasies"—segues into comments on the demand for Sennett's new comedies featuring the Bathing Beauties. But as the act ends, a nostalgic, pensive Mack toys with the napkin ring that Mabel left and, as the lights dim, sings a reprise of "I Won't Send Roses."

Act two begins five years later. The public is no longer taken with Sennett's half-nude beauties, and Mabel Norman has appeared in a string of pretentiously bad pictures under Taylor's direction. Frank suggests that Mack ask Mabel to come back under his aegis. Reluctantly, Mack relents, asks her back with the intention of doing a romantic, noncomedic film. Mabel arrives for filming early the next morning before the crew is on the set. Now the night watchman begins one of Herman's most infections numbers, "When Mabel Comes in the Room."

This song has often been compared with "Hello, Dolly!" and sometimes with "Mame," all being songs of return and praise for a heroine. Indeed, there are surface similarities, since Herman uses the can't-fail technique of sequence, pitching the second phrase of each song a tone higher than the first. But the motif of Mabel's song being chromatic (in contrast to the scaline idea of "Dolly" and "Mame"), besides creating a most infectious, joyful song, is redolent of 1920s moviemaking. Each of these songs is cast in a different form, "Dolly" being ABAC, "Mame" ABAB, and "Mabel" in ABCA, the only one with a release or bridge.* Herman uses the form in its true sense of relief or contrast. The catchy little motif that earlier went up chromatically now descends scalewise.

Mack is overjoyed to be working with Mabel again, but his urge to add comedic touches to pictures will not be denied, and he asks Mabel to wait in her dressing room while he films some background material featuring two clumsy policemen. Unable to stop himself, he adds more mayhem, turning these officers into the Keystone Kops. Mabel is fuming while waiting in the dressing room, as Mack, losing track of time, sings "Hit 'Em on the Head." The song turns into a Keystone Kops production number, which goes a long way toward explaining why violence on the screen can be perceived as being hilarious. I quote from the last chorus:

Cause a little wreck, ha, ha, ha,
Break somebody's neck, ha, ha, ha,
Shoot a little gun, yes, folks, it's scintillating.
Watch the fellow reel and slip on that banana peel, ha, ha,
The public finds it's fun when it's excruciating.
Everybody loves to see policemen futile
In breaking up a brawl that's been divinely brutal,
So, bite 'em in the calf, ha, ha, ha,
Listen to 'em laugh, ha, ha, ha,

* See Glossary for an explanation of different forms of showtunes.

Robert Preston (Mack) rehearses the Keystone Kops in "Hit 'Em on the Head" in previews in San Francisco. Considered too violent, it was cut before the show reached Broadway. Museum of the City of New York.

Make a little slash, make a wider gash,
Hit 'em on the head!

The Kops are wildly successful with the public, while Mabel Normand, who has long since left her dressing room, is about to sail for Europe with Taylor to research backgrounds for a new movie. To avert this, Mack swallows his pride and goes down to the dock just before the liner pulls out.

When the lights come up, Mabel is looking after the loading of some personal belongings, while Mack pretends to have come to the pier to see some other friends off. In his roundabout way he proposes marriage, and she almost accepts. When he says he plans to star her in a serious picture, she is ecstatic. But before he can stop himself, he mentions the comedy role she would play in the film after that. As she turns away, he asks whether he had "said the wrong thing." "You said the only words you could, Mack" she replies, letting us know that the emotion she felt a moment ago has evaporated.

As Mack leaves, Taylor, who has observed the scene, comes down the gangplank intent on altering Mabel's mood. He offers her a drink, which she refuses, and then insists she take a whiff of angel dust. Reluctantly, she does, saying she will forget Mack in time. This is the cue for one of Herman's ballads that is in the top echelon of dramatic art. "Time Heals Everything" was called "one of the greatest theatrical moments of our time," by the chanteuse Mabel Mercer. And who could not agree?

This song shows us many things about Herman's command of his genre. First, it proves that songwriting is not about rhyme. It contains only two, but its clipped, almost clinical prosody (*April, August, patient, break, mend, forget, hell,* all words ending with strong consonants) reveals the power of language to indicate the torture that Mabel—or any person hopelessly in love—is suffering. Besides the sound of the words, there are the lyrical references to the slow passage of time, doled out at the end of each phrase. The musical motif on these semigasped words (*Tuesday, Thursday, April, August*) is a descending second, an appoggiatura—wrong note to right—that sounds like a sob. In the second part of the song the singer interrupts herself by gathering her references and extending the musical continuity in their reiteration (purposely clinging to the same almost boring pair of notes to indicate time's dragginess) before she gives us a riveting scream of pain. On the last repetition of the title, she has skipped to the cruelest interval, a major seventh, at the top of her vocal range. It is as though she is keening to convince herself that "Time Heals Everything." But the song's message is clear. We almost don't need her final three words. We already know that time heals nothing.

> Time heals everything, Tuesday, Thursday,
> Time heals everything, April, August.
> If I'm patient the break will mend,
> And one fine morning, the hurt will end.
> So make the moments fly, autumn, winter,
> I'll forget you by next year, some year.
> Though it's hell that I'm going through,
> Some Tuesday, Thursday, April, August,
> Autumn, winter, next year, some year,
> Time heals everything, time heals everything—
> But loving you.

A blackout with Mabel on the steamship, and the lights come up on Mack, who now fills the audience in on Mabel's sordid affair and how Frank has left to write pictures with "spoken words." He concludes his soliloquy by telling us about how Lottie, "that broken-down hoofer," hit it big. "Hell," he admits, "if you could say words on that screen, you could sing. And if you could sing . . . you could dance!"

This brings on one of Herman's most charming and campiest numbers, "Tap Your Troubles Away." Although it has been criticized for having some images in poor taste, its lyric really reflects the crudeness, body jokes, and child porn that had invaded the early talkies. This song skewers the reigning tap dancers of the early Vitaphone Varieties—Ruby Keeler, Eleanor Powell, and the other tightfisted, bent-kneed tappers. The lyrics are hilarious, and like Cole Porter's, they get funnier with each succeeding verse. I quote from my own favorite, the second one:

Tap your troubles away.
You're sued for divorce,
Your brother gets locked up.
Tap your troubles away,
You're fat as a horse,
And find that you're knocked up.
When you need something to turn your mind off,
Why not try tapping your poor behind off?
Your boat goes over the falls,
The plane you're on stalls,
The pilot yells, "Pray!"
When your parachute strap
Is beginning to snap,
Smile a big smile and
Tap, tap, tap, your troubles away.

In between the second and third choruses Stewart has inserted a dumb-show of the scandalous murder of William Desmond Taylor, followed by a newsboy shouting "Extra, Extra!"

And then we are back in Mack's studio, where Kleinman is exulting over Lottie's success while Mack wonders why Mabel doesn't fight the adverse publicity, bordering on libel, with which the tabloids have hit her. Believing in her innocence, Mack confronts Mabel to tell her of his resolve to make the serious picture he had promised her before she went off to Europe. When she accepts his offer, he brings out the napkin ring and reminds her of her lines, changing them to "when two people get married, even for a single *picture*, they need a ring." Mabel begins to weep, and Sennett, always the director, orders her to stop: "One, you turn. Two, you wipe your eyes. Three, smile. Four, you smile." And the music comes up on the final wedding song, "I Promise You a Happy Ending," which, if it had a less interesting melodic line or less adventurous harmonic underpinning, could be maudlin. (Note the quasi-religious use of the I III V I chords and the wonderful "blue note," the A flat in third and fourth bars of the melody, against a bright dominant chord. Its elegaic melody belies the "happy ending" Mack has promised.)

I promise you a happy ending
Like the ones that you see on the screen.
So if you've had a bad beginning
Love will come out winning in the closing scene.
And when you find it rough contending
With the grind that the world puts us through,
I can promise you a happy ending,
That has you loving me,
Loving you.

The almost-wedding is followed by Mack's final speech, back on his old soundstage. He recounts the story of the making of Mabel's last picture, *Molly-O,* and its failure, which broke Sennett financially. Then Mack gives some of the details of Mabel's death in 1930, reminding us that the entire musical has been a flashback.

Dispensing with reality, he calls all the cast together for a happy ending, the way he would have liked the story to end had he been in charge. When the cast exits, leaving only Mack and Mabel, one sees their figures receding, a common fadeout device in the silent era, alone, silhouetted against a red Hollywood sky. Curtain.

With the Michael Stewart's sensitive libretto completed and Herman's atmospheric score awaiting orchestration, the team brought the project to Gower Champion, who had contributed so much to the success of *Hello, Dolly!* Champion's career had been in decline in recent years, with only a restaging of the old operetta, *Irene,* on the plus side, heavily counterbalanced by the flops of *The Happy Time* and *Prettybelle.* The director needed a superhit to revive his flagging reputation, and he accepted the assignment eagerly. When Champion suggested David Merrick as producer for this project, Herman, recalling the torturous weeks Merrick had put him through in the *Hello, Dolly!* days, was less than enthusiastic. But on second thought, Herman realized that then he had then been a neophyte; now, with two gigantic hits to his credit, he could no longer be placed in such an inferior position by Merrick. He went along with Champion's choice. The Dolly trio—Herman, Stewart, and Champion—felt confident that with the addition of Merrick their early-movie odyssey was in capable hands. A Broadway opening was planned for early October 1974, following a healthy break-in tour across the country, starting in San Diego. Merrick had reserved one of Broadway's best houses for musicals, the Majestic, as the home for what promised to be a rousing success.

Herman supervised the selection of the splendid cast, headed by Robert Preston. Preston had appeared as Beauregard in the movie *Mame,* which was to open at the Radio City Music Hall only a few months before *Mack and Mabel* hit New York. Herman had worked with Preston a decade before, when he had written "To Be Alone with You," to be interpolated into *Ben Franklin in Paris.* That song had become the hit of the show.

Bernadette Peters, then an up-and-coming musical star, was not the first choice for the role of Mabel.* Herman wanted Marcia Rodd, a strong

---

* Bernadette Peters (1948–) born Bernadette Lazarra in Queens, has become one of the Broadway musical's most bankable leading ladies. She has been in the limelight since she was three. So as not to be typed in ethnic Italian roles, she changed her name at nine (taking her father's first name for her last). She made her Broadway debut in 1967 in *No Trump.* The next year she appeared in *George M* and was a sensation as the star of off-Broadway's *Dames at Sea.* In 1969 she created the sensitive Gelsomina in *La Strada,* and that year she received her first Tony nomination for her role of Brunhilde Esterhazy in the revival of *On the Town.* She finally took home the award for Best Actress in a Musical in 1986, when she starred in *Song and Dance.*

A baby-faced Herman, backstage at an early rehearsal of 1974's *Mack and Mabel,* **with Robert Preston (Mack), Bernadette Peters (Mabel), and librettist Mike Stewart. Photograph: Martha Swope.**

singer, but Champion was going for a name. The group auditioned Kelly Garrett, who had done feature roles on Broadway and who could really belt out the songs. Again Champion nixed this dynamo. At last, Herman suggested Peters. "She has the voice," he said, "she has the humor, and is absolutely unique." Champion auditioned her and agreed.

For the important featured role of Lottie, Champion chose Lisa Kirk, who had been doing supper club acts since her heyday in the late 1940s, when she was featured in *Allegro* and *Kiss Me Kate.* By 1974 both Kirk and Preston, seasoned troupers that they were, were beyond the age when they could muster the youthful vitality needed to portray young blood in a brand new industry, but their names were well known, and they both knew how to put over a song.

Trouble started from the day Champion decided to use a unit set. Designer Robin Wagner worked imaginatively within the very limited concept to keep the action in one corner of a huge soundstage. The idea was an intriguing one, but it proved to be much too static. The permanently angled walls of the set made it impossible to use flies to bring in new backdrops or change scenery. According to Herman, "It became boring, but by the time we realized it, it was too late to change."

Merrick flew into a rage when he saw the design for the set and told Herman and Stewart that he wanted to fire Champion. They talked him out of it, pointing out that they "owed this man *Hello, Dolly!* and everything we've gotten from the superhit," Herman said. "I never thought the mockup of the set was a good idea, but I trusted Gower and said, 'If he wants to do it in a corner, we'll do it in a corner.' When the set went up, we realized how depressing, dark, and unrelenting it was, and David came to me and said, 'I can't afford to do a new set, and I fear we've lost our show.'"[3]

Sylvia Hersher, the production associate, put her finger on another weakness besides the set. "The concept was wrong. Dark. The show takes place in California, and should have been light, open. Then in the moments when Mack is torn, the contrast becomes that much greater."[4]

Herman blames Champion, too, for devoting too much time to one production number that involved the Keystone Kops at the expense of other scenes. Certainly Champion was trying to re-create one of the high spots in all musical theater—"The Waiters' Gallop," the glorious mayhem that preceded Dolly's entrance. "This time he created a fantastic sequence in which the cops came running when a fire broke out in a hospital," he recalled. "Bells and sirens went off and there were hoses and ladders and actors running around in all directions. It was a spectacular dance piece and very cleverly done. But that number took most of our rehearsal time, most of our preview time before Gower realized that you can't make living human beings on a stage look like silent movie characters."

Before the San Diego opening, Herman began to realize that neither Mack nor Mabel made a truly lovable musical hero or heroine. Sennett, being a tough black-Irish businessman who was totally wrapped up in making movies, and Mabel, willful, vulnerable, and likable but without the great force that is essential in a musical theater character, made for a constrained relationship. "Besides," Herman stated, "even when you put these people together they were not intrinsically lovable." It is permissible, Herman feels, "to have a hero and heroine without personality, but then you must create great empathy for them—and only in opera can you get away with a heroine who dies unhappily."

"The line that announced Mabel's death in 1930 used to take all the air out of the audience," Herman recalled. "You could actually hear them deflating." Herman begged Gower and Mike not to end the show like that, especially since Mabel went on to live, presumably happily, with Cody for seven years before she died. Besides, he argued, stark truth was not the point here, since Stewart had beautifully fictionalized the early scenes, making Mabel a deli delivery girl instead of the model she really was. "But Gower was going through what I call his Chekhov period," Herman said, "and had taken on *Mack and Mabel* because it was a more serious musical. He wanted to take it one step further and make it even darker."

After the San Diego premiere, which was well received by press and public, the show went on to Los Angeles for further work. Again it got enthusiastic approval, and all concerned felt sure that, with a few minor revisions, they would have a hit. Then, in the trek East, Merrick booked the show into Muni, the 11,000-seat outdoor arena run by the St. Louis Municipal Opera Company. The booking was a terrible mistake. The place was so enormous that the principals couldn't possibly bring any subtlety or charm to the characters. Preston and Peters had to overplay their parts on that enormous stage, and in their overacting they pulled the show, a simple human comedy, drastically out of shape.

The problems got worse when the show got to Washington en route to New York. "Nothing was working," Herman remembered. Champion became frantic, restaging scenes that had worked well on the West Coast. Herman, wanting to be a good collaborator, could do nothing but agree. The Keystone Kops number featuring "Hit 'Em in the Head," which had taken so much time in rehearsal, was replaced. Champion, fearing that critics would compare his ballet to Jerome Robbins's 1947 revered Kops ballet in *High Button Shoes,* wanted a new number here. On the road Herman turned out the milder "Every Time a Cop Falls Down."*

"Gower choreographed a charming softshoe for the new song, but it never had the vitality of the original Kops number," Herman felt. "That was a loss, not a gain, and it was typical of the tinkering done on the show, which was fatally overworked on the road. Instead of concentrating on its true weaknesses, we spent months and months fixing things that didn't need to be fixed." So when it finally opened on Broadway, Herman felt, for the first time in his career, "The show was *less* polished and *less* perfect than the production that had opened in the West four months earlier."

Opening night, 6 October 1974 in New York, was disastrous: an onstage accident "was fatal to the show, and almost fatal to members of the cast," ac-

---

* Softpedaling the violence in the title, and making it sound more like a ballad, the song was listed in the program as "My Heart Leaps Up."

cording to Herman. In the middle of "Tap Your Troubles Away," a huge piece of the background set crashed down. It came near crushing Lisa Kirk and some of the girls in the chorus. They stopped tapping and stood frozen with fear. All theatrical illusion was lost, and it was hard to get the show going again once the debris was cleared. The cast never recovered and neither did the show.

Critics were kind enough not to mention the accident, but the reviews were harsh. Clive Barnes in the *New York Times* gave the most positive review. He rather enjoyed the show's score, saying it contained "one or two catchy, and one or two lushly attractive songs." He summed it up as "a musical in the old and true tradition—tuneful music, lively staging, and a bundle of pretty girls in classy costumes by Patricia Zipprodt, and imaginative settings by Robin Wagner."[5]

All the others seemed gleeful to take potshots at the show and especially at Herman. None of them seemed to agree as to what the musical's main trouble was. Douglas Watt in the *Daily News* accused the songs of "sounding pretty much alike—brisk and empty."[6] He was joined by most of his colleagues in panning the whole "When Mabel Comes in the Room" segment as a rehash of the Harmonia Gardens scene in *Hello, Dolly!* One critic accused Champion of consistently using the same cakewalk style that sparked the earlier musical, adding that Herman seemed "to fall back on this whenever he feels the need for a sure-fire number—and the more he does it, the less sure fire it is."[7]

Other aisle sitters voiced different complaints: the use of flashback to tell the story, Stewart's juggling the true facts of Mabel's early and late years, the lack of chemistry between a "grandfatherly Robert Preston" and a "too cutesy Bernadette Peters." *Newsweek*'s Jack Kroll mixed his media by calling *Mack and Mabel* "a bollixed up show that should have been as good as *Singin' in the Rain.*"[8]

Audiences responded enthusiastically to the show, but coming in at the enormous cost of almost a million dollars, and with a very large cast to support, the musical needed rave reviews to fill a large theater like the Majestic. The show was building its audience slowly, and seemed to be getting a toehold when David Merrick abruptly decided to close it after eight weeks. Stewart and Herman begged him to keep it running because word of mouth was excellent, but Merrick, who usually initiated intensive advertising campaigns to combat so-so or bad reviews, could not be swayed. The Shuberts, who owned the Majestic, were no help, as they had no interest in keeping *Mack and Mabel* on the boards. They had booked the theater for *The Wiz,* which, from the advance reports, looked like a big hit. According to the final tally, as listed in *Variety, Mack and Mabel* had lost almost its entire investment.

Herman was devastated when he heard about the Tony nominations that spring, for though *Mack and Mabel* received eight nominations in major categories, two more than the eventual winner, *The Wiz*, his score was completely ignored.* To flesh out to four the number of nominees for Best Score of a Musical, after citing *Shenandoah* and *The Wiz*, the Tony committee had to scrape the barrel and add *The Lieutenant*, a depressing rock opera based on the My Lai incident in Vietnam, and *A Letter for Queen Victoria*, a stream-of-consciousness play without continuity. Each of these abject failures closed within a week. Nominations for these avant-garde shows leave no doubt that the critics were looking for the outré that year.

But that was not to be the end of the road for this, Herman's best-loved of all his works. Like *Dear World, Mack and Mabel* was to become a revered cult musical, and an especial favorite of gay audiences after it was featured in the movie version of *Love! Valour! Compassion!* The show was to have many revivals, a strong rebirth in Britain and, even as I write, a planned restaging on Broadway. Besides that, the original cast recording is still selling briskly.

The late choreographer Ron Field mounted the first "corrective" production, starring Lucie Arnaz and David Cryer, and shortly after that the Papermill Playhouse in New Jersey staged another version which restored the gutsy "Hit 'Em on the Head." When Herman saw that version, he says, "I knew what had to be done to fix the show."

In 1984, after the British ice skating team of Torville and Dean used *Mack and Mabel*'s overture as the music for their gold medal–winning Olympic figure skating competition, the BBC was inundated with calls asking what the music was. In response to the interest, the recording company rereleased the original cast album. The record rose to number six on the charts—unheard of for a show album, especially one that is ten years old.

Then in 1988 Herman and producer Barry Mishon put together an all-

---

* Besides a nomination as Best Musical of the Season, nominations were given to Bernadette Peters (Best Actress in a Musical), Robert Preston (Best Actor in a Musical), Robin Wagner (Best Scenic Design), Patricia Zipprodt (Best Costume Design), Michael Stewart (Best Book of a Musical), and Gower Champion (Best Choreographer and Best Director of a Musical). None won a Tony.

star charity concert. George Hearn sang "Movies Were Movies," Georgia Brown did "Time Heals Everything," and Tommy Tune danced his heart out to "Tap Your Troubles Away." Sheridan Morley, Britain's premier theatrical critic, called the score "one of the richest and most distinctive in the whole postwar history of Broadway."

While all this was going on, the producer Jon Wilner, a longtime Herman fan, worked toward remounting the show. "I don't want to live in a world without his songs," he said, "and needed to do something about it."[9] He commissioned the late Mike Stewart's sister, the writer Francine Pascal, to revise scenes and especially the ending of the musical, so as to eliminate the "downer effect."[10] The script now ends when Mabel returns to Mack's studio to make her comeback movie. Mack knows that the project is hopeless and will ruin him financially, but he makes the movie anyway. This romantic ending seems most appropriate to these somewhat cardboard characters, for the whole show seems a fantasy, far removed from reality.

In 1995 Wilner reopened the show in England's favorite try-out town, Leicester. Because there were new orchestrations and many book changes, Herman flew over to supervise the production. Early feedback was so glorious that the show accumulated a million pounds in advance receipts before it opened in London—topping the reigning hit, George and Ira Gershwin's *Crazy for You.* Two months later Wilner brought it to London's cavernous Piccadilly Theatre.

Since the Piccadilly, off the main stem, is hidden from tourists, Wilner had the theater painted red and rented a big neon sign in Piccadilly Circus to announce *Mack and Mabel*'s presence. He needn't have bothered. The British critics loved the show, would have discovered it had it been playing in a back alley, and were quick to give it headlines. The *Financial Times* reviewer wrote, "The brilliance and intelligence of Jerry Herman's lyrics match the songs with a fizz that has seldom been found in the musical theatre of the last thirty years." Two weeks later *Mack and Mabel* won one of England's most prestigious prizes, the *Evening Standard* Award for Best Musical. The show played successfully for ten months, and though it did not turn a profit—because of its large cast and costly sets—it did break even.

Francine Pascal's much improved book was used again in 1999 for the Barrington Stage production in Great Barrington, Massachusetts, directed by Julianne Boyd, as well as in the Los Angeles Reprise Production in 2000.

Turning a failed show into a big hit a quarter-century later is not unique. It is often hard to see the faults in the limited time allotted to

Jerome Lawrence, left, and Jerry Herman, right, receive the Zeta Beta Tau Man of Distinction award from Burton Litwin. Lawrence and Herman were ZBT brothers during their college days. Zeta Beta Tau Fraternity Archives.

mount, rehearse, and premiere a show en route to Broadway. Hammerstein spent years tinkering with the second act of *Show Boat* and rewriting *Allegro*. Sondheim constantly works with producers to polish his shows so that they may have a continuing life, and Lloyd-Webber has been known to close down a show in performance in order to accomplish a complete rewrite.

Herman's unique score needed no reworking, but the critics, heeding Hammerstein's dictum that "the book is paramount," dismissed Stewart's prosaic libretto, and overlooked the most atmospheric score of the decade. But in Herman's own words, time heals everything, and from the vantage point of a quarter-century later *Mack and Mabel*'s score is on a par with *Mame,* Herman's finest.

Herman is overjoyed that his show has joined *Hello, Dolly!, Mame,* and *La Cage aux Folles* as his "fourth big hit" and feels that henceforth it will never again be perceived as a failure. "The most beautiful thing about Jerry," says Sylvia Hersher, "is that when he says, 'I Promise You a Happy Ending,' he truly tries to make it."[11] Herman, always positive, agrees and crows that he was able to turn the fate of this show around—"the single most gratifying accomplishment of my career."

But no matter how he tinkered with it, his next show, *The Grand Tour,* would remain unfixable.

11

the grand tour

By the beginning of 1975, after *Mack and Mabel*'s abrupt close, Jerry Herman felt like a fish whose tank has run dry. Accustomed throughout the sixties to having two, sometimes three shows running on Broadway, he now had none. Worse, with the critiques for his last two flops resounding in his ears, he realized that the kinds of musicals he felt comfortable attending—or writing—were quickly disappearing. The concept musical that had begun as far back as *Love Life* (1948), and was nurtured with shows like *Cabaret* (1966), had come to full flowering in *Company* (1970). Shows like these made Herman feel that his type of old-fashioned scene-followed-by-song musical was passé. Topical revue was still popular, with shows like *Rodgers and Hart* and *A Musical Jubilee* scheduled for production that spring, but that was a form he had outgrown by the time he was thirty.

What affected Herman most was that rock, a form he did not understand, had taken over the pop charts, and seemed poised to envelop musical theater. *Hair* in 1968 had not been a mere blip on the screen; it had proved that rock would find a long-running place on Broadway. *Godspell, Jesus Christ Superstar, Grease,* and *The Rocky Horror Show* all had recently explored that idiom in intriguing ways. *The Wiz,* a rock version of *The Wizard of Oz,* had even ousted *Mack and Mabel* from its theater. Musicals whose songs had previously made "Your Hit Parade" were dodos of a bygone age. Herman deplored that he hadn't been born thirty years earlier so that he might have written "twenty shows before my musical era came to an end." Although he continued his love affair with the piano, able to lose himself for hours replaying his own music, and the songs of his generation, he refused to think of trying to change his style. Actually, he would not have known how.[1]

After the Tony Awards in the spring of 1975 Herman was so affected by the uncanny dismissal of what he considered his finest score that he decided to stop writing musicals entirely. Hefty royalties were still rolling in from touring and local productions of *Hello, Dolly!* and *Mame,* and, with dozens of annual high school and college productions, they had become "standards" whose income seemingly would never dry up. Additionally, recordings, original cast, and cover versions were selling briskly, not only of the big hits but even of *Milk and Honey* and *Dear World.* One could live luxuriously throughout the sixties and seventies solely from the income from the more than 130 different recordings of the single song "Hello, Dolly!"[2] Besides that, Herman had amassed a fortune from the sale of his two blockbusters to the movies.

Uninterested in the new librettos offered for his consideration, Herman returned them unread. But the lack of musical creation, and of the joy he got from collaboration, left a big hole in Herman's life. He filled it by overseeing small or touring productions of his hit shows, visiting his large circle of friends, taking cruises, and shuttling between New York and his second love, southern California—specifically Beverly Hills and Palm Springs. Once the bloom wore off this dolce far niente life, the man, energetic to the point of obsessiveness, turned his mind to his second love: interior design.

Herman's experience in creative design had started back in his revue years, when he had redone his tiny Greenwich Village walk-up by removing the plaster and exposing raw brick. Alice Borden, who rehearsed there, frequently termed it "a daring innovation in those days, so chic."[3] After *Milk and Honey* opened, Herman could afford a garden apartment, which allowed him more leeway. He took off all the doors and made new ones to simulate barn doors, turning the urban setting into a country one with stripped light pine floors and natural brick. His choice (then and now) of unusual color schemes defines Herman's style: beige or white with a single color accent. In his Greenwich Village days the accent had been royal blue.

After *Hello, Dolly!* opened and was a tremendous hit, he bought his first real home, Edward Albee's dark, depressing town house on West Tenth Street. Installing a copper and glass skylight, he transformed it into a sunny showplace worthy of a lead article in *House Beautiful,* an eight-page, full-color spread.[4]

As Herman became more successful in his musical career, he felt himself capable of taking time off to expand his designing skills. Back in 1962, he had had the audacity to be his own architect and built a splendid, mostly glass beach house on Fire Island that brought reflections of sand and sea inside.

Feeling himself now capable of any architectural challenge, he bought a large duplex penthouse in an art deco building at 55 Central Park West which came with a roof garden that he knew he "could turn into something marvelous."

Herman moved right in and started tearing the place apart. It wasn't musical theater, he acknowledged, but it gave him something creative to wake up to every morning. To help him in this endeavor he contacted his longtime friend, the building contractor Charles "Chuck" Fultz. "We work together nicely," says Fultz. "I love tearing walls down and he loves watching them go up so he can decorate them."[5]

Not only did Herman design the job, he shopped it, contracted it, and oversaw all the work, turning the eight smallish rooms into four comfortable living spaces. With twelve workmen working for a full year, at last he had created something spectacular. The new rooms had sleek lines with glorious views of the park and walls covered in gray flannel. Herman furnished the rooms with Lucite coffee tables and a staircase worthy of Ziegfeld, embedded with little twinkling lights that led to the roof garden. The composer lived happily for a year in what he called "my fantastic stage set," and then decided to sell it when Calvin Klein made him an offer he couldn't refuse.

The experience of designing this penthouse whetted his appetite, and a year later, when his restlessness impelled him to leave New York for Hollywood, he decided to further indulge his love for interior design and buy a house in Beverly Hills, live in it while he fixed it up, and then sell it—as he says, "for a lot of money."

After that, Herman began thinking of interior design not as a hobby but as a tandem profession along with his music, and he gave it his usual passion. He has since won prestigious awards for his dozens of houses. Among his most cherished honors is one from his alma mater, the Parsons School of Design.

He has an uncanny eye for choosing the site, believes the old adage "location, location, location," and is not afraid to pay top dollar for superb residential property. Besides his strong sense of architectural design, according to Fultz, he has a strong aptitude for nuance. "He loves the color mushroom, and senses all the subtlety of the variations within it. 'Does it have a little blue, a little green, a little red?' he will say. And although the impression of the neutrality is on one level, he sees far more variation and depth to this color than one could ever imagine. In a way, that's who he is. But in creating that perception of a pale background color, Jerry contrasts it vibrantly with any of the other colors of the rainbow."

One of the first West Coast houses Herman redid had been the honeymoon home of Elizabeth Taylor and Michael Wilding. Although the house was desperately in need of work when Herman bought it in the mid-1960s, its location high on a hillside in Beverly Hills was ideal, commanding a spectacular panoramic view. He relished the fact that one "could wake up in the morning, take your cup of tea outside and gaze at the Pacific Ocean, miles away." He did not think he overpaid when he bought the property for a million dollars—an enormous sum at the time.

Herman turned that house into an English gentleman's abode by putting down hardwood floors and covering the walls with hand-loomed fabric, finishing the place with comfortable armchairs "to make it cozy" and imported antiques to give it "style." By the time the house was completed, in the late 1960s, the real estate market had dropped, and Herman, ready to go back to New York, feared he would have to take a loss to unload this property.

That was at the time of the London opening of *Hello, Dolly!*, when Herman flew from Hollywood to be consulted on any of the show's last-minute changes. Charles Lowe, Carol Channing's husband, insisted that Herman accompany Lady Rothmere, whose husband owns the *Daily Mail*, to the premiere. Always a bundle of nerves on opening nights, Herman objected vociferously but to no avail. The account from his memoir gives a glimpse of his style—and acumen:

> So on opening night, I arrived in front of the Savoy. Standing right in front was my date, an enormous woman . . . wearing a pink gown with tiers and tiers of pink tulle that went all the way to the floor. She looked like a living lampshade. All I could think of was that scene in *Dolly* when Ernestina dresses up in all her gaudy finery.
>
> I almost told the cab driver to keep on going. Of course, I didn't, but under my breath I said, "Charles Lowe, I'm gonna get you for this." Then I stepped out of the cab, gave my hand to my guest, and was as charming as I could be.
>
> Lady Rothmere—"Bubbles" was what she asked me to call her—turned out to be a very lovely lady with very bubbly personality. She almost smothered me in the taxicab with all that pink tulle, but I survived—and on the way to the theater I sold her my house for two million dollars.[6]

Herman's self-imposed exile from the theater ended after Michael Stewart called one day and said he had the "perfect play for us to set." It was based on S. N. Behrman's adaptation of *Jacobowsky and the Colonel,* which had been successfully presented on Broadway in 1943, then in 1958 made into a second-rate film starring Danny Kaye and Kurt Jurgens. Herman read the play and found it "interesting," but he really didn't want to write a musical about a man running from the Nazis. "I would rather do something with showgirls," he ventured. "Okay, forget about it," said Stewart, and Herman promptly forgot about it until six months later, when Stewart called again.

"We've got the money, we've got the Palace Theatre, and we've got Joel Grey to star," he announced. Tempted he was, but still Herman was not convinced that the project was for him until Stewart came over the next day with producer Diana Shumlin. She was certain that Herman's kind of songs was just what was needed for this musical. When Mike reminded him how long it had been since they had had a show on Broadway, and how joyously they had worked together, Herman began to weaken. In rereading the play, looking for spots for musicalization, he found plenty of places that, as he says, "needed to sing." A few weeks later the trio, Herman, Stewart, and Shumlin, began work.

The creation of *The Grand Tour,* as the musical was called, was incredibly smooth, compared to the journey to the stage of its progenitor *Jacobowsky and the Colonel.* The drama began at a dinner party, where Gottfried Reinhardt, son of the famed director Max Reinhardt, heard a gripping story told by the raconteur Franz Werfel.* Werfel recounted the saga of the escape over the Alps of his friend the Stuttgart banker S. L. Jacobowicz. Reinhardt thought that these adventures, in which the fugitive outwitted the Nazis at every turn, would make a wonderful play, but Werfel felt the stories were merely after-dinner tales of high adventure, too slight for an evening in the theater. Reinhardt persisted and offered Werfel a 50 percent share if he would let him turn this picaresque saga into a play. Eventually Werfel capitulated.

Reinhardt chose to collaborate with well-known playwright S. N. Behr-

---

* Franz Werfel (1890–1945), Czech born poet, playwright, and novelist, was the author of such best-sellers as *Forty Days of Musa Dagh* and his most popular work, *The Song of Bernadette.* The latter book had its origin when Werfel, a Jew, found solace in the pilgrimage town of Lourdes, where St. Bernadette had had visions of the Virgin. Werfel promised to "sing her song" if he ever reached the United States. Fleeing the Nazis, he crossed the Pyrenees on foot and eventually made his way to California, where he wrote the promised book, as well as *Jacobowsky and the Colonel.*

man.* The trio were halfway through when Werfel changed his mind and decided to dramatize the story himself. Furious, Behrman and Reinhardt threatened a lawsuit, but Werfel ignored them.

When the Theater Guild rejected his play as overlong and preachy, Werfel started afresh with Clifford Odets as collaborator. To add to Werfel's problems, S. L. Jacobowicz, who had not been consulted about the dramatization, heard about the race to produce a play based on his life and demanded a share of the project. He threatened an injunction against the work, now subtitled by Werfel "The Comedy of a Tragedy." Werfel agreed reluctantly to cut Jacobowicz in. Once again his play was offered to the Guild and deemed not stageworthy. Werfel rewrote, this time collaborating with the producer Jed Harris. They had not quite finished the last rewrite when the Guild optioned Behrman's version and opened it on Broadway, starring Louis Calhern as the Colonel and Oscar Karlweiss as Jacobowsky. The play was an immediate hit, and eventually the royalty arrangements were sorted out, but the animosity remained, and many said that the stress contributed to Werfel's premature death two years later.

Mike Stewart's version (written in collaboration with his friend Mark Bramble) was a very free adaptation of the Jacobowsky saga as outlined by Werfel at that dinner table twenty years earlier. Aiming to point the austere story in the direction of musical comedy, Stewart excised Werfel's protracted philosophical discussions between the two thousand-year old Wandering Jew and St. Francis in favor of endless confrontations between Jacobowsky and the Colonel for the love of the Colonel's inamorata, Marianne. For excitement, he substituted scenes which transported the audience to a carnival. He had Jacobowsky stumble on a Jewish wedding so that he might have the opportunity to bring on the ensemble. With the Nazis in hot pursuit of a little band of survivors, the musical had the feeling of a *Fiddler on the Roof* redux, fifteen years too late.

The show's "Prologue" finds Jacobowsky on stage alone. He sings one of Herman's most meaningful songs, "I'll Be Here Tomorrow," which gives us insight into the flight of Jacobowsky—and all the European Jews—from

---

* S[amuel] N[athaniel] Behrman (1891–1972) usually wrote plays set in genteel upper-class drawing rooms, dramatizing conflicts of conscience among wealthy privileged characters. He produced a series of urbane and curiously impersonal high comedies such as *The Second Man* (1927), *Biography* (1932), *End of Summer* (1936), and *No Time for Comedy* (1939).

land to land. The verse of this important statement, a kind of recitative, sets the scene:

> Mama took the dishes, the furniture,
> Mama took the pillows, the candlesticks,
> Mama took the children and fled to Berlin.
> I grew into manhood, a citizen,
> I went into business, a patriot,
> Foolishly believing I belonged in Berlin.
> Then that knock on the door
> In the dead of the night.
> And that voice saying
> "Run! The sky is falling. Run! The ship is sinking!"
> Through the blind confusion I remember still what I was thinking—

Then the chorus:

> I'll be here tomorrow, alive and well and thriving,
> I'll be here tomorrow, my talent is surviving.
> If before the dawn this fragile world might crack,
> Someone's gotta try to put the pieces back.
> So, from beneath the rubble, you'll hear a little voice say,
> "Life is worth the trouble,
> Have you a better choice?"
> So let the skeptics say, "Tonight we're dead and gone,"
> I'll be here tomorrow—simply going on.*

Succeeding verses, wherein the music is a free recitative, talk about Jacobowsky's flight to Vienna, and from there to Paris. The long soliloquy becomes an expository aria, an intriguing contrast to the chorus, whose melody is simple, matter-of-fact, and sequential. This very effective preamble gives us great insight to Jacobowsky's character and sets out the ultra-serious tone of the musical to come. It pokes a hole into costar Ron Holgate's thesis that "I'll Be Here Tomorrow" opens the show with the wrong

---

* On 10 November 2001 Jerry Herman was honored with the Nedda Harrington Logan award, the highest honor the Actors' Fund can bestow. To conclude the all-star program, Herman himself performed this song, changing "I'll" to "We'll," thereby making it relevant to the September 11 calamity at New York's World Trade Center. The song, with lines like "from beneath the rubble," and "simply going on," resonated deeply in the audience's consciousness and seemed to possess a freshly minted quality.

thought. "The show is not about the Diaspora," Holgate, who played Colonel Tadeusz Stjerbinsky, maintains, "but it's about the conflict between the Jewish guy and the Polish guy."[7] Unfortunately, Holgate misses the point that Stewart and Herman were trying to make, for by the time the musical reached Broadway, Werfel's thesis, the clash of cultures, had been downsized and Jacobowsky's part had been built up. This scene and song limn Jacobowsky better than a drawing might have, for they distill the optimism that has kept this plucky character alive and one step ahead of the Nazis.

The actual play begins after Jacobowsky's credo. We are at a small hotel in Montmartre, where both Jacobowsky and Colonel Stjerbinsky are staying. It is the morning of an air raid, and the Colonel, headstrong and too imperious to retire to the shelter, is receiving important war papers listing the names of Polish underground forces.* He is instructed that he is to travel to St. Nazaire and meet up with another agent, who will be wearing a boutonniere. He is to give him the password, "For Liberty," and take the boat to London, where he will deliver the papers to a representative of the Polish government in exile. Should the papers fall into the hands of the Gestapo, it would mean the death of dozens of Polish patriots.

Jacobowsky, meanwhile, has arranged to buy a large touring Rolls-Royce. But once it is delivered, he realizes he does not know how to drive it, and he tries to intrigue the Colonel and his orderly to accompany him to the border, for he, like all the rich Jews, is fleeing the Nazis. The snobbish, anti-Semitic officer refuses to join Jacobowsky, and they have their first confrontation—a war of words which ends in a tie, after Jacobowsky has sung a rousing rah-rah march, and the residents of the hotel have joined him. Finally the Colonel relents and says he will do it, "For Poland." "For keeping the Fatherland out and the Motherland free," sings the Colonel. "This horrendous trip I'm taking / And the sacrifice I'm making? I'll be making for P-O-L-A-N-D."

The Colonel insists that they must take a route to the sea through St. Cyrille, where his lady love, Marianne, lives. The route is foolhardy and perilously close to where the Nazis are encamped, and Jacobowsky tries unsuccessfully to dissuade him. Ultimately he has no choice but to accept that road the hardheaded Colonel has chosen.

In the next scene we meet Marianne. Her companion has tried to cajole her into fleeing, but she, fiercely patriotic and certain her Colonel will keep

---

* Both Werfel's and Behrman's versions of the play begin with a sense of imminent danger, at night, in the cellar of the hotel during an air raid.

his promise to come for her, now sings one of the show's most operatic and ardent songs, "I Belong Here." Built on lower and upper appoggiatura, as well as using a wonderfully wide range, it wrings out the emotions, making it one of Herman's most original creations.*

> I belong here, where a dusty road curls by,
> I belong here, where the birches touch the sky,
> There's nothing splendid or remarkable in any way
> But I open the shutter each day
> And it dazzles my eye.

The Colonel and Jacobowsky appear, but by this time Marianne has gone into the house. Heedless of the danger of Germans lurking nearby, the chivalrous Colonel launches into a touching serenade, "Marianne" Its melody, built mostly on the gentle interval of the third, is felicitous, but the lyric—comparing the inamorata to Jennies, Janes, Janets, pearls from Manila or ginger, lime, and vanilla—seems to go for easy rhymes and tired metaphors, making it more suited to a catalogue than a love song. Still, the melody will not be denied, and when its gentle climax falls on the lovely 9th of the chord (see * in the example on page 215), it is truly an affecting moment.

Marianne, whom Jacobowsky dubs "the spirit of France," refuses to leave her country and go with them even though Jacobowsky points out that the Colonel risked all their lives to come and save her. At last, when they tell her that they need her to help the cause of France and Poland, she agrees to leave with them, and to sew the important papers the Colonel is carrying into the lining of a hat which she stows away in her ever-present hatbox.

With the Germans only ten kilometers away, the fugitives load every-

---

* Lower appoggiatura are marked *; upper ones are marked **.

Don't speak of gin - ger or lime or va - nil - la un -
til you have kissed Mar - i - anne.

thing into the car, then find it out of gas, so Jacobowsky and the adjutant are forced to push it to the station, where they will board a dilapidated train.*

The scene that follows is one of the musical's best inventions. Crowded into a crumbling third-class carriage with passengers, luggage, and livestock, the quartet attempt to divert the other passengers with their optimistic travelogue. The production number, "We're Almost There," sounds like a French can-can and brings the first real sense of joy to the show:

> We're almost there, we're almost there,
> Though there's a million more kilometers to go,
> The window clatters, the engine spatters,
> But with a glass of wine you'll never know.
> A spicy joke, a hand of bridge,
> And we'll forget the trip is tedious and slow.
> The car is musty, the track is rusty,
> We'll end up God knows where.
> But with diversion, its an excursion,
> And so we're almost there.

At the end of the number the conductor announces that the track ahead has been cut by the Germans, and everyone is forced to disembark. The resourceful Stewart has Jacobowsky discover the Manzoni carnival troupe, a touring Hungarian circus, ahead. He convinces the kindly owner to take them along. As luck and operatic coincidence would have it, the troupe's

---

* The use of a train was Michael Stewart's inspiration. Both Behrman's and Werfel's versions continued the entire journey by automobile, Jacobowsky wheedling a certificate for a tankful of *essence* from an off-duty *gendarme.*

strong man has quit earlier that day, and they need someone to fill the costume of "The Hungarian Hercules." Incongruous as it sounds, little Jacobowsky is elected. Throughout the scene, one can sense that Marianne is growing fonder of Jacobowsky, admiring his bravura and acumen for getting them out of every jam. She laughs with him at the joke that life has played on them—much to the Colonel's annoyance. Eventually Marianne bursts out with a song, a stylized tango, "More and More," only to be answered by the Colonel in counterpoint with "Less and Less." The two melodies fit neatly together:

So much potential	When he smiles
He has to still explore,	He aggravates my sinus,
(A genie in a bottle)	When he laughs
If they would listen	He gives me nervous stress.
He could resolve the war,	She thinks he's cuddly,
My Polish Aristotle	As a pup,
His allure,	I think
His charm and his candor,	I'm going
Make this tour seem grander	
and grander	To throw up!
Moment to moment	More and more
I like him more and more!	I like him less and less!

The animosity between the men has built to the point where the Colonel challenges Jacobowsky to a duel. With his adjutant offering to be the Colonel's second, Marianne steps forward as the second for Jacobowsky. Ready to pace and fire, they are interrupted by the appearance of an SS captain and two soldiers. Jacobowsky boasts that he is Hercules, the Hungarian superstrong man who is shot out of a cannon at each performance. Amused, the SS man agrees not to arrest them, but announces that he and other German officers will be at the show. He threatens to send the whole troupe to the concentration camp if they are not who they say they are. This leads to the big finale of the act. As the scene changes to the circus ring, the highly chromatic song, "One Extraordinary [pronounced "Ec-straw-din-nary] Thing" has a calliope sound. The song's lyrical concept is similar to "One Person" from *Dear World* and not very fresh, but that matters little because of the mayhem that is going on on stage:

Change tomorrow's course, do one extraordinary thing,
With inhuman force do one extraordinary thing.

Sail the skies and plumb the depths of the ocean,
Thrill the world and make the universe sing.
Have no great remorse for all the deeds you've never done,
As long as you accomplish one
Extraordinary thing!

As the circus progresses and the Colonel, adjutant, Marianne, and Jacobowsky play their parts, we finally see Jacobowsky being loaded into the cannon. The SS officer asks him a question in Hungarian, to which he replies to the audience, "Seven languages I speak, but no Hungarian." The SS man, realizing the fraud, orders everyone to halt, but Marianne has already lit the cannon fuse, and Jacobowsky is shot across the arena.* In the ensuing mayhem, Jacobowsky, who has somehow emerged unharmed, has found a man with a truck hauling nets to the coast. He has places for three more passengers, and Jacobowsky persuades him to take the Colonel, Marianne, and the adjutant with him. When they object to the separation, he reminds them how disastrous it would be for the names of those free men fighting for Poland to fall into Nazi hands, and convinces them to leave at once. Marianne still objects, but Jacobowsky says he will be safe by going south to Spain, and thence across to America. They say their goodbyes and he is left alone on stage. Just before the act ends, Jacobowsky picks up Marianne's hatbox, looks inside, and exclaims, "My God! That schlemiel has forgotten the papers!" Then, smiling at the thought of seeing Marianne again, he resolves to change his course, vowing to meet up with them despite the risk to his life. As he promises to deliver the papers and reprises "One Extraordinary Thing," the curtain falls.

Act two finds Jacobowsky ensconced on a barge in the southwest of France. In a charming song, "Mrs. S. L. Jacobowsky," he fantasizes on what life would be like if he were married to Marianne. The melody, with two bars in a major key followed by two in the minor indicates, according to Herman, "the Christian-Jewish combination." With lines like "We'll artfully combine, her old world with mine," it shows Herman's utter control of his materials. The lyric ends reflectively:

---

* A dummy is shot across the stage, but one critic remarked that it *looked* like a dummy. Could that critic seriously have expected Joel Grey to consent to being shot from a cannon eight times a week?

And when it's almost over and I'm gray and bent
Trying to remember where the years all went,
Trying to recall how much each moment meant
And looking for the meaning of my life.
When not a soul remembers what my name is,
My lasting claim to fame is
Mrs. Jacobowsky was my wife.

Jacobowsky finally makes it to St. Nazaire, hoping somehow to connect
with the agent for the Polish government to whom he can deliver the docu-
ments. He intrudes on a Jewish wedding and assumes that the father of the
bride, who wears a flower in his lapel, is the agent the Colonel was to meet.
The bride's father mistakes Jacobowsky for the rabbi hired to perform the
ceremony. Herman sets the scene to music, again showing his mastery of the
integrated musical:

Jacobowsky	What a lovely boutonniere you're wearing
	It shows such culture, such style and grace,
	The colonel will be joining us in just a little while,
Bride's Father	I'll tell my wife to set an extra place.
Jacobowsky	Have no fear, the little hat is with me.
	In my safekeeping, and no one knows
Bride's Father	We'll need it for the ceremony. Is it black or white?
Jacobowsky	It's beige and has a veil and little bows.
Bride's Father	Oh, a reformed rabbi!

The song continues in the same amusing vein until Jacobowsky, wanting this presumed agent to recognize him, offers a toast with the code word,
"To Liberty." The father of the bride responds with his own toast, "Mazeltov." This leads into typical Jewish wedding *freilach*. The song is not particularly memorable, but the dance arrangement by Peter Howard and Phil
Lang's orchestrations are splendid.

At the end of the dance one of the wedding guests warns the revelers
that the Germans have crossed the little bridge into the town, so they dis-
perse. Observing that German officers are reluctant to enter a ladies room,
Jacobowsky hides there, and after the enemy departs, he emerges to organize a search party to find the Colonel and Marianne.

They are found on the road nearby. The Colonel is in the agony of self-
abnegation, feeling he has betrayed his country by foolishly losing the papers, while Marianne tries to comfort him and make him think about the

Joel Grey, who starred in Herman's 1979 musical *The Grand Tour,* caught
here during a sensitive moment singing the reprise of "Marianne."
Photofest, Inc.

qualities of the man who began as his adversary and now has become his savior. He talks about what it is like to lie in a ditch hoping not to be discovered by the enemy. From the hunter he has metamorphosed into the prey. In one of Herman's most compelling songs, "I Think, I Think," the Colonel has his own epiphany. He admits that he has finally come to understand another hunted person, "a Jacobowsky," but of course, as his last lines indicate, his understanding is self-referential:

> I too have smiled at the danger pretending life doesn't hurt,
> I too have dreamed of the sunlight and had to hide in the dirt.
> I think I used to think "How sad to be a Jacobowsky"
> I think it's far that I have traveled since this traveling began,
> Today I think I think it's not so bad to be a Jacobowsky,
> I think I think someone so much like me must be a very special man.

Herman has a chance to write some liturgical music as the scene shifts to a convent, where the Colonel and Jacobowsky meet up at last. Knowing that the SS is nearby, our quartet get into nuns' habits and outwit the Germans, sending them—in a scene not unlike the ending of *Dear World*—down into the coal pit beneath the abbey and locking the door after them. The Colonel is so grateful to Jacobowsky that he decides to adopt him as an honorary Pole. The two sing the rousing "You I Like," a sort of Yiddish polka full of sequences. The song is in showtune form—that is, ABAB—and its first A is bouncy and fresh. Unfortunately, its tired B section is almost a direct crib from *Mame*'s "It's Today."

> You I like so let me tip my hat,
> In your path I spread my welcome mat.
> You I like, can you imagine that?

Although your ways may be strange
And there's much that I'd change, somehow,
You I like.

The last scene is on the old wharf. The four are waiting for the launch
that will take them to England. Marianne sings a reprise of "I Belong Here,"
but this time the music swells more romantically as the lyric refers to Marianne being enfolded in her Colonel's arms. When the little boat comes
alongside the pier, the captain says he has room only for one, possibly for
two. The orderly decides to make his way somehow back to Poland, and Jacobowsky gives up his place to Marianne. He remains on stage as the
Colonel and Marianne, promising they will all three meet again, depart.
Starting in slow tempo but gradually accelerating to a kind of jaunty tempo,
he sings "I'll Be Here Tomorrow" as the curtain falls.*

Since Michael Stewart was running the enterprise before Herman became involved, he was the one who chose the producers, new to Herman.
James Nederlander and Jack Schussel, in addition to Diana Schumlin, who
had cajoled Herman into coming aboard in the first place, put together a
first-rate production. The director was Gerald Freedman, who, except for
Hair in its original downtown incarnation, was better known for serious
drama than for musicals.† Because of his attention to minutiae, when the
musical opened in San Francisco, it was far too long. Herman did not seem
to mind the inordinate length; he is well-used to whittling shows to size, and
as he says, "It is easier to cut down a show than to flesh one out."

Freedman is the kind of director who takes his time with staging a show,
and, according to Ron Holgate, who played the Colonel, the troupe re-

---

* Both Werfel and Behrman end their dramatizations with Jacobowsky and the
Colonel going off to England, the former to be part of British intelligence and the latter as one of the voices of Free Poland. As their launch sails out, each man promises to
return for Marianne.

† Gerald Freedman (1927–) began his career as an assistant on *Bells Are Ringing* and
made his Broadway debut as director of the revival of *On the Town* in 1959. In 1960 he
began a long association with the New York Shakespeare Festival with an Obie-win-
ning *Macbeth* and served as the festival's artistic director from 1967 until 1971. From
1974 to 1977 he was codirector of the Acting Company. At the time of *The Grand Tour*
he was also director of the American Shakespeare Festival in Stratford, Connecticut,
and worked with New York's Roundabout Theatre. Since 1991 he has been dean of the
North Carolina School of Fine Arts.

hearsed some sections "forever." As a consequence, the scene in the railroad station with everybody crammed into the car took more time than it should have, and "We were late getting into rehearsal where we should have been doing run-throughs. It wasn't until just a day or two before we left for San Francisco that we had any kind of run-through, so we didn't know how long the show ran. Then we got to San Francisco and there were set complications. It had a treadmill going across the stage—and there was a problem getting things on that treadmill so they came out at the right time. A lot of time was spent on that and the technical rehearsal, so when we had the first performance we were a good half-hour over. Mike [Stewart] went ballistic. 'None of my shows ever runs too long,' he yelled. So we came in the next day for rehearsal and he had cut the show down, just disemboweled it, took the life out of it. He ran away from the controversy of the show."

As we have seen, Holgate feels that the show is about a Polish aristocrat and a Jewish refugee. "They can't see each other. Prejudice on both sides. One is a romantic, the other is practical. I remember one thing that shocked both Joel and myself and we didn't know what to do about it. [Stewart] cut out the line where I asked, 'Where do you come from?' and Jacobowsky says, 'Shtutvill,' and I say, 'Ah, Shtutvill. My father had great estates there; your father was a dealer in lending money, no doubt.' And Mike screamed, 'Cut the line!' And I said, 'Why are you cutting this line out?' and he said, 'I felt the audience go—uuh—wince when you said it.' 'What's wrong with that?' I yelled. 'Prejudice, that's what the show's about.' And he didn't appreciate the controversy, and we spent the rest of the time trying to get him to put things back into the show, and he made my part into more of a buffoon, a comic, and took away the point of view of the Colonel—a sort of romantic, heroic quality and how the two get together—so that in the end they both have their pluses and minuses. But much of what he did deballed the show.

"The funny thing is that a few weeks after we opened I went to a performance of *Sweeney Todd,* and Mike was there and came over to me saying, 'What a great show!' And if he thought *Sweeney,* rough and tough as can be, is great, why couldn't he do that with our show?"

What Holgate felt about *The Grand Tour* makes some sense, but he does not observe that Stewart, famed for high comedic librettos, was not musicalizing *Jacobowsky and the Colonel* but writing a musical based on the peregrinations of a Pole, a Frenchwoman, and a Jew. Perhaps if he had hewed more closely to the original confrontational template, the libretto would have gained the depth it lacked. But the seriousness with which Stewart had approached *Mack and Mabel,* and its attendant dismissal by the critics, was still in his craw, and here he returned to light musical comedy, his usual and most comfortable métier. This was reflected in the reviews, for one critic wrote that so earnestly did Herman's and Stewart's musical steer away from controversy that "the word Jew is not used until the final scene."

When the show opened on 11 January 1979, many critics thoroughly enjoyed it. Clive Barnes, writing in the *New York Post,* indulged in superlatives. "I loved *The Grand Tour,*" he wrote. "Joel Grey is one of the consummate artists of our time. I liked Jerry Herman's unaffected and cast iron tuneful melodies embellished with his own slick lyrics." Then he went all-out (as did most of the other critics) in writing about the visual aspects, Ming Cho Lee's magnificent sets. "It is in the actual look of the stage," he wrote, "that the show comes closest to having that unique profile that all the great musicals have possessed."[8]

Edwin Wilson in the *Wall Street Journal* and John Beaufort in the *Christian Science Monitor* singled out Joel Grey as a "sparkling" and "lively" star, while, on the negative side, Dennis Cunningham on CBS-TV announced that the main problem with the show was "that first and foremost it's a star vehicle—and Joel Grey is not a star."[9]

The other critiques were mixed. Richard Eder in the *New York Times* dubbed the show "often amiable and sometimes more"—tantamount to death on Broadway. Eder went on to give the musical the coup de grace, saying that it had "a lot of first rate talents working at their second best."[10] In the *Daily News,* Douglas Watt, a habitual Herman basher, was harsher, calling the show "chock full of pretty little Jerry Herman songs with nothing out of place, including its sentimental greasepaint heart. Why, you'd hardly know there was a war going on as the Polish Catholic colonel and the meek little Polish Jew pursued their sweet adventure." He ended his review, "There is nothing to dislike about *The Grand Tour* unless it's the insistent mediocrity."[11]

Still, one wonders why, with so many pluses going for it, *The Grand Tour,* which cost the then-astronomical sum of a million dollars to produce, closed after only sixty-one performances. Certainly a more publicity minded group of producers might have kept the show running longer. But as theater aficionados have always known, the Palace is an enormous theater, a bit off the main stem of theater row, and it takes a hefty advance and/or a star with a magnetic draw to make for a long run.

Herman's own feeling about the show is primarily one of gratitude, because it got him writing again. He enjoyed the social aspect of this musical because he had friends in the cast. "My best friend, Carol Dorian, was in the chorus, and my love Florence Lacey was playing Marianne." He is reluctant to say that he likes *The Grand Tour* less than any of his other shows. "It is one of my children," he reasons, "and there are some lovely things in it. The story is quite charming and I believe it has humor and a lot of heart."

I feel that *The Grand Tour* is a show written when Herman's heart was elsewhere. Herman was accustomed to writing for strong women, but Stewart's libretto afforded him no opportunity to fill out Marianne's personality in song. Although he gives her a sumptuous ballad in "I Belong Here," she remains merely a colorless female, caught between the two dominating protagonists.

As for the other songs, it must be admitted that nowhere in Herman's oeuvre do we find such uninspired lyrics as in "Marianne" or such forced rhymes as in "For Poland" ("so . . . the sheep'll get shorn" rhyming predictably with "the land where you were born"), or a tired concept like "Mazeltov" executed with such lackluster. Yet Herman's knack for writing memorable songs was not to desert him. "I Belong Here," "I'll Be Here Tomorrow," "We're Almost There," and "I Think, I Think" are fine theater pieces affirming the professionalism of *The Grand Tour*.* As beautiful as the show was to look at, as exquisitely as it was orchestrated and conducted, the score lacked the ebullient lift alternating with the emotional tug that is the hallmark of a Jerry Herman show.

So ended Herman's miserable decade. Just around the corner was the one when he would bounce back on top. And what a smash hit bounce that would be.

---

* "I'll Be Here Tomorrow" has had a most successful life beyond the show. It was adapted as the unofficial song of the Gay Men's Health Crisis, its message of survival seemingly giving hope to those affected with AIDS and those who test HIV positive, that with medication, treatment, and a positive outlook, they too will be here for many tomorrows.

12

la cage aux folles

In 1978 Jerry Herman and Chuck Fultz went to the 68th Street Playhouse to see *La Cage aux Folles,* the film version of a humorous French play about a gay couple who operate a drag club in St. Tropez. Fultz remembered, "Jerry was so excited by this film that he squoze my arm so tightly that after the movie I still had a mark. And as we were leaving the theater, he said, 'That's my next musical, I know just what to do with it.'"[1]

First thing the next morning Herman telephoned his agent, Biff Liff, to see about acquiring the film's musical rights. That afternoon Liff called back with the distressing news that those rights had already been optioned. Allan Carr and a group of investors had acquired the property some time before, were already far beyond the planning stage, and intended to take their proposed musical adaptation to Broadway.*

Carr and his partners had moved the setting of the story to New Orleans. The libretto, now retitled *The Queen of Basin Street,* was the work of

---

* The cinema version of *La Cage aux Folles* was based on Jean Poirot's French play which ran in Paris for five years in the seventies. The film, directed by Edward Molinaro, starred Ugo Tognazzi as Georges and Michel Serrault as Albin, the star of the cabaret, known on stage as Zaza. It was one of the most successful foreign films ever released. Two sequels, *La Cage aux Folles II* (1980) and *La Cage aux Folles: The Wedding* (1985), have been made. The first is dreary, with the gay couple getting involved in a spy ring, and the second is only slightly more amusing. In this one Albin is in line for a big inheritance if he marries and produces an heir. The original film of *La Cage,* its setting changed from St. Tropez to Miami's South Beach, was tastelessly remade in 1996 as *The Birdcage.* Directed by Mike Nichols, it starred Robin Williams as Georges and Nathan Lane as Albin.

Jay Presson Allen, known for her adaptations of *The Prime of Miss Jean Brodie, Forty Carats,* and the screenplay for *Cabaret.* Music and lyrics were in the process of being written by Maury Yeston (who was even then preparing *Nine,* an adaptation of Fellini's *8½*). Mike Nichols was the superstar director, and choreography was being handled by Tommy Tune. The fact that the project had advanced so far and so fast under these seasoned professionals seemed to ring the death knell to any hope that Herman would ever attain the rights.

This was doubly disappointing to Herman, who had been searching for nine years, since *Mack and Mabel,* for a story that might revivify his creativity. (It must be remembered that he had accepted *The Grand Tour* only as a stop-gap project, a favor to his buddy Mike Stewart.) For all of 1980 and 1981, even though he was involved in other projects, the loss of *La Cage* nettled and saddened him. But Herman, who is a fatalist, recently told me that during those years when the property was not his, he never lost the positive feeling that somehow, despite the seeming hopelessness of it, the project would bounce itself into his corner.[2]

Luckily, Alex Cohen, who had produced *Dear World* years before, and with whom Herman had a close friendship, called one morning asking him to come to Baltimore to see the madcap revue called *A Day in Hollywood/A Night in the Ukraine,* in previews before a Broadway run. Cohen and choreographer Tommy Tune, who was now the director, felt the first act was "50 percent there, but something [was] missing." The second part of the show moved smoothly, according to the producer, including a hilarious story about the Marx Brothers being cast in a pre-Soviet film. The songs that had been written for their insane shenanigans seemed amusing enough, but the first part, set in the lobby of Grauman's Chinese Theatre, which was supposed to take sophisticated slaps at Hollywood's deities, needed some work. Tune and Cohen turned to Herman for help. Herman abhorred the role of musical doctor, never forgetting how he had squirmed in Detroit when David Merrick brought in others to "fix" *Hello, Dolly!* Still, he relished the feeling of "being wanted" to help a colleague like Tune. And he welcomed the diversion, which turned his mind away from dwelling on the loss of *La Cage.* When he saw the show he felt that he knew exactly what was needed.

"We went out to dinner afterward," Herman recalled, "and I said, 'This show needs an opening number that will tell the audience where they are and what it is about. You have nothing about movies. You need a serious song for Priscilla Lopez [the female lead], instead of the one she has—

which is terrible. And a crazy comedy song for the comedienne. That's all that's wrong. The rest is delicious."

"Would you write them?" Cohen asked.

"Not before talking with the composer-lyricists," Herman replied.

Dick Vosburgh and Frank Lazarus, whose first show this was, were called to join in the discussion. "We think your idea is a good one, but we don't know *how* to do it," they admitted. Then they asked Herman to help them out.

Herman contributed three gems to the show. One of them, a paean to the cinema he grew up on, "Just Go to the Movies," is top-notch Herman; the other two, "Nelson" and "The Best in the World," are a bit bizarre, but still interesting.

"Just Go to the Movies" has a jaunty, whistlable theme, a curious kind of little motive that hooks itself onto one's brain. Its two-bar motive begins on the tonic and with each succeeding repetition keeps wandering downward until we come to the title phrase. Herman has the good sense to modulate up a third and to stretch this two-bar idea into four for the bridge (and the technique to bring us neatly back for the final section). The song, an anthem for late-night movie buffs, has become popular in cabaret.

> Need to relax? Need to escape?
> Go see Fay Wray in the paw of an ape.
> Watch Errol Flynn shooting his bow,
> Just go to the movies, just go to a picture show, oh,
> When your morale needs some repairs
> Watch Busby's beauties descending the stairs
> Hundreds of girls doin' high kicks,
> Just go to the movies, just go to the flicks.
> And all for the sum of a quarter life is peachy,
> You can become Alice Faye or Don Ameche.
> Swamped with your bills? Late with your rent?
> Watch Bette Davis run out on George Brent,
> See Fred Astaire steppin' in style,
> When everything's dark and upset,
> Go calling on Clark and Claudette,
> Just go to a marvelous movie and smile.

One must not forget that Herman is a philosopher who can sprinkle his optimistic lyrics not only with stardust but with muddy realism. In this

Need to re-lax? Need to es-cape? Go see Fay Wray in the paw of an ape. Watch Er-rol Flynn shoot-ing his bow, Just go to the mov-ies Just go to a pic-ture show, Oh,

song he plunged his mind back into the 1930s, the Depression era he grew up in. The movies were often the public's only escape, offering, as he says, "for twenty-five cents, two or three hours of pure illusion." Hence lines like

> So when your life seems a bit lean
> Just let some shadows appear on the screen
> Shine like a star
> For a brief while. . . .
> Just go to a marvelous movie and smile!"

"Nelson" is almost pure camp, a rangy waltz with its melody centering around the Oo oo oo of the "Indian Love Call," in which Jeanette MacDonald joined voice with her longtime on-screen lover, Nelson Eddy. Again Herman shatters the Hollywood illusion. Goody-two-shoes MacDonald becomes a bitch and completely decimates her stalwart Nelson, confiding that Eddy must "stand on a box," and "acts like a lox." She builds to a climactic couplet, revealing that they are

> A pair made in heaven, the fans love to say,
> But each time we kiss, I could swear that he's gay.

Herman's third entry in *A Day in Hollywood* was the first "story-song" he had written since his days in revue. In essence it is actually a miniscene, a solo playlet. In its four verses, over a ruminative blues theme, it tells the tale of a young usherette in Cincinnati whose father assures her, "You're too good to be holding doors. . . . With a face like yours, there's a fortune out there that you just gotta go and get." So, repeating her father's mantra, "You're the best in the world," she turns in her flashlight and cape and hitches her way out to the Coast. After several lean years she gets a part in a movie and then eventually is given a starring role. Papa flies out to witness her moment of glory—but the film bombs and closes after only a few days.

Back in Cincinnati she applies for her old job of usherette, and in perhaps the most ironic and touching moment in the song, the manager asks if she has had any experience. This gives her the opportunity to belt her last chorus:

> "Sir," I said, "I'm the best! I'm the best in the world!
> I'm the bright little star that stands out from the rest.
> If I make it or not, don't forget what I've got,
> It's been drummed in my head
> Papa said, Papa said, Papa said
> I'm the best!"

Depending on how it is performed and one's personal taste, this saga built on the fifteen-minutes-of-fame parable can be pathetic or bathetic. But besides pointing out again the tawdry illusion that is behind most Hollywood sagas, it is the kind of showbiz lyric that could not have been written by anyone other than Jerry Herman. Its genuine surprise is the non-Hermanesque blues figure in the verse, accompanying the usherette's lyric, and the dissonant sharp 9th chord that ends each phrase. To contrast this, Herman reverts to his typical showtune chorus for the father's words. The idea is viable, but the melodic line of the chorus is not strong enough to support the jarring gearshift that the juxtaposition of these two styles creates.

With Herman's input into the show, *A Day in Hollywood/A Night in the Ukraine,* which opened in May 1980, was able to survive a full year on Broadway, turn a small profit, and garner a Tony Award for Priscilla Lopez. Showbiz denizens know that her performance of "The Best in the World" won the statue for her.

Hollywood/Ukraine was the last show Herman's father, Harry, attended. Living contentedly in Miami, Harry and his wife, Edna, traveled to New York to attend every one of his son's premieres. In September 1981 Harry

Priscilla Lopez in 1980's *A Day in Hollywood / A Night in the Ukraine,* another show to which Herman contributed three songs. His "The Best in the World" won Lopez the Tony. Photofest, Inc.

had a massive stroke and died before Jerry could get to see him. Certainly Harry Herman (and Edna, who lived on a decade after Harry's demise) recognized Jerry's accomplishments—although the two men looked at life through different prisms. In *Showtune* Herman tells a story about the opening of *Mame* that illustrates the pride the elder Herman took in his son:

> On his way to the orchestra pit, Don [Pippin, the conductor] noticed his father sitting in the third row. He smiled and gave his father a little nod of recognition. The elder Mr. Pippin was so thrilled that he turned to the gray-haired gentleman sitting next to him, who was an absolute stranger, and said, "That's my son conducting." The stranger smiled back and said, "He's conducting my son's music."[3]

After Harry's funeral the son learned that his father had willed him a small annuity. In no need of money, he left it in a bank at favorable interest. Herman said recently that the annuity "has mounted up to a sizable sum. It will make a nice scholarship when I go, perhaps at a theater camp for underprivileged youngsters, and I will name it in honor of my father."[4]

When *Jacques Brel Is Alive and Well (and Living in Paris)* and Noël Coward's *Sweet Potato* opened on Broadway in 1968, they started a vogue for the retrospective revue devoted to the work of a single artist that has not abated even to the excellent *A Class Act*, featuring the songs of Edward Kleban, in 2000. Stephen Sondheim's *Side by Side—by Sondheim* arrived in April 1977, and Thomas "Fats" Waller was immortalized in *Ain't Misbehavin'*, which reached Broadway in May 1978. It is amazing that with so many extractable and varied songs in his dossier, Herman's oeuvre had to wait until 1981, when the producer Larry Alford came to him with an idea: an all-girl retrospective revue with the Herman point of view of femininity, to be called *Jerry's Girls*. Alford wanted to try the show at Ted Hook's ever-popular Backstage cabaret, a supper club off Broadway on 46th Street. He planned to use four singers (Evalyn Baron, Alexandra Korey, Leila Martin, and Pauletta Pearson) and a three-woman orchestra. Herman would sometimes come in and take part in the finale, singing his signature song "I'll Be Here Tomorrow," but he would also be represented by four life-size cardboard cut-outs of himself, dressed as the waiters in the "Hello, Dolly!" number.

Putting the show together was a joy for these young women. Leila Martin remembered that since "there were only the four of us, Jerry held rehearsals at his place on Fire Island. Just like in a Hollywood movie, he moved the grand piano out to the pool and we rehearsed around it. We had a fabulous lunch and stayed over. So relaxed—it was more like a holiday than a rehearsal."[5]

But once they got on stage, it was professionalism all the way. Cheryl Hardwick led her orchestra and put her singers through their paces with an iron hand.[6] These thirty-seven songs, beginning with a list of all the women who had played in Herman shows (set to the tune of "It's Today"), packed them in nightly at Backstage, as it did in the expanded cabaret called On-stage. John Wilson gave it a rave review in the *New York Times*, and it soon became Broadway's "hot ticket." It ran there for two years, and producer Alford talked to Herman about sending it out on tour.

One night during the Backstage run, Herman was invited to dinner with Fritz Holt and Barry Brown, who were associate producers with Allan Carr of *La Cage*. He suspected that they were interested in sending *Jerry's Girls* on tour. But immediately upon sitting down they asked him whether he had any interest in doing the score to *La Cage*. His answer—reminiscent of the invitation to write *Mame*—was wildly affirmative. Although noted for his hearty appetite, Herman remembered the evening with a smile. "I could hardly eat a bite," he recalled, "so excited was I by the news." Nor did he sleep that night, waiting for the call from producer Carr with a bona fide offer. Carr called the next morning, explaining that he had had "artistic and financial difficulties with Mr. Nichols and Mr. Tune," and that Mr. Yeston had withdrawn from the project to complete his work on *Nine*. He did not discuss Ms. Allen's libretto but did specify that he wanted to start all over again—sticking to the film's original St. Tropez background—and that the songs were paramount. So the first to be hired was the composer-lyricist, and he thought that Herman would be an ideal choice to write this score.[7]

He wanted to know whether Herman had any ideas for the other two most important collaborators: librettist and director. Herman immediately suggested Arthur Laurents to write the book, having long admired Laurents's librettos for *West Side Story* and especially *Gypsy*, which Herman, with most theater professionals, considers the finest book ever written for a musical.* When Laurents was contacted, he expressed enthusiasm for what looked like a most interesting project—not as librettist, but as director.

---

* Arthur Laurents (1918–) has been associated with some of the biggest hits of the American theater—both in musicals and drama. He is the author of *Home of the Brave* (1945) and *The Time of the Cuckoo* (1952), among other plays, as well as the librettos of *West Side Story* (1957), *Gypsy* (1959), *Anyone Can Whistle* (1964), *Do I Hear a Waltz?* (1965), and *Hallelujah, Baby* (1968). His only experiences in directing on Broadway were *Anyone Can Whistle* (1964) and the revivals of *Gypsy* in 1974 and 1989.

By the early 1980s musical directors, led by Jerome Robbins, were considered "conceptualists"—that is, they had progressed from merely blocking actors to rewriting lines and actually conceiving the shape of the musical.* The producers and Herman felt that the involvement in any capacity of Laurents, one of the towering figures in twentieth-century musicals, could only be a plus for their property. As conceptualist-director, it was hoped that he would shape and elevate the piece from a sentimental farce into a trenchant musical play.

Laurents says that he agreed to direct the musical of *La Cage* because Fritz Holt asked him to, but he "never thought it would get off the ground."[8] Still, Laurents's agent specified that his client's name be in almost the same size type as that of the author, composer, lyricist, and stars of the musical. And, knowing his client would be contributing lines to the script, he secured 10 percent of the librettist's royalties for the director.

As for librettist, Laurents suggested Harvey Fierstein, the young man who had written three one-act plays and cobbled them together to make *Torch Song Trilogy,* which was then packing them in off Broadway. After seeing Fierstein's portrayal of a Jewish drag queen in his play, Herman and Carr agreed that the man understood transvestitism and could write dynamic and moving dialogue. They noted, too, that his play revealed great insight into the gay lifestyle and that his characters had a mordant, biting humor. That he was a generation younger than Laurents, a decade and a half younger than Herman, and a great deal more militant than either of them assured them that their musical would have an up-to-date point of view of the contemporary gay scene.

As soon as the contracts were signed, the three went to work—usually meeting at Jerry Herman's East 61st Street town house. Fierstein's and Laurents's sensitivity to their subject won out over their lack of extensive experience in the field of playwriting and directing. That the triumvirate was gay was a bonus. Who other than three homosexual men could hope to write Broadway's first musical about a gay couple?

La Cage aux Folles,† whose action takes place in a single day, begins with a short overture. (As with *Hello, Dolly!,* the overture was added after the

---

* The standard Dramatists Guild contract, by which all directors and authors are bound, forbids directors from rewriting the script without the author's approval.

† As we have seen, *folle* is the feminine form of *fou.* Thus the title translates literally as *The Cage for Crazies.* But *folle* is also derogatory French slang for "mad homosexual queen."

show's premiere, in this case because the more dramatic opening of the play, directly on the cabaret stage, was deemed too abrupt.) During this overture the audience sees a sunny pastel St. Tropez as midafternoon turns to twilight. In contrast to some of the provocative lines to come in the text, wholesomeness and elegance at the outset is the byword for sets and costumes.

When the traveler curtain opens, we are in front of the cabaret, La Cage aux Folles. A cymbal crash brings on a dapper Georges, who presents his ballyhoo for the evening's early show, over a steady vamp from the orchestra: "Bon soir! . . . Welcome to the fifteenth edition of the world-famous revue starring the one and only Zaza and featuring the notorious and dangerous Cagelles," he declaims. He goes on to offer some intriguing and conspiratorial lines about remaining "in your seats, or the management will not be responsible for the consequences."

The curtains open on a striking tableau: twelve figures in glamorous evening coats, their backs to us.* The orchestra maintains a steady "stop time" beat, as they turn around one by one. They seem to be an assortment of beautiful women with decidedly deep voices.

> We are what we are
> And what we are is an illusion.
> We love how it feels
> Putting on heels, causing confusion.
> We face life, though it's sometimes sweet and sometimes bitter,
> Face life with a little guts and lots of glitter.
> Look under our frocks, girdles, and jocks,
> Proving we are what we are.
>
> We are what we are,
> Half a brassiere, half a suspender.
> Half real and half fluff,
> You'll find it tough guessing our gender.
> So just *(whistle)* if we please you, that's the way to show us,
> Just *(whistle)* cause you'll love us once you get to know us.
> Look under our glitz, muscles, and tits,
> Proving we are what we are.

The song, actually only a stanza that is but eighteen bars long, has an in-

---

*In the New York production two of the twelve were female, added for brightness of tone, and, as Herman's lyric notes, "confusion."

teresting musical construction, as though the music itself doesn't know to which gender it belongs. Its first half, starting with jagged syncopations, is followed by legato phrases which give way to a rising minor scale line before the first phrase returns in conclusion. But what is more interesting here is that the title is a throwaway, seemingly unimportant in the scheme of the musical. It is a nugget to be squirreled away in the audience's subconscious and brought forth for the shattering conclusion of the act.

The disparate elements of the song fit neatly together to form backgrounds in succeeding choruses which introduce each of the Cagelles, who performs his or her specialty. Chantal sings an extended stratospheric cadenza; Hanna, the group's dominatrix, cracks her whip; and Phaedra sticks out an enormously provocative tongue. As the number ends, they remove their wigs, now a tradition, but formerly required by French law at any transvestite entertainment. Backstage, as they taunt Zaza for being too old, too fat, or too frequently late, the cabaret stage moves off as the apartment Georges and Albin share moves on. Georges is pounding on the dressing room door trying to avert a calamitous domestic scene and get Albin/Zaza to dress for his appearance. At last, when the door opens, Zaza's confidant, the maid/butler Jacob, who is keen for a chance to debut in the nightclub revue, comes out in full drag. Georges brushes him aside, still threatening to break down the door, until Albin, wearing a tattered bathrobe, enters from the kitchen with flour-caked hands, complaining loudly that Georges missed a gala lunch that he had prepared. "Now," he says, when Georges reluctantly kneels to put on Zaza's ankle bracelets, "you start missing meals, then you won't put on my ankle bracelets, then separate bedrooms—then some young brunette." Georges protests that there is no one else, never has been, convincing an overly dramatic Albin to move to the dressing room and prepare for his turn in the show. He does so with a theatrical sigh.

The rest of the apartment disappears as Albin sits disconsolately before his mirror and puts on makeup, dazzling sequined dress, glamorous wig, and jewels which transform him from a frumpy, balding, unhappy man into the extraordinary Zaza. Herman visualized this alchemy as he wrote the song. When he first presented it to the director, he told Laurents that he saw Albin putting on his plumage on stage. Herman knew what stage business was to happen on exactly which words. The work bears a similarity in that respect to Stephen Sondheim's "The Worst Pies in London" from *Sweeney Todd*, in which the composer created the scene while staging the number with pounding, kneading, stamping, and other effects all built into the score. Both bear the authentic mark of a veteran theater visionary.

Hearn as Zaza, the drag queen, in the opening number, shown here with the support of the Cagelles. Photofest, Inc.

When Laurents first heard Herman's scene/song, he said, "We'll stage it right in front of the audience." He arranged for a giant wardrobe to be on stage, with dressers hidden inside to reach out and zip or tuck Albin into his clothes. Everything had to go on at the precise moment on exactly the proper word.[9] George Hearn, who played the role on Broadway, said it was the most difficult number he ever had to learn, but it was worth it because audiences cheered the song's courage.

"A Little More Mascara" presents a raison d'être for transvestism to a straight audience more clearly than an hourlong lecture on the psychology of cross-dressing ever could, and brings tremendous honesty to the character in the play. Herman expanded on the song's meaning in his memoir:

> When Albin sings these thoughts, you realize that this song is not about a man who is putting on a dress. It's about a man who is becoming another human being. During that one sequence he leaves behind his dull, ordinary middle-aged life, and transforms himself into this divine creature who is everything that he thinks of as exquisite and elegant.

To me, this song works because it establishes a motive for Albin's transformation. It explains something that the movie of *La Cage* treated as a cute, quirky aberration, and never did explain—which is *why* a man would want to spend his life in drag.[10]

VERSE (*Albin before the mirror*)
Once again I'm a little depressed by this tired old face that I see,
Once again it is time to be someone, who's anyone other than me.
With a rare combination of girlish excitement and manly restraint
[*checking make-up*]
I position my precious assortment of powders, pencils, and paint,
[*Putting on headband*]
So whenever I feel that my place in the world is beginning to crash,
I apply one great stroke of mascara to my rather limp upper lash,
[*He does so*]
And I can cope again,
[*He does the second lash and looks front*]
Good God! There's hope again!
[*Puts down the mascara*]
CHORUS
When life is a real bitch again
[*Putting on eye blush*]
And my old sense of humor has up and gone,
It's time for the big switch again—
I put a little more mascara on.
[*Looking in the mirror*]
When I count my crow's feet again
[*now doing his cheeks*]
And tire of this perpetual marathon,
I put down the john seat again
And put a little more mascara on.
And everything's sparkle dust, bugle beads, ostrich plumes,
[*putting on eyelash*]
When it's a beaded lash that you look through,
Cause when I feel glamorous, elegant, [*second eyelash*] beautiful,
The world that I'm looking at's beautiful too!
[*He puts on dress and earrings*]
When my little road has a few bumps again and I need something
   level to lean upon,

I put on my sling pumps again, and wham!—this ugly duckling
  is a swan!
[*He picks up lipstick*]
So when my spirits start to sag, I hustle out my highest drag,
And put a little more mascara on.

As the song goes into its second chorus, Albin gets into the wig, applies
the final cosmetic touches, and dons his jewelry. With the metamorphosis
complete, a lighted staircase appears magically from under his dressing
room table, and with the Cagelles singing backup, we are suddenly transported to the nightclub stage where Albin is displaying this transformation
as a part of the show. The fluid staging was Laurents's idea, and it is something that adds to the seamlessness of the libretto throughout the musical.

While Albin goes on with his encore at the club, Jacob, the maid, pulls
Georges back to the apartment, where a handsome brunette is draped
across the sofa. The libretto tries to give us the idea (initiated in the original
movie) that this is a quick sexual fling for Georges, but luckily for the story's
believability, this deception does not go on too long, and we are informed
that this is George's son, Jean-Michel, home on a visit. George's love for his
offspring, we see, is real and paternal.

Jean-Michel has come to tell his father that he is engaged to be married
to Anne, a young woman he met on a recent holiday. When Georges com-
plains that the boy is too young to marry, Jean-Michel says he's twenty-four,
but that's not their problem. The difficulty is that the father of his proposed
bride is Edouard Dindon,* deputy general of the Tradition and Morality
Party, the very same man who is running for office on his pledge to close
down all the transvestite clubs in St. Tropez. Jean-Michel assures Georges
that Anne is nothing like her parents and then drops the bombshell that
"they are on their way here from Paris to meet you."

The boy, who has told his prospective father-in-law that his father is retired from the French Foreign Service, suggests that they seal the door that
leads from their quarters to the club. He also insists that Georges remove
some of the obvious homosexual statues and artifacts from the apartment.
Then he hurls the thunderbolt that his father must send Albin, whose femininity is undisguisable, away for this evening.

Georges calls Jean-Michel a traitor and points out that Albin has raised
the young man with a mother's love, but Jean-Michel, seeing no harm in

---

* "Dinde" translates from the French as "turkey." "Dindon" means "turkey-cock" and,
in slang, "ninny, blockhead."

George Hearn as Albin and Gene Barry as Georges in the Broadway production of *La Cage aux Folles*. The show won the Tony as Best Musical, and Hearn won for Best Actor in a Musical. Photofest, Inc.

this deception, repeats that "it's only for one evening" and goes into a jaunty song about his beloved Anne:

> Life is in perfect order with Anne on my arm,
> It makes my shoulders broader with Anne on my arm.
> Even when things won't jell and the pieces won't fit.
> I'm suddenly in,
> I'm suddenly on,
> I'm suddenly it!

Georges realizes through the song that Jean-Michel is deeply in love and promises—with a heavy heart—to tell Albin that he is not to be present that evening. He even accedes to the boy's request that he invite his birth mother, Sybil, to join them for dinner. An excited Albin bursts in upon the scene (having heard the news of the betrothal from Jacob). He is thrilled that their son is home for a few days and delighted by the prospect of the up-coming wedding, but as Jean-Michel retires, Albin throws a jealous tantrum when he hears Georges plans to invite Sybil to meet the new in-laws. Georges decides that a walk by the sea might make it easier to give Albin the troubling news that he is to be barred from meeting the Dindons. The scene gives the musical a chance to show these two lovers in a spirited dance to the same tune that Jean-Michel introduced, now retitled "With You on My Arm."

Originally the libretto did not have this reprise but went directly into Georges's lovely "Song on the Sand," but the light dance and lively "Prome-nade" for Jean-Michel and Anne was added in Boston, as well as the intro-duction of Jacqueline, a cabaret-owning friend, to brighten the mood. The scene gives the principals a chance to stop the show with an old-fashioned soft-shoe, then segues into the first romantic scene between the two men. They are at a little café table with the shoreline of St. Tropez in the back-ground. A string of David Mitchell's candy-colored lights hang over them as Georges begins what sounds like a nostalgic recitative. But as the gentle melody of the chorus pours out of him, the song soon turns into an ardent duet.

> Do you recall that windy little beach we walked along,
> That afternoon in fall, that afternoon we met?
> A fellow with a concertina sang. . . . What was the song?
> It's strange what we recall, and odd what we forget . . .
> I heard la, da da, dah, da, da dah, as we walked on the sand.

I heard la, da, da, dah I believe it was early September.
Through the crash of waves I could tell that the words were romantic,
Something about sharing, something about always . . .

As the song goes on it delves deeper into the lovers' reminiscences and concludes with "I hear la, da, da, dah . . . and I'm young and in love."

Although the music has somewhat the feel of a slow waltz, it is actually written in 4/4 time with triplets that create the feeling of the rolling surf.* The melody, though rangy, and needing an accomplished singer, is one of Herman's finest and is especially moving, orchestrated as it was in the show, featuring an atmospheric concertina.

After the applause Albin realizes that this wedding is all about love, not jealousies or old wounds, and agrees to let Sybil come. "And the three of us shall bear witness," he adds, "to our son's marriage together. Hand in hand . . . in hand." But Georges is unable to break the news that Jean-Michel is ashamed of him, and, as Albin rushes them back to the club for the second show, Georges laments, "Tonight, for the first time in his life, he has to be on time."

* The Broadway, British, and Australian recordings of *La Cage* treated this music as written, in four, but the German conductor performs the music, especially in its reprise, as though it had been written by Johann Strauss.

Back at La Cage, Georges discovers that Jean-Michel has rented a van to move out all the statues, furniture, and paintings that might look too gay, and seeing this, father cautions son to think over what he has asked him to do. Jean-Michel takes the warning lightly, and with the impetuousness of youth, even removes Zaza's drag costumes so that Sybil will have room for any clothes she brings.

Now we get the title song, "La Cage aux Folles" a description of the cabaret sung by Albin and the Cagelles. It is full of verve and perfect for this show, having a kind of minor verse with a major can-can chorus that lends itself to individual specialties and wild dancing. The music is typical of the Lido, a high-class Parisian boîte, only better, and supports the biggest production number in the show. The lyrics describing this high-class clip-joint are raunchy and funny:

> It's rather gaudy, but it's also rather grand,
> And while the waiter pads your check he'll kiss your hand.
> The clever gigolos romance the wealthy matrons
> At La Cage aux Folles.
> It's slightly Forties and a little bit New Wave,
> You may be dancing with a girl who needs a shave,
> Where both the riffraff and the royalty are patrons
> At La Cage aux Folles.

After the mayhem, as Albin is changing for his next number, he notices furniture and costumes coming down the stairs. "Spring cleaning is one thing," he remarks, "but where are you going with my gowns?"

Georges tries to temporize, but Jean-Michel's impatient "Haven't you told him yet?" brings the dreaded moment to a head. Trying to explain matters as calmly as he can, while Albin is dressing behind a screen, Georges knows that what he has to say will wound his lover deeply, and so he ends his speech with "Believe me, this will be one of those stories we'll laugh about for the rest of our lives. So what do you say?" A stoic, silent Albin brushes by his lover with the tight-lipped remark, "Excuse me, I have a show to finish," and walks to the cabaret stage, the stage moving with him. He tries to sing "We Are What We Are" with the Cagelles but is unable to get the words out. At last he holds up his hands for silence, and each chorus member, now intimidated, slinks off. He stands immobile, thoughtful for what seems an eternal moment, and then with measured pace and no accompaniment begins one of music theater's supremely tense moments. Albin chooses each word carefully, and after the first phrase the orchestra leader brings in the instruments on tiptoe, one by one, to follow him:

I . . . am . . . what . . . I . . . am,
I am my own special creation.
So come take a look,
Give me the hook, or the ovation.
It's my world that I want to have a little pride in,
My world, and it's not a place I have to hide in.
Life's not worth a damn till you can say,
"Hey, world, I am what I am."

Adapting the lyrics to the theme of "We Are What We Are," was Herman's canny manipulation, for the number now serves a double purpose: it is both reprise, one of the cornerstones of the lyric theater, and something totally new. By the second chorus, Albin is singing full-voiced with tremendous confidence, and the orchestra, now a tone higher, is backing him with a metered martial arrangement.

I am what I am,
I don't want praise, I don't want pity.
I bang my own drum,
Some think it's noise, I think it's pretty.
And so what, if I love each feather and each spangle,
Why not try to see things from a different angle.
Your life is a sham till you can shout out loud,
"I am what I am."

Now the accompaniment is moving twice as fast, allowing the singer to broaden his tempo. The key has been lifted another half-tone, landing us in the bright key of C major and permitting the singer, at the top of his range, to sting us with a resolve he has never shown before:

I am what I am
And what I am needs no excuses.
I deal my own deck,
Sometimes the ace, sometimes the deuces.
There's one life,
And there's no return and no deposit,
One life,

So it's time to open up your closet.
Life's not worth a damn till you can say
"Hey, world, I am what I am!"*

As he ends the song, Albin takes off his wig, flings it in George's face, and walks offstage, down the aisle, and out of the theater. Georges is left holding the wig and reaching out to Albin as the curtain falls.

Act two finds the lovers again by the sea. Georges apologizes to an obdurate Albin for allowing himself to be manipulated into permitting his lover to be banished, even for a single evening. At last, he softens Albin's and the audience's hearts with a reprise of "Song on the Sand," and the pair join in this nostalgic melody now meltingly sung in thirds. Rather than hiding Albin for the evening, he hatches a plan to make him "presentable." He wants to masculinize him and introduce him as Jean-Michel's Uncle Al. In an amusing martial song he tries to teach him to slouch, to walk like John Wayne, and to eat his food in a virile manner—and not to worry if he makes a mistake, but to try again to master this machismo before nightfall.

Think of this as masculine toast and masculine butter,
Ready for spreading by a masculine hand.
Pick up that knife and make believe it's a machete,
It'll take all your strength and steady nerves
For hacking your way through the cherry preserves.
Think of John Wayne and Jean Paul Belmondo,
Think of the Legionnaires and Charlemagne's men.
So, like a stevedore you grab your cup,
And if, God forbid, that your pinkie pops up
You can climb back up the mountain once again.

As the scene shifts, we see the transformation Jean-Michel has wrought on the apartment. It has been stripped bare, except for a large wooden crucifix and a few pieces of unadorned dark furniture. Jacob is dressed as a butler—albeit from the period of Louis Quinze, and promises to tone down his outrageous behavior in exchange for Jean-Michel's assurance that he will talk to his father about a spot for him in the show.

* Herman wrote this song overnight, and in the same keys as were used in the New York production. When he presented the work with its accompanying figures and tempi to Don Pippin, he asked if changes were necessary. "Not a thing," Pippin replied, "We'll have it orchestrated exactly as you just played it."

When Georges presents Albin, looking ridiculously mincing as "Uncle Al," Jean-Michel is certain the Dindons will see through the deception and he will lose Anne. He lashes out at his father, saying that Georges has no consideration for what *he* wants. All the embarrassments of having been brought up by his father's swishing lover spew out of him. "The razzings I took in school. The beatings I got defending him. People staring as we'd walk down the street because he'd insist we stroll arm in arm. I'd ask for a shirt, he'd buy me a blouse."

Georges counters with his own speech about how Albin always offered help with Jean-Michel's homework, and reminds his son of entire nights when Albin nursed him through his childhood illnesses. He caps the speech with one of Herman's most original and powerful lyrics. It is set to a strong, scale-like minor melody that is accompanied by a hemiolic rhythm.*

How often is someone concerned with the tiniest thread of your life,
Concerned with whatever you feel and whatever you touch?
Look over there, look over there,
Somebody cares that much.
How often does somebody sense that you need them without
    being told
When you have a hurt in your heart you're too proud to disclose?
Look over there, look over there,
Somebody always knows.
When you world spins too fast
And your bubble has burst,
Someone puts himself last
So that you can come first.
So count all the loves who will love you from now to the end
    of your life,
And when you have added the loves who have loved you before,
Look over there, look over there,
Somebody loves you more.

When Jean-Michel, faced with his loyalty to Albin and his love for Anne, cannot cope with his emotions and leaves the room, Albin reveals

---

* Hemiola is defined as the deceptive change of meter achieved by false emphasis. In this case, although the melody is clearly in triple time, the accompanying figure is in duple. The contrast not only sets off the vocal line interestingly but gives the song a churning intensity.

that a telegram has come from Sybil, saying that she is off on a vacation and will not be able to attend the party. Knowing how disappointed Jean-Michel will be, Albin excuses himself just as the Dindons arrive.

After the usual pleasantries, Georges sings the first part of what will become four songs written to counterpoint one another; this one, fictionalizing his days in the foreign service, ends

> With men who loved their camels, and their brandy, and, I swear,
> Nobody dished, nobody swished
> When I was a Foreign Legionnaire.

As he sings, Mrs. Dindon is rhapsodizing about the hors d'oeuvres dishes which bear pictures of naked boys "playing leap-frog." Dindon comments on the strangeness of this household, hoping he can talk his daughter out of the engagement. Jacob offers his own song, insulting the Dindons, calling the father "a prig" and the mother "a pill."

The songs fit neatly together, but unfortunately for this exercise none of the quartet has a real melody to sing—and the words are repeated twice more to make sure we get them. It is all very much like the trio in *Dear World,* but a bit more pretentious and less interesting in both music and lyric. This ensemble number builds suspense, for it seems as if Georges and Albin are certain to be found out. But Albin saves the day. As the quartet ends, he appears in maternal drag and announces "Here's Mother!"

With a gray wig, a flowered dress, and tied-up shoes, Albin looks and plays the part of a dowdy matriarch perfectly. He charms all three Dindons while his own family stands by agasp. After cocktails, he rings the bell for dinner to be served, and when Jacob opens the kitchen door, a belch of smoke cascades into the room. Albin realizes the dinner is ruined but recovers quickly, reserving places for them all at Jacqueline's restaurant next door. The living room set dissolves into a chic nightclub. Jacqueline introduces Albin as "the one and only Zaza," begging him to sing. Ham that he is, Albin as Zaza cannot refuse, and he dedicates the song to his future daughter-in-law, Anne.

It is an infectious sing-along, full of the repetition Jerry Herman writes better than anyone. Called "The Best of Times," it resembles "Those Were the Days" in rhythm and élan. It has very little to do with the plot, but it wells up such a spirit of bonhomie, optimism, and well-being that has become a standard:

> The best of times is now.
> What's left of summer but a faded rose?
> The best of times is now.
> As for tomorrow, well, who knows, who knows, who knows?
> So hold this moment fast
> And live and love as hard as you know how,
> And make this moment last
> Because the best of times in now.
> Now! Not some forgotten yesterday,
> Now! Tomorrow is too far away.

The song is so enthusiastically received by the on-stage audience that Zaza forgets the circumstances of being at Jacqueline's, or the presence of the Dindons, and, in his habitual gesture after applause, automatically removes his wig.

Dindon suddenly realizes the truth of what he has been suspecting all along. He shouts "Cults, cats, punks, perverts!" Suddenly, the restaurant disappears and we are back in the apartment. As Dindon insists that his wife and Anne must leave this place immediately, his daughter defects and says she is going to remain with Jean-Michel. "What good can come of this marriage to the son of someone brought up by two transvestite homosexuals?" Dindon fulminates. "One transvestite," Albin corrects. "One plain homosexual," Georges adds.

Jean-Michel tells Dindon that he has made a terrible mistake, and that he will spend the rest of his life trying to make up for his thoughtlessness. Dindon refuses to accept his apology, but Jean-Michel stops him and says, "It wasn't to you I was apologizing. It was to my parents." Singling out Albin, he directs a heartfelt reprise of "Look Over There" to him.

Now, self-serving Jacqueline enters, saying that publicity for her restaurant never hurts. She reveals that she has invited a raft of local photographers, who are waiting outside, to photograph Dindon and his family in the company of the homosexuals he has campaigned so ardently against. Georges uses a little blackmail to wrest a promise that Dindon will not stand in the way of their children's marriage if he gets the deputy out of this pickle and safely away from St. Tropez. He dresses everyone in drag—even Dindon as an ugly woman—so they can all be part of the finale of the show. And then after everyone has danced their way up the aisle and the Dindons have eluded the press, Georges and Albin appear on stage alone. The muted setting of the opening drops down behind them, and the pale blue light of early morning over St. Tropez filters in as they sing of their continuing love in "Song on the Sand." And the curtain falls.

Writing this remarkable score was, according to Herman, "a joy. The songs and their stagings just seemed to pour out of me." Laurents too found it "glitchless" and called the rehearsals, previews, and even the New York run "one of his happiest theater experiences."[11]

Putting the show together through the early months of 1983 was one of Herman's smoothest working times. "We gave to each other easily. When Harvey came in with Albin's speech for the end of the first act," Herman recalled, "I said, 'If you give me those five words, "I am what I am," I think I know what to do with them.' The next day—we usually met for lunch and discussed the show over food—as soon as they got there I ushered them right to the piano and sang them the act one finale. Arthur jumped up and said, 'It's perfect! I can see the whole thing as he exits up the aisle, out of the theater and onto Broadway!' And Harvey tried to hide the tear in his eye." Herman knew that this intense song would trumpet the show's real messages: personal dignity, self-respect, and honesty. He felt that it would even broaden the show's concept to include intolerance—toward gay or straight, men or women, or people of color.

One song, "Have a Nice Day," written to be sung by Dindon, was cut before the tryouts in Boston. Full of racial and ethnic slurs, its premise was that if it weren't for the dykes, the kikes, the wops, and the Japs, we could all have a nice day. Herman, who gave me access to all his musical and lyrical oeuvre, would not permit any quotation from this song and is reticent about having it performed. "It has the most awful words," he says; "you wouldn't believe they came out of me." The performers, the rest of the cast, the backstage crew, and even Jay Garner, who played Dindon, found it hilarious. Laurents, too, felt that it worked well within the show. He tried to coax Herman to keep it in, finally asking the composer to try it once for a preview audience, but Herman vetoed its use in the show.*

Perhaps more important than the casting in any Herman show was the exact tone and vocal range of the two major characters, Georges and especially Albin. Laurents was the first to suggest George Hearn, whose enormous range, from deep bass to near falsetto, brought out the masculine/feminine colors in the role of Albin.† The director insisted that Hearn do his audition in drag, after which Hearn was given a standing ovation and quickly signed. Herman calls him a liberal thinker, so sure of his masculinity that he courted and wed Leslie Stevens (one of the Cagelles) during the run of the play.

Early in the rehearsal period the actor who was originally signed for the role of Georges was let go. Allan Carr, who knew of Gene Barry's musical background, asked him to come in for an audition at a theater in Los Angeles, where he lives.‡ Barry easily passed that audition, and he and his wife

---

* Herman used the song in *Jerry's Girls* and admits, "It stopped the show every night when Dorothy Louden, dressed in evangelistic white robes with a doo-wop apple-cheeked chorus behind, sang it over radio station WKKK. People were crying with laughter then, but I would never allow it to be recorded." Indeed, it was omitted from the original cast album of *Jerry's Girls*.

† George Hearn (1934–) began his acting career in the early 1960s with performances in various roles with the New York Shakespeare Festival and the Theatre at Lincoln Center. He first garnered a notice as John Dickinson in *1776* and later worked opposite Liv Ullmann in *I Remember Mama* (1979). That year he replaced Len Cariou as *Sweeney Todd* in Stephen Sondheim's thriller and later toured in the production opposite Angela Lansbury, the original Mrs. Lovett. Recorded for Showtime, his TV performance garnered him an Emmy. He followed *Sweeney* with a Tony-nominated performance in *Watch on the Rhine* (1980) and *A Doll's Life* (1983) before being cast as Albin.

‡ Gene Barry (1919–) (b. Eugene Klaas) is perhaps best known for his work on television and in the movies, although he began his career on the musical stage. Selected by Max Reinhardt to appear in *Rosalinda*, the Broadway adaptation of *Die Fledermaus*, Barry played the original title role, the Bat, under conductor Erich Korngold. He also starred in *Polonaise* with Jan Kiepura and Martha Eggert before going on to Mike Todd's production of *The Would-Be Gentleman* and *Bless You All* on Broadway. But it was his work on television, as Bat Masterson (1958–1961) and as Amos Burke in

were flown to New York. "I went to the theater," he remembers, "I got up and sang a song, they gave me a standing ovation. The company manager then brought out this actor who was waiting in the wings, and we did a scene together and it was a wrap." Balancing Barry's lyric tenor as the more masculine of the couple against Hearn's deep baritone for the drag queen was brilliant, nontraditional casting. It helped to banish the gay stereotype that the French play and the film promulgated. And as Gene Barry later said, "using two nongay actors made the musical more acceptable to a straight audience."

On the first day of rehearsal, when Laurents told the cast he was a Stanislavski-type director, Barry felt at ease, because it is his custom to "get into a role gradually." Barry was thrown, however, when Laurents asked for a more or less polished performance almost from the next day. "I wasn't expecting Arthur to be so demanding," Barry recalled. "In television you get into the part quickly because you are doing so little—but in the theater you can't do that. My recall is that he expected too much too fast."[12]

Laurents, who was trying to give up smoking at the time, was understandably testy. He complained in his biography, *Original Story By*, that there were too many nervous producers hanging about and that Herman and Fierstein "gave me notes at breakfast every morning in Boston during the tryouts." He also remembered that "one of the two stars," implying that it was Barry, "would have to be fired, but a replacement couldn't be found. Somehow I had to get a performance out of him." He needn't have worried, for Barry, accustomed to working slowly into a role, came to own the part of Georges by the time of the Boston previews.

"The strength of the show eventually fell on my back," Gene Barry mentioned recently. "It was tough to solidify that role in terms of the audience, but eventually they went with me in the terms of being a father." Barry's sensitivity to his own children was the keynote of his interpretation.

The opening performance in Boston had to be canceled because the moving stage panels didn't work. Worse, Herman, Laurents, and Fierstein were not convinced this was the right city to preview the first musical about a gay couple. Herman was the most worried of all and was certain that the uptight Boston Brahmins would never accept a show about homosexuals.

On the first night the three were sitting a row behind an elderly

---

Burke's Law, that brought him near to household-name status. His movie credits include *Atlantic City* (1952), *Soldier of Fortune* (1955), *China Gate* (1957), and *Sodom and Gomorrah* (1980).

couple—he with the old-school tie, she with the blue-rinsed upsweep—who gave only tepid applause to some of the early numbers. "When Georges and Albin got to 'Song on the Sand,'" Herman recalled, "they turned to each other and smiled. I saw him reach over and take her hand, and I could feel their own love and their enjoyment. I nudged Arthur and Harvey and we, all three, were moved and had difficulty swallowing. We knew we had reached our goal and the show would be a hit with straight audiences."[13]

Gene Barry has his own remembrances of that Boston opening night. "When we did the final chorus of 'The Best of Times,' a sea of gray hair stood up—all those older people out there." The show was so effective that Barry's wife, Betty, knowing they were in for the long run, flew home to Los Angeles the next day to pack up the things she and her husband would need to spend the next year in New York.

Audiences and reviewers all seemed ecstatic. When the city fathers announced *La Cage aux Folles* Day, some three thousand people assembled at the Boston City Hall, and the engagement in that notoriously prudish town was completely sold out.

Opening night, 21 August 1983, on Broadway at the Palace Theatre was an unqualified success. The critics raved. Everybody connected with the show was mentioned: Herman's score was given top billing, then Theoni Aldredge was praised for her "exquisite pastel costumes," David Mitchell for his "superbly eloquent settings," Jules Fisher for the "atmospheric lighting," choreographer Scott Salmon for his "sensitive Parisian show routines," and Don Pippin for conducting the orchestra "with verve and vivacity."

Although the usually dour Laurents appreciated the show's success, he alone among its creators made little of what others called a "landmark musical." He has written that *La Cage* "is about a drag queen who wants to be accepted as a mother," but he quite underestimates the power of Herman's score to champion human dignity. "Broadway at this moment," he told an interviewer at the time, "is mindless glamour and glitter, and the audience loves it. They're so busy loving it that they accept two men as a couple, with a son. It's agitprop in sequins."[14] Still, although unable to analyze the reasons for the show's success, he did come to ameliorate his opinion of the musical. "I've been in the theater for a long time, but I have never seen an audience respond as they do with this show," he told Jack Kroll in *Newsweek*. "It's not the greatest story or the greatest music—or the greatest direction, but something, when all this is put together is at work that can't be analyzed logically."[15]

The reviews were splendid. Each critic had a good time, and almost all

Hearn reviews the show's title song during the recording session with
Thomas Z. Shepard, producer of the original cast album for RCA.
Photofest, Inc.

of them had a high opinion of Herman's music and lyrics. Howard Kissel of *Women's Wear Daily* led the pack, saying that "*La Cage* seems unquestionably Jerry Herman's most accomplished score. If the standout numbers in his other shows were tributes to larger-than-life women, here they are celebrations of love, and the ability to savor life. The lyrics are sharp and clever; the occasional coyness which has marred past Herman lyrics here seems in character. The tunes are lilting and bright."[16] Clive Barnes in the *New York Post* seconded the praise, finding Herman's "music and lyrics, his best yet—happier, more assertive, more buoyant than *Hello, Dolly!* or *Mame*."[17] The *New York Times*'s Frank Rich, who never had seemed to care much for Herman's oeuvre, did an about-face: "We expect snappy, old-style Broadway melodies from [Herman] but we don't expect passion. This time we get that passion, and it is Mr. Herman's score . . . that gives the charge to every genuine sentiment in the show."[18] Even Gerald Clark in *Time* gave a long list of the show's faults but had to add that it resembled "a chemical equation that makes gross faults appear small, minor virtues look large and major achievements seem more so. Despite its gay theme, it is a sentimental show that extols the values of love, honor and fidelity to home and family; consequently it seems to have drawn audiences that are largely straight."[19]

The two stars, Barry and Hearn, came in for raves as well. Hearn, with the more flamboyant role, seemed singled out more often than his partner, and he commented wryly on his drag role that "after three marriages and as many divorces, I should know something about women."[20] Barry, when asked about the subtleties of playing the role of a homosexual who could slip unnoticed into society, said, "You don't play gay. It simply comes in as a final thing, if you care for this man. The father part of the role was the leveler that the nongay audience could accept."[21]

Both stars seem to have so admirably succeeded that one critic wrote, "Straightness aside, still Hearn and Barry are the most romantic couple of the year."[22]

13

after *la cage*

With *La Cage* launched at the Palace and doing capacity business, Herman had more time to attend to his personal life. He had always been caring and responsive to his large circle of theatrical friends and had kept contact with acquaintances from his childhood and camp days. He paid special attention to the many older women from his mother's circle, now in their seventies. These he looked after with particular attention, as he no doubt would have cared for Ruth, had she remained alive. He remembered who was sick, who had lost a close family member, and he made sure that these survivors received an orchid on their birthdays and on Valentine's Day. Now his calendar was even fuller, for, having written the first gay musical, there were a raft of gay men who wanted to meet him.

He was fifty-two—for a homosexual man, even in the best of health, generally a time when popularity wanes. But as the invitations poured in, Herman enjoyed "feeling wanted" and relished the clamor of good-looking men eager to invite him out. "Success is a powerful aphrodisiac," Herman observed, adding, "I was a nice-looking guy, and thought it wonderful that at a gay party people would slip their cards and addresses in my pocket. It was good for my ego. If I had been a straight man I would have liked girls to suddenly become interested in me. Who wouldn't? I'm positive that men like Lerner, Loewe, Rodgers, and the other notorious womanizers [of the musical theater] enjoyed having all those chorines flocking about them. Like them, I had a healthy interest in sex, and I slept with a lot of different people. I guess you would say I was promiscuous."[1]

At this time in his life, perhaps too much was not enough. Herman admits that in spite of "sleeping around," he was looking desperately for a lasting relationship. But it must be added that according to Priscilla Morgan, the agent who managed him through a large part of his career, "He kept his homosexuality discrete and sotto voce. Behind the façade I think there was a pretty wild scene that went on in Fire Island or 61st Street, but I never saw any of it. He was always outwardly very elegant and very private about his personal life."[2] Herman is extremely inner-directed and yet sometimes— amid all the hoopla and over-the-top hilarity of the gay scene—he can appear very lonely.

So it was on a dreary Sunday in December 1983 that he decided to go alone to a well-known gay meeting place, The Loft, in Greenwich Village. A crowded pre-Christmas party was in session, but Herman, who is always shy in large groups, sat by himself. Eventually a casual acquaintance offered to introduce him to anyone he fancied in the room. Herman pointed out a tall, good-looking younger man with a thick walrus moustache, also alone, on the other side of the room. A few minutes later he shook hands with Marty Finkelstein, who turned out to be the great love of Jerry Herman's life.

They went over to the bar, picked up Cokes (Marty, like Jerry, being a teetotaler), and spent the whole of that early evening talking about theater, music, and art. By deep nightfall Herman discovered that Marty, who was thirty-four, sixteen years younger than himself, came from Philadelphia, had studied architecture, and was working for a design firm—but was interested in doing something of a more creative nature. He was passionate about the restoration of many old buildings then going on in the Center City in Philadelphia. Proudly, he revealed that the city fathers had constructed a new public fountain from his design, a fountain from which the water, as it came through the pipe, made interesting patterns on the stones. Of course, Marty knew who Jerry was and was familiar with many of his songs. Every theater aficionado in most metropolitan cities had seen pictures of the gay triumvirate who had produced *La Cage aux Folles*.

After this long discussion of their mutual interest in creative work, Herman invited his new friend to his house, but Finkelstein declined, explaining he had been living with a rather straitlaced physician named Ben for a number of years and had to get back to Philadelphia. "Somehow," Herman remembered, "I got up the courage to ask him what he was doing the next weekend. Would he like to see a show with me? And to my surprise he said, 'I'd love to see you,' and I said 'Why don't you drive up again and stay at my house?' And he came to my town house on 61st Street the next weekend, and it was one of those times when you really know that something is happening."

Nonetheless, possessing a strong conscience in matters of the heart, Herman told the younger man "I'm not a homebreaker. I don't want to interfere with what you have with your friend." Marty replied by inviting him to come down to Philadelphia to meet Ben. Herman drove there a few weeks after the new year and met "a lovely, quite distinguished man." Feeling even more caddish about coming between Marty and Ben because he *liked* the other man, Herman announced that he did not want "to get in the middle of this" long-standing relationship. "You'll have to make your decision," he told Marty, "and when you do—I'm here." Since he wasn't seeing anybody at the time and it was long after his relationship with Joe Masiell, Herman bided his time. Finally Finkelstein called one day in March 1984 to say that he would really like to spend more time with Herman. He said he had explained it to Ben, who had understood. Then he and Herman started to see each other on a steady basis. Herman firmly believed that he had found his soul mate, and the two were to spend the next seven years together.[3]

Alice Borden, who was then living in California, used to come to New York twice a year to stay with Jerry. She remembers that Marty would often be there. "If Jerry was busy, Marty and I would just go out and do our own thing. Marty was very warm, very sweet. This was the first time I discovered that Jerry actually lived with another person and had a relationship with him. When I stayed there, I would often go into the living room and Jerry and Marty would just be sitting there watching television like an ordinary couple—it was sweet and wonderful." For someone who saw her friend as a most glamorous person, observing this tranquil domestic life was "a bit of a shock—not out of prudishness, but simply because it deglamorized him."[4]

Since Finkelstein was close to his parents and two sisters, he and Herman would often drive to Philadelphia to visit them, or they would invite them to New York. Herman fitted his career into this domestic situation. He admired Marty's warm friendliness, as well as his sense of humor. He was also impressed with Marty's architectural renderings, which revealed a considerable talent. It was important to him that Marty have the opportunity to fulfill his potential, and he decided to take some steps to put their relationship on an equal footing.

"I was in a position in my life," Herman recalled, "where I did not have to compromise on just about anything. Suddenly I found myself with another human being who needed and deserved his own place in the sun. . . . I realized that if I wanted this relationship to work, I could not allow this man to live in my shadow. He needed his own dignity."

Herman suggested that they visit the Florida Keys for a weekend. They flew to Miami, and in the center of Key West found a real estate agent who showed them two side-by-side Victorian houses on Fleming Street that had been built for two sisters. "The gingerbread was falling off and the paint was in disrepair," Herman remembered, "and I asked Marty, 'How would you like to start a little business?' and I introduced the idea of our redoing houses together. I needed it like an extra nostril because I was so busy with my shows, but I wanted Marty to have something of his own. I didn't want him to be Mr. Jerry Herman."

Herman bought those huge, imposing, and quite splendid houses, which needed what Herman calls "more restoration than renovation." He and Marty kept the original architecture intact down to the last detail but returned the homes to their original luster. They saved their modernization for the kitchens and bathrooms, which they made state-of-the-art. They installed magnificent swimming pools in the rear of each lot, and they finished their transformation by landscaping the entire area with elegant plantings. The houses sold immediately on completion, at a substantial profit. Herman and Finkelstein were now entrepreneurs.

They bought a third house, moved into it, and became copartners in business. They combined their first names and called the company MaJer Design. Herman says, "Marty had very good taste, but he let me have the upper hand when we did houses because I had so much experience. Besides that, he was colorblind, so he had to let me make all decisions in terms of color." After their first year together, Finkelstein decided to move permanently to Key West. Herman, with houses in Manhattan, Beverly Hills, and now Key West, could come and go at will to look after the many projects in which he was involved. When Herman had to be away, sometimes for extended periods, Finkelstein could take care of managing, decorating, selling, or renting vacant property.

Over the next four years the firm remodeled and sold many houses. Eventually, the two men moved into two adjacent houses. The move was important for both of them. For Finkelstein, it allowed him to seek out his own friends and offered him the space to decorate as he chose, without Big Brother looking on. If he chose, he was now able to ask his family down to stay with him.

Herman, too, is a private person, needing time to be alone. He demands total privacy when he is working on a show. Protective of his work, and unwilling when he is composing music or lyrics to expose an unfinished song even to those closest to him, he will very often play the music over and over, fortissimo. Sometimes he will tramp from room to room singing at the top of his lungs. Only when a song is set and polished will he perform it for his collaborators and later for friends.

Working with the local architect Tom Pope, MaJer Design put together fifteen houses in all, decorating and selling each one, often for many times what the firm had paid. Because Finkelstein now had something of his own, was self-sufficient, and had a comfortable income, his family was delighted with Herman's influence on the younger man. Herman, in turn, was especially thrilled that "his parents accepted me as a son."

Herman was riding high that spring, for the Tony committee had given nine nominations to *La Cage aux Folles*. Besides putting the show up for the coveted Best Musical award, the committee nominated both Gene Barry and George Hearn for Best Actor in a Musical; Herman for Best Score; Arthur Laurents for Best Director of a Musical; Harvey Fierstein for Best Book; Theoni Aldredge for costumes; Jules Fisher for lighting; and Scott Salmon for choreography. The show's major competition was the Sondheim-Lapine *Sunday in the Park with George,* a show rooted in Georges Seurat's pointillism. It had received ten nominations and looked like a shoo-in for Best Musical because many of the more "intellectual" critics had raved about the artistic aspirations of the work.* Chief among them was the powerful Frank Rich of the *New York Times,* originally an art critic, whose reviews always praised the avant-garde over the establishment.

Almost as a surprise, *La Cage aux Folles* won in all its nominated categories except for lighting and choreography. When a grinning Herman bounced up on the platform to accept his Tony, he held the statue aloft for a moment. "There's been a rumor," he said beamingly, "that the simple hummable showtune is dead on Broadway." Then after a pause for approving applause and whistles, he crowed, "Well, it's alive and well at the Palace!" At which point pandemonium broke out.

Many took Herman's remarks as a slur to Sondheim, but the composer mentioned that he admires Sondheim's work tremendously. He told me that his speech was misunderstood. He meant to let the audience know that he envisions a multimusical Broadway, where his style of songwriting is still welcomed—a place where a Sondheim musical, a Lloyd-Webber through-

---

* *Sunday in the Park with George's* ten nominations were for Best Musical; Actor in a Musical (Mandy Patinkin); Actress in a Musical (Bernadette Peters); Featured Actress in a Musical (Diana Ivey); Director (James Lapine); Book (James Lapine); Score (Stephen Sondheim); Scenic Design (Tony Straiges); Costumes (Patricia Zipprodt and Ann Hould-Ward); and Lighting (Richard Nelson). It won Tonys only in the Scenic and Lighting categories. However, it was awarded a Pulitzer Prize later that year.

sung extravaganza, a Herman showtune-y show, an operetta, a revival, a rock musical, and an experimental show can all play side by side.[5] But one must admit that Herman's use of the phrase "simple, hummable showtune" could be construed as a dig at Sondheim, his less accessible melodies, and his intellectual lyrics.

Shortly after he won the Tony, Herman flew back to Key West, where MaJer Design was to receive an award from the chamber of commerce for giving the city a face-lift. When it came time to receive the plaque, Herman made Finkelstein go to the stage and accept it. Marty gave, according to Herman, "a lovely speech," mentioning both their backgrounds. Herman is proudest of having given Finkelstein "the feeling of having his own business and happier for that award than for having won the Tony."

La Cage went from hot to hotter ticket after the Tonys were announced, and Herman was frequently called back from Key West to approve of casting changes and the road companies that would soon be proliferating. He also flew frequently to wherever *Jerry's Girls* was playing, once it had closed at Ted Hook's On Stage. The producer Zev Buffman decided to take the show out on a cross-country tour—hoping eventually to bring it to Broadway. He cast it cleverly, finding variety in his choice of singing actresses: Carol Channing, Leslie Uggams, and Andrea McArdle. In the 1983–1984 season the tour crisscrossed the country, with sold-out engagements in New Haven, Nashville, Washington, Houston, San Diego, and Oklahoma City, among others. Herman often joined the show for the finale, invariably bringing down the house with his rendition of "I'll Be Here Tomorrow."

In 1985 Buffman brought the show to Broadway, booking the St. James Theatre, where *Hello, Dolly!* had played so many record-breaking performances two decades earlier. Carol Channing had other commitments and was replaced by the equally hilarious comedienne-singer Dorothy Louden, and since Herman wanted a strong dancer as part of his trio, he chose Chita Rivera, Broadway's top female hoofer, who is also a superb belter. The only one retained from the old gang was the elegant Leslie Uggams.

Because it was in a Broadway house, the orchestra for *Jerry's Girls* was expanded from twelve to twenty-four, and a chorus of eight singers was added to the principals to give the show heft. In order to freshen well-known songs, most of the numbers were reconceived and fitted out with new arrangements. "Hello, Dolly!," for example, was spoofed first by Dorothy Louden as a cocktail pianist reluctantly playing it as a request, then as a commercial for Oscar Mayer wieners ("Hello, Deli"), and finally as a Lyndon Johnson campaign song. "Mame" was sung in a whisper instead of

Herman, surrounded by Jerry's Girls, the principals in his 1985 Broadway revue: Dorothy Louden, Chita Rivera, and Leslie Uggams. Photofest, Inc.

its usual ear-splitting sound, and "La Cage aux Folles" was sung by Chita Rivera in male drag to a disco beat. Perhaps the freshest idea of the evening was a bevy of sunbathing beauties lolling on a Caribbean island and crooning "We Need a Little Christmas." The show opened in December 1985 and received excellent notices, except from Herman's bête noir, Frank Rich, in the *New York Times. Backstage* found the show "in the finest tradition of the Ziegfeld Follies," and Clive Barnes raved that "it can stay at the St. James Theatre forever, at the very least."[6] Business was so good that the show seemed as if it might carry out Mr. Barnes's prophecy. But six months into the run, Chita Rivera, who lives outside of New York City, had a serious automobile accident while driving home after a Sunday matinee. Substitutes were found, but without Rivera, who was pivotal to the show, *Jerry's Girls* soon ran out of steam and was forced to close.

Rivera calls *Jerry's Girls* a "wonderful but hard luck show. Dorothy Louden broke two toes during the previews, and then this happened to me. I can't think of anything worse happening to any show," Rivera adds sanguinely, "unless it is for an actress to die on stage."[7]

But even though *Jerry's Girls* had a curtailed New York run, it has not lacked for other companies in smaller venues. It is, in a way, a distillation of the essence of Herman, a collection of larger-than-life women whose voices he always hears in his head when he writes his songs—what Carol Channing rightly calls "an avalanche of amazonian females."[8]

Jerry's Girls closed in April 1986, and although it did not run as long as Herman had hoped it might, it and *La Cage* were continuing successes that helped to make his and Finkelstein's life an idyllic one. That is, until one evening just a few months later, when, at his house in Key West, Marty got a tearful phone call from Ben, who broke the news that he had just been diagnosed with AIDS. Neither Finkelstein nor Herman was particularly worried, because they showed no outward symptoms, and they had already been together for four years. A few weeks later, Ben died. That autumn Marty came down with what was thought to be a bronchial infection which simply wouldn't go away. He was admitted to a hospital in Key West.

"I'll never forget the day the doctor came into the room," Herman recalled, "and said, 'Can I talk to the two of you?' and closed the door, and he said that Marty had AIDS. I could not hold it together, and I went to the little sink in the corner of his room and wept into it. Marty was worried about *me,* worried about my having fallen apart. I'll never forget that. He recovered from that infection, and we hoped that the medication he would be on would enable us to beat the illness."

Herman was disconsolate, as he says, "not only for him but for me. I knew I was not going to be far behind. But I was more devastated for him because he was thirty-three years old. But he was very brave about it and handled it with much maturity and intelligence. Much better than I did. I went to my own doctor and discovered, without too much surprise, that I was HIV positive, and I started on medication. A year later, Marty had a second bout of pneumonia while we were down in Key West. I found myself spending more and more time down there and became very close to his family. His two sisters and his mother and father treated me—and still do—as part of their family, always talking positively even though a dark cloud hung over us. In 1989, two and a half years after he had first been diagnosed, in the middle of a brutally cold winter, Marty went back to Philadelphia to visit the family and came down with another chest infection. This time it was a fungal one and he was taken to the Hanniman Hospital there. I rented a room at the Hershey Hotel, around the corner from the hospital, so that I could be with him every day. And one day the doctor took me aside and said, 'We cannot fight this fungus and he is going to leave us.' When I went back home to get a change of clothes, he went into a coma, and I was told not to come back because the doctor didn't want me to remember him like that. And two days after I left, he died. I was with the family throughout the funeral and beyond. I stayed in his parents' house, in the room he grew up in. It was probably the most painful experience I can relate to you, but I'm very grateful I was able to spend such good years with him. Because the illness did not stop us from doing houses, from going to dinner, or cooking together, or loving each other. The illness was very brief, comparatively. I never thought he was going to die. I thought he would have the dog luck that I have had. The only tragedies I have had in my life were my mother's death and Marty's. I loved him and I felt loved by him, and I'm grateful that I had that experience and that I know what love feels like."

After Marty's death it was hard for Herman to return to Key West, but he did go back the next winter to create a memorial to his lover, a hospice in his honor called Marty's Place. It was actually an old motel that Herman redesigned completely so that each individual unit has its own kitchen, bedroom, and bath. Facing onto gardens with lush tropical plantings, green lawns, and lawn chairs, the whole is centered around a large swimming pool. Herman supports the hospice, which has become one of the most successful places in the world for buoying AIDS patients. Because of the great demand for admittance into this comfortable and comforting environment, Herman has recently supervised and financed the addition of three additional units.

By 1992, after several memory-filled seasons in Key West, Herman decided that he could no longer bear the reminders that living in that area brought with it, and he sold his houses in Florida. It had been an especially distressing winter with the death of his close chum, Carol Dorian, with whom Herman could trace a special friendship back to college days.

But fortunately—although he had not written a new show in a decade—there were his past successes to supervise. *Dolly, Mame,* and *La Cage* had touring companies to look in on, and new productions seemed to be sprouting all over the world. A splendid album conducted by Don Pippin and titled *Jerry Herman's Broadway* was released by RCA Victor in 1992, and Herman was asked by the singer-pianist Michael Feinstein to collaborate on an album in his retrospective series featuring the works of famous songwriters like Irving Berlin, Jule Styne, and Burton Lane. This vibrant album, *Michael Feinstein Sings the Jerry Herman Songbook,* contains such gems as the entire "Penny in My Pocket" cut from *Dolly* and the male version of *Mame's* standard, now retitled "If She Walked into My Life," which works almost as well as the original.

And then on 30 June 1993, for the first of many Herman retrospectives, a crowd of eleven thousand assembled at the Hollywood Bowl to listen to the Los Angeles Philharmonic and a galaxy of stars pay homage to the composer. The following year the producer Manny Kladitus asked Herman to supervise a revival of *Hello, Dolly!* which would star the seventy-year-old and seemingly inexhaustible Carol Channing. It was Herman's chance to change the design of the all-important staircase in the second act and to have the orchestration of "Ribbons Down My Back" reassessed. These were all to the show's good, and when *Dolly* came back to the Lunt-Fontanne Theatre for an interim booking the next year, it was heartily welcomed by the critics. Vincent Canby, who said he had heard that this was a "one-song show," wrote that he was pleasantly surprised to find Herman's score "packed with wit and melody."[9] Carol Channing, displaying boundless energy, was for more than three months once again the toast of Broadway.

During his time in New York that winter, Herman had lunch with his first agent, Priscilla Morgan, who suggested that he write a special for television. She put him in touch with some of the producers at CBS, who proposed that he write a special built around a particular holiday: Valentine's Day, Thanksgiving, or Christmas.[10] Always eager for a new challenge, Her-

Michael Feinstein and Jerry Herman record *The Jerry Herman Songbook*.
Photofest, Inc.

man got an idea for a plot that turned out to be an annual TV Christmas
show. It did not take him long to come up with the theme, since he is most
comfortable writing about women, and especially older women. This one is
ageless, and the title, *Mrs. Santa Claus,* popped into his head from the outset. With ten new songs, most of them in the best Herman tradition, and a

sensible story, it has become a Christmas perennial on the Hallmark Entertainment Channel.

Even while the idea was still forming in his head, Herman phoned Angela Lansbury to ask her to portray the woman behind Santa who is always in the background—this time coming to the foreground. Lansbury thought it was "a delicious idea" and asked Herman to call her when he had written some of the music.

Working without a deadline was a joy for Herman. He soon enlisted the help of the dramatist Mark Salzman, who outlined a colorful story set in 1910, but one that fit the preoccupation of social activists of the mid-1990s—women's as well as workers' rights—and left room for a lot of Hermaniana: love, honor, and romance. Salzman's themes are far more adult than the usual Christmas storybook fare, and although this show was intended for the living room, Herman never wrote down for the medium—as, say, Cole Porter had for his only TV special, *Aladdin*. This score is top-drawer Herman, on a par with Rodgers and Hammerstein's *Cinderella*.

The story begins at the North Pole, where, because of Mrs. Claus's clever planning, Santa's elves have finished making all their toys with a week to spare before Christmas. Since there are so many more children in the world than in bygone days, Mrs. Claus has dreamed up a new, more direct route to speed Santa's deliveries, but he will not hear of it. Feeling neglected and rejected, she decides to try out the new navigational plan on her own, intending to be back by morning, she hitches up the reindeer to Santa's sled and takes off to a jaunty tune:

> I'm Mrs. Santa Claus, the invisible wife,
> And Mrs. Santa Claus needs a change in her life.
> I've been manning the business and planning each holiday plan,
> And I'm tired of being the shadow behind the great man.

Somewhere over New York City she runs into a blizzard and is forced to make a crash landing on a cobblestone street. She is unharmed, but reindeer Cupid has hurt his leg. Fortunately there is a stable nearby run by the young, friendly Marcello, who examines the animal and says that he must rest for a few days if the leg is to heal properly. Before he takes Mrs. Claus on a tour of the area, Marcello finds her a room in Mrs. Lowenstein's boarding house and shows her the ethnic world, mostly Jewish, Irish, and Italian—what Herman calls "the great big bouillabaisse" of the teeming Lower East Side of

1910. The melody, with repeated notes beginning in A minor, has a very Yiddish sound, but it quickly reverses directions and sequences into C major. It reflects the polyglot culture of the area, as do Herman's rhymes, using "pickled herring, lasagna, and chow mein on the same tray," or music that the "saxophone will play," all rhyming with "Avenue A." The song is perfect for the big, colorful production number that was given splendid, screen-filling choreography by Rob Marshall:

> Welcome to the world of Avenue A
> Where you hear "Come sta?" and "Bless my soul," and "Oy vay!"
> Rosie Finkelstein and Michael Monahan are still going steady,
> Mrs. Brandenheim is yelling out the window, "Dinner is ready!"

Mrs. Claus, calling herself Mrs. North, soon meets the other members of Mrs. Lowenstein's household: her daughter, known as Soapbox Sadie because of her custom of assembling crowds and preaching women's right to vote, and young Nora Kilkenny, who came over from Ireland with her father. Both Kilkennys work long hours, hoping to save enough to bring over Nora's mother and baby brother.

Nora, not much more than a child, takes "Mrs. North" over to the Tavish Toy factory where she is employed, and Mr. Tavish, seeing that this lady knows something about making toys, gives her a job. She is shocked when she sees the shoddy merchandise he is turning out, and the sweatshop—or, rather, freezeshop—conditions under which the employees, many of them children, must work.

Herman has written an ideal villain song, full of octave skips that sound like the grinding of machine cogs. It was composed with heavy Terrence Mann in mind, and he plays it to the hilt:

> The red balloons may stain your ceiling, and the fire engine's
>   paint is peeling
> But my heart just squeals with joy,
> I've just made a Tavish toy. (It only has to last till Christmas.) . . .

Mrs. North decides to outsmart this villain and starts by amusing the children with a gentle soft shoe, "Almost Young":

> My walk is swift and sporty
> My disposition is evergreen
> Why say "I'm over forty?"
> I'm over seventeen.

Like *La Cage*'s "With Anne on My Arm" or *Dear World*'s "Tomorrow Morning," it is what is known as a "charm song," a genre in which Jerry Herman has no peer.

After winning the hearts of the children who work at Tavish's, Mrs. North decides to improve their lot, but being a stranger to the area, she seeks advice from Sadie. Sadie's problems now take over the story, and the two march together, collecting supporters of women's suffrage as they go. Marcello, smitten with Sadie, tags along as the only man to join this considerable group of females. The tune here (with appropriate lyrics) is the "Mrs. Santa Claus" of the opening, and it serves as the frequent Herman standby: reprise.

When they are alone, Marcello and Sadie sing a duet in the Rodgers and Hart tradition, not unlike "Isn't It Romantic?" or "It's Got to Be Love," called "We Don't Go Together at All." The title reveals the theme, and the song seems predictable until near the end, when Herman pulls a switch: "But I like your spunk," "And I like your pride," they sing in alternating lines. And then together:

> So I'll still be there, marching at your side.
> So I guess, my friend, we must admit the simple fact
> That opposites, oh yes, opposites attract!

And they seal it with a peck on the cheek.

During all the happenings on Avenue A—Sadie and Marcello's romance, Nora and Mrs. North's growing mother-daughter involvement, in short, more plot than is needed—there are frequent scene shifts to Santa at the North Pole, and even a joyous interpolation of Herman's classic "We Need a Little Christmas," as the elves try to cheer up their boss. When the head elf, Arvo, brings Santa a hot chocolate, and he turns his nose up at the taste, he demands a cup of his wife's chocolate, insisting that Anna is the only one who knows how a hot chocolate should be made. Arvo reveals that Mrs. Claus has been gone for two days—and this is the first he has asked about her. A contrite Santa realizes that he has been taking this good woman for granted. Now the elf convinces Santa to change his ways and suggests that he start by writing her a letter telling her as much. To yet another reprise of the "Mrs. Santa Claus" melody, Santa promises "a drastic change." The tempo slows and the song ends movingly with an imaginative Herman caboose:

> So I wish on the moon
> You'd come home to me soon
> Because
> You'll never know how Santa misses
> Missus Claus.

Back at the toy factory, the plot becomes overly thick as Mrs. Claus institutes a works slowdown, which only infuriates Tavish. He retaliates by making the children work on Christmas. But Nora and Mrs. Claus will not be stopped: the youthful workers go out on strike, urging all the children of New York to discard these defective toys. As toys fly from windows across the city, the factory is closed. We never know what happens to their jobs, but we have more weighty matters to concern us. It is Christmas Eve, and after Mrs. Claus has bolstered a romance between Mrs. Lowenstein and a policeman, she goes out on a balcony, looks up at the North Star, and sings her big ballad, "He Needs Me." The rangy melody is a bit fresher than its overused title and lyrics, which nonetheless climax nicely: "I need him much more."

The reverie is interrupted when Marcello tells Mrs. Claus that the reindeer is fully recuperated, but as she enters the stable she runs into villain Tavish. In a Dickensian finale (somewhat reminiscent of the Herman-Mosel *Madame Aphrodite*), she steers him into a tearful confession that he had a teddy bear whose seams split when he clutched it tightly. Its loss ruined his Christmas, and ever since, he has had the urge to spoil everybody's

Christmas. His confession having cleansed Tavish psychologically, we assume his factory will now produce only well-made toys.

In a twinkling, Mrs. Claus is back in the North. Santa bids her to close her eyes and dresses her in a chic floor-length fur-lined red coat (designed by Bob Mackie), and off they go, this time together, singing what has by now almost become another Christmas perennial, "The Best Christmas of All":

> Though the wind may be strong
> I will never complain, dear,
> I'm happy as long
> As there's you and my reindeer. . . .
> When you're no longer kids and have kids of your own,
> You'll remember what somebody said to you when you were small,
> As long as you love one another,
> You'll have the best Christmas of all.

There is something very charming about a mature woman's space and time travel, and Lansbury—with her braided gray hair, a dead ringer for Maria von Trapp—and Charles Durning, an Everyman version of Kris Kringle, play and sing like the true pros they are. Their ease makes one overlook the social messages that clutter the plot.

Mrs. Santa Claus, the most successful television film of 1996, has played every December since, and it probably will continue for years to come. Herman counts it as one of his most joyous experiences "because Angela, who was a big star because of *Murder, She Wrote,* was in such a happy frame of mind. At Universal Studios, we saw a whole section of old New York— horses and carriages and such a *tummel,* and as Angela and I walked down this new-old street we both started to laugh."[11] One can conjecture that neither of these people can believe their enormous success, and only with a kindred soul can they let their happiness spill out.

Nothing gives Jerry Herman more pleasure than accompanying an artist singing his original songs. To this end, in 1997 he devised a program of his music called *An Evening with Jerry Herman,* which was designed to create a relaxed, living-room retrospective of his work. He enlisted charming Florence Lacey, who had been his Marianne in *The Grand Tour,* and the flamboyant Leroy Reams, who had played Cornelius Hackl in the most recent *Dolly* revival, to sing and cavort. The show, a typical summer stock experience, tried out for a couple of weeks at the Westport Playhouse and was eminently successful—until Herman, who cannot brook any halfway mea-

Charles Durning as Santa is welcomed home by Angela Lansbury in the Hallmark television special *Mrs. Santa Claus*. Photofest, Inc.

sures, overdid his own intensity and suffered the warning symptoms of a heart attack. Doctors rushed him to the hospital and performed a most successful triple bypass the next morning.

His goddaughter, Jane Dorian, knowing that his operation was scheduled for 8:00 A.M., got to the hospital at five in the morning to see him before he underwent surgery. He smiled weakly and held her hand, felt the comfort knowing that she and Sheila Mack were there. And after the operation, when he regained consciousness, these two women were nearby. "P. A. I. N.," he wrote in the air as he started the recuperative process.

Two weeks later he was back at the Rainbow and Stars, stamping his foot in time with the music, holding nothing back, upsetting some of the old women, friends of his mother's who he had invited to the performance.

"Jerry," one cautioned, "you shouldn't play so hard. You'll give yourself another heart attack. But talking to an artist is like talking to the wall."

It was indeed.

For a large part of the 1990s Herman grieved for Marty Finkelstein and would not let himself become involved emotionally, and certainly not sexually, with another human being. When he wasn't looking in on one of his show revivals which were dotting the country, he spent most weekends in his house in Palm Springs. That city has a large gay community, and Herman knows many of its residents, having performed frequently at charity concerts and fund-raisers. In 1999 he was still an active, if mature, man of sixty-eight, with a healthy interest in sex. When his doctors told him that his T-cells were under control, and they assured him that "he would not die of AIDS," he began to hint to his friends that he would be interested in meeting a sensitive person "for companionship, maybe more."

In August of that year one of his friends arranged a blind date with sandy-haired Terry Marler—tall, blue-eyed, good-looking, and fifteen years younger than Herman. Marler, when asked about his relationship with Herman, confessed that he had "been in love with the man and his music since as a kid of sixteen I first heard *Milk and Honey* in 1962. Some years later when I attended the first San Diego preview of *Mack and Mabel,* that clinched it. Ever after I followed his career and his shows on records. You can imagine how excited I was that evening. The fact that I was finally meeting my idol was thrilling to me."

Marler had been a music major with a keen interest in photography in college. After graduation, when he found himself unable to find work in his chosen field, he got a job in real estate photography. Palm Springs was experiencing a real estate boom at the time, so he had plenty of work.

"But once I met Jerry," Marler said, "since I knew a great deal about the homes I had photographed, he suggested that I get my real estate license. So I did, and now I specialize in brokering apartment rentals and real estate office buildings."

The relationship blossomed from that first night: first, occasional meetings; later, almost every weekend together. Now they are what Marler calls "life partners," even though they choose not to live together. Marler's career centers around Palm Springs, where he keeps his apartment, while Herman, although he has a residence in that city, considers his primary residence to be in Beverly Hills. When asked why they opted to live apart, Marler explained that Herman "doesn't like to have anybody around when he is creating music. And he is used to being self-sufficient, quite capable of being alone. Jerry could survive on a desert island, but," Marler added, "we are working on the idea of spending more and more time together—we're up to fifty percent now."[12]

14

the road ahead

At seventy-three, his HIV-positive status under control so that it is "almost imperceptible," Jerry Herman, who follows a prudent lifestyle, "hopes to be able to write at least one or two more Broadway musicals." Since the phenomenal success of *La Cage aux Folles* he has been bombarded with playscripts, constantly having to turn them down, either because they do not inspire him or because, if he finds them inspiring and doable, he usually also finds them dated. The libretto for *A Pocketful of Miracles,* a charmer about Apple Annie, a poor lady who pretends to be rich, is the kind of feel-good musical that came across his desk recently, and one he might have set to music back in the sixties, but now he says he wouldn't know how to handle such an old-fashioned idea.

Bullets over Broadway, Woody Allen's zany film about a gangster who wants to be a producer, was offered to him, and although he found the plot hilarious, he didn't find anything in the story "to sing about." In 1999, when Mel Brooks thought of making a Broadway musical of his film *The Producers,* he asked Herman to write the songs. Knowing he would have to include "Springtime for Hitler" from the movie (which did become the centerpiece of the musical) reminded Herman of the agony he had suffered when David Merrick added interpolations* to the score of *Hello, Dolly!* What clinched

---

* In earlier times composers often added uncredited songs to a troubled musical. Jerry Bock and Sheldon Harnick contributed several to *Her First Roman,* the musical version of Shaw's *Caesar and Cleopatra,* and to the Sherlock Holmes musical *Baker Street.* Herman's interpolations in *Ben Franklin in Paris* were uncredited, but he did receive program credit for his three songs added to *A Day in Hollywood/A Night in the Ukraine,* since it was a sort of revue. Herman refused to interpolate songs into the Styne-Merrill

Herman's turndown of *The Producers—The Musical* was that it needed, as he says, "shtick," which he couldn't provide. Instead, Herman gave Brooks confidence by pointing out the filmmaker's own musical talent and assuring him that songs from the original *Producers* and from *Blazing Saddles* could be perfectly viable theater music. "'Springtime for Hitler,'" he told Brooks, "is as good as anything I might write. On stage it will play like wildfire."[1]

One project he did not turn down, the only major one since his television special *Mrs. Santa Claus*, came to him from the Las Vegas entrepreneur Steve Wynn, who built the luxurious Bellagio and owned the Treasure Island and Mirage hotels. Wynn flew Herman to Las Vegas to talk about a new musical. "I went to the airport and got on a plane—more like a whole house," Herman recalled. When Herman dined that evening with Wynn and his wife, the entrepreneur boasted that he had five of the greatest restaurants in the world, his own art gallery, *Cirque de Soleil*, and most of the best hotels in Las Vegas. "The only thing I lack," he added "is a Jerry Herman musical." "If you talk to me like that," Herman remembers retorting, "you can have anything I own."

"I want you to write something for a new theater I'd like to build in this hotel," Herman recalls Wynn saying. "I'll leave it up to you, and when you have finished something, contact me."

He drew up a very generous and fair contract that included an advance of half a million dollars, $250,000 on signing and the balance on delivery of the score. A fortune would have come in royalties because Vegas shows generally have a life of five or more years.

Herman came back a few weeks later and played Wynn "Vegas," an irresistible, swinging Sinatra-type song whose lyric might have been written by the city's chamber of commerce—if they had any talent:

> Vegas . . . that great sensation where nothing is quite what it seems,
> Vegas, a combination of thrills and excitement and dreams,
> Where ev'ry ordinary civilian
> Can turn a half-a-buck into half a million.
> You'll find your cares are lighter whenever they turn on those lights,
> You won't know which is brighter, the stars or the star-studded nights.
> Come find a brand new girlfriend, or bring your wife,
> Las Vegas will light up your life

Sugar (based on *Some Like It Hot*) and the Strouse-Maltby *Nick & Nora* (based on *The Thin Man*). In both cases the directors, not the composers, sought his help.

According to Herman, Wynn "loved it," and with such enthusiastic approval of his initial offering, he went forward to work out the plot.

"I got the idea of using a contest sponsored by a fictional hotel called The Spectacular," he said, "that is looking for an identifiable personage, a spokesperson. They organize a competition that welcomes entrants from all over the country. I thought up a name, Sara Jane Hotchkiss, for my heroine.* She is a simple girl from Ohio who thinks she can win this contest. At work her boss always garbles her name: 'Miss Hitchcock,' 'Miss Harrison,' and after constant corrections by another secretary, he finally begins asking for 'Miss What's-her-name.' And that's how I got the idea for the opening number, which is 'Miss What's-Her-Name (Is Stopping the Show).' By the time I had the whole plot worked out I went to Robert Freedman, who had cowritten the script of *Mrs. Santa Claus,* for the most minimal amount of talk. I didn't want people in Las Vegas to have to sit through six pages of dialogue."

Herman remembered how interesting daydreams could be and molded his plot after James Thurber's *Secret Life of Walter Mitty,* with perhaps a touch of Moss Hart's *Lady in the Dark.* The heroine finds herself in different situations always triggered by the sound of a big slot machine spitting out masses of jingling coins. "In one episode she imagines herself a princess who lacks everything but a lover, and I wrote 'Where in the World Is My Prince?' And I also knew there'd be a conflict between Charlie, her boyfriend, and the hotel's lounge singer climaxing in an imaginary *High Noon* shoot-out number. I saw a Western bar with guns going off around her, somewhat like Marlene Dietrich in *Destry Rides Again.* I almost heard it sung in a Kurt Weill–like German-accented English: 'I want to live each night like it's my last one . . .'

"Then I thought, what could be better than if she pictures herself the star of the *Ziegfeld Follies?* I'm known for girls, and I said to Steve, 'I've written something, but it needs at least thirty-five girls.' He said, 'I love it. You've got it.' Then the charming thing at the end where Charlie says to her, 'My great dream is a simple dream, not anything like yours—a little house, a sweet wife.' And she accepts that.

"The end of the show has Charlie and Sara Jane being married by a preacher in a plastic Las Vegas chapel. She's in a little housedress when she

* Just as Herman used his father's and uncle's names in *Hello, Dolly!* and the names of his lover, Marty Finkelstein, in *Mrs. Santa Claus,* so in this work did he honor his goddaughter, Jane Dorian, and her daughter, Sarah Haspel.

hears the next couple make a big slot machine win. It sends her off again into the most glorious wedding with a new bride and groom, and a forty-foot bridal train held by all thirty-five showgirls—a perfect spot for reprises of all my score.

"I thought I had a jewel that could play for ten years. It's colorful, humorous, wholesome, and it's fun. And Steve Wynn was in love with it. He was so much in love with it that when I came to him one day and said, 'I'd love to do a concept recording of my material and use a different star on each number. I don't want it to be like an original-cast album, but I would like to get different people who would be right for each particular song. For example, I'd like Steve Lawrence to sing 'Vegas,' because he has that Sinatra sound, and he said 'Go have it done. Send me the bill.' And he loved everything I was doing, and I said to myself, 'This kind of producer is made in heaven.' So I had Larry Blank, a wonderful orchestrator, a disciple of Phil Lang, orchestrate the songs, and each one sung by a handpicked artist.

"The next thing I know is that I read in *Variety* that Wynn sells his entire holdings in Vegas, not only every hotel but every contract. And I thought 'Oh, my god! What now?' I had been so euphoric about this project and all of a sudden it was not there. And after all the warm feelings we had for each other, I think he was embarrassed. I know I was terribly depressed."

One can understand Herman's shock at this unforeseen cancellation of his show. Shows have closed for additional work in Boston or Philadelphia after tryouts—some never to reopen—but to halt a show which has all indications of becoming a big hit, with an excellent prerecorded score, is unprecedented. Herman, who received his down payment but not the second quarter-million dollars, says he didn't care because he knew the balance of his money would come from royalties.

When I first began writing this book in November 1999, Herman came to my apartment in New York and played me the demo recording of *Miss Spectacular* that had recently been made. He was understandably euphoric (as was I) because material, performers, orchestrations, and recording were top-notch. A year later, Herman called his agent, Biff Liff, and asked him to inform MGM that it now owned the contract with Jerry Herman. After the call, Liff told his client that the top brass of the organization expressed their regrets about the way the matter had been handled, and said that they would have put on *Miss Spectacular* if they had had no show running at the MGM Grand. But they were showing a typical Vegas spectacular, one which cost $20 million. This extravaganza would probably play for the next ten years. Not wanting to hold Herman's work in limbo, they gave the agent back total rights to the show.

Liff believes that "since we finally got the rights back, we'll do it somewhere. We'll get it on someday because it really belongs in Las Vegas."[2] Herman, too, believing it to be Las Vegas material, traveled there in the fall of 2001 to scout other venues, but it was shortly after the 9/11 calamity, and nobody was interested in new shows. Optimist that he is, he believes *Miss Spectacular* will be produced in the near future.

Herman has good reason to be optimistic about the eventual fate of this score because the consensus from the professionals who have heard it (myself included) is that it is top-notch Herman, with at least three zingers besides the Vegas number that could become standards.* "Where in the World Is My Prince?" was first performed in public—to an enthusiastic reception—by a recumbent Nancy Dussault at the S. T. A. G. E. 10 November 2001 Tribute to Jerry Herman. The number is a prime candidate for sophisticated cabaret divas:

I have countries and counties and physical bounties,
And orchards of orchids and quince,
I have barrels of rubies and breathtaking boobies,
But where in the world is my prince?
Ev'ry day Nieman-Marcus massages my carcass,
Sassoon gives my tresses a rinse.
I've been trained by Nijinsky and coached by Lewinsky,
So where in the world is my prince?
Then along came a man from a land that was far, far away.
He was strong, he was smart, he was sweet, he was rich—he was gay.
I have ladies in waiting and Ford's highest rating,
It shouldn't be hard to convince
Some young duke to devour me, to come and deflower me,
Oh, where in the world is my prince?

"Ziegfeld Girl" is one of Herman's most haunting melodies. Perhaps it is the use of the augmented chord at the end of the first phrase, or the song's

---

* DRG Records remastered the *Miss Spectacular* recording and released it commercially, with much hoopla, in July 2002. It is conducted by Don Pippin and features Debbie Gravitte, Steve Lawrence, Michael Feinstein, Faith Prince, Karen Morrow, Christine Baranski, and David Gaines.

release, which goes up the interval of a fourth to the top of the singer's range. This, combined with an almost visual lyric, gives the song great seductiveness. It feels like it could be by Irving Berlin, but is far more sensual. It could only have been written by a man like Herman who has gone on record that he "adores beautiful women." Herman's frequent connection with staircases, as evidenced in *La Cage, Mame,* and certainly *Dolly,* serves him well in this lyric, too, as the listener almost becomes a voyeur, watching these long-stemmed beauties insinuating themselves provocatively down the stairs:

> Ziegfeld Girl, show us your crimson lips and sapphire eyes,
> Show us the beauty that your name implies.
> We'll never tire of watching you descend the stairs.
> Oh, Ziegfeld Girl, show us the glamour that your name defined,
> Show us the figure that the gods designed,
> We'll never tire of watching you descend the stairs.
> We're hypnotized by ev'ry graceful movement that you make,
> We're mesmerized by ev'ry song you sing, and ev'ry silken step
>   you take.
> Oh, Ziegfeld Girl, we know you'll leave us in a little while,
> With just the mem'ry of your haunting smile,
> And just the thrill of watching you descend the stairs.

"No Other Music" reminds one a bit of Harold Arlen or Jule Styne at their most rhapsodic. With octave skips and a lush harmonization, it is just the kind of big ballad that every Jerry Herman show needs. The lyrics are suitably fervent:

No other music takes my breath away,
Only the magic of your song.
Your la, da, da, de, da, da, dah,
Makes the voice in my heart sing along.
And no other music has such majesty,
No other mem'ry is as strong.
Just sing that strain, that soft refrain,
And the tunes in my ear all at once disappear,
And there's no other music
But your sweet song!

While Herman is waiting for *Miss Spectacular* to open as a Las Vegas revue, he has not been inactive. As a composer and lyricist whose great popularity lies with audiences, he is most interested in encouraging youthful musical theatergoers, and to this end has been instrumental in developing the ASCAP Jerry Herman Legacy Series: free theatrical performances for teenage students. The series consists of a pair of shows for young audiences. First, a program called *Hello, Jerry,* a retrospective starring Karen Morrow, Jason Graae, and Paige O'Hara, with Don Pippin at the piano, and an appearance by Herman himself. This is followed by a touring Broadway musical on the following night—so that youthful audiences may have a double immersion in this art form. Not only does Herman give his time and support to this program, and his own show, but he actually pays for five hundred tickets to the second night's performance, sending these youngsters to see whatever musical is playing in their city or one nearby. In the summer of 2001 the Herman show was followed by a performance of *Funny Girl.* In March of 2002 the series continued in Savannah and Chicago, and in November 2002 in Santa Ana, California.

Biff Liff, Herman's agent, feels he knows why young people "are even now finding Herman's music so interesting: People who know nothing about the theater like it because it's tuneful and direct. And youthful audiences need to hear and heed some of the important things in his shows, like the ugliness of greed, the message in *Dear World.* They also simply *enjoy* the bygone era that *Mack and Mabel* summons up—its songs almost bring the flickering screen to life."

The near future also holds a great many Herman projects. At present writing, in spring 2004, producer Marty Richards is planning to bring *La Cage aux Folles* back to Broadway (perhaps to Studio 54, whose current occupant is *Cabaret*). It would be, according to Herman, "the gritty, grungy show, taking place in a milieu more like a true drag club, that Harvey and I wanted originally."[3]

Two of Herman's shows that were poorly received in their original Broadway performances will have recorded reassessments in 2003. Finsworth Alley, having bought the rights from Columbia, will release a new CD of *The Grand Tour,* for which Herman will write the liner notes. Another production of *Mack and Mabel* is also scheduled at a new theater in Houston, as well as an all-star concert version in Carnegie Hall. The improved book, rewritten by Francine Pascal, is much leaner than the original Broadway version.

Herman is never idle. He continues to work a daily schedule that includes overseeing new productions of his oeuvre, while looking for that rare book or idea that might be transformed into a musical. He honors many requests to appear for charitable causes, such as the recent "Jerry's Boys" concert of the Gay Men's Chorus, which raised a tidy sum to fight the scourge of AIDS. In this and other concert appearances he ends the program by playing and singing his "I'll Be Here Tomorrow," a song with a deeply felt message of hope.

It seems that none of Herman's shows lies unperformed. *Tune the Grand Up,* which began in San Francisco, had a successful engagement on the East Coast in July 2003, and *Jerry's Girls* is scheduled to tour Australia for the fourth time. And the list of Hermaniana above does not include the dozens of amateur performances of *Dolly, Mame,* and *La Cage* that are presented year-round by high schools, colleges, and community theater groups.

Where do Herman's works fit into twentieth-century musical theater? Chita Rivera describes his contribution from the viewpoint of a theatrical professional: "Jerry hands you his soul on a silver platter. For an actor that is everything. And then it's up to you to take care of it."[4]

But Herman is more than an actor's or singer's dream.

Certainly his musicals were the most successful of the 1960s. His tunefulness and optimism distilled the essence of the feel-good musical, acting as a welcome antidote to that violent decade. By the middle of the next decade the musical itself had stagnated and reached an impasse. And just as Richard Rodgers, nearing the end of his collaboration with Lorenz Hart, felt that he could write no more songs in the musical comedy genre and had to turn in the direction of musical play with Oscar Hammerstein 2nd, so the musical needed to revivify itself. Herman practiced, and still practices, the classic musical comedy, and nobody does it better. As Martin Gottfried notes in his massive *Broadway Musicals*, "He will never be one of those composers who stretches the limits of theater music, but his knack for the showtune is irresistible, and his melodies are delicious—they need no justification. Many a trained composer would sell his soul for such tunes."[5]

Agreed. But why the subtitle of this book? How is Herman "the poet of the showtune"? Granted, his poetry is not of the Oscar Hammerstein variety, nor does it contain the perceptiveness or intellectuality of a Sondheim. There is very little communication with nature, no larks who are learning to pray, but the subtleties of "and then he walked away and took my smile with him" or "and now the years blur by" (both from "And I Was Beautiful"), or "someone puts himself last so that you can come first" (from "Look Over There"), resonate in our minds. Poetic insights abound, as when Mame realizes she "never found the boy before she lost him," or Dolly pleads with the world to "take me back," or personifies love and entreats it to "look in my window, come in and stay a while."

And there is humor, never ribald, always benevolent and apt for the story, as when Gooch, who has taken her guru's advice about opening new windows, laments "and who would suppose it was so hard to close it," or when Dolly, offering her services, proclaims (in "Just Leave Everything to Me"), "If you want your children coddled, corsets boned or furs remodeled, or some nice fresh fricassee."

Herman's lyrics have never lacked optimism. But this quality is built into the man; he truly believes what he says in "One Person," that "one little voice that's squeaking a song can make a million voices strong," or later, "it isn't the size of the fist, it's the size of the dream." He observes that "there'll be no blue Monday in your Sunday clothes," and rejects the skeptic's prediction in "I'll Be Here Tomorrow" that "tonight we're dead and gone." Herman's contradiction avows, "we'll be here tomorrow, simply going on."

In the 1970s and 1980s new ground needed to be broken, and Kander and Ebb, Sondheim, Tim Rice, and Lloyd-Webber brought shattering controversy, new forms, adult themes, the concept musical, and even rock to the stage to dominate the musicals of their eras. But we cannot underestimate the pure melodic—and often lyrical—genius that infuses Herman's best work, for though there are better-trained and more ambitious composer-lyricists, he is, again as Gottfried observes, "the one closest to the musical theater's original spirit; the one most similar to the giants [of the musical stage]."[6]

From his teens Herman never chose to be an iconoclast. He wanted his audiences to enjoy themselves. He aimed to emulate Irving Berlin, to give the public "songs they could whistle as they left the theater and take home in their pockets," and to write for larger-than-life females. In both those areas he has succeeded surpassingly. But there is more, for his scores speak in his own distinctive voice, they elucidate character without preaching, and they are far more showbiz, more emotional, certainly more immediate than Berlin's. His great standards, like "Hello, Dolly!" "Before the Parade Passes By," "Mame," "If He Walked into My Life," "Time Heals Everything," and "The Best of Times," have become American perennials. He has also given Broadway three of its most theatrically durable characters: Dolly, Mame, and Zaza.

Herman's oeuvre is small by Broadway standards: seven book musicals, a TV special, a revue (Parade), an off-Broadway oddity (Madame Aphrodite), two retrospectives (Jerry's Girls and Tune the Grand Up), and an extravaganza (Miss Spectacular). Because of their scores, three of them, Milk and Honey, Dear World, and Mack and Mabel (arguably Herman's finest, most atmospheric score), have developed a considerable following.

His long-running superhits, Dolly, Mame, and La Cage, each have imperishable, singable melodies that have the potential to pull us from laughter to tears—and back again. In each of these musicals it is Herman's score that transforms the ordinary comedy, from which it is derived, into a dramatic musical milestone. Because of his songs Mame's character is fathoms deeper than Patrick Dennis's or Lawrence and Lee's script limns her. Herman's contribution imbues La Cage's couple with a dignity that quashes the farcical movie and makes their show one of the landmark musicals of its decade. Of the trio, Dolly's libretto most needed Herman's artistry to transform a garrulous, bossy female into a beloved American icon. Had he written no more than these three seminal works, his shining place in the pantheon of the American musical theater would have been assured.

But Dear World's Countess Aurelia, Milk and Honey's Ruth, and Mack's Mabel are catching up in popularity, completing a sextet unique in showbusiness history. Each of these characters speaks/sings through Herman in his or her own distinctive voice. He writes a kind of Broadway poetry and seats it on a fountain of melody.

Miss Spectacular's splendid score shows that Herman's songwriting skills are as refined and sharp as ever, and, if we agree with Martin Gottfried when he says, "nobody does it better," in truth, as Jerry Herman sings his way into the twenty-first century, nobody even comes close.

SONGS, SHOWS, MUSIC IN PRINT, AND RECORDINGS

PARADE
Music and lyrics by Jerry Herman
Opened in New York 20 January 1960, Players' Theatre
Original cast: Charles Nelson Reilly, Dody Goodman, Richard Tone, Fia Karen,
  Lester James, with Jerry Herman at the piano

Songs
 1 "Gypsy Dance"
 2 "Don't Tear Down the House of Detention"
 3 "Your Hand in My Hand"
 4 "Confession to a Park Avenue Mother"
 5 "Two-a-Day"
 6 "Hail the TV Commercial"
 7 "The Last Rockette"
 8 "The Antique Man"
 9 "Just Plain Folks"
10 "The Next Time I Love"
11 "Naughty Forty-Second Street"
12 "How Hollywood Actresses Find Their Names"
13 "We Put the Music"
14 "Showtune in 2/4"
15 "Paris, I'm Prepared"
16 "Your Good Morning"
17 "Tenement Scene"
18 "Get Off My Lawn" (Music used in *Mack and Mabel* as "Call the Cops" but
   deleted)
19 "Where's Boris?"
20 "Another Candle"
21 "Truth and Consequences"
22 "Maria in Spats"
23 "The Audition"
24 "Jolly Theatrical Season"
25 "Parade"

Songs Added to the West Coast Version
26 "Skip the Opening Number"
27 "Parade"

Recordings

A. Original cast (Kapp KDL [M] KDS 7005); contains an overture and 2, 3, 4, 5, 8, 9, 10, 14, 16, 20, 22, 24, 25
B. Private tape of Los Angeles and San Francisco versions (1961, casts not identified); contains 3, 4, 5, 6, 7, 8, 10, 11, 12, 14, 16, 17, 18, 20, 23, 25, 26, 27
C. "Jolly Theatrical Season," "Your Good Morning," Charles Nelson Reilly with Robert Morse (Capitol T (MYST[S]), 186 2
D. "Your Hand in My Hand," The Melcharino Strings (RCA LPM[M] SPS 3323)
E. "Showtune in 2/4," Paige O'Hara (Columbia)

MILK AND HONEY

Music and lyrics by Jerry Herman
Book by Don Appell
Directed by Albert Marre
Choreographed by Donald Saddler
Orchestrations by Hershey Kay and Eddie Sauter
Choral arrangements by Robert de Cormier
Dance arrangements by Genevieve Pitot
Opened in New York 10 October 1961, Martin Beck Theatre (543 performances)
Original cast: Robert Weede (Phil), Mimi Benzell (Ruth), Molly Picon (Clara), Tommy Rall (David), Ronald Holgate (Policeman), Juki Arkin (Adi), Ellen Madison (Zipporah)

Songs

1 Overture
2 "Shalom"
3 "Independence Day Hora"
4 "Milk and Honey"
5 "There's No Reason in the World"
6 "Chin Up, Ladies"
7 "That Was Yesterday"
8 "Let's Not Waste a Moment"
9 "The Wedding"
10 Entr'acte
11 "Like a Young Man"
12 "I Will Follow You"
13 "Hymn to Hymie"
14 "As Simple as That"
15 Finale

Recordings
A. Original cast (RCA 09026-61997-2)

Music Publications
Piano/vocal score, Hal Leonard 384240
Piano/vocal selections, Hal Leonard 384251
Piano/vocal sheet music
  "Shalom," Hal Leonard 382050

MADAME APHRODITE
Music and lyrics by Jerry Herman
Book by Tad Mosel
Opened in New York, 29 December 1961, Orpheum Theatre (13 performances)
Original cast: Jack Drummond (Barney), Nancy Andrews (Madame Aphrodite),
  Cherry Davis (Rosemary), Red Colbin (Fiffy), Jane Hyer (Rita LaPorte), Joyce
  Hines (Mrs. Rooney)

Songs
1 "I Don't Mind"
2 "Sales Approach"
3 "Beat the World"
4 "Euclid Avenue"
5 "Beautiful"
6 "You I Like"
7 "And a Drop of Lavender Oil"
8 "The Girls Who Sit and Wait"
9 "Afferdyte"
10 "There Comes a Time"
11 "Only Love"
12 "Take a Good Look Around"

Recordings
A. Studio cast: John Richard, demo recording
B. Private tape; contains 5, 8, 11, 12

HELLO, DOLLY!
Music and lyrics by Jerry Herman
Book by Michael Stewart (based on Thornton Wilder's *The Matchmaker*)
Opened in New York 16 January 1964, St. James Theatre (2,844 performances)
Original Broadway cast: Carol Channing (Dolly Levi), David Burns (Horace Van-
  dergelder), Eileen Brennan (Irene Molloy), Sondra Lee (Minnie Fay), Charles
  Nelson Reilly (Cornelius Hackl), Jerry Dodge (Barnaby Tucker), Mary Jo Catlett
  (Ernestina), Igors Gavon (Ambrose Kemper), David Hartman (Rudolph), Gor-
  don Connell (Judge), Ken Ayers (Court Clerk)

Opened in London 2 December 1965, Drury Lane Theatre (794 performances)

Original touring cast and original London cast: Mary Martin (Dolly), Loring Smith, Marilyn Lovell, Coco Ramirez, Beverly Weir, Bohn Beecher, Mark Alden, Judith Drake, Skedge Miller, Robert Hocknell, Garrett Lewis. Conducted by Alyn Ainsworth

Songs

1 "Call on Dolly"
2 "I Put My Hand In"
3 "It Takes a Woman"
4 "Put on Your Sunday Clothes"
5 "Ribbons Down My Back"
6 "Motherhood March"
7 "Dancing"
8 "Before the Parade Passes By"
9 "Elegance"
10 "The Waiters' Gallop"
11 "Hello, Dolly!"
12 "Come and Be My Butterfly" (later replaced with "The Polka Contest")
13 "It Only Takes a Moment"
14 "So Long, Dearie"

Songs Cut Before New York Opening

15 "World, Take Me Back" (reinstituted when Ethel Merman took over the role)
16 "Love, Look in My Window" (reinstituted when Ethel Merman took over the role)
17 "Penny in My Pocket"
18 "You're a Damned Exasperating Woman"
19 "No, a Million Times, No"
20 "The Goodbye Song" (replaced by 14)

Song Written for the Film Version

21 "Just Leave Everything to Me"

Recordings

A. Original cast (RCA LOCD [M] and P [CD] [S]1087), contains 1–9, 10–14; also reissued on Time-Life P-16382 (S) set STL-AM13 with *Mame* and *The Music Man*, set titled Meredith Willson–Jerry Herman

B. Original London cast (E/RCA RD [M]/SF [S]7768, RCA LOCD [M]), contains same as B

C. Excerpts

   i. "Elegance," Carol Channing (OC Command RS880 SD [S]), with new lyrics by Jerry Herman

ii. "Hello, Dolly!" Ginger Rogers (RC [8-65] Curtain Calls CC [M]), from TV
Betty Grable (RC [5-67] Curtain Calls CC 100/5), from TV
Carol Channing, private tape (M), from TV
Pearl Bailey, private tape (M), from TV
Jerry Herman, *Hello, Jerry* (United Artist UAL 343)

iii. "Before the Parade Passes By," Ginger Rogers (RC [8-65] Curtain Calls)
Barbra Streisand (with "Love Is Only Love") (Columbia 4S45072[S])
Paige O'Hara sings Jerry Herman (RCA)

iv. "World Take Me Back," "Love, Look in My Window," Ethel Merman (Bar Mike EM1, 45 RPM); sold only in the theater during Merman's run in the show

v. "Ribbons Down My Back," Jerry Herman and orchestra (UA [M]) 3432)

vi. "Put on Your Sunday Clothes," "So Long, Dearie," Carol Channing (RCA 17-8350 [M] 45 RPM)

vii. "Penny in My Pocket," Michael Feinstein sings the Jerry Herman Songbook

D. Cast albums

viii. Original replacement cast: Martha Raye, Max Showalter, Will Mackenzie, Jon Mineo, June Hilmers, Alix Elias, Richard Hermin, Alice Playton. Conducted by Peter Howard (private recording)

ix. Original London replacement cast: Dora Bryan, Julie Dawn, Bernard Spear (E/HMVCPL [M]CSD [S]3545); also reissued by World Records (ST-1027)

x. Original all-black replacement cast: Pearl Bailey, Cab Calloway, Jack Crowder, Winston deWitt Hemsley, Roger Lawson, Emily Yancy, Chris Calloway. Conducted by Saul Schechtman (RCA LOC [M]:SO [S] 1147-2 JRG)

xi. Original German cast: Tatjana Iwanow, Wolfgang Aras, Ingid Ernest, Sigfried Siegert, Evelyn Baiser, Wolfgang Reinbacher. Conducted by Klaus Doldinger (Columbia OL-6710/OS-3110)

xii. Original French cast: Annie Corday, Jacques Mareuil, Jean Pamarez, Pierette Delange, Arlette Partick. Conducted by Carvelli

xiii. Original Israeli cast: Hanna Maron, Shraga Friedman, Gadi Yagil (I/CBS 7S70047)

xiv. Original Austrian cast: Malka Roekk, Kurt Humer, Heinz Zuber (Metronome KMLP-332 [S])

xv. Studio cast: Beryl Reid, Arthur Haynes, Patrica Routledge, Tony Adams, Richard Fox, Sylvia King, Eula Parker (Music for Pleasure MFP 1066)

xvi. Selections: "Just Leave Everything to Me," "Before the Parade Passes By," Lisa Kirk; "Put on Your Sunday Clothes," Jerry Herman and Joe Masiell; "Ribbons Down My Back," Carol Dorian; "It Only Takes a Moment," Joe

Masiell; "Hello, Dolly!" Jerry Herman, Joe Masiell, Carol Dorian, and Lisa Kirk; all selections with Jerry Herman at the piano (Laureate 1L-505 [S])

E. Cinema version, soundtrack, 20th Century–Fox film with Barbra Streisand, Walter Matthau, Michael Crawford, Louis Armstrong. Conducted by Lennie Hayton and Lionel Newman (20th Century–Fox Records DTCS-5103 [S]); contains a short prologue and 2, 4, 5, 7, 8, 9, 11, 13, 14, 21, 23

Music Publications

Piano/vocal score, Hal Leonard 383731

Piano/vocal elections, Hal Leonard 383730

Piano/vocal sheet music

"Hello, Dolly!" Hal Leonard 380882

"Put On Your Sunday Clothes," Hal Leonard 381890

Choral

"Hello, Dolly!" SATB (arr. Kirby Shaw), Hal Leonard 8621213

"Hello, Dolly!" SAB (arr. Kirby Shaw), Hal Leonard 8621214

"Hello, Dolly!" instrumental, Hal Leonard 8621216

"Hello, Dolly!" Sho Trax, Hal Leonard 8621217

"Hello, Dolly!" SATB (arr. Clay Warnick), Hal Leonard 8647725

BEN FRANKLIN IN PARIS

Music by Mark Sandrich

Lyrics by Sydney Michael

Opened in New York 27 October 1965, Lunt-Fontanne Theatre (215 performances)

Jerry Herman wrote two songs that were uncredited and interpolated into the production:

Songs

1 "To Be Alone with You"

2 "Too Charming"

Recording

A. Original cast (Capitol VAS [M] SVAS [S] 2191

B. Excerpt

i. "To Be Alone with You," Jerry Herman and Orchestra, *Hello, Jerry* (UAL 3432)

MAME

Music and lyrics by Jerry Herman

Book by Jerome Lawrence and Robert E. Lee, based on the novel *Auntie Mame* by Patrick Dennis and the play of the same title by Jerome Lawrence and Robert E. Lee

Opened in New York 24 May 1966, Winter Garden Theatre (1,508 performances)

Original Broadway cast: Angela Lansbury (Mame) Bea Arthur (Vera), Jane Connell (Gooch), Willard Waterman (Babcock), Charles Braswell (Beauregard),
Jerry Lansing (Patrick), George Coe (Lindsay), Frankie Michaels (Young Patrick), Sab Shimono (Ito)
Opened in London 20 February 1969, Drury Lane Theatre (443 performances)

Songs

1 "St. Bridget"
2 "It's Today" (music partly based on "Showtune in 2/4" from *Parade*)
3 "Open a New Window"
4 "The Man in the Moon"
5 "My Best Girl"
6 "We Need a Little Christmas"
7 "The Fox Hunt"
8 "Mame"
9 "The Letter" (reprise of "Mame")
10 "Bosom Buddies"
11 "Gooch's Song"
12 "That's How Young I Feel"
13 "If He Walked into My Life"

Songs Cut Before New York Opening

14 "Camouflage"
15 "Sterling Silver Boy"
16 "Love Is Only Love" (cut from *Mame* and reinstated in film version of *Hello,
Dolly!*)

Recordings

A. Original cast (as listed above) (Columbia KOL-6600 [M] KOS 6600 [S] and E/
CBS 7051 [M]); contains an overture and 1–6, 8–13
B. Original cast (as listed above) (remastered on Sony Classical/Columbia Leg-
acy SK 60959); in addition to tracks listed in A, contains bonus demo tracks
of 1, 2, 3, 8, and "Camouflage," from a demo tape, Jerry Herman with Alice
Borden
C. Also reissued on Time-Life P-16381 Set STL AM13 with *Hello, Dolly!* and *The
Music Man;* set titled Jerry Herman–Meredeth Willson
D. Excerpts
    i. "That's How Young I Feel," Ginger Rogers (OLC-Curtain Call Records 100/
21 [M]), from TV
    ii. "Open a New Window," "We Need a Little Christmas," "Mame," "That's
How Young I Feel," "If He Walked into My Life," studio cast: Mary Louise,
the Michael Brothers (Diplomat Records DS-2385 [X])
    v. "It's Today," "Open a New Window," "My Best Girl," "We Need a Little

Christmas," with other material, Cheltenham Chorus and Orchestra (Wyn-cote W-9147 [M] [S])

   vi. "It's Today," "Open a New Window," "If He Walked into My Life," with other songs, Paige O'Hara sings Jerry Herman

E. Cinema version, soundtrack, Warner Brothers film with Lucille Ball, Robert Preston, Bea Arthur, Jane Connell, and Kirby Furlong. Conducted by Fred Werner (Warner Brothers W-2773); contains an overture and all selections except 7, 12, 14, 15, 16

Music Publications

Piano/vocal score, Hal Leonard 384224
Piano/vocal selections, Hal Leonard 384226
Piano/vocal sheet music
   "The Best of Times," Hal Leonard 380201
   "If He Walked into My Life," Hal Leonard 381065
   "We Need a Little Christmas," Hal Leonard 382520
   "We Need a Little Christmas," piano duet, Hal Leonard 388520
Band/orchestra
   "We Need a Little Christmas," Easy Concert Band, Hal Leonard 4001624
   "We Need a Little Christmas," string, Hal Leonard 4849885
Choral
   "Open a New Window," two-part (arr. Mac Huff), Hal Leonard 8621137
   "Open a New Window," Sho Trax, Hal Leonard 8621137
   "We Need a Little Christmas," SATB (arr. Mac Huff), Hal Leonard 8200228
   "We Need a Little Christmas," SAB (arr. Mac Huff), Hal Leonard 8200229
   "We Need a Little Christmas," two-part (arr. Mac Huff), Hal Leonard 8200230
   "We Need a Little Christmas," Sho Trax, Hal Leonard 8200231
   "We Need a Little Christmas," SATB (arr. Kerr), Hal Leonard 8565913
   "We Need a Little Christmas," SSA (arr. Kerr), Hal Leonard 8565914
   "We Need a Little Christmas," SAB (arr. Kerr), Hal Leonard 8565915
   "We Need a Little Christmas," two-part (arr. Kerr), Hal Leonard 8599625
   "We Need a Little Christmas," SATB (arr. Albert), Hal Leonard 8649280

DEAR WORLD

Music and lyrics by Jerry Herman
Book by Jerome Lawrence and Robert E. Lee, based on the play *The Madwoman of Chaillot* by Jean Giraudoux, as adapted by Maurice Valency
Opened in New York 6 February 1969, Mark Hellenger Theatre (132 performances)
Original cast: Angela Lansbury (Countess Aurelia), Milo O'Shea (Sewerman), Jane Connell (Madwoman of Montmartre), Carmen Matthews (Madwoman of the Flea Market), Kurt Peterson (Julian), and Pamela Hill (Nina), with William Larsen, Michael Davis, Joe Masiell. Conducted by Donald Pippin

Songs

1 "The Spring of Next Year"
2 "Each Tomorrow Morning"
3 "I Don't Want to Know"
4 "I Never Said I Love You"
5 "Garbage"
6 "Dear World"
7 "Kiss Her Now"
8 "Memory"
9 "Pearls"
10 "Dickie"
11 "Voices"
12 "Thoughts"
13 "And I Was Beautiful"
14 "One Person"

Songs Cut Before Opening

15 "I Like Me"
16 "Have a Little Pity"
17 "A Sensible Woman" (restored in the November 2000 revival)
18 "Really Rather Rugged to be Rich"
19 "Through the Bottom of the Glass"

Recordings

A. Original cast (Columbia BOS-3260 [S]); reissued as Columbia Special Products ABOS-3260 (S); contains an overture and 1–14

B. Unidentified cast, demo recording (private LP LP-666 [M]); contains an overture, entr'acte, and 1–14

C. Excerpts
   i. "A Sensible Woman," M'el Dowd (Lansbury's understudy), private tape
   ii. "I Like Me," Kurt Peterson, private tape
   iii. "Really Rather Rugged to Be Rich," Milo O'Shea, private tape
   iv. "I Don't Want to Know," "And I Was Beautiful," Joe Masiell and Lisa Kirk (Laureate Records LL606)

Music Publications

Piano/vocal selections, Hal Leonard 383360

MACK AND MABEL

Music and lyrics by Jerry Herman
Book by Michael Stewart
Opened in New York 6 October 1974, Majestic Theatre (65 performances)
Original cast: Robert Preston (Mack), Bernadette Peters (Mabel), Lisa Kirk (Lottie), James Mitchell (William Desmond Taylor), Jerry Dodge (Frank), Christo-

pher Murney (Charlie), Tom Batten (Mr. Kleinman), Bert Michaels (Mr. Fox), Nancy Evers (Ella), Robert Fitch (Wally), Stanley Simmonds (Eddy the Watchman). Conducted by Donald Pippin

Songs

1 "Movies Were Movies"
2 "Look What Happened to Mabel"
3 "Big Time"
4 "I Won't Send Roses"
5 "I Wanna Make the World Laugh"
6 "Wherever He Ain't"
7 "Hundreds of Girls"
8 "When Mabel Comes in the Room"
9 "My Heart Leaps Up"
10 "Time Heals Everything"
11 "Tap Your Troubles Away"
12 "I Promise You a Happy Ending"

Songs Cut Before New York Opening
13 "Call the Cops" (same music as "Get Off My Lawn" from *Parade*)
14 "Hit 'Em in the Head"
15 "Today I'm Gonna Think About Me"

Recordings

A. Original cast (ABC—ABCH-830); contains 1–8, 10–13
B. Private tape of the complete show (M/A), recorded in Los Angeles, before New York opening; contains an entr'acte and 1–8, 10–13
C. Excerpts
   i. "Movies Were Movies," Jerry Herman; "I Won't Send Roses," Joe Masiell; "Time Heals Everything," Carol Dorian; "Tap Your Troubles Away," Lisa Kirk; all with Jerry Herman at piano (Laureate Records II-606)

Music Publications

Piano/vocal selections, Hal Leonard 384205
Piano/vocal sheet music
   "Time Heals Everything," Hal Leonard 382312

THE GRAND TOUR

Music and lyrics by Jerry Herman
Book by Michael Stewart and Mark Bramble, based on the book *Jacobowsky and the Colonel* by Franz Werfel and the American play based on Werfel's book by S. N. Behrman.
Opened at New York 11 January 1979, Palace Theatre (61 performances)
Original cast: Joel Grey (Jacobowsky), Ronald Holgate (the Colonel), Florence Lacey (Marianne), and Stephen Vinovich (Szabuniewicz), with George Hein-

hold, Gene Varrone, Chevi Colton, Grace Keagy, Travis Hudson. Conducted by Wally Harper

Songs

1 "I'll Be Here Tomorrow"
2 "For Poland"
3 "I Belong Here"
4 "Marianne"
5 "We're Almost There"
6 "More and More/Less and Less"
7 "One Extraordinary Thing"
8 "Mrs. S. L. Jacobowsky"
9 Wedding Conversation
10 "Mazeltov"
11 "I Think, I Think"
12 "You I Like"

Songs Cut Before New York Opening
13 "I Want to Live Each Night"
14 "What Am I with You"
15 "Two Possibilities"
16 "Having Someone There"
17 "Song of Advice" (melody later used for "Nelson" in *A Day in Hollywood/ A Night in the Ukraine*)

Recordings

Original cast (Columbia JS 35761 [S]); contains an overture and 1–12

Music Publications

Piano/vocal selections, Hal Leonard (out of print)
Choral
　　"I'll Be Here Tomorrow," SATB (arr. Lojeski), Hal Leonard 8621244
　　"I'll Be Here Tomorrow," SAB (arr. Lojeski), Hal Leonard 8621245
　　"I'll Be Here Tomorrow," SSA (arr. Lojeski), Hal Leonard 8621246
　　"I'll Be Here Tomorrow," instrumental, Hal Leonard 8621247
　　"I'll Be Here Tomorrow," Sho Trax (arr. Lojeski), Hal Leonard 8621248

A DAY IN HOLLYWOOD/A NIGHT IN THE UKRAINE

Music mostly by Frank Lazarus
Lyrics mostly by Dick Vosburgh
Three songs in act one, music and lyrics by Jerry Herman:

Songs

1 "Just Go to the Movies"
2 "Nelson"
3 "The Best in the World"

Recordings

A. Herman's songs included in the original cast recording
B. Excerpt
   i. "Just Go to the Movies," Michael Feinstein sings Jerry Herman

Music Publications

Piano/vocal selections

"Just Go To the Movies," "Nelson," "The Best In the World," included in Regent Music Folio 4649

JERRY'S GIRLS

Songs and Medleys

1 "Jerry's Girls" (to the tune of "It's Today")
2 Optimist Medley ("Put on Your Sunday Clothes," "Open a New Window," "Chin Up, Ladies")
3 "It Only Takes a Moment"
4 "Wherever He Ain't"
5 "We Need a Little Christmas"
6 "I Won't Send Roses"
7 "Tap Your Troubles Away"
8 Vaudeville Medley ("Two a Day," "Bosom Buddies," "I Want to Make the World Laugh," "The Man in the Moon")
9 "If He Walked into My Life"
10 "Hello, Dolly!"
11 Movies Medley ("Just Go to the Movies," "Movies Were Movies," Look What Happened to Mabel," "Nelson")
12 "Take It All Off"
13 "Shalom"
14 "Milk and Honey"
15 "Time Heals Everything"
16 "Mame"
17 "Kiss Her Now"
18 "The Tea Party" ("Dickie," "Voices," "Thoughts")
19 "And I Was Beautiful"
20 "Gooch's Song"
21 "Before the Parade Passes By"
22 "I Don't Want to Know"
23 "I'll Be Here Tomorrow"

Music Publication

Piano/vocal selections, Jerryco Music/Hal Leonard

LA CAGE AUX FOLLES

Music and lyrics by Jerry Herman

Book by Harvey Fierstein, based on the French film by Jean Poiret
Opened in New York, 21 August 1983, Palace Theatre (1,761 performances)
Original cast: George Hearn (Albin), Gene Barry (Georges), John Weiner (Jean-Michel), Leslie Stevens (Anne), Jay Garner (Dindon), and Merle Louise (Mme Dindon), with William Thomas Jr., Walter Charles, Sydney Anderson, David Cahn, Dennis Calahan. Conducted by Donald Pippin

Songs

1 Prelude
2 "We Are What We Are"
3 "A Little More Mascara"
4 "With Anne on My Arm"
5 "With You on My Arm"
6 "Song on the Sand"
7 "La Cage aux Folles"
8 "I Am What I Am"
9 "Masculinity"
10 "Look Over There"
11 "The Best of Times"

Recordings

Original cast (RCA Victor RCD1-4824)

Music Publications

Piano/vocal score, Hal Leonard 313003
Piano/vocal selections, Hal Leonard 284040
Piano/vocal sheet music
    "The Best of Times," Hal Leonard 380201
    "I Am What I Am," Hal Leonard 380987
    "Song on the Sand," Hal Leonard 382139
Band/orchestra
    "La Cage aux Folles," full orchestra, Hal Leonard 4500742

MRS. SANTA CLAUS

Music and lyrics by Jerry Herman
Book by Mark Saltzman
Directed by Terry Hughes
Choreography by Rob Marshall
Television special, first presentation December 1996
Original cast: Angela Lansbury (Mrs. Santa Claus), Charles Durning (Santa), Michael Jeter (Arvo), Terrence Mann (Tavish), David Naroma (Marcello), Debra Wiseman (Sadie), Rosalind Harris (Mrs. Lowenstein), Bryan Murray (Officer Doyle). Conducted by Don Pippin

Songs

1 Overture
2 "Seven Days 'Til Christmas"
3 "Mrs. Santa Claus"
4 "Avenue A"
5 "A Tavish Toy"
6 "Almost Young"
7 "Suffragette March"
8 "We Don't Go Together at All"
9 "Whistle"
10 "Dear Mrs. Santa Claus"
11 "He Needs Me"
12 "The Best Christmas of All"

Recordings

Soundtrack (RCA Victor 09025-68665-2)

Music Publications

Piano/vocal selections, Hal Leonard 385010

MISS SPECTACULAR

Music and lyrics by Jerry Herman
Book by Jerry Herman and Robert Freedman
Based on an idea by Jerry Herman
Concept album, recorded August 1998
Orchestrations and arrangements by Larry Blank
Vocal arrangements and conducting by Don Pippin
Produced by Steve Wynn for Mirage Entertainment

1 Overture, Orchestra
2 "Miss What's-Her-Name," Debbie Gravitte
3 "Las Vegas," Steve Lawrence
4 "Ziegfeld Girl," Michael Feinstein
5 "Sarah Jane," Chorus
6 "Ziegfeld Girl" (reprise), Chorus
7 "Where in the World Is My Prince?" Faith Prince
8 "No Other Music," Karen Morrow
9 "I Wanna Live Each Night," Christine Baranski
10 "Miss Spectacular," Debbie Gravitte
11 "My Great Dream," Davis Gaines
12 "Finale," Chorus
13 Exit, Orchestra

Recording

DRG Theater Records 12995

Music Publications

Piano/vocal selections, Hal Leonard 385033

THE JERRY HERMAN SONGBOOK

A selection of seventy Herman songs, Hal Leonard 00385217

NOTES

CHAPTER 1 **If You Believe**

1 *New York Post,* 26 January 1962.
2 Author interview with Jerry Herman, 14 November 1999.
3 Author interview with Jerry Herman, 22 January 2000. All quotations from Herman in this chapter not otherwise cited are from this interview.
4 Herman, *Showtune,* p. 63.
5 *Hello, Dolly!* Prompt book, Tams-Witmark Music Library, p. 24.
6 Herman, *Showtune,* p. 4.
7 Ibid.
8 Ibid., p. 65.
9 Author interview with Alice Borden, 18 February 1999; Herman interview, 14 November 1999.
10 Borden interview, 18 February 1999.
11 Author interview with Alice Borden, 22 March 2000.

CHAPTER 2 **Early Days**

1 Author interview with Jerry Herman, 14 November 1999. All quotations from Herman in this chapter not otherwise cited are from this interview.
2 Herman, *Showtune,* p. 3.
3 Author interview with Claire Tannenbaum, 10 March 2000.
4 Herman interview, 14 November 1999.
5 Author interview with Jerry Herman, 3 March 2000.
6 Author interview with Alice Borden, 22 March 2000. All quotations from Borden in this chapter not otherwise cited are from this interview.
7 Herman, *Showtune,* p. 12.
8 Author telephone interview with Jerry Herman, 19 September 2001.
9 Author interview with Phyllis Newman, 10 June 2000.

CHAPTER 3 **College and Beyond**

1 Herman, *Showtune,* p. 23.
2 Ibid., p. 24.
3 Author interview with Jerry Herman, 3 March 2000. All quotations from Herman in this chapter not otherwise cited are from this interview. Author interview with Jane Dorian, 20 July 2001.
4 Margery Nagel, letter to author, 10 November 2000.
5 Author telephone interview with Jerry Herman, 4 September 2002.

6   Author telephone interview with Louis Hertz, 10 February 2001.

7   Author interview with Jerry Herman, 2 March 2000.

8   Herman interview, 2 March 2000.

9   *New York Times,* 10 October 1954.

10   *New York World-Telegram,* 10 October 1954.

11   Author interview with Priscilla Morgan, 14 April 2000. All quotations from Morgan in this chapter not otherwise cited are from this interview.

12   Author telephone interview with Ruth Pearlman, 10 March 2000.

13   Herman, *Showtune,* p. 26.

14   Author interview with Jim Paul Eilers, 14 July 2000. All quotations from Eilers in this chapter not otherwise cited are from this interview.

15   Author interview with Jerry Herman, 14 November 1999.

16   *New York Post,* 19 May 1958.

17   Herman, *Showtune,* p. 33.

18   Author interview with Charles Nelson Reilly, 10 April 2002.

19   Zadan, *Sondheim & Co.,* p. 232.

20   Citron, *Sondheim and Lloyd-Webber,* p. 43.

CHAPTER 4 *Milk and Honey*

1   Author interview with Priscilla Morgan, 14 March 2000.

2   Author interview with Jerry Herman, 3 March 2000. All quotations from Herman in this chapter not otherwise cited are from this interview.

3   Author interview with Irma Oestreicher, 10 December 1999. All quotations from Oestreicher in this chapter not otherwise cited are from this interview.

4   Picon, *Molly,* p. 218.

5   Ibid., p. 220.

6   Author interview with Ronald Holgate, 15 April 2000. All quotations from Holgate in this chapter not otherwise cited are from this interview.

7   From a lecture at New York's 92nd Street Y, 10 November 1971.

8   Picon, *Molly,* pp. 217, 218.

9   Author telephone interview with Luther Henderson, 10 September 2000.

10   *New York Times,* 11 October 1961; *Herald-Tribune,* 11 October 1961; *Mirror,* 11 October 1961.

11   Herman, *Showtune,* p. 55

12   Author interview with Jerry Herman, 2 March 2000.

13   Bordman, *American Musical Theatre,* p. 678.

14   Author telephone interview with Tad Mosel, 10 March 2000.

CHAPTER 5 *A Damned Exasperating Woman*

1   Author interview with Jerry Herman, 14 November 1999. All quotations from Herman in this chapter not otherwise cited are from this interview.

2   Kissel, *David Merrick,* p. 77

3   Ibid., p. 87.

4 Harrison, *Thornton Wilder,* p. 189.

5 Quoted in Kissel, *David Merrick,* p. 106.

6 Kissel, *David Merrick,* p. 106.

7 Author interview with Carol Channing, 10 November 2001.

8 Author interview with Madeline Gilford, 14 July 2000.

9 Gottfried, *Broadway Musicals,* pp. 304–305.

CHAPTER 6 *Hello, Dolly!*

1 Author interview with Jerry Herman, 14 November 1999. All quotations from Herman in this chapter not otherwise cited are from this interview.

2 Kissel, *David Merrick,* p. 292.

3 Ibid., p. 293.

4 Author interview with Madeline Gilford, 14 July 2000.

5 *Herald-Tribune,* 17 January 1964.

6 *New York Times,* 17 January 1964.

7 *New York Post,* 17 January 1964.

8 Herman, *Showtune,* pp. 97–98.

9 *Boston Globe,* 12 October 1964.

10 Facts of depositions conveyed in author interview with Jerry Herman, 3 March 2000.

11 Author interview with Jerry Herman, 2 March 2000.

12 Rogers, *Ginger,* pp. 355–357.

13 Kissel, *David Merrick,* pp. 295–296.

14 Herman interview, 2 March 2000.

15 Herman, *Showtune,* p. 156.

16 Herman interview, 2 March 2000.

17 Edwards, *Streisand,* p. 261.

18 Herman interview, 3 March 2000.

CHAPTER 7 *Mame*

1 Jordan, *But Darling,* p. 216.

2 Leslie Bennetts, profile of Edward Tanner III, *Vanity Fair,* September 2000, p. 186.

3 Author interview with Jerome Lawrence, 12 July 1999.

4 Jordan, *But Darling,* p. 74.

5 Author interview with Jerry Herman 20 August 2001. All quotations from Herman in this chapter not otherwise cited are from this interview.

6 Gottfried, *Balancing Act,* p. 209.

7 Quoted ibid., p. 212.

8 Ibid., p. 218.

9 Author interview with Angela Lansbury, 10 November 2001.

CHAPTER 8 *Mame—and Its Movie*

1 Author interview with Jerry Herman, 20 August 2001. All quotations from Herman in this chapter not otherwise cited are from this interview.

2 Author interview with Jerry Herman, 10 September 2001.

3   *New York Herald-Tribune,* 25 May 1966.

4   *New York Times,* 25 May 1966.

5   *New York Post,* 25 May 1966.

6   *New York Times,* 2 June 1968.

7   Herman interview, 10 September 2001.

8   *New York Times,* 6 June 1968; *New York Times,* 4 June 1969.

9   *New York Times,* 25 July 1983.

10   *Daily News,* 24 July 1983.

11   *Women's Wear Daily,* 24 July 1983.

12   Leslie Bennetts, profile of Edward Tanner III, *Vanity Fair,* September 2000, p. 186.

13   Jordan, *But Darling,* p. 275.

14   *New York Times,* 28 May 1974.

15   *New Yorker,* 31 March 1974.

16   *Newsweek,* 29 March 1974.

17   Jordan, *But Darling,* p. 266.

CHAPTER 9 *Dear World*

1   Author interview with Jerry Herman, 10 April 2002.

2   Herman, *Showtune,* pp. 169–170.

3   Reilly, *Jean Giraudoux,* pp. 24–25.

4   Quoted in Edwards, *A Remarkable Woman,* p. 353.

5   Author interview with Jerry Herman, 10 September 2001.

6   Gottfried, *Balancing Act,* pp. 263–264.

7   Herman interview, 10 September 2001.

8   Author interview with Samuel Liff, 28 August 2001.

9   *New York Times,* 7 February 1969.

10   *Time,* 11 February 1969.

11   *New York Times,* 16 February 1969.

12   *Women's Wear Daily,* 7 February 1969.

13   Author interview with Sally Ann Howes, 27 August 2001.

CHAPTER 10 *Mack and Mabel*

1   Author interview with Jerry Herman, 2 March 2000.

2   Ibid.

3   Author interview with Jerry Herman, 14 April 2000. All quotations from Herman in this chapter not otherwise cited are from this interview.

4   Author interview with Sylvia Hersher, 22 December 1999.

5   *New York Times,* 7 October 1974.

6   *Daily News,* 7 October 1974.

7   Martin Gottfried, *New York Post,* 7 October 1974.

8   *Time,* 21 October 1974; Jack Kroll, *Newsweek,* 21 October 1974.

9   Author interview with Jon Wilner, 10 January 2000.

10 Author telephone interview with Francine Pascal, 5 April 2001.

11 Author telephone interview with Sylvia Hersher, 12 March 2000.

CHAPTER 11 *The Grand Tour*

1 Author interview with Jerry Herman, 14 April 2000. All quotations from Herman in this chapter not otherwise cited are from this interview.

2 *Variety* (14 March 1973) reported that 132 recordings of "Hello, Dolly!" had been released.

3 Author interview with Alice Border, 18 February 1999.

4 *House Beautiful,* November 1970.

5 Author interview with Charles Fultz, 10 September 2001. All quotations from Fultz in this chapter not otherwise cited are from this interview.

6 Herman, *Showtune,* p. 155.

7 Author interview with Ronald Holgate, 15 April 2000. All quotations from Holgate in this chapter not otherwise cited are from this interview.

8 *New York Post,* 12 January 1979.

9 *Wall Street Journal,* 12 January 1979; *Christian Science Monitor,* 17 January 1979; WCBS-TV, 11 January 1979.

10 *New York Times,* 12 January 1979.

11 *Daily News,* 12 January 1979.

CHAPTER 12 *La Cage aux Folles*

1 Author interview with Charles Fultz, 10 September 2001.

2 Author interview with Jerry Herman, 16 May 2001. All quotations from Herman in this chapter not otherwise cited are from this interview.

3 Herman, *Showtune,* pp. 134–135.

4 Author interview with Jerry Herman, 10 August 2002.

5 Author interview with Leila Martin, 4 September 2001.

6 Ibid.

7 Author interview with Jerry Herman, 2 October 2000.

8 Laurents, *Original Story By,* p. 412.

9 Ibid.

10 Herman, *Showtune,* p. 232.

11 Laurents, *Original Story By,* p. 213.

12 Author interview with Gene Barry, 14 August 2001. All quotations from Barry in this chapter not otherwise cited are from this interview.

13 Herman interview, 2 October 2000.

14 Laurents, *Original Story By,* p. 412.

15 *Newsweek,* 27 January 1983; Laurents, *Original Story By,* p. 414.

16 *Women's Wear Daily,* 22 August 1983.

17 *New York Post,* 22 August 1983.

18 *New York Times,* 22 August 1983.

19 *Time,* 29 August 1983.
20 Author telephone interview with George Hearn, 4 October 2001.
21 Barry interview, 14 August 2001.
22 Gerald Clarke in *Newsweek,* 29 August 1983.

CHAPTER 13 **After *La Cage***

1 Author interview with Jerry Herman, 14 December 1999.
2 Author interview with Priscilla Morgan, 14 April 2000.
3 Herman interview, 14 December 1999.
4 Author interview with Alice Borden, 22 March 2000.
5 Author interview with Jerry Herman, 12 February 2001. All quotations from Herman in this chapter not otherwise cited are from this interview.
6 *New York Post,* 19 December 1985.
7 Author interview with Chita Rivera, 15 July 1999.
8 Author interview with Carol Channing, 23 November 2001
9 *New York Times,* 17 January 1994.
10 Morgan interview, 14 April 2000.
11 Author interview with Jerry Herman, 2 October 2000.
12 Author interview with Terry Marler, 7 November 2003.

CHAPTER 14 **The Road Ahead**

1 Author interview with Jerry Herman, 12 February 2001.
2 Author interview with Biff Liff, 5 September 2001. All quotations from Liff in this chapter not otherwise cited are from this interview.
3 Author interview with Jerry Herman, 15 September 2002.
4 Author interview with Chita Rivera, 14 July 1999.
5 Gottfried, *Broadway Musicals,* p. 304.
6 Ibid., p. 306.

GLOSSARY OF MUSICAL, LYRIC,
AND THEATRICAL TERMS

AABA The commonest song form (usually called the "pop" form), in which the first theme (usually eight bars in length) is repeated and then followed by a contrasting theme. The first theme then returns to conclude the song. All A's must be essentially the same; however, their endings may vary.

ABAC The most common showtune form. The A theme, usually eight bars in length, is followed by a contrasting eight-bar theme. The first theme then returns, and the last section can be similar to the original B section or totally different.

alla breve 4/4 time played rather quickly so that there are only two counts to the bar. Indicated on the sheet as a large C with a line through it. Popular musicians call it "cut time." See Jerry Herman's "Showtune in 2/4."

anticipation A rhythmic variant in which the melody or chords intended to be sounded on the first beat of the bar are played an eighth or sixteenth note earlier. Rhythmic anticipation is often used to give a jazz or swing feeling. Melodic anticipation is akin to suspension.

appoggiatura From the Italian meaning "to lean." A decorative pitch not belonging to the indicated chord, usually approaching its resolution from above. Appoggiatura creates mild dissonance and can add great intensity to a melodic line.

arpeggio From the Italian word for harp, *arpa*. An arpeggio is a chord whose members are sounded individually. A series of arpeggios can create a banal flourish.

augmented chord A chord whose fifth has been raised a half tone.

belting A woman singer's use of her chest voice rather than letting air pass over the diaphragm to create what is known as a soprano or head sound.

bridge The B section of a AABA song. The bridge usually contrasts to the A section. It is also known as *release* or *channel*.

canon Two or more melodic lines that enter at different times, such as "Frere Jacques" or "Sheep Song" from Herman's *Milk and Honey*. May be a "round" (more technically called canon at the octave.)

channel See **bridge**.

charm song A lighthearted song in duple meter intended for tap or soft-shoe dancing.

chorus In form, the main section of the song; the refrain.

chromaticism The use of tones falling outside the prevailing key signature.

circle of chords The natural progression of dominant sevenths to tonics. This series of chords usually written in circular fashion.

$$
\begin{array}{ccc}
 & C7 & \\
G7 & & F7 \\
D7 & & B\flat 7 \\
A7 & & E\flat 7 \\
F7 & & A\flat 7 \\
B7 & & D\flat 7 \\
 & G\flat 7 &
\end{array}
$$

coda An extension. In popular music it is called a tag.

commercial bridge The eight bars that comprise the majority of releases use the following sequences: I dominant 7th, IV, II dominant 7th, V. In the key of C this translates to C7, F, D7, G7. Each chord lasts two bars.

contrary motion See **motion**

counterpoint Literally, note against note. The technique of using two or more distinct melodic lines in such a way that they establish a harmonic relationship while retaining their linear individuality.

crotchet The British term for quarter note.

cut time See **alla breve**

diminished The word usually refers to the diminished 7th chord, which is a series of three superimposed minor thirds. There are only three possible combinations for diminished chords: one starting on C (C, E$\flat$, G$\flat$, A), on C$^\sharp$ (C$^\sharp$, E, G, B$\flat$), or on D (D, F. A$\flat$, B). Diminished chords can be superdramatic. They are most effective when used with an appoggiatura or suspension.

diminished cliché My own term for a series of four chords comprising the tonic (I), a diminished seventh (usually built on the tonic or lowered supertonic) (I dim or $^\sharp$I dim), the minor supertonic (II), and the dominant (V). These four chords are common in popular and show music as the I, VI, II, V sequence.

dominant The chord built on the fifth note of the diatonic scale (G or G7 in the key of C). The dominant is one of the three basic chords of the key.

downbeat The first beat of the measure. A strong entry.

dummy lyrics/tune Temporary lyrics or melody line that will be changed eventually. Dummy lyrics or tune are usually used in drafting a song so as not to impede the artistic or creative flow.

duple meter Indicating a time signature of 4/4 or 2/4.

evaded ending Use of a series of chords to avoid ending a song. Usually a III (often with flatted fifth) followed by VI or VI dominant. See Jerry Herman's "I've Never Said I Love You."

extractability In musicals, a song's ability to create a life of its own apart from the show. Songwriters formerly sought several extractable songs in each musical. Today such songs are less important.

fake book A collection of "lead sheets" used originally by instrumentalists and singers who would "fake" or improvise on the written melodies and chords.

fourth A musical interval; C to F, for example.

fifth A rather wide musical interval; C to G, for example.

Gold Record A standard set by the Recording Industry Association of America. To reach this standard a recording must sell a half-million units and achieve $1 million in wholesale U.S. revenues.

grace note A non–chord member struck on the beat—usually a tone or half-tone above or below the chord member.

hemiola A rhythmic device consisting of superimposing two notes in the time of three, or three notes in the time of two. Hemiola can often enliven a routine melodic passage.

hold book To assist at rehearsal once the actors have memorized their lines. Holding book implies prompting and checking to see that the author's exact lines are spoken.

lead sheet Shorthand to a piano-vocal arrangement. Lead sheets list the essentials: melody, chords, and lyrics. Performers create their own arrangements from these essences. Lead sheets give only an approximation of the composer's intentions. A bound collection of lead sheets is called a fake book.

leading tone The seventh note of the scale, so called because it leads smoothly back to the tonic.

legit A shortening of the term *legitimate,* implying proper or operatic singing using resonating head tones rather than chest or "belt" singing.

libretto The book of a musical or opera. A printed libretto also includes lyrics to songs and/or arias.

librettist One who writes the book of a musical or opera.

list song A song whose lyric comprises a list of items. See Jerry Herman's "Just Leave Everything To Me" or Cole Porter's "Let's Do It."

lyric(s) The words to a song.

lyricist The contemporary term for the person who writes words to a song.

major scale A progression from a keynote (called the tonic) up two whole tones and a halftone, followed by three more whole tones and a halftone. On the keyboard, CDEFGABC.

measure (1) A musical unit divided by a bar line. (2) A synonym for bar.

melisma The use of more than one pitch on a single verbal syllable. Melismatic passages are most often associated with baroque music but are also frequently found in oriental, religious, Hebraic, or "soul" music. See excerpt from Jerry Herman's "St Bridget."

minor scale The pure minor scale (Aeolian mode) comprises the notes A B C D E F G A; the melodic minor, A B C D E $F^\sharp$ $G^\sharp$ A; the harmonic minor, which is often used in Yiddish or klezmer music, is A B C D E F $G^\sharp$ A. *Milk and Honey's* score relies heavily on all three forms of the scale.

modality Indicating the use of a scale other than the common major (Ionian mode) or minor (Aeolian mode).

modulation Changing from one key to another. Unlike transposition, which is done to accommodate a singer, modulation is used to create interest or to progress smoothly from one section of a song to another.

motion The movement of the melody in relation to the bass. There are three kinds of movement: in parallel motion the bass and soprano move in the same direction; in contrary motion they move in opposite directions; and in oblique motion one voice stays on the same pitch while the other moves.

motive (or **motif**): The basic germ of a musical idea. A series of notes set in a rhythm that will be used again and again in various ways throughout the entire composition.

octave A musical interval. The eighth full tone above a given tone, having twice as many vibrations per second, or below a given tone, having half as many vibrations per second.

oleo A painted backdrop on a horizontal scroll that is unrolled to simulate background scenes. Short for *oleograph.*

one-six-two-five A harmonic pattern usually expressed as I VI II V, indicating a series of chords upon which countless popular songs have constructed. As the underpinning of songs from "Heart and Soul" to many country and rock songs of the 1960s and beyond, this cliché is the granddaddy of them all.

piano/vocal score The musical as it will be performed in the theater at rehearsal, and later published. The accompaniment does not always include the melody. Some composers insert instrumental suggestions in their piano/vocal scores.

Platinum Record A standard set by the Recording Industry Association of America. To reach this standard a recording must sell a million units and achieve $2 million in wholesale U.S. revenues.

presto A musical term for very fast. A step beyond *vivace.*

prosody The wedding of words to music. Good prosody coupled with an artist's clear diction make a lyric understandable.

punchline song A song whose lyric contains a surprise at its conclusion—preferably in the very last syllable. See Jerry Herman's "Dickie" from *Dear World* or Arthur Segal's "Guess Who I Saw Today."

quarter note The basic pulse of most popular music. The British term is *crotchet.*

ragtime A rhythmic style popular from 1890 to 1914 with much anticipation and syncopation.

range The vocal palette. In popular songs before the 1960s it was limited to a tenth (an octave and a third). Show music was permitted a somewhat wide latitude, but it was not until works by Bernstein, Bacharach, Sondheim, and Lloyd-Webber demanded an even wider range that a singer's full capabilities began to be used in musicals.

refrain The main body of the song. Interchangeable with *chorus.*

release See **bridge**.

reprise Repetition of a song in a musical. Often used by a composer to make a song indelible. Reprise is one of the favored devices of Jule Styne and Jerry Herman.

roman numeral system A shorthand used to refer to chords built on scale tones. In the key of C, for example, I is built on C, II on D, III on E, and so on. Thus the chord relationships remain the same even if the song is transposed to another key.

scrim A painted drop curtain that becomes transparent when lit from behind.

second A musical interval; the next nearest note. C to D, for example.

segue Italian for "follow." A musical direction meaning to proceed to the next section without pause or break.

semitone A half tone, the next nearest pitch. In the Western musical system, the octave is divided into twelve semitones.

sequence A succession of phrases based on the same melodic pattern but repeated at different pitches, sometimes in different keys.

seventh A wide musical interval, A going upward to G, for example.

skip A musical interval that is larger than a whole step.

stop time A slow 4/4 (which implies four beats to a measure). The first two beats are generally accented, while the rest of the measure is left empty for singing or tap dancing.

spotting In the creation of a musical, finding the actual spot where songs will be inserted.

story song A song whose narrative is its most important feature. See Jerry Herman's "Penny in My Pocket" and "The Best in the World."

subdominant The fourth degree of the diatonic scale. The subdominant (F triad in the key of C) is of one of the three basic chords.

suspension A non–chord member that according to classical harmony was obliged to resolve to a chord member. Suspensions no longer need to resolve. The most frequently used suspensions are those of the 4th and the 9th. The suspended 4th is generally listed as either A47 or A7 sus 4, while the 9th is always listed as A7 sus 9.

syncopation Misplacing accents which would normally be felt on the first and third beats of the bar.

third A musical interval; the next but one note above or below. Thirds can be strung together for a tender melodic line, as in Herman's "Marianne."

tag An extension to a song. Sometimes called a *coda*.

tessitura The general range of a composition. Songs that remain largely around the top of the singer's range are said to have a high tessitura; those that keep punching out the middle or low tones would have a low tessitura.

tonic The first tone or keynote of a diatonic scale.

transposition Changing the key of a song or composition. In musicals (but rarely in opera) music is generally transposed to place it within the best possible range of the singer.

triad The basic chord of three notes. Two superimposed thirds.

tritone The interval of the diminished fifth (or augmented fourth). C to $F^\sharp$ for example. The tritone was known as the sound of the devil's violin (achieved by retuning), and is assiduously avoided in all exercises in harmony and composition. However, it can be stunningly beautiful. See the motive of Bernstein's "Maria."

twofer Two tickets for the price of one, or a coupon to buy a ticket to a show at reduced price.

underscoring Music under dialogue. Underscoring is an effective and often emotion-heightening device musicals borrowed from the cinema. See the last scene of *The King and I*.

upbeat A lead-in or pick-up. The beat before the bar line, or downbeat.

vamp A repeated chord pattern or motive, usually ad-libbed until the entrance of the soloist.

verse Before 1960, the mood-setting, expendable introductory section preceding an ABAC or AABA refrain. After 1960, a short refrain, usually one of several.

whole tone A full step; two half steps.

BIBLIOGRAPHY

Ball, Lucille. *Love, Lucy.* New York, Putnam's, 1996.

Bonano, Margaret Wander. *Angela Lansbury.* New York, St. Martin's, 1964.

Bordman, Gerald. *American Musical Theatre.* New York, Oxford University Press, 2001.

Brady, Kathleen. *Lucille: The Life of Lucille Ball.* New York, Hyperion, 1994.

Burr, Charles. *Notes on* Dear World. New York, Sony-Broadway, 1994.

Citron, Stephen. *The Musical from the Inside Out.* Chicago, Ivan R. Dee, 1992.

———. *Sondheim and Lloyd-Webber.* New York, Oxford University Press, 2001.

Dennis, Patrick. *Auntie Mame.* New York, Vanguard, 1955.

Edelman, Rob, and Audrey Kupferberg. *Angela Lansbury.* Secaucus, N.J., Citadel, 1998.

Edwards, Anne. *A Remarkable Woman: Katharine Hepburn.* New York, Morrow, 1985.

———. *Streisand.* New York, Little, Brown, 1996.

Engel, Lehman. *The American Musical Theater.* New York, Macmillan, 1975.

Fowler, Gene. *Father Goose: The Mack Sennett Story.* New York, Covici-Friede, 1934.

Furia, Philip. *The Poets of Tin Pan Alley.* New York, Oxford University Press, 1990.

Fussell, Betty Harper. *Mabel.* New Haven, Ticknor and Fields, 1982.

Gottfried, Martin. *Balancing Act.* New York, Pinnacle, 1999.

———. *Broadway Musicals.* New York, Abrams, 1979.

Gurnsey, Otis. *Broadway Song and Story.* New York, Dodd, Mead, 1985.

Harrison, Gilbert. *The Enthusiast: Thornton Wilder.* New Haven, Ticknor and Fields, 1983.

Herman, Jerry. *Showtune.* New York, Penguin, 1996.

Herman, Jerry, with Ken Bloom. *The Lyrics: A Celebration.* New York, Routledge, 2003.

Ilson, Carol. *Harold Prince.* New York, Limelight, 1992.

Jordan, Richard Tyler. *But Darling, I'm Your Auntie Mame!: The Amazing History of the World's Favorite Madcap Aunt.* Santa Barbara, Capra, 1998.

Jungk, Peter Stephan. *Franz Werfel.* New York, Grove/Weidenfeld, 1990.

Kissel, Howard. *David Merrick.* New York, Applause, 1993.

Laufe, Abe. *Broadway's Greatest Musicals.* New York, Funk and Wagnalls, 1977.

Laurents, Arthur. *Original Story By.* New York, Knopf, 2000.

Lemaitre, Georges. *Jean Giraudoux.* New York, Frederick Unger, 1971.

LeSage, Laurent. *Jean Giraudoux.* University Park, Pennsylvania State University Press, 1959.

Logan, Joshua. *Josh.* New York, Dell, 1976.

Martin, Mary. *My Heart Belongs.* New York, Warner, 1977.

Mordden, Ethan. *Broadway Babies.* New York, Oxford University Press, 1983.

————. *Open a New Window.* New York, St. Martin's, 2001.

Morley, Sheridan. *Spread a Little Happiness.* London, Thames and Hudson, 1987.

Ostrow, Stuart. *A Producer's Broadway Journey.* Westport, Conn., Praeger, 1999.

Picon, Molly. *Molly.* New York, Simon and Schuster, 1980.

Prince, Hal. *Contradictions.* New York, Dodd, Mead, 1974.

Reilly, John. *Jean Giraudoux.* Boston, G. K. Hall, 1978.

Rich, Frank. *Hot Seat.* New York, Random House, 1998.

Sennett, Mack. *King of Comedy.* New York, Doubleday, 1954.

Stevenson, Isabelle. *The Tony Award.* Portsmouth, N.H., Heinemann, 1994.

Suskin, Steven. *Show Tunes.* New York, Oxford University Press, 2000.

Wilder, Thornton. *The Matchmaker.* New York, Harper and Row, 1957.

————. *The Merchant of Yonkers.* New York, Harper and Row, 1939.

Zadan, Craig. *Sondheim & Co.* New York, Harper and Row, 1974.

SONG CREDITS

"Almost Young," music and lyric by Jerry Herman. © 1996 Jerry Herman. All rights controlled by Jerryco Music Co. Exclusive agent: Edwin H. Morris and Co., a division of MPL Communications, Inc. All rights reserved. Used by permission.

"And I Was Beautiful," music and lyric by Jerry Herman. © 1968 (renewed) Jerry Herman. All rights controlled by Jerryco Music Co. Exclusive agent: Edwin H. Morris and Co., a division of MPL Communications, Inc. All rights reserved. Used by permission.

"The Antique Man," music and lyric by Jerry Herman. © 2002 Jerry Herman. All rights controlled by Jerryco Music Co. Exclusive agent: Edwin H. Morris and Co., a division of MPL Communications, Inc. All rights reserved. Used by permission.

"As Simple as That," music and lyric by Jerry Herman. © 1961 (renewed) Jerry Herman. All rights controlled by Jerryco Music Co. Exclusive agent: Edwin H. Morris and Co., a division of MPL Communications, Inc. All rights reserved. Used by permission.

"Avenue A," music and lyric by Jerry Herman. © 1996 Jerry Herman. All rights controlled by Jerryco Music Co. Exclusive agent: Edwin H. Morris and Co., a division of MPL Communications, Inc. All rights reserved. Used by permission.

"Beautiful," music and lyric by Jerry Herman. © 1961 (renewed) Jerry Herman. All rights controlled by Jerryco Music Co. Exclusive agent: Edwin H. Morris and Co., a division of MPL Communications, Inc. All rights reserved. Used by permission.

"Before the Parade Passes By," music and lyric by Jerry Herman. © 1964 (renewed) Jerry Herman. All rights controlled by Edwin H. Morris and Co., a division of MPL Communications, Inc. All rights reserved. Used by permission.

"The Best Christmas of All," music and lyric by Jerry Herman. © 1996 Jerry Herman. All rights controlled by Jerryco Music Co. Exclusive agent: Edwin H. Morris and Co., a division of MPL Communications, Inc. All rights reserved. Used by permission.

"The Best in the World," music and lyric by Jerry Herman. © 1980 Jerry Herman. All rights controlled by Jerryco Music Co. Exclusive agent: Edwin H. Morris and Co., a division of MPL Communications, Inc. All rights reserved. Used by permission.

"The Best of Times," music and lyric by Jerry Herman. © 1983 Jerry Herman. All rights controlled by Jerryco Music Co. Exclusive agent: Edwin H. Morris and

Co., a division of MPL Communications, Inc. All rights reserved. Used by permission.

"Big Time," music and lyric by Jerry Herman. © 1974 (renewed) Jerry Herman. All rights controlled by Jerryco Music Co. Exclusive agent: Edwin H. Morris and Co., a division of MPL Communications, Inc. All rights reserved. Used by permission.

"Bosom Buddies," music and lyric by Jerry Herman. © 1966 (renewed) Jerry Herman. All rights controlled by Jerryco Music Co. Exclusive agent: Edwin H. Morris and Co., a division of MPL Communications, Inc. All rights reserved. Used by permission.

"La Cage aux Folles," music and lyric by Jerry Herman. © 1983 Jerry Herman. All rights controlled by Jerryco Music Co. Exclusive agent: Edwin H. Morris and Co., a division of MPL Communications, Inc. All rights reserved. Used by permission.

"Chin Up, Ladies (Somewhere over the Rainbow There's a Man)," music and lyric by Jerry Herman. © 1961 (renewed) Jerry Herman. All rights controlled by Jerryco Music Co. Exclusive agent: Edwin H. Morris and Co., a division of MPL Communications, Inc. All rights reserved. Used by permission.

"Confession to a Park Avenue Mother," music and lyric by Jerry Herman. © 2002 Jerry Herman. All rights controlled by Jerryco Music Co. Exclusive agent: Edwin H. Morris and Co., a division of MPL Communications, Inc. All rights reserved. Used by permission.

"Dancing," music and lyric by Jerry Herman. © 1963 (renewed) Jerry Herman. All rights controlled by Edwin H. Morris and Co., a division of MPL Communications, Inc. All rights reserved. Used by permission.

"Dear World," music and lyric by Jerry Herman. © 1968 (renewed) Jerry Herman. All rights controlled by Jerryco Music Co. Exclusive agent: Edwin H. Morris and Co., a division of MPL Communications, Inc. All rights reserved. Used by permission.

"Dickie," music and lyric by Jerry Herman, © 1968, 1969 (renewed) Jerry Herman. All rights controlled by Jerryco Music Co. Exclusive agent: Edwin H. Morris and Co., a division of MPL Communications, Inc. All rights reserved. Used by permission.

"Each Tomorrow Morning." *See* "Tomorrow Morning."

"Elegance," music and lyric by Jerry Herman. © 1964 (renewed) Jerry Herman. All rights controlled by Edwin H. Morris and Co., a division of MPL Communications, Inc. All rights reserved. Used by permission.

"Garbage," music and lyric by Jerry Herman, © 1968, 1969 (renewed) Jerry Herman. All rights controlled by Jerryco Music Co. Exclusive agent: Edwin H. Morris and Co., a division of MPL Communications, Inc. All rights reserved. Used by permission.

"The Girls Who Sit and Wait," music and lyric by Jerry Herman. © 1961 (renewed) Jerry Herman. All rights controlled by Jerryco Music Co. Exclusive agent: Edwin H. Morris and Co., a division of MPL Communications, Inc. All rights reserved. Used by permission.

"Gooch's Song," music and lyric by Jerry Herman. © 1966 (renewed) Jerry Herman. All rights controlled by Jerryco Music Co. Exclusive agent: Edwin H. Morris and Co., a division of MPL Communications, Inc. All rights reserved. Used by permission.

"Hello, Dolly!" music and lyric by Jerry Herman. © 1963 (renewed) Jerry Herman. All rights controlled by Edwin H. Morris and Co., a division of MPL Communications, Inc. All rights reserved. Used by permission.

"Hit 'Em on the Head," music and lyric by Jerry Herman. © 1974 (renewed) Jerry Herman. All rights controlled by Jerryco Music Co. Exclusive agent: Edwin H. Morris and Co., a division of MPL Communications, Inc. All rights reserved. Used by permission.

"How to Be a Clown," music and lyric by Jerry Herman. All rights controlled by Jerryco Music Co. Exclusive agent: Edwin H. Morris and Co., a division of MPL Communications, Inc. All rights reserved. Used by permission.

"Hundreds of Girls," music and lyric by Jerry Herman. © 1974 (renewed) Jerry Herman. All rights controlled by Jerryco Music Co. Exclusive agent: Edwin H. Morris and Co., a division of MPL Communications, Inc. All rights reserved. Used by permission.

"Hymn to Hymie," music and lyric by Jerry Herman. © 1961 (renewed) Jerry Herman. All rights controlled by Jerryco Music Co. Exclusive agent: Edwin H. Morris and Co., a division of MPL Communications, Inc. All rights reserved. Used by permission.

"I Am What I Am," music and lyric by Jerry Herman. © 1983 Jerry Herman. All rights controlled by Jerryco Music Co. Exclusive agent: Edwin H. Morris and Co., a division of MPL Communications, Inc. All rights reserved. Used by permission.

"I Belong Here," music and lyric by Jerry Herman. © 1978, Jerry Herman. All rights controlled by Jerryco Music Co. Exclusive agent: Edwin H. Morris and Co., a division of MPL Communications, Inc. All rights reserved. Used by permission.

"I Don't Want to Know," music and lyric by Jerry Herman, © 1968, 1969 (renewed) Jerry Herman. All rights controlled by Jerryco Music Co. Exclusive agent: Edwin H. Morris and Co., a division of MPL Communications, Inc. All rights reserved. Used by permission.

"If He Walked into My Life," music and lyric by Jerry Herman. © 1966 (renewed) Jerry Herman. All rights controlled by Jerryco Music Co. Exclusive agent: Edwin H. Morris and Co., a division of MPL Communications, Inc. All rights reserved. Used by permission.

"I'll Be Here Tomorrow," music and lyric by Jerry Herman, © 1979 Jerry Herman. All rights controlled by Jerryco Music Co. Exclusive agent: Edwin H. Morris and Co., A division of MPL Communications, Inc. All rights reserved. Used by permission.

"I Promise You a Happy Ending," music and lyric by Jerry Herman. © 1974 (renewed) Jerry Herman. All rights controlled by Jerryco Music Co. Exclusive agent: Edwin H. Morris and Co., a division of MPL Communications, Inc. All rights reserved. Used by permission.

"I Put My Hand In," music and lyric by Jerry Herman. © 1964 (renewed) Jerry Herman. All rights controlled by Edwin H. Morris and Co., a division of MPL Communications, Inc. All rights reserved. Used by permission.

"I Think, I Think," music and lyric by Jerry Herman, © 1979 Jerry Herman. All rights controlled by Jerryco Music Co. Exclusive agent: Edwin H. Morris and Co., A division of MPL Communications, Inc. All rights reserved. Used by permission.

"It Only Takes a Moment," music and lyric by Jerry Herman. © 1963 (renewed) Jerry Herman. All rights controlled by Edwin H. Morris and Co., a division of MPL Communications, Inc. All rights reserved. Used by permission.

"It's Not My Fault," music and lyric by Jerry Herman. All rights controlled by Jerryco Music Co. Exclusive agent: Edwin H. Morris and Co., a division of MPL Communications, Inc. All rights reserved. Used by permission.

"It's Today," music and lyric by Jerry Herman. © 1966 (renewed) Jerry Herman. All rights controlled by Jerryco Music Co. Exclusive agent: Edwin H. Morris and Co., a division of MPL Communications, Inc. All rights reserved. Used by permission.

"It Takes a Woman," music and lyric by Jerry Herman. © 1963, 1964 (renewed) Jerry Herman. All rights controlled by Edwin H. Morris and Co., a division of MPL Communications, Inc. All rights reserved. Used by permission.

"I've Never Said I Love You," music and lyric by Jerry Herman, © 1968, 1969 (renewed) Jerry Herman. All rights controlled by Jerryco Music Co. Exclusive agent: Edwin H. Morris and Co., a division of MPL Communications, Inc. All rights reserved. Used by permission.

"I Wanna Make the World Laugh," music and lyric by Jerry Herman. © 1974 (renewed) Jerry Herman. All rights controlled by Jerryco Music Co. Exclusive agent: Edwin H. Morris and Co., a division of MPL Communications, Inc. All rights reserved. Used by permission.

"I Will Follow You," music and lyric by Jerry Herman. © 1961 (renewed) Jerry Herman. All rights controlled by Jerryco Music Co. Exclusive agent: Edwin H. Morris and Co., a division of MPL Communications, Inc. All rights reserved. Used by permission.

"I Won't Send Roses," music and lyric by Jerry Herman. © 1974 (renewed) Jerry Herman. All rights controlled by Jerryco Music Co. Exclusive agent: Edwin H. Morris and Co., a division of MPL Communications, Inc. All rights reserved. Used by permission.

"Just a Little Bit More," music and lyric by Jerry Herman. © 1968 (renewed)

Jerry Herman. All rights controlled by Jerryco Music Co. Exclusive agent: Edwin H. Morris and Co., a division of MPL Communications, Inc. All rights reserved. Used by permission.

"Just Go to the Movies," music and lyric by Jerry Herman. © 1980 Jerry Herman. All rights controlled by Jerryco Music Co. Exclusive agent: Edwin H. Morris and Co., a division of MPL Communications, Inc. All rights reserved. Used by permission.

"Just Leave Everything to Me," music and lyric by Jerry Herman. © 1968, 1969 (renewed) Jerry Herman. All rights controlled by Jerryco Music Co. Exclusive agent: Edwin H. Morris and Co., A division of MPL Communications, Inc. All rights reserved. Used by permission.

"Kiss Her Now," music and lyric by Jerry Herman. © 1968 (renewed) Jerry Herman. All rights controlled by Jerryco Music Co. Exclusive agent: Edwin H. Morris and Co., a division of MPL Communications, Inc. All rights reserved. Used by permission.

"Las Vegas," music and lyric by Jerry Herman. © 2002 Jerry Herman. All rights controlled by Jerryco Music Co. Exclusive agent: Edwin H. Morris and Co., a division of MPL Communications, Inc. All rights reserved. Used by permission.

"Let's Not Waste a Moment," music and lyric by Jerry Herman. © 1961 (renewed) Jerry Herman. All rights controlled by Jerryco Music Co. Exclusive agent: Edwin H. Morris and Co., a division of MPL Communications, Inc. All rights reserved. Used by permission.

"A Little More Mascara," music and lyric by Jerry Herman. © 1983 Jerry Herman. All rights controlled by Jerryco Music Co. Exclusive agent: Edwin H. Morris and Co., a division of MPL Communications, Inc. All rights reserved. Used by permission.

"Look Over There," music and lyric by Jerry Herman. © 1983 Jerry Herman. All rights controlled by Jerryco Music Co. Exclusive agent: Edwin H. Morris and Co., a division of MPL Communications, Inc. All rights reserved. Used by permission.

"Look What Happened to Mabel," music and lyric by Jerry Herman. © 1974 (renewed) Jerry Herman. All rights controlled by Jerryco Music Co. Exclusive agent: Edwin H. Morris and Co., a division of MPL Communications, Inc. All rights reserved. Used by permission.

"Love Is Only Love," music and lyric by Jerry Herman. © 1966, 1968, 1969 (renewed) Jerry Herman. All Right Controlled by Jerryco Music Co. Exclusive agent: Edwin H. Morris and Co., a division of MPL Communications, Inc. All rights reserved. Used by permission.

"Love, Look in My Window," music and lyric by Jerry Herman. © 1970 (renewed) Jerry Herman. All rights controlled by Jerryco Music Co. Exclusive agent: Edwin H. Morris and Co., a division of MPL Communications, Inc. All rights reserved. Used by permission.

"Loving You," music and lyric by Jerry Herman. © 1973, 1974 (renewed) Jerry Herman. All rights controlled by Jerryco Music Co. Exclusive agent: Edwin H. Morris and Co., a division of MPL Communications, Inc. All rights reserved. Used by permission.

"Mame," music and lyric by Jerry Herman. © 1966 (renewed) Jerry Herman. All rights controlled by Jerryco Music Co. Exclusive agent: Edwin H. Morris and Co., a division of MPL Communications, Inc. All rights reserved. Used by permission.

"The Man in the Moon," music and lyric by Jerry Herman. © 1966 (renewed) Jerry Herman. All rights controlled by Jerryco Music Co. Exclusive agent: Edwin H. Morris and Co., a division of MPL Communications, Inc. All rights reserved. Used by permission.

"Marianne," music and lyric by Jerry Herman, © 1978, 1979 Jerry Herman. All rights controlled by Jerryco Music Co. Exclusive agent: Edwin H. Morris and Co., a division of MPL Communications, Inc. All rights reserved. Used by permission."

"Masculinity," music and lyric by Jerry Herman. © 1983 Jerry Herman. All rights controlled by Jerryco Music Co. Exclusive agent: Edwin H. Morris and Co., a division of MPL Communications, Inc. All rights reserved. Used by permission.

"Mazeltov," music and lyric by Jerry Herman, © 1979 Jerry Herman. All rights controlled by Jerryco Music Co. Exclusive agent: Edwin H. Morris and Co., A division of MPL Communications, Inc. All rights reserved. Used by permission.

"Milk and Honey," music and lyric by Jerry Herman. © 1961 (renewed) Jerry Herman. All rights controlled by Jerryco Music Co. Exclusive agent: Edwin H. Morris and Co., a division of MPL Communications, Inc. All rights reserved. Used by permission.

"Mrs. Santa Claus," music and lyric by Jerry Herman. © 1996 Jerry Herman. All rights controlled by Jerryco Music Co. Exclusive agent: Edwin H. Morris and Co., a division of MPL Communications, Inc. All rights reserved. Used by permission.

"Mrs. S. L. Jacobowsky," music and lyric by Jerry Herman, © 1979 Jerry Herman. All rights controlled by Jerryco Music Co. Exclusive agent: Edwin H. Morris and Co., A division of MPL Communications, Inc. All rights reserved. Used by permission.

"More and More/Less and Less," music and lyric by Jerry Herman. © 1978, Jerry Herman. All rights controlled by Jerryco Music Co. Exclusive agent: Edwin H. Morris and Co., a division of MPL Communications, Inc. All rights reserved. Used by permission.

"Motherhood March," music and lyric by Jerry Herman. © 1964 (renewed) Jerry Herman. All rights controlled by Edwin H. Morris and Co., a division of MPL Communications, Inc. All rights reserved. Used by permission.

"Movies Were Movies," music and lyric by Jerry Herman. © 1974 (renewed) Jerry Herman. All rights controlled by Jerryco Music Co. Exclusive agent: Edwin

H. Morris and Co., a division of MPL Communications, Inc. All rights reserved. Used by permission.

"My Best Girl," music and lyric by Jerry Herman. © 1966 (renewed) Jerry Herman. All rights controlled by Jerryco Music Co. Exclusive agent: Edwin H. Morris and Co., a division of MPL Communications, Inc. All rights reserved. Used by permission.

"My Type," music and lyric by Jerry Herman. © 1986 Jerry Herman. All rights controlled by Jerryco Music Co. Exclusive agent: Edwin H. Morris and Co., a division of MPL Communications, Inc. All rights reserved. Used by permission.

"Nelson," music and lyric by Jerry Herman. © 1980 Jerry Herman. All rights controlled by Jerryco Music Co. Exclusive agent: Edwin H. Morris and Co., a division of MPL Communications, Inc. All rights reserved. Used by permission.

"Nice Running Into You," music and lyric by Jerry Herman. © 2002 Jerry Herman. All rights controlled by Jerryco Music Co. Exclusive agent: Edwin H. Morris and Co., a division of MPL Communications, Inc. All rights reserved. Used by permission.

"No Other Music," music and lyric by Jerry Herman. © 2002 Jerry Herman. All rights controlled by Jerryco Music Co. Exclusive agent: Edwin H. Morris and Co., a division of MPL Communications, Inc. All rights reserved. Used by permission.

"One Extraordinary Thing," music and lyric by Jerry Herman. © 1978, Jerry Herman. All rights controlled by Jerryco Music Co. Exclusive agent: Edwin H. Morris and Co., a division of MPL Communications, Inc. All rights reserved. Used by permission.

"One Person," music and lyric by Jerry Herman, © 1968, 1969 (renewed) Jerry Herman. All rights controlled by Jerryco Music Co. Exclusive agent: Edwin H. Morris and Co., a division of MPL Communications, Inc. All rights reserved. Used by permission.

"Only, Only Love," music and lyric by Jerry Herman. © 1961 (renewed) Jerry Herman. All rights controlled by Jerryco Music Co. Exclusive agent: Edwin H. Morris and Co., a division of MPL Communications, Inc. All rights reserved. Used by permission.

"Open a New Window," music and lyric by Jerry Herman. © 1966 (renewed) Jerry Herman. All rights controlled by Jerryco Music Co. Exclusive agent: Edwin H. Morris and Co., a division of MPL Communications, Inc. All rights reserved. Used by permission.

Opening Act II, *Mame,* music and lyric by Jerry Herman. © 1966 (renewed) Jerry Herman. All rights controlled by Jerryco Music Co. Exclusive agent: Edwin H. Morris and Co., a division of MPL Communications, Inc. All rights reserved. Used by permission.

"Pearls," music and lyric by Jerry Herman, © 1968, 1969 (renewed) Jerry Herman. All rights controlled by Jerryco Music Co. Exclusive agent: Edwin H. Morris and Co., a division of MPL Communications, Inc. All rights reserved. Used by permission.

"A Penny in My Pocket," music and lyric by Jerry Herman. © 1963 (renewed) Jerry Herman. All rights controlled by Edwin H. Morris and Co., a division of MPL Communications, Inc. All rights reserved. Used by permission.

"Put on Your Sunday Clothes," music and lyric by Jerry Herman. © 1963 (renewed) Jerry Herman. All rights controlled by Edwin H. Morris and Co., a division of MPL Communications, Inc. All rights reserved. Used by permission.

"Ribbons Down My Back," music and lyric by Jerry Herman. © 1963 (renewed) Jerry Herman. All rights controlled by Edwin H. Morris and Co., a division of MPL Communications, Inc. All rights reserved. Used by permission.

"St. Bridget," music and lyric by Jerry Herman. © 1966 (renewed) Jerry Herman. All rights controlled by Jerryco Music Co. Exclusive agent: Edwin H. Morris and Co., a division of MPL Communications, Inc. All rights reserved. Used by permission.

"Sheep Song," music and lyric by Jerry Herman. © 1963 (renewed) Jerry Herman. All rights controlled by Jerryco Music Co. Exclusive agent: Edwin H. Morris and Co., a division of MPL Communications, Inc. All rights reserved. Used by permission.

"Show Tune in 2/4" (also called "There's No Tune Like a Show Tune"), music and lyric by Jerry Herman. © 1960 (renewed) Jerry Herman. All rights controlled by Edwin H. Morris and Co., a division of MPL Communications, Inc. All rights reserved. Used by permission.

"So Long, Dearie," music and lyric by Jerry Herman. © 1964 (renewed) Jerry Herman. All rights controlled by Edwin H. Morris and Co., a division of MPL Communications, Inc. All rights reserved. Used by permission.

"Song on the Sand," music and lyric by Jerry Herman. © 1983 Jerry Herman. All rights controlled by Jerryco Music Co. Exclusive agent: Edwin H. Morris and Co., a division of MPL Communications, Inc. All rights reserved. Used by permission.

"The Spring of Next Year," music and lyric by Jerry Herman, © 1968, 1969 (renewed) Jerry Herman. All rights controlled by Jerryco Music Co. Exclusive agent: Edwin H. Morris and Co., a division of MPL Communications, Inc. All rights reserved. Used by permission.

"Tap Your Troubles Away," music and lyric by Jerry Herman. © 1974 (renewed) Jerry Herman. All rights controlled by Jerryco Music Co. Exclusive agent: Edwin H. Morris and Co., a division of MPL Communications, Inc. All rights reserved. Used by permission.

"A Tavish Toy," music and lyric by Jerry Herman. © 1996 Jerry Herman. All rights controlled by Jerryco Music Co. Exclusive agent: Edwin H. Morris and Co., a division of MPL Communications, Inc. All rights reserved. Used by permission.

"That Was Yesterday," music and lyric by Jerry Herman. © 1961 (renewed)

Jerry Herman. All rights controlled by Jerryco Music Co. Exclusive agent: Edwin H. Morris and Co., a division of MPL Communications, Inc. All rights reserved. Used by permission.

"There's No Reason in the World," music and lyric by Jerry Herman. © 1961 (renewed) Jerry Herman. All rights controlled by Jerryco Music Co. Exclusive agent: Edwin H. Morris and Co., a division of MPL Communications, Inc. All rights reserved. Used by permission.

"There's No Tune Like a Show Tune." *See* "Show Tune in 2/4."

"Through the Bottom of the Glass," music and lyric by Jerry Herman. © 1968 (renewed) Jerry Herman. All rights controlled by Jerryco Music Co. Exclusive agent: Edwin H. Morris and Co., a division of MPL Communications, Inc. All rights reserved. Used by permission.

"Time Heals Everything," music and lyric by Jerry Herman. © 1974 (renewed) Jerry Herman. All rights controlled by Jerryco Music Co. Exclusive agent: Edwin H. Morris and Co., a division of MPL Communications, Inc. All rights reserved. Used by permission.

"To Be Alone with You," music and lyric by Jerry Herman. © 1964 (renewed) Jerry Herman. All rights controlled by Morley Music Co. All rights reserved. Used by permission.

"Tomorrow Morning" (also called "Each Tomorrow Morning"), music and lyric by Jerry Herman. © 1968 (renewed) Jerry Herman. All rights controlled by Jerryco Music Co. Exclusive agent: Edwin H. Morris and Co., a division of MPL Communications, Inc. All rights reserved. Used by permission.

"(The Wonderful World of the) Two a Day," music and lyric by Jerry Herman. © 1961 (renewed) Jerry Herman. All rights controlled by Jerryco Music Co. Exclusive agent: Edwin H. Morris and Co., a division of MPL Communications, Inc. All rights reserved. Used by permission.

"Voices," music and lyric by Jerry Herman, © 1968, 1969 (renewed) Jerry Herman. All rights controlled by Jerryco Music Co. Exclusive agent: Edwin H. Morris and Co., a division of MPL Communications, Inc. All rights reserved. Used by permission.

"We Are What We Are," music and lyric by Jerry Herman. © 1983 Jerry Herman. All rights controlled by Jerryco Music Co. Exclusive agent: Edwin H. Morris and Co., a division of MPL Communications, Inc. All rights reserved. Used by permission.

"We Don't Go Together at All," music and lyric by Jerry Herman. © 1996 Jerry Herman. All rights controlled by Jerryco Music Co. Exclusive agent: Edwin H. Morris and Co., a division of MPL Communications, Inc. All rights reserved. Used by permission.

"We Need a Little Christmas," music and lyric by Jerry Herman. © 1966 (renewed) Jerry Herman. All rights controlled by Jerryco Music Co. Exclusive agent: Edwin H. Morris and Co., a division of MPL Communications, Inc. All rights reserved. Used by permission.

"We're Almost There," music and lyric by Jerry Herman. © 1978, Jerry Herman. All rights controlled by Jerryco Music Co. Exclusive agent: Edwin H. Morris and Co., a division of MPL Communications, Inc. All rights reserved. Used by permission.

"When I Was a Foreign Legionnaire," music and lyric by Jerry Herman. © 1983 Jerry Herman. All rights controlled by Jerryco Music Co. Exclusive agent: Edwin H. Morris and Co., a division of MPL Communications, Inc. All rights reserved. Used by permission.

"Where in the World Is My Prince?" music and lyric by Jerry Herman. © 2002 Jerry Herman. All rights controlled by Jerryco Music Co. Exclusive agent: Edwin H. Morris and Co., a division of MPL Communications, Inc. All rights reserved. Used by permission.

"Wherever He Ain't," music and lyric by Jerry Herman. © 1974 (renewed) Jerry Herman. All rights controlled by Jerryco Music Co. Exclusive agent: Edwin H. Morris and Co., a division of MPL Communications, Inc. All rights reserved. Used by permission.

"With Anne on My Arm" (also called "With You on My Arm"), music and lyric by Jerry Herman. © 1983 Jerry Herman. All rights controlled by Jerryco Music Co. Exclusive agent: Edwin H. Morris and Co., a division of MPL Communications, Inc. All rights reserved. Used by permission.

"With You on My Arm." *See* "With Anne on My Arm."

"World, Take Me Back," music and lyric by Jerry Herman. © 1970 (renewed) Jerry Herman. All rights controlled by Jerryco Music Co. Exclusive agent: Edwin H. Morris and Co., a division of MPL Communications, Inc. All rights reserved. Used by permission.

"You I Like," music and lyric by Jerry Herman, © 1978, 1979 Jerry Herman. All rights controlled by Jerryco Music Co. Exclusive agent: Edwin H. Morris and Co., a division of MPL Communications, Inc. All rights reserved. Used by permission.

"Ziegfeld Girl," music and lyric by Jerry Herman. © 2002 Jerry Herman. All rights controlled by Jerryco Music Co. Exclusive agent: Edwin H. Morris and Co., a division of MPL Communications, Inc. All rights reserved. Used by permission.

INDEX

Note: An *n* following the page number refers to a footnote; an *f* refers to a figure (including musical examples); a page number in **boldface** refers to a photograph.